Financial Engineering
Principles

Founded in 1807, John Wiley & Sons is the oldest independent publishing company in the United States. With offices in North America, Europe, Australia, and Asia, Wiley is globally committed to developing and marketing print and electronic products and services for our customers' professional and personal knowledge and understanding.

The Wiley Finance series contains books written specifically for finance and investment professionals as well as sophisticated individual investors and their financial advisors. Book topics range from portfolio management to e-commerce, risk management, financial engineering, valuation, and financial instrument analysis, as well as much more.

For a list of available titles, please visit our Web site at www.WileyFinance.com.

Financial Engineering
Principles

A Unified Theory for Financial
Product Analysis and Valuation

Perry H. Beaumont, PhD

WILEY

John Wiley & Sons, Inc.

Copyright © 2004 by Perry H. Beaumont, Ph.D. All rights reserved.

Published by John Wiley & Sons, Inc., Hoboken, New Jersey.

Published simultaneously in Canada.

No part of this publication may be reproduced, stored in a retrieval system, or transmitted in any form or by any means, electronic, mechanical, photocopying, recording, scanning, or otherwise, except as permitted under Section 107 or 108 of the 1976 United States Copyright Act, without either the prior written permission of the Publisher, or authorization through payment of the appropriate per-copy fee to the Copyright Clearance Center, Inc., 222 Rosewood Drive, Danvers, MA 01923, 978-750-8400, fax 978-750-4470, or on the web at www.copyright.com. Requests to the Publisher for permission should be addressed to the Permissions Department, John Wiley & Sons, Inc., 111 River Street, Hoboken, NJ 07030, 201-748-6011, fax 201-748-6008, e-mail: permcoordinator@wiley.com.

Limit of Liability/Disclaimer of Warranty: While the publisher and author have used their best efforts in preparing this book, they make no representations or warranties with respect to the accuracy or completeness of the contents of this book and specifically disclaim any implied warranties of merchantability or fitness for a particular purpose. No warranty may be created or extended by sales representatives or written sales materials. The advice and strategies contained herein may not be suitable for your situation. You should consult with a professional where appropriate. Neither the publisher nor author shall be liable for any loss of profit or any other commercial damages, including but not limited to special, incidental, consequential, or other damages.

For general information on our other products and services, or technical support, please contact our Customer Care Department within the United States at 800-762-2974, outside the United States at 317-572-3993 or fax 317-572-4002.

Wiley also publishes its books in a variety of electronic formats. Some content that appears in print may not be available in electronic books.

For more information about Wiley products, visit our web site at www.wiley.com.

Library of Congress Cataloging-in-Publication Data
Beaumont, Perry H., 1961-
Financial engineering principles: a unified theory for financial
product analysis and valuation / Perry H. Beaumont.
  p. cm. — (Wiley finance series)
Published simultaneously in Canada.
  ISBN 0-471-46358-2 (cloth)
  1. Financial engineering. I. Title. II. Series.
  HG176.7.B42 2003
  658.15'224—dc21   2003011338

Printed in the United States of America.

10 9 8 7 6 5 4 3 2 1

For my wife, Alexandra, with love and devotion

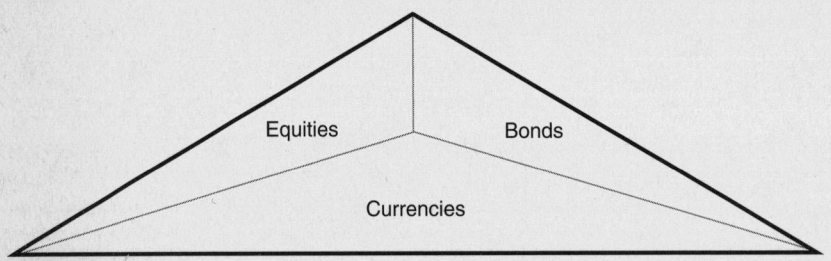

Contents

FOREWORD — IX

PREFACE — XI

INTRODUCTION — XVII

PART ONE
Products, Cash Flows, and Credits — 1

CHAPTER 1
Products — 3

CHAPTER 2
Cash Flows — 15

CHAPTER 3
Credit — 73

PART TWO
Financial Engineering, Risk Management, and Market Environment — 111

CHAPTER 4
Financial Engineering — 113

CHAPTER 5
Risk Management — 171

CHAPTER 6
Market Environment — 241

INDEX — 271

Foreword

Casting aside the traditional notion of financial products grouped within distinct, relatively isolated asset classes, Beaumont insightfully uncovers common characteristics that allow the practitioner to better understand interrelationships between bonds, equities, and currencies. Importantly, the author drafts a hands-on roadmap to help investors manage these asset management building blocks within an integrated portfolio context.

Moving aggressively away from "box thinking," the author creatively develops an applied geometry of self-contained triangles to accent the essential functional qualities of various product or cash flow categories. Macrotopics are then added around the perimeter of these triangles to illustrate common traits or themes that the author pulls together to help weave the complex fabric of financial engineering.

The text and the entire Appendix for Chapter 4 are peppered with practical examples that give *Financial Engineering Principles* a "real world" flavor. In this way, professionals and laypersons alike have access to a virtual Global Positioning System to safely and swiftly navigate the most challenging of financial straits, even as the market environment changes, strategic courses are recalibrated, and new investment vehicles evolve.

Particularly timely, in a global financial arena marked by periods of excessive volatility and widespread uncertainty, Beaumont devotes an entire chapter to strategies and instruments that can help the portfolio manager better quantify, allocate, and manage (or hedge) critical investment risks. By employing a fresh cross-market approach, the author draws not just on product-related risk drivers, but also on cash flow and credit interrelationships to develop a richer, more powerful approach to risk management.

Financial Engineering Principles combines the best of a well-crafted "practitioner's guide" with an invaluable "reference work" to give readers a financial engineering tool that will undoubtedly become one of the most used tools in their investment management tool chest.

Gilbert A. Benz
Executive Director
Investment Solutions
UBS, Zurich, Switzerland

Preface

After nearly 20 years in the financial industry, and with assignments that have taken me to every corner of the globe, it is only now that I feel this book could be written.

In my first text, *Fixed Income and Synthetic Assets,* the idea was to trek from the front of the yield curve to the back and provide ideas for how a properly equipped financial toolbox could help identify trading strategies and perhaps even assist with creating new financial products in the world of fixed income.

Here my goal is to introduce a unifying theory among the various factors that make up the world of finance. The three fundamental factors to this unified theory are products, cash flows, and credit. With a solid grounding in these first principles, we will show how any financial security can be better understood by financial professionals, students, or individual investors who desire to go beyond more basic financial concepts.

After having spent years teaching about the financial markets, I continue to find it disheartening that some students feel that global markets are far more disparate than they are similar and shy away from thinking in a more eclectic and encompassing way about the world. There are many common elements across markets, and the potential insights to risk and reward that can be gained from a more unified approach are simply tremendous.

While one overall goal of the book is to highlight the unifying aspect of my approach to these key financial markets, the chapters can be quite instructive on a stand-alone basis. By this I mean that a reader who is primarily interested in bonds will not have to read any chapters beyond those within the bond sections to fully capture the essence of that product type. To this end, it bears emphasizing that when I refer to a unifying theory of the financial markets, I am referring both to a unifying aspect within each market segment and across them.

We are most certainly at a crucial juncture of the markets today. Recent lessons have shown us that a new market dialogue is required. The generic labels commonly used within finance today do not convey the same meaning and value that they did years ago. A blanket reference to a bond versus an equity ought no longer to evoke a sense of the former being a safer investment than the latter; just the opposite may be true in today's highly engineered marketplace. Unfortunately, the new kind of dialogue that financial professionals must now practice does not fit the easy classifications that suited the marketplace for decades if not centuries. It is not nearly enough

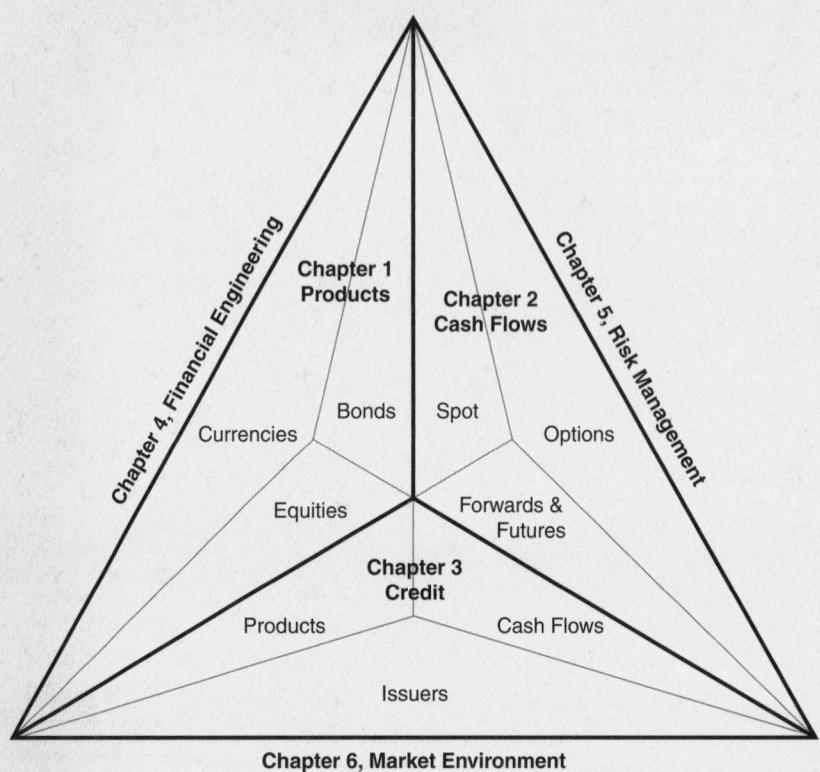

FIGURE P.1 High-level overview of chapters and topics.

to state that credit is a factor that permeates all markets, or that legal considerations are key when determining what happens in the event of a default. What is now absolutely essential is a clear understanding of the interrelationships among these (and many other) market dynamics and how the use of such tools as probability theory and historical experience can help to guide informed and prudent decision making.

The world of finance is not necessarily a more complex place today, but it is most certainly a different place. A large step toward understanding the new order is to embrace the notion of how similar financial products truly are rather than to perpetuate outlived delineations of how they are so different. The dialogue in support of this evolution does not require a new, different vocabulary; rather we must use our existing vocabulary in a richer and more meaningful way to portray more accurately a relevant perspective of a security's risk and reward profile. Terms like "duration" and "beta" have been around for a long time and are commonly used, though they are woefully insufficient now as stand-alone concepts; they are much more valuable to investors when seen in broader context alongside other financial measures. This text shows why and presents new ways that long-standing metrics of risk and return can be combined to assist with divining creative and meaningful market insights.

Figure P.1 presents the layout of the entire book within a single diagram. The concepts of products (bonds, equities, and currencies), cash flows (spot, forwards and futures, and options), and credit (products, cash flows, and issuers) are intended to represent more specific or micro-oriented considerations for investors. Conversely, the concepts of financial engineering (product creation, portfolio construction, and strategy development), risk management (quantifying risk, allocating risk, and managing risk), and market environment (tax, legal and regulatory, and investors) are intended to represent more general or macro-oriented considerations. While the microtopics are presented pictorially as self-contained triangles to suggest that these are the building blocks of finance, the macrotopics are presented around the perimeter of the triangle to suggest that these are broader and more encompassing concepts. Two of the three topics in Chapter 3 are the titles of Chapters 1 and 2. The significance of this is twofold: It highlights the interrelated nature of markets, and it points out that credit is an extremely important aspect of the market at large.

Let's begin!

Acknowledgments

A work of this type typically is successful only because of the support and assistance of a variety of individuals, and for me this is one of the most rewarding aspects of engaging in a project such as this. The sacrifices asked of immediate family, in particular, are usually great, and I am most grateful to my wife, Aly, and my sons, Max, Jack, and Nicholas, for indulging their husband and father in this latest work. Another dimension of this book is that during the time of its writing I had the good fortune to live and work on two continents and with global responsibilities. These experiences provided considerable food for thought, and I am grateful for that. I also want to thank the anonymous reviewers of this text, though I fully accept any errors as being completely my own. Finally, for their assistance with preparing this book, I want to thank Elena Baladron and Thomas Cooper.

Introduction

This text presents, for the first time, a single unified approach to building bridges across fundamental financial relationships. The top layer of this new methodology is comprised of products, cash flows, and credit. Products are financial securities including equities, bonds, and currencies. "Cash flow" refers to the structure of a security and denotes if the asset is a spot, forward or future, or option. Credit is a factor that winds its way through all of the above. As recent market events readily attest, understanding credit risk is paramount to successful investing.

While laying the fundamental groundwork, the text examines implications for investment-making decisions and develops a framework for how investors and portfolio managers can evaluate market opportunities. Specific trading strategies are presented, including detailed suggestions on how portfolio managers can build optimal portfolios.

In short, this text provides a simple yet powerful introduction to identifying value in any financial product. While primarily intended for professional portfolio managers, individual investors and students of the financial markets also will find the text to be of value. Key financial terms are highlighted in italics throughout the book for easy reference and identification.

While one obvious benefit of specialized texts is that they offer an in-depth view of particular classes of financial products, an obvious shortcoming is that readers gain little or no appreciation for hybrid securities or alternative investments. Is a preferred stock an equity by virtue of its credit rating and the fact that it pays dividends, or is it a bond owing to its fixed maturity date and its maturity value of par? With the rapid pace of financial innovation, convenient labels simply do not apply, and this is especially the case today with credit derivatives. Thus, by virtue of its focus on the dynamics of processes and interrelationships as opposed to more definitional and static concepts, this text provides a financial toolbox that is equipped to build or deconstruct any financial product that may evolve. To reinforce this, each chapter builds on the previous one, and key concepts are continuously reinforced.

Each chapter begins with a reference to a triangle of three themes that will be explored within the chapter. A convenient property of any triangle is that it has three points. Accordingly, if we were to label these three points as A, B, and C respectively, point A is always one step away from either B or C. The same can be said for point B relative to points A and C, or for point C relative to A and B. This is a useful consideration because it supports the notion that while I may refer to three distinguishable niches of the marketplace (as with equities, bonds, and currencies), I wish also to stress how the three particular niches are also related—that they are always just one step away from one another.

Chapter 1 provides fundamental working definitions of what is meant precisely by equities, bonds, and currencies.

Chapter 2 presents cash flows—the way that a product is structured. The three basic cash flow types are spot, forwards and futures, and options.

Chapter 3 presents credit. In its most fundamental form, credit risk is the uncertainty that a counterparty cannot or will not honor its promise to provide a good, service, or payment, and in a timely fashion. The chapter examines credit risk from the perspective of products, cash flows, and issuers.

Chapter 4 demonstrates intra- and interrelationships among the triangles presented in previous chapters and in a product creation context and shows how hybrids can be analyzed. Indeed, with the new building block foundation, the text demonstrates how straightforward it can be to construct or decompose any security. Also presented are ideas on how to construct and trade optimal portfolios relative to various strategies including indexation.

Chapter 5 continues the presentation of the unifying methodology in the context of risk management and considers risk: quantifying, allocating, and managing it.

Chapter 6 presents the market environment, by which is meant the more macro-influences of market dynamics. Three fundamental macro-influences include tax, legal and regulatory, and investor considerations.

Many senior institutional investors and those with considerable market experience traditionally have viewed the bond, equity, and currency markets as rather distinct and generally differentiated asset classes. Indeed, it would not be too difficult at all to assemble a list of how these asset types are unique. For example, the stock market is generally an *exchange-traded* or *listed* market (including the New York Stock Exchange, NYSE), while the currency market is generally an *unlisted* or *over-the-counter* (OTC) market, (meaning not on an exchange), while bonds are more OTC than not, although this situation is changing rapidly. Another point of distinction is that over long periods of time (several years), equities generally have sported superior returns relative to bonds, although also with a greater level of risk. In this context, *risk* is a reference to the variability of returns. That is, the returns of equities may be more variable year-to-year relative to bonds, but over a long period of time the return on equities tends to be greater.

However, similarities among the big three products (equities, bonds, and currencies) are much more dominating and persuasive than any differences. But before listing these similarities, it is worthwhile to list the three points of conventional wisdom that places these asset types into three very different spheres.

1. Stemming largely from their different risk-reward profiles, market professionals who actively trade within these three asset classes generally tend to specialize. Accordingly, equity trading often is protected and isolated from bond trading, and vice versa; currencies also are typically seen as being in their own world.
2. If only from a pure marketing perspective, if asset classes are "packaged" differently and are marketed as truly unique and individual products, it is perhaps easy to understand why the firms that sell these products (as well as many that buy them) are keener to accept differences than similarities.
3. Some powerful ideas within portfolio theory suggest that meaningful diversification can allow for appreciable return enhancement opportunities while also reducing risk profiles. With this particular orientation, the drive to carve out separate and distinct asset classes becomes more understandable.

To avoid misunderstanding, I must emphasize that I do not mean to suggest that equities, bonds, and currencies are identical or even virtually so. However, I do wish to show how these broad asset classes are interrelated and to indicate that while they typically have different characteristics in different market environments, the big three are best understood as being more like one another than unlike. That is, the big three have many things in common, and a pedigogical approach that embraces these commonalities has theoretical and practical value.

Consider the following example. Typically, interest rate risk is perceived to be dominant among bonds while price risk is perceived to be the purview of equities. But consider the risk profile of a long-dated stock option. This instrument type actually trades on the Chicago Board of Options Exchange and is known as a LEAP (for long-term equity anticipation securities). As any knowledgeable LEAP trader will readily state, interest rate risk is quite easily a LEAP's single greatest vulnerability among the key market variables that are used to value an option. Why? Since an option can be seen as a leveraged play on the market, and since leverage means financing, the cost of that financing is measured by an interest rate. The longer the time that a strategy is leveraged, the greater the overall contribution that is being made by the relevant financing rate. Indeed, in some instances, an option need not have a final expiration much beyond six months to have a situation where, all else being equal, the price value of the LEAP responds more to an incremental change in the finance rate than an incremental change in the LEAP's underlying equity price. In other words, for certain longer-dated stock options, the greatest risk at a particular point in time may be the risk associated with financing rather than the underlying equity. Thus, the dominant risk of an equity future may not be an equity price risk but an interest rate risk: the dominant risk of bonds. Some LEAP traders actually buy or sell Eurodollar interest rate futures in combination with their equity option trades so as to help minimize any unwanted interest rate (financing risk) exposure. More on this later.

Without question, global financial markets do encompass much more than equities, bonds, and currencies. To name but a few other key market segments, there are also precious metals and commodities of every shape, size, color, and taste. By choosing to focus primarily on equities, bonds, and foreign exchange, this text highlights the commonality among these three markets; I do not mean to understate the depth and breadth of other financial markets. Indeed, Chapter 5 attempts to link the unified approach to these other markets. The underlying principles for the big three are applicable to every type of financial product.

Why focus on equities, bonds, and currencies? They are well-established markets, they are very much intertwined with one another, and collectively they comprise the overwhelming portion of global trading volume. Investors do themselves a disservice if they attempt to define the relative value of a particular corporate bond to the exclusion of balance sheet and income statement implications of that firm's equity outlook, and vice versa. And certainly both equity and bond investors are well advised to monitor the currency profile of their investments consistently. Even for locally based portfolio managers who are interested solely in locally denominated products (as with a U.S.-domiciled investor interested only in U.S.-dollar-denominated securities), the proliferation of venues to hedge away the currency component of a given security provides the ability to embrace a global investment outlook. With an American Depository Receipt (ADR), for example, a U.S.-based investor can purchase a U.S.-dollar-denominated equity listed with a U.S. equity exchange but with the equity issuer actually domiciled outside of the United States.

As an overlay to the analysis of key financial products, the text devotes considerable attention to credit issues and the ways that certain uses of capital can have profound implications. The notion of symmetry across a firm's capital structure and associated financial instruments is not necessarily a new idea, although it has become increasingly deserving of new and creative insights. In an important paper written in 1958 entitled "The Cost of Capital, Corporate Finance, and the Theory of Investment," Franco Modigliani and Merton Miller first suggested, among other propositions,

Introduction

that the financial instrument used by a firm to finance an investment is irrelevant to the question of whether the instrument is worthwhile; issuing debt to finance an acquisition, for example, will not make it a more profitable investment than issuing equity.[1] While the "M&M propositions" came under much attack when first introduced (notably for what were decried as unreasonable assumptions underlying the propositions), in 1990 Miller received the Nobel Prize in economics, largely due to his work in the area of capital structure, and Modigliani received the same prize in 1985.

It has been said that a useful way of thinking about the various (perhaps even heroic) assumptions[2] underlying the M&M propositions is that they at least contribute to a framework for analysis. If the framework argues for a particular type of symmetry between bonds and equities, asymmetries may be exposed in the process of questioning key assumptions. The same spirit of questioning ought also to be encouraged to better understand any practical or theoretical framework. Thus, students and practitioners of finance must question how existing financial relationships differ (or not) from theoretical contexts and explore the implications. In essence, such exploration is the mission of this text, which provides an innovative way to think about market linkages and synergies and sketches a practical blueprint that both students and practitioners can use for a variety of applications.

---

[1] Franco Modigliani and Merton Miller, "The Cost of Capital, Corporate Finance, and the Theory of Investment," *American Economic Review*; December 1958, pp. 261–297.

[2] Within the theoretical context of presenting their ideas, Miller and Modigliani assumed that companies don't pay taxes and that all market participants have access to the same information. In actuality, companies certainly do pay taxes, and in most instances worldwide there is a tax advantage with debt offerings over equity offerings.

Financial Engineering
Principles

PART ONE

Products, Cash Flows, and Credit

CHAPTER 1

Products

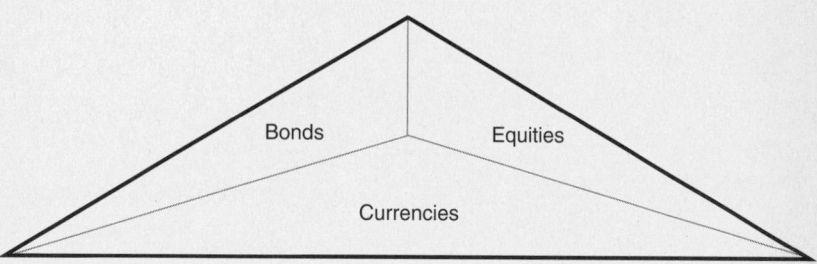

This chapter provides working definitions for bond, equity, and currency, and discusses similarities and differences between bonds and equities.

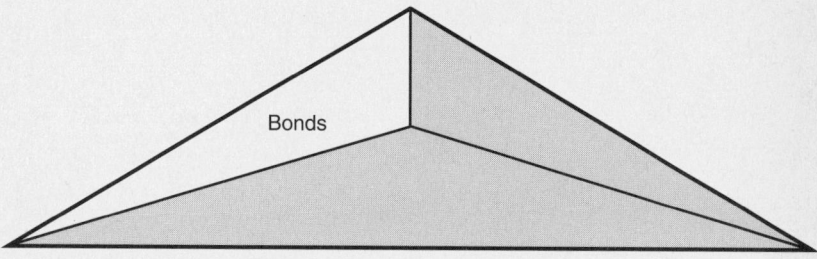

Perhaps the most basic definition of a bond[1] is that it is a financial instrument with a *predetermined life span* that embodies a *promise* to provide one or more *cash flows*. The life span of the security is generally announced at the time it is first launched into the market, and the longest *maturities* tend to be limited to about 30 years.[2]

---

[1] A bond typically is viewed as a fixed income instrument with more than 10 years to maturity, while a note typically is viewed as a fixed income security with 10 years or less to maturity. Fixed income securities with a year or less to maturity are typically referred to as money market instruments. In this text, all fixed income products are referred to as bonds.

[2] From time to time so-called century bonds are issued with a life span of 100 years.

Cash flows generally consist of periodic *coupons* and a final payment of *principal*. Coupons typically are defined as fixed and regularly paid amounts of money, and usually are set in relation to a percent of the principal amount. For example, if the coupon of a bond is set at 8 percent and is paid twice a year over five years, and if the principal of the bond is valued at $1,000, then every six months the investor will receive $40.

$$\$1,000 \times 8\%/2 = \$40$$

A bond *issuer* is the entity selling the bonds to *investors*. The issuer then has the opportunity to use the money received to finance various aspects of its business, and the investor has the opportunity to earn a rate of return on the money lent. In sum, the issuer has incurred a *debt* that is owed to the investor. If the issuer becomes unable to pay back the investor (as with a *bankruptcy*), the bond investor generally is protected by law to have a *priority ranking* relative to an equity investor in the same company. Priority ranking means that a bondholder will be given preference over an equity holder if a company's assets are sold off to make good on its obligations to investors. Chapter 3 presents more information on bankruptcy.

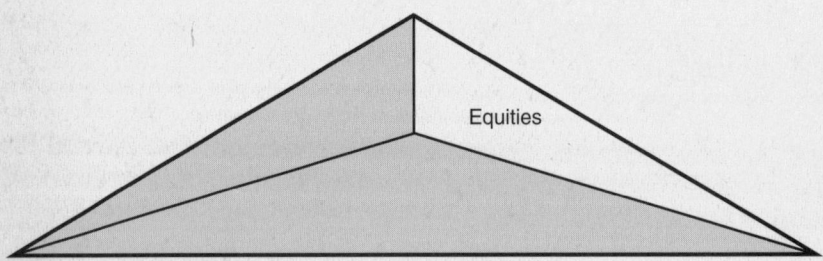

Perhaps the most basic definition of equity is that it's a financial instrument without a predetermined life span. An equity may or may not pay cash flows called *dividends*. Dividends typically are paid on a quarterly basis and usually are paid on a per-share basis. For example, if a dividend of 34 cents per share is declared, then every *shareholder* receives 34 cents per share. Unlike a bond, an equity gives an investor the right to vote on various matters pertaining to the issuer. This right stems from the fact that a *shareholder* actually owns a portion of the issuing company. However, unlike a bondholder, a shareholder does not enjoy a preferential ranking in the event of a bankruptcy.

With the benefit of these working definitions for bonds and equities, let us consider what exactly is meant by the words "promise," and "priority," and when and by what criteria a bond might begin to look more like an equity and vice versa.

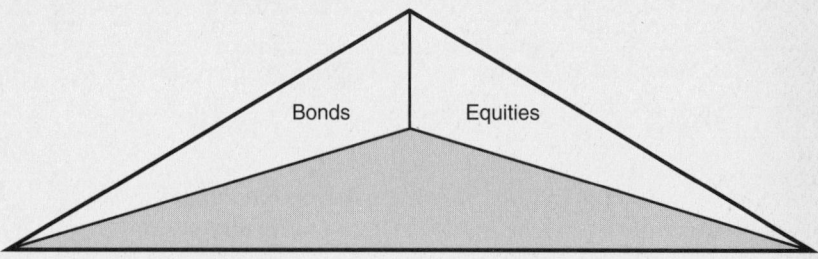

PROMISES AND PRIORITIES

At issue here is not so much the sincerity of an issuer wanting to keep a promise, but rather the business realities affecting an issuer's ability to make good on the financial promises it has made. Ability, in turn, involves any number of factors, including *financial fundamentals* (as with key financial ratios), quality of company management, economic standing relative to *peer group* (other comparable companies if there are any), and the *business cycle* (strength of economy).

Various entities within the marketplace have an interest in monitoring a given company's likelihood of success. These entities range from individual investors who use any number of valuation techniques (inclusive of visiting the issuer to check out its premises and operations) to governmental bodies (e.g., the Securities and Exchange Commission). Increasingly the *investment banks* (firms that assist issuers with bringing their deals to market) also are actively practicing *due diligence* (evaluation of the appropriateness of funding a particular initiative.)

A bond issuer that fails to honor its promise of paying a coupon at the appointed time generally is seen as suffering very serious financial problems. In many instances the failure to make good on a coupon payment equates to an automatic *distressed* (company is in serious financial difficulty) or *default* (company is unable to honor its financial obligations) scenario whereby bondholders are immediately vested with rights to seize certain company assets. By contrast, companies often choose to dispense with otherwise regularly scheduled dividend payments and/or raise or lower the dividend payment from what it was the previous time one was granted. While a skipped or lowered dividend may well raise some eyebrows, investors usually look to the explanation provided by the company's officers as a guide. For example, a dividend might be lowered to allow the company to build up a larger cash reserve that it can use for making strategic acquisitions, and shareholders might especially welcome such an event.

When a bankruptcy or distressed or default situation does arise, it is imperative to know exactly where an investor stands in regard to collecting all or a portion of what the issuer originally had promised to pay. As stated, bondholders stand in line ahead of equity holders. However, there are various classifications of bondholders and shareholders, and there are materially different priorities as to how these categories are rated and treated. Chapter 3 delves into the nuances of what these classifications mean. Figure 1.1 presents a continuum of investment products that depicts investor rankings in an event of default.

Table 1.1 summarizes this section on bonds and equities. These characteristics are explored further in later chapters, where it is shown that while these characteristics may hold true generally as meaningful ways to differentiate a bond from an equity, lines also can become blurred rather quickly.

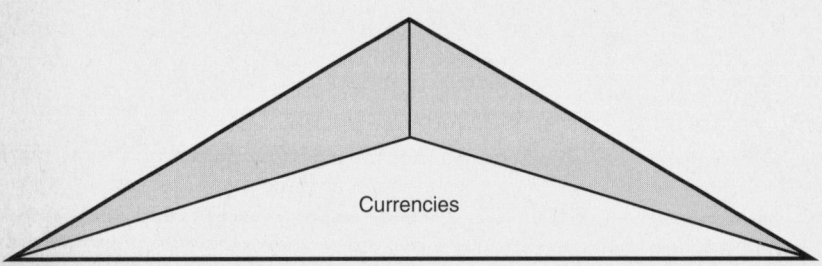

Like equities and bonds, currencies are also investment vehicles, a means to earn a return in the marketplace. Investors based in country X might choose to save *local currency* (U.S. dollar for the United States) holdings in something like an interest-bearing checking account or a three-month *certificate of deposit* (a short-term money market instrument) or they might even stuff it under a mattress. Alternatively, they might choose to spend local currency

| Common equity holders | Preferred equity holders | Junior subordinated bondholders | Senior subordinated bondholders | Senior bondholders | Senior secured bondholders |

Low ──► High

FIGURE 1.1 Continuum of product rankings in the event of default (from lowest credit protection to highest).

TABLE 1.1 Similarities and Differences of Equities and Bonds

	Equities	Bonds
Entitles holder to vote	√	
Entitles holder to a preferable ranking in default		√
Predetermined life span		√
Has a price	√	√
Has a yield	√	√
May pay a coupon		√
May pay a dividend	√	

by purchasing goods or services or other investment vehicles, including equities, bonds, real estate, precious metals, or even other currencies.

A currency typically is thought of as a unit of *implied value*. I say "implied value" because in contrast with times past, today's coins and paper money are rarely worth the materials used to make them and they tend not to be *backed by* anything other than faith and trust in the government minting or printing the money. For example, in ancient Rome, the value of a particular coin was typically its intrinsic value—that is, its value in its natural form of silver or gold. And over varying periods of time, the United States and other countries relied on linking national currencies to gold and/or silver where paper money was sometimes said to be backed by gold or subject to a *gold standard*—that is, actual reserves of gold were set aside in support of outstanding supplies of currency. The use of gold as a centerpiece of currency valuation pretty much faded from any practical meaning in 1971.

Since the physical manifestation of a currency (in the form of notes or coins) is typically the responsibility of national governments, the judgment of how sound a given currency may be generally is regarded as inexorably linked to how sound the respective government is regarded as being. Rightly or wrongly, national currencies today typically are backed by not much more than the confidence and expectation that when a currency (or one of its *derivatives*, as with a check or credit card) is presented for payment, it typically will be accepted. As we will see, while the whole notion of currencies being backed by precious metals has faded as a way of conveying a sense of discipline or credibility, some currencies in the world are backed by other currencies, for reasons not too dissimilar from historical incentives for using gold or silver.

While the value of a stock or bond generally is expressed in units of a currency (e.g., a share of IBM stock costs $57 or a share of Société Generale stock costs €23), a way to value a currency at a particular time is to measure how much of a good or service it can purchase. For example, 40 years ago $1 probably could have been exchanged for 100 pencils. Today, however, 100 pencils cost more than $1. Accordingly, we could say that the value of the dollar has *depreciated*; it buys fewer pencils today than it did 40 years ago. To express this another way, today we have to spend more than $1 to obtain the same 100 pencils that people previously spent just $1 to obtain. Spending more money to purchase the same goods is a classic definition of *inflation*, and inflation certainly can contribute to a currency's *depreciation* (weakening relative to another currency). Conversely, *deflation* is when the same amount of money buys more of a good than it did previously, and this can contribute to the *appreciation* (strengthening relative to another currency) of a currency. Deflation may occur when there is a technological advancement with how a good or service is created or provided, or when there is a surge in the *productivity* (a measure of efficiency) involved with the creation of a good or providing of a service.

Another way to value a currency is by how many units of some other currency it can obtain. An *exchange rate* is defined simply as being the measure of one currency's value relative to another's. Yet while this simple definition of an exchange rate may be true, it is not very satisfying. Exchange rates generally tend to vary over time; what influences how one currency will trade in relation to another? Well, no one really knows precisely, but a couple of theories have their particular devotees, and they are worth mentioning here. Two of the better-known theories applied to exchange rate pricing include the theory of interest rate parity and purchasing power parity theory.

INTEREST RATE PARITY

Assume that the annual rate of interest in country X is 5 percent and that the annual rate of interest in country Y is 10 percent. Clearly, all else being equal, investors in country X would rather have money in country Y since they are able to earn more *basis points*, or *bps* (1% is equal to 100 bps), in country Y relative to what they are able to earn at home. Specifically, the *interest rate differential* (the difference between two yields, expressed in basis points) is such that investors are picking up an additional 500 basis points of yield. However, by investing money outside of their home country, investors are taking on exchange rate risk. To earn the rate of interest being offered in country Y, investors first have to convert their country X currency into country Y currency. At the end of the investment horizon (e.g., one year), international investors may well have earned more money via a rate of interest higher than what was available at home, but those gains might be greatly affected (perhaps even entirely eliminated) by swings in the value of respective currencies. The value of currency Y could fall by a large amount relative to currency X over one year, and this means that less of currency X is recovered.

Indeed, the theory of interest rate parity essentially argues that on a fully hedged basis, any differential that exists between the interest rates of two countries will be eliminated by the differential in exchange rates between those two countries. Continuing with the preceding example, if a forward contract is purchased to exchange currency Y for currency X at the end of the investment horizon, the pricing embedded in the forward arrangement will be such that the currency loss on the trade will exactly offset the gain generated by the interest rate differential. That is, currency Y will be priced so as to depreciate relative to currency X, and by an equivalent magnitude of 500 bps. In short, whatever interest rate advantage investors might enjoy initially will be eliminated by currency depreciation when a strategy is executed on a hedged basis.

When currency exposures are left unhedged, countries' interest rates and currency values may move in tandem or inversely to other countries' interest rates and currency values. Given the right timing and scenario, international investors could not only benefit from the higher rate of interest provided by a given market, but at the end of the investment horizon they might also be able to exchange an appreciated currency for their weaker local currency. Accordingly, they obtain more of their local currency than they had at the outset, and this is due to both the higher interest rate and the effect of having been in a strengthening currency. Nonetheless, many portfolio managers swear by the offsetting nature of yield spreads and currency moves and argue that, over time, these variables do manage to catch up to one another and thus mitigate long-term opportunities of any doubling of benefits in total return when investing in nonlocal currencies. Figure 1.2 illustrates this point. As shown, there is a fairly meaningful correlation between these two series of yield spread and currency values.

In summary, while interest rate differentials may or may not have meaningful correlations with currency moves when currencies are unhedged, on a fully hedged basis there is no interest rate or currency advantage to be gained. As is explained in the next chapter, interest rate differentials are a key dynamic with determining how *forward exchange rates* (spot exchange rates priced to a future date) are calculated.

PURCHASING POWER PARITY

Another popular theory to explain exchange rate valuation goes by the name of purchasing power parity (PPP).

The idea behind PPP is that, over time (and the question of what period of time is indeed a relevant and oft-debated question), the purchasing ability

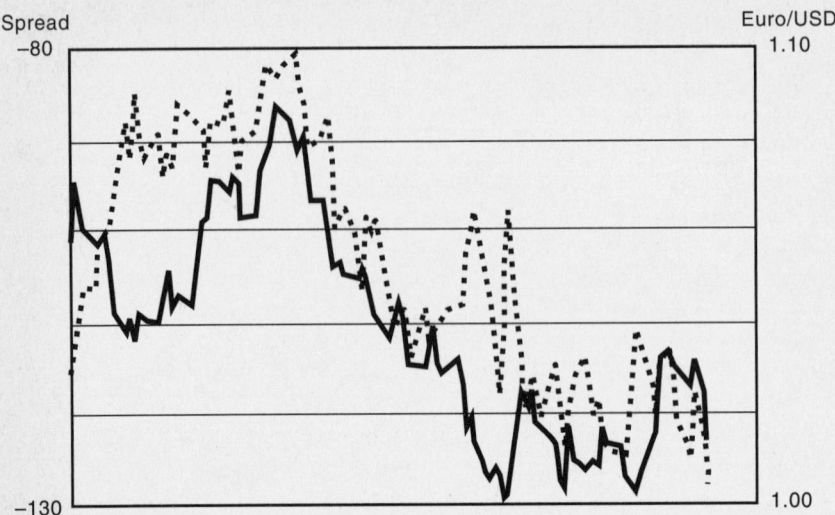

FIGURE 1.2 Yield spread between 10-year German and U.S. government bonds and the euro-to-dollar exchange rate, September 1, 1999, to January 15, 2000.

of one currency ought to adjust itself to be more in line with the purchasing power of another currency. Broadly speaking, in a world where exchange rates are left free to adjust to market imbalances and disequilibria in a price context, exchange rates can serve as powerful equalizers. For example, if the currency of country X was quite strong relative to country Y, then this would suggest that on a relative basis, the prices within country Y are perceived to be lower to consumers in country X. Accordingly, as the theory goes, since consumers in country X buy more of the goods in country Y (because they are cheaper) and eventually bid those prices higher (due to greater demand), an equalization eventually will materialize whereby relative prices of goods in countries X and Y become more aligned on an exchange rate–adjusted basis.

Although certainly to be taken with a grain of salt, *Economist* magazine occasionally updates a survey whereby it considers the price of a McDonald's Big Mac on a global basis. Specifically, a Big Mac price in local currency (as in yen for Japan) is divided by the price for a Big Mac in the United States (upon conversion of yen into dollars). This result is termed "purchasing power parity," and when compared to respective actual dollar exchange rates, an over- or undervaluation of a currency versus the dollar is obtained. The presumption is that a Big Mac is a relatively homogeneous product type and accordingly represents a meaningful point of reference. A rather essential (and perhaps heroic) assumption to this (or any other comparable PPP exercise) is that all of the ingredients that go into making a Big Mac are accessible in each of the countries where the currencies are being compared. Note that "equal" in this scenario does not necessarily have to mean that access to goods (inputs) is 100 percent free of tariffs or any type of trade barrier. If trade were indeed completely unfettered then this would certainly satisfy the notion of equally accessible. But if all goods were also subject to the same barriers to access, this would be equal too, at least in the sense that equal in this instance means equal barriers. Yet the vast number of trade agreements that exist globally highlights just how bureaucratic the ideal of free trade can become even if perceptions (and realities) are such that trade today is generally at the most free it has ever been. Another important and obvious consideration is that certain inputs might enjoy advantages of proximity. Beef may be more plentiful in the United States relative to Japan, for example.

The very fact that there is both an interest rate theory to explain currency phenomenon and a notion of purchasing power parity tells us that there are at least two different academic approaches to thinking about where currencies ought to trade relative to one another. No magic keys to unlocking unlimited profitability here! But like any useful theories commonly applied in any field, here they are popular presumably because they manage to shed at least some light on market realities. Generally speaking, market participants tend to be a rather pragmatic and results-oriented lot; if something does not "work," then its wholesale acceptance and use is not very likely.

So why is it that neither interest rate parity nor purchasing power parity works perfectly? The answer lies within the question: The markets themselves are not perfect. For example, interest rates generally are influenced to an important degree by national central banks that are trying to guide an economy in some preferred way. As interest rates can be an important tool for central banks, these are often subject to the policies dictated by well-meaning and certainly well-informed people, yet people do make mistakes. Monetarists believe that one way to eliminate independent judgment of all kinds (both correct and incorrect) is to allow a country's monetary policy to be set by a fixed rule. That is, instead of a country's money supply being determined by human and subjective factors, it would be set by a computer programmed to allow only for a rigid set of money growth parameters.

As to other price realities in the marketplace that may inhibit a smoother functioning of interest rate or PPP theories, there are a number of considerations, including these three.

1. Quite simply, the supply and demand of various goods around the world differ by varying degrees, and unique costs can be incurred when special efforts are required to make a given good more readily available. For example, some countries can produce and refine their own oil, while others are required to import their energy needs.

2. The cost of some goods in certain countries are subsidized by local governments. This extra-market involvement can serve to skew price relationships across countries. One example of how a government subsidy can skew a price would be with agricultural products. Debates around these subsidies can become highly charged exchanges invoking cries of the need to take care of one's own domestic producers, to appeal for the need to develop self-reliant stores of goods so as to limit dependence on foreign sources. Accordingly, by helping farmers and effectively lowering the costs borne to produce foodstuffs, these savings are said to be passed along to consumers who enjoy lower-cost items relative to the price of imported things. Ultimately whether this practice is good or bad is not likely to be answered here.
3. As alluded to above, tariffs or even total bans on the trade of certain goods can have a distorting effect on market equilibriums.

There are, of course, many other ways that price anomalies can emerge (e.g., with natural disasters). Perhaps this is why the parity theories are most helpful when viewed as longer-run concepts.

Is there perhaps a link of some kind between interest rate parity and purchasing power parity? The answer to this question is yes; the link is inflation. An interest rate as defined by the Fischer relation is equal to a real rate of interest plus expected inflation (as with a measure of CPI or Consumer Price Index). For example, if an annual nominal interest rate is equal to 6 percent and expected inflation is running at 2.5 percent, then the difference between these two rates is the real interest rate (3.5 percent). Therefore, inflation is an important factor with interest rate parity dynamics. Similarly, price levels within countries are affected by inflation phenomena, and so are price dynamics across countries. Therefore, inflation is an important factor with PPP dynamics as well. In sum, whether via a mechanism where an interest rate is viewed as a "price" (as in the price to borrow a particular currency) or via a mechanism where a particular amount of a currency is the "price" for obtaining a certain good or service, inflation across countries (or, perhaps more accurately, inflation differentials across countries) can play an important role in determining respective currency values.

As of this writing, there are over 50 currencies trading in the world today.[3] While many of these currencies are well recognized, such as the U.S. dollar, the Japanese yen, or the United Kingdom's pound sterling, many are not as well recognized, as with United Arab Emirates dirhams or Malaysian ringgits. Although lesser-known currencies may not have the same kind of recognition as the so-called majors (generally speaking, the currencies of the

---

[3]International Monetary Fund, *Representative Exchange Rates for Selected Currencies*, November 1, 2002.

Group of Seven, or G-7), lesser-known currencies often have a strong price correlation with one or more of the majors. To take an extreme case, in the country of Panama, the national currency is the U.S. dollar. Chapters 3 and 4 will discuss this and other unique currency pricing arrangements further.

The G-7 (and sometimes the Group of Eight if Russia is included) is a designation given to the seven largest industrialized countries of the world. Membership includes the United States, Japan, Great Britain, France, Germany, Italy, and Canada. G-7 meetings generally involve discussions of economic policy issues. Since France, Germany, and Italy all belong to the European Union, the currencies of the G-7 are limited to the U.S. dollar, the pound sterling, Canadian dollar, the Japanese yen, and the euro. The four most actively traded currencies of the world are the U.S. dollar, pound sterling, yen, and euro.

CHAPTER SUMMARY

This chapter has identified and defined the big three: equities, bonds, and currencies. The text discussed linkages among equities and bonds in particular, noting that an equity gives a shareholder the unique right to vote on matters pertaining to a company while a bond gives a debtholder the unique right to a senior claim against assets in the event of default. A discussion of pricing for equities, bonds, and currencies was begun, which is developed further in a more mathematical context in Chapter 2.

As a parting perspective of the similarities among bonds, equities, and currencies, it is well to consider if one critical element could serve effectively to distinguish each of these products. In the case of what makes an equity

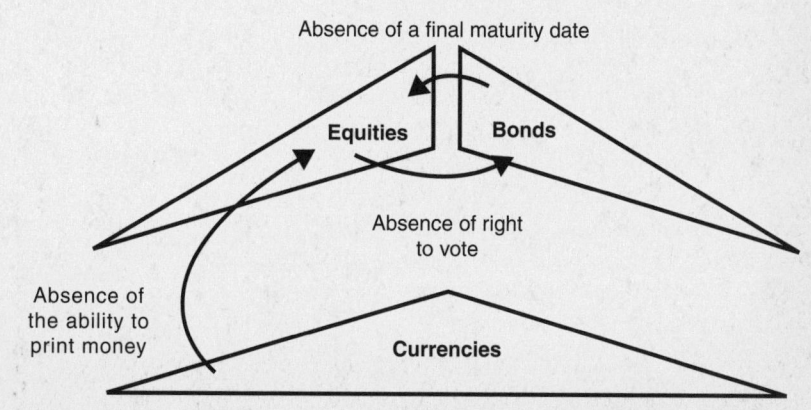

FIGURE 1.3 Key differences among bonds, equities, and currencies.

an equity, the Achilles' heel is the right to vote that is conveyed in a share of common stock. Without this right, an equity becomes more of a hybrid between an equity and a bond. In the case of bonds, a bond without a stated maturity immediately becomes more of a hybrid between a bond and an equity. And a country that does not have the ability to print more of its own money may find its currency treated as more of a hybrid between a currency and an equity. Figure 1.3 presents these unique qualities graphically. The text returns time and again to these and other ways of distinguishing among fundamental product types.

CHAPTER 2

Cash Flows

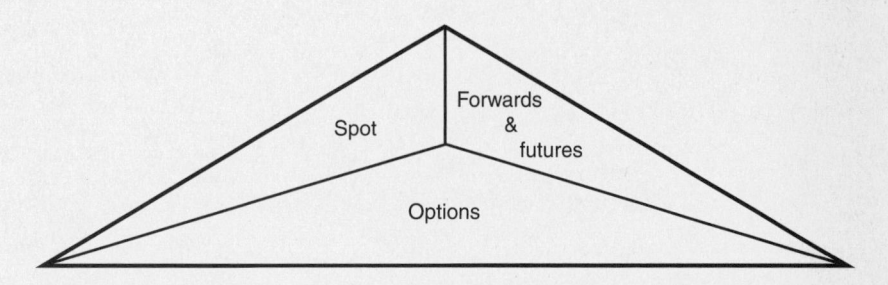

```
         Forwards
  Spot      &
          futures

       Options
```

If the main thrust of this chapter can be distilled into a single thought, it is this: Any financial asset can be decomposed into one or more of the following cash flows: spot, forwards and futures, and options. Let us begin with spot.

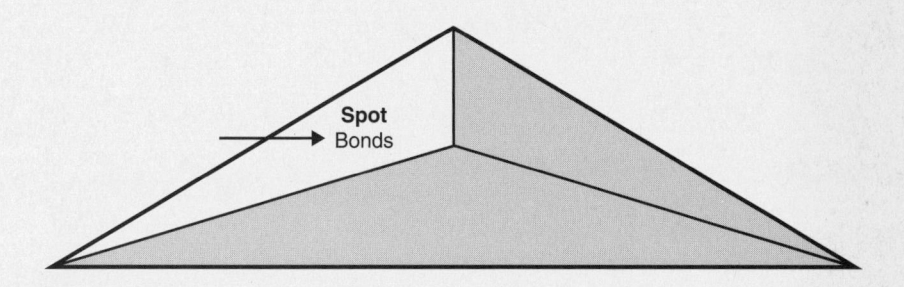

```
   Spot
 → Bonds
```

"Spot" simply refers to today's price of an asset. If yesterday's closing price for a share of Ford's equity is listed in today's *Wall Street Journal* at $60, then $60 is Ford's spot price. If the going rate for the dollar is to exchange it for 1.10 euros, then € 1.10 is the spot rate. And if the price of a three-month Treasury bill is $983.20, then this is its spot price. Straightforward stuff, right? Now let us add a little twist.

In the purest of contexts, a *spot price* refers to the price for an immediate exchange of an asset for its cash value. But in the marketplace, immediate may not be so immediate. In the vernacular of the marketplace, the sale and purchase of assets takes place at agreed-on *settlement dates*.

15

For example, a settlement that is agreed to be *next day* means that the securities will be exchanged for cash on the next business day (since settlement does not occur on weekends or market holidays). Thus, for an agreement on a Friday to exchange $1,000 dollars for euros at a rate of 1.10 using next day settlement, the $1,000 would not be physically exchanged for the € 1,100 until the following Monday.

Generally speaking, a settlement day is quoted relative to the day that the trade takes place. Accordingly, a settlement agreement of *T plus 3* means three business days following trade date. There are different conventions for how settlement is treated depending on where the trade is done (geographically) and the particular product types concerned.

Pretty easy going thus far if we are willing to accept that the market's judgment of a particular asset's spot price is also its *value* or true *worth* (valuation above or below the market price of an asset). Yes, there is a distinction to be made here, and it is an important one. In a nutshell, just because the market says that the price of an asset is "X" does not have to mean that we agree that the asset is actually worth that. If we do happen to agree, then fine; we can step up and buy the asset. In this instance we can say that for us the market's price is also the worth of the asset. If we do not happen to agree with the market, that is fine too; we can *sell short* the asset if we believe that its value is above its current price, or we can buy the asset if we believe its value is below its market price. In either event, we can follow meaningful strategies even when (perhaps especially when) our sense of value is not precisely in line with the market's sense of value.

Expanding on these two notions of price and worth, let us now examine a few of the ways that market practitioners might try to evaluate each.

Broadly speaking, price can be said to be definitional, meaning that it is devoid of judgment and simply represents the logical outcome of an equation or market process of supply and demand.

Let us begin with the bond market and with the most basic of financial instruments, the Treasury bill. If we should happen to purchase a Treasury bill with three months to maturity, then there is a grand total of two cash flows: an outflow of cash when we are required to pay for the Treasury bill at the settlement date and an inflow of cash when we choose to sell the Treasury bill or when the Treasury bill matures. As long as the sale price or price at maturity is greater than the price at the time of purchase, we have made a profit.

A nice property of most fixed income securities is that they mature at par, meaning a nice round number typically expressed as some multiple of $1,000. Hence, with the three-month Treasury bill, we know with 100 percent certainty the price we pay for the asset, and if we hold the bill to maturity, we know with 100 percent certainty the amount of money we will get in three months' time. We assume here that we are 100 percent confident that the U.S. federal government will not go into default in the next three months and renege on its debts.[1] If we did in fact believe there was a chance that the U.S. government might not make good on its obligations, then we would have to adjust downward our 100 percent recovery assumption at maturity. But since we are comfortable for the moment with assigning 100 percent probabilities to both of our Treasury bill cash flows, it is possible for us to state with 100 percent certainty what the total return on our Treasury bill investment will be.

If we know for some reason that we are not likely to hold the three-month Treasury bill to maturity (perhaps we will need to sell it after two months to generate cash for another investment), we can no longer assume that we can know the value of the second cash flow (the sale price) with 100 percent certainty; the sale price will likely be something other than par, but what exactly it will be is anyone's guess. Accordingly, we cannot say with 100 percent certainty what a Treasury bill's total return will be at the time of purchase if the bill is going to be sold anytime prior to its maturity date. Figure 2.1 illustrates this point.

Certainly, if we were to consider what the price of our three-month Treasury bill were to be one day prior to expiration, we could be pretty confident that its price would be extremely close to par. And in all likelihood

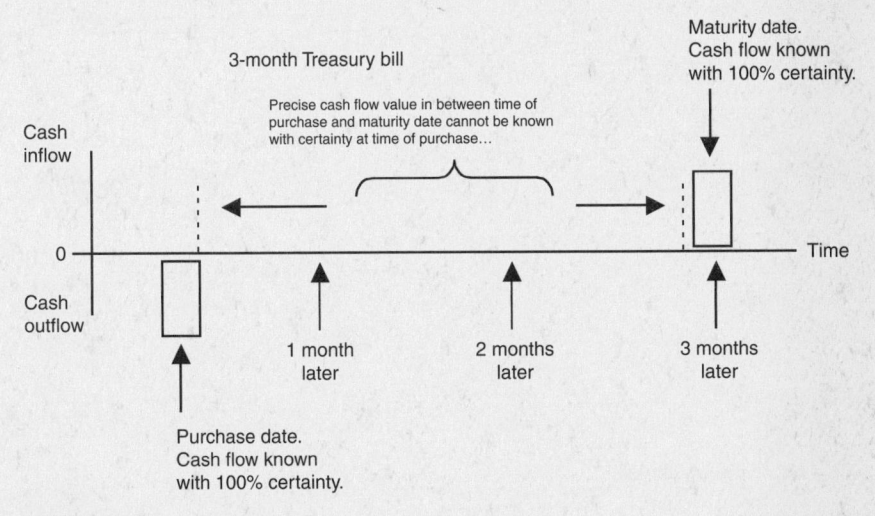

FIGURE 2.1 Cash flows of a 3-month Treasury bill.

---

[1]If the government were not to make good on its obligations, there would be the opportunity in the extreme case to explore the sale of government assets or securing some kind of monetary aid or assistance.

the price of the Treasury bill one day after purchase will be quite close to the price of the previous day. But the point is that using words like "close" or "likelihood" simply underscores that we are ultimately talking about something that is not 100 percent certain. This particular uncertainty is called the *uncertainty of price*.

Now let us add another layer of uncertainty regarding bonds. In a coupon-bearing security with two years to maturity, we will call our uncertainty the *uncertainty of reinvestment*, that is, the uncertainty of knowing the interest rate at which coupon cash flows will be reinvested. As Figure 2.2 shows, instead of having a Treasury security with just two cash flows, we now have six.

As shown, there is a cash outlay at time of purchase, coupons paid at regular six-month intervals, and the receipt of par and a coupon payment at maturity; these cash flows can be valued with 100 percent certainty at the time of purchase, and we assume that this two-year security is held to maturity. But even though we know with certainty what the dollar amount of the intervening coupon cash flows will be, this is not enough to state at time of purchase what the overall total return will be with 100 percent certainty. To better understand why this is the case, let us look at some formulas.

First, for our three-month Treasury bill, the annualized total return is calculated as follows if the Treasury bill is held to maturity:

$$\frac{Cash\ out\ -\ cash\ in}{Cash\ in} \times \frac{365}{90} = Annualized\ total\ return$$

Accordingly, for a three-month Treasury bill purchased for $989.20, its annualized total return is 4.43 percent. The second term, 365/90, is the *annualization term*. We assume 365 days in a year (366 for a leap year), and

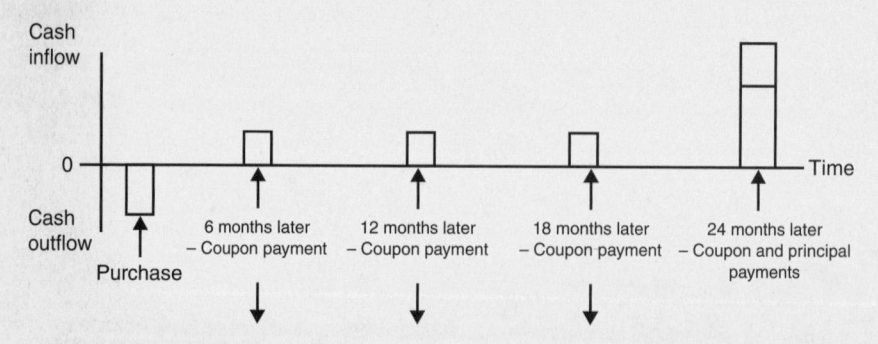

FIGURE 2.2 Cash flows of a 2-year coupon-bearing Treasury bond.

90 days corresponds to the three-month period from the time of purchase to the maturity date. It is entirely possible to know at the time of purchase what the total return will be on our Treasury bill. However, if we no longer assume that the Treasury bill will be held to maturity, the "cash-out" value is no longer par but must be something else. Since it is not possible to know with complete certainty what the future price of the Treasury bill will be on any day prior to its maturity, this uncertainty prevents us from being able to state a certain total return value prior to the sale date.

What makes the formula a bit more difficult to manage with a two-year security is that there are more cash flows involved and they all have a time value that has to be considered. It is material indeed to the matter of total return how we assume that the coupon received at the six-month point is treated. When that coupon payment is received, is it stuffed into a mattress, used to reinvest in a new two-year security, or what? The market's convention, rightly or wrongly, is to assume that any coupon cash flows paid prior to maturity are reinvested for the remaining term to maturity of the underlying security and that the coupon is reinvested in an instrument of the same issuer profile. The term "issuer profile" primarily refers to the quality and financial standing of the issuer. It also is assumed that the security being purchased with the coupon proceeds has a yield identical to the underlying security's at the time the underlying security was purchased,[2] and has an identical *compounding frequency*. "Compounding" refers to the reinvestment of cash flows and "frequency" refers to how many times per year a coupon-bearing security actually pays a coupon. All coupon-bearing Treasuries pay coupons on a semiannual basis. The last couple of lines of text give four explicit assumptions pertaining to how a two-year security is priced by the market. Obviously, this is no longer the simple and comfortable world of Treasury bills.

Coupon payments prior to maturity are assumed to be:

1. Reinvested.
2. Reinvested for a term equal to the remaining life of the underlying bond.
3. Reinvested in an identical security type (e.g., Treasury-bill).
4. Reinvested at a yield equal to the yield of the underlying security at the time it was originally purchased.

---

[2] It would also be acceptable if the cash flow–weighted average of different yields used for reinvestment were equal the yield of the underlying bond at time of purchase. In this case, some reinvestment yields could be higher than at time of original purchase and some could be lower.

To help reinforce the notion of just how important reinvested coupons can be, consider Figure 2.3, which shows a five-year, 6 percent coupon-bearing bond. Three different reinvestment rates are assumed: 9 percent, 6 percent, and 3 percent. When reinvestment occurs at 6 percent (equal to the coupon rate), a zero contribution is made to the overall total return. However, if cash flows can be reinvested at 9 percent, then at the end of five years an additional 7.6 points ($76 per $1,000 face) of cumulative dollar value above the 6 percent base case scenarios is returned. By contrast, if rates are reinvested at 3 percent, then at the end of five years, 6.7 points ($67 per $1,000 face) of cumulative dollar value is lost relative to the 6 percent base case scenario.

Figure 2.3 portrays the assumptions being made.

The mathematical expression for the Figure 2.4 is:

$$\text{Price at time of purchase} = \frac{C}{(1+Y/2)^1} + \frac{C}{(1+Y/2)^2}$$

$$+ \frac{C}{(1+Y/2)^3} + \frac{C \& F}{(1+Y/2)^4} = \$1{,}000$$

The C in the equation is the dollar amount of coupon, and it is equal to the *face amount* (F) of the bond times the coupon rate divided by its compounding frequency. The face amount of a bond is the same as the par value received at maturity. In fact, when a bond first comes to market, face, price, and par values are all identical because when a bond is launched, the coupon

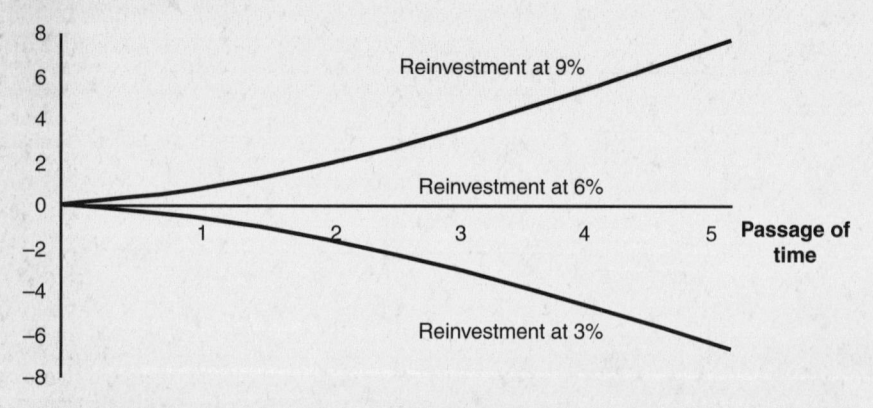

FIGURE 2.3 Effect of reinvestment rates on total return.

rate is equal to Y. The Y in the equation is yield, and it is the same value in each term of the equation. This is equivalent to saying that we expect each coupon cash flow (except the last two, coupon and principal) to be reinvested for the remaining life of the underlying security at the yield level prevailing when the security was originally purchased. Accordingly, the price of a 6 percent coupon-bearing two-year Treasury with a 6 percent yield is $1,000 as shown in the next equation.

$$\frac{\$60/2}{(1 + 6\%/2)^1} + \frac{\$60/2}{(1 + 6\%/2)^2} + \frac{\$60/2}{(1 + 6\%/2)^3} + \frac{\$60/2 \; \& \; \$1,000}{(1 + 6\%/2)^4} = \$1,000$$

If yield should happen to drop to 5 percent after initial launch, the coupon rate remains at 6 percent and the price increases to $1,018.81. And if the yield should happen to rise to 7 percent after launch, the price drops to 981.63. Hence, price and yield move inversely to one another. Moreover, by virtue of price's sensitivity to yield levels (and, hence, reinvestment rates), a coupon-bearing security's unhedged total return at maturity is impossible to pin down at time of purchase. Figure 2.4 confirms this.

Figure 2.5 plots the identical yields from the last equation after reversing the order in which the individual terms are presented. This order rever-

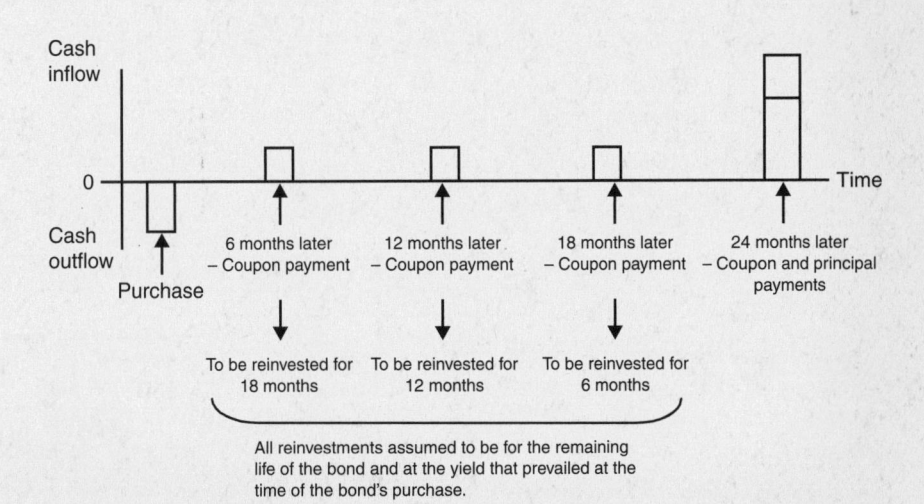

FIGURE 2.4 Reinvestment requirements of a 2-year coupon-bearing Treasury bond.

$$\frac{(\$60/2)\&\$1{,}000}{(1+6\%/2)^4} + \frac{\$60/2}{(1+6\%/2)^3} + \frac{\$60/2}{(1+6\%/2)^2} + \frac{\$60/2}{(1+6\%/2)^1} = \$1{,}000$$

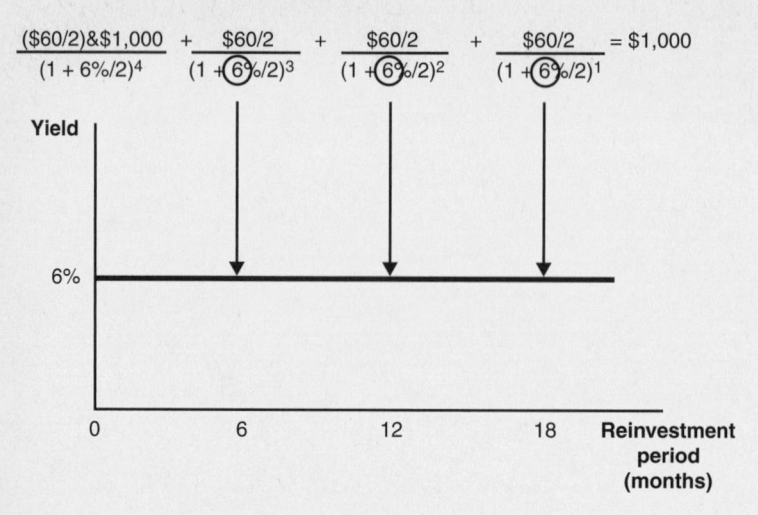

[Graph: Yield of 6% (flat) plotted against Reinvestment period (months) at 0, 6, 12, 18, with downward arrows at 6, 12, and 18 months.]

FIGURE 2.5 Reinvestment patterns for cash flows of a 2-year coupon-bearing Treasury bond.

sal is done simply to achieve a chronological pairing between the timing of when cash flows are paid and the length of time they are reinvested. Note how the resulting *term structure* (a plotting of yields by respective dates) is perfectly flat.

Note too that when a reinvestment of a coupon cash flow is made, the new security that is purchased also may be a coupon-bearing security. As such, it will embody reinvestment risk. Figure 2.6 illustrates this.

Let us now add another layer of uncertainty, called the *uncertainty of credit quality* (the uncertainty that a credit may drift to a lower rating or go into default). Instead of assuming that we have a two-year security issued by the U.S. Treasury, let us now assume that we have a two-year bond issued by a U.S. corporation. Unless we are willing to assume that the corporation's bond carries the same credit quality as the U.S. government, there are a couple of things we will want to address. First, we will probably want to change the value of Y in our equation and make it a higher value to correspond with the greater risk we are taking on as an investor. And what exactly is that greater risk? To be blunt, it is the risk that we as investors may not receive *complete* (something less than 100 percent), and/or *timely payments* (payments made on a date other than formally promised) of all the cash flows that we have coming to us. In short, there is a risk that the company debt will become a victim of a distressed or default-related event.

Clearly there are many shades of real and potential credit risks, and these risks are examined in much more detail in Chapter 3. For the time being,

Cash Flows 23

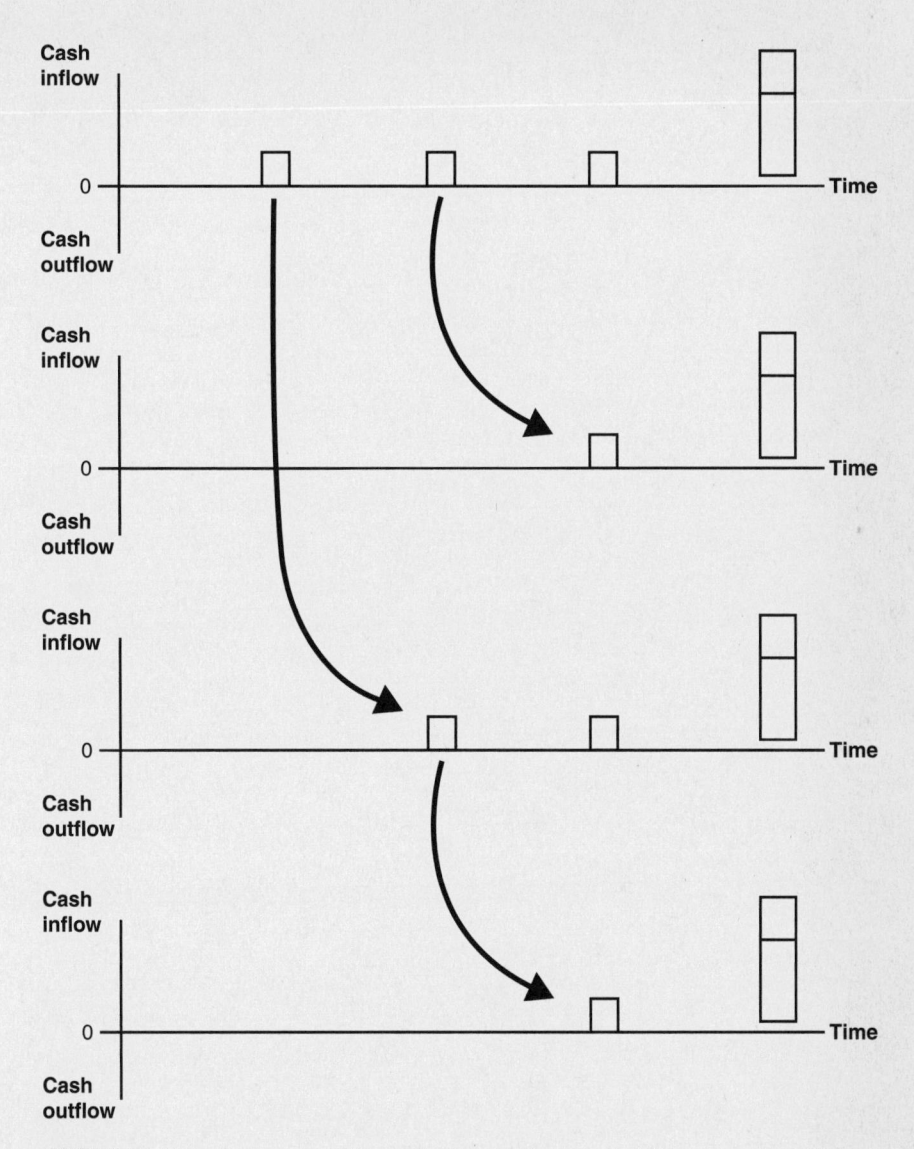

FIGURE 2.6 How coupon cash flows of a 2-year Treasury bond give rise to additional cash flows.

we must accept the notion that we can assign credit-linked probabilities to each of the expected cash flows of any bond. For a two-year Treasury note, each cash flow can be assigned a 100 percent probability for the high likelihood of full and timely payments. For any nongovernmental security, the probabilities may range between zero and 100 percent. Zero percent? Yes. In fact, some firms specialize in the trading of so-called distressed debt, which can include securities with a remaining term to maturity but with little or no likelihood of making any coupon or principal payments of any kind. A firm specializing in distressed situations might buy the *bad debt* (the downgraded or defaulted securities) with an eye to squeezing some value from the seizure of the company's assets. Bad debt buyers also might be able to reschedule a portion of the outstanding sums owed under terms acceptable to all those involved.

If we go back to the formula for pricing a two-year Treasury note, we will most certainly want to make some adjustments to identify the price of a two-year non-Treasury issue. To compensate for the added risk associated with a non-Treasury bond we will want a higher coupon paid out to us— we will want a coupon payment above C. And since a coupon rate is equal to Y at the time a bond is first sold, a higher coupon means that we are demanding a higher Y as well.

To transform the formula for a two-year Treasury—

$$Price = \frac{C}{(1 + Y/2)^1} + \frac{C}{(1 + Y/2)^2} + \frac{C}{(1 + Y/2)^3} + \frac{C \& F}{(1 + Y/2)^4} = \$1{,}000$$

from something that is Treasury-specific into something that is relevant for non-Treasury bonds, we can say that Y_i represents the yield of a like-maturity Treasury bond plus some incremental yield (and hence coupon) that a non-Treasury bond will have to pay so as to provide the proper incentive to purchase it. In the bond market, the difference between this incremental yield and a corresponding Treasury yield is called a *yield spread*. Rewriting the price formula, we have:

$$Price = \frac{C}{(1 + Y_i/2)^1} + \frac{C}{(1 + Y_i/2)^2} + \frac{C}{(1 + Y_i/2)^3} + \frac{C \& F}{(1 + Y_i/2)^4} = \$1{,}000$$

Since the same number of added basis points that are now included in Y_i are included in C, the price of the non-Treasury bond will still be par at

Cash Flows

the time of original issue—at least when it first comes to the marketplace. Afterwards things change; yield levels are free to rise and fall, and real and perceived credit risks can become greater or lesser over time. With regard to credit risks, greater ones will be associated with higher values of Y_i and lower ones will translate into lower values of Y_i.

So far, we have uncovered three uncertainties pertaining to pricing:

1. Uncertainty of price beyond time of original issue.
2. Uncertainty of reinvestment of coupons.
3. Uncertainty of credit quality.

To understand the layering effect, consider Figure 2.7. The first layer, uncertainty of price, is common to any fixed income security that is sold prior to maturity. The second layer, uncertainty of reinvestment, is applicable only to coupon-bearing bonds that pay a coupon prior to sale or maturity. And the third layer, uncertainty of credit quality, generally is unique to those bond issuers that do not have the luxury of legally printing money (i.e., that are not a government entity; for more on this, see Chapter 3).

SPOT PRICING FOR BONDS

Unlike equities or currencies, bonds are often as likely to be priced in terms of a dollar price as in terms of a yield. Thus, we need to differentiate among a few different types of yields that are of relevance for bonds.

The examples provided earlier made rather generic references to "yield." To be more precise, when a yield is calculated for the spot (or present) value of a bond, that yield commonly is referred to as *yield-to-maturity, bond-equivalent yield,* or *present yield*. There are also *current yields* (the result of dividing a bond's coupon by its current price), and *spot yields* (yield on bonds with no cash flows to be made until maturity). Thus, a spot yield could be

Rising uncertainty ↑		
	Uncertainty of credit quality	Generally when a security is a nongovernmental issue
	Uncertainty of reinvestment	When a coupon is paid prior to sale or maturity
	Uncertainty of price	For any fixed income security

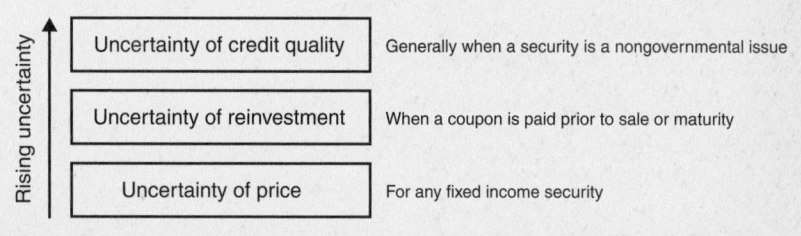

FIGURE 2.7 Layers of uncertainty among various types of bonds.

a yield on a Treasury bill,[3] a yield on a coupon-bearing bond with no remaining coupons to be paid until maturity, or a yield on a zero-coupon bond. In some instances even a yield on a coupon-bearing bond that has a price of par may be said to have a spot yield.[4] In fact, for a coupon-bearing bond whose price is par, its yield is sometimes called a *par bond yield*. For all of the yield types cited, annualizing according to U.S. convention is assumed to occur on the basis of a 365-day year (except for a leap year). Finally, when an entire *yield curve* is comprised of par bond yields, it is referred to as a *par bond curve*. A yield curve is created when the dots are connected across the yields of a particular issuer (or class of issuers) when its bonds are plotted by maturity. Figure 2.8 shows a yield curve of Treasury bonds taken from November 2002.

As shown, the Treasury bond yield curve is upward sloping. That is, longer-maturity yields are higher than shorter-maturity yields. In fact, more

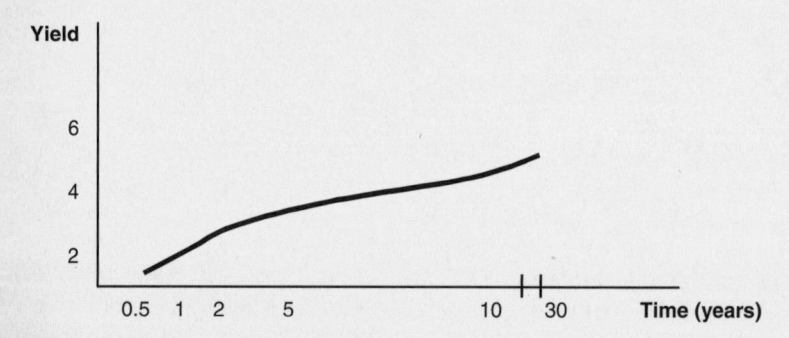

FIGURE 2.8 Normal upward-sloping yield curve.

---

[3] As a money market instrument (a fixed income security with an original term to maturity of 12 months or less), a Treasury bill also has unique calculations for its yield that are called "rate of discount" and "money market yield." A rate of discount is calculated as price divided by par and then annualized on the basis of a 360-day year, while a money market yield is calculated as par minus price divided by par and then annualized on the basis of a 360-day year.

[4] The reason why a coupon-bearing bond priced at par is said to have a yield equivalent to a spot yield is simply a function of algebraic manipulation. Namely, since a bond's coupon rate is equal to its yield when the bond is priced at par, and since its price and face value are equivalent when yield is equal to coupon rate, letting $C = Y$ and $P = F$ and multiplying through a generic price/yield equation by $1/F$ (permissible by the distributive property of multiplication) we get $1 = Y/2/(1 + Y/2)^1 + Y/2 /(1 + Y/2)^2 + ...$ In short, C drops away.

Cash Flows

often than not, the Treasury bond yield curve typically reflects such a positive slope.

When a bond is being priced, the same yield value is used to *discount* (reduce to a present value) every cash flow from the first coupon received in six months' time to the last coupon and face amount received in 2 or even 30 years' time. Instead of discounting a bond's cash flows with a single yield, which would suggest that the market's yield curve is perfectly flat, why not discount a bond's cash flows with more representative yields? Figure 2.9 shows how this might be done.

In actuality, many larger bond investors (e.g., bond funds and investment banks) make active use of this approach (or a variation thereof) to pricing bonds to perform *relative value* (the value of Bond A to Bond B) analysis. That is, if a bond's market price (calculated by market convention with a single yield throughout) was lower than its theoretical value (calculated from an actual yield curve), this would suggest that the bond is actually trading cheap in the marketplace.[5]

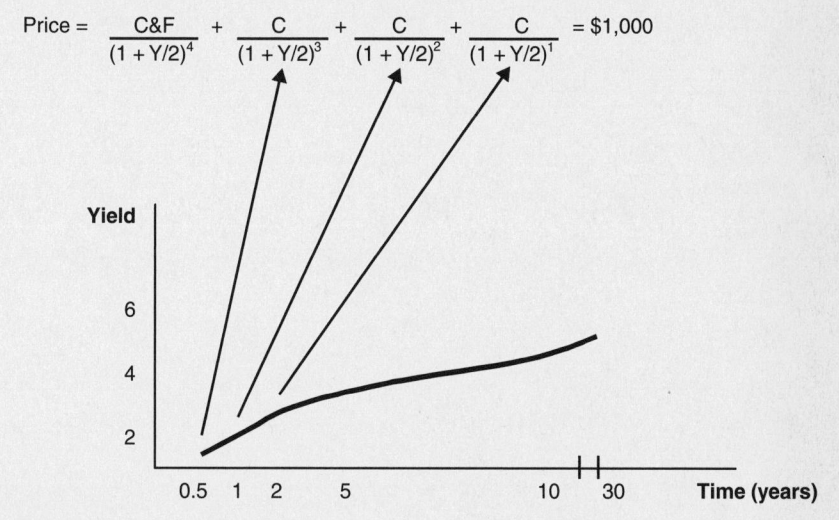

$$\text{Price} = \frac{C\&F}{(1+Y/2)^4} + \frac{C}{(1+Y/2)^3} + \frac{C}{(1+Y/2)^2} + \frac{C}{(1+Y/2)^1} = \$1,000$$

FIGURE 2.9 Using actual yields from a yield curve to calculate a bond's price.

---

[5]It is important to note that it is theoretically possible for a given bond to remain "cheap" (or rich) until the day it matures. A more likely scenario is that a bond's cheapness and richness will vary over time. Indeed, what many relative value investors look for is a good amount of variability in a bond's richness and cheapness as a precondition for purchasing it on a relative value basis.

While there is just one spot price in the world of bonds, there can be a variety of yields for bonds. Sometimes these different terms for yield apply to a single value. For example, for a coupon-bearing bond priced at par, its yield-to-maturity, current yield, and par bond yield are all the same value.

As previously stated, a yield spread is the difference between the yield of a nonbenchmark security and a benchmark security, and it is expressed in basis points.

Yield of nonbenchmark − Yield of benchmark = Spread in basis points

Therefore, any one of the following things might cause a spread to narrow or become smaller (where the opposite event would cause it to widen or become larger):

A. If the yield of the nonbenchmark (YNB) issue were to . . .
   i. . . . decline while the yield of the benchmark (YB) issue were to remain unchanged
   ii. . . . rise while the YB rose by more
   iii. . . . remain unchanged while the YB rose
B. If the yield of the benchmark issue (YB) were to . . .
   i. . . . rise while the yield of the nonbenchmark (YNB) issue remained unchanged
   ii. . . . decline while the YNB fell by more
   iii. . . . remain unchanged while the YNB fell

Thus, the driving force(s) behind a change in spread can be attributable to the nonbenchmark, the benchmark, or a combination of both. Accordingly, investors using spreads to identify relative value must keep these contributory factors in mind.

Regarding spreads generally, while certainly of some value as a single static measure, they are more typically regarded by fixed income investors as having value in a dynamic context. At the very least, a single spread measure communicates whether the nonbenchmark security is trading *rich* (at a lower yield) or *cheap* (at a higher yield) to the benchmark security. Since the benchmark yield is usually subtracted from the nonbenchmark yield, a positive yield spread suggests that the nonbenchmark is trading cheap to the benchmark security, and a negative yield spread suggests that it is trading rich to the benchmark security. To say much beyond this in a strategy-creation context with the benefit of only one data point (the one spread value) is rather difficult. More could be said with the benefit of additional data points.

For example, if today's spread value is 50 basis points (bps), and we know that over the past four weeks the spread has ranged between 50 bps and 82 bps, then we might say that the nonbenchmark security is at the *richer* (narrower) end of the range of where it has traded relative to the benchmark issue. If today's spread value were 82 bps, then we might say that the nonbenchmark security is at the *cheaper* (wider) end of the range of where it has been trading. These types of observations can be of great value to fixed income investors when trying to decipher market trends and potential opportunities. Yet even for a measure as simple as the difference between two yields, some basic analysis might very well be appropriate. A spread might change from day to day for any number of reasons. Many bond fund managers work to know when and how to trade around these various changes.

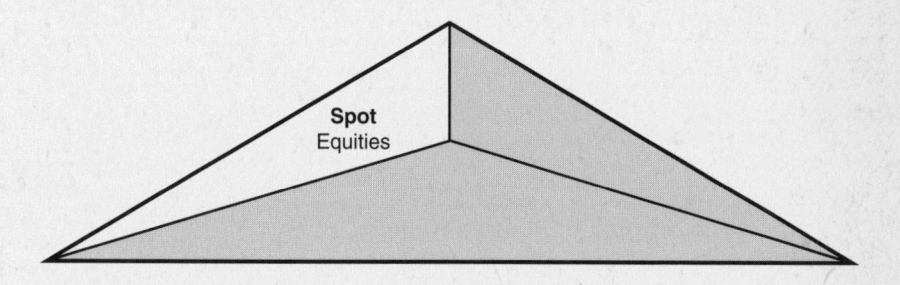

Spot
Equities

Now we can begin listing similarities and differences between equities and bonds. Equities differ from bonds since they have no predetermined maturity. Equities are similar to bonds since many equities pay dividends, just as most bonds pay coupons. However, dividends of equities generally tend to be of lower dollar amounts relative to coupons of bonds, and dividend amounts paid may vary over time in line with the company's profitability and dividend-paying philosophy; the terms of a bond's coupon payments typically are set from the beginning. And while not typical, a company might choose to skip a dividend payment on its equity and without legal consequences, while a skipped coupon payment on a bond is generally sufficient to initiate immediate concerns regarding a company's ongoing viability.[6] Occasionally a company may decide to skip a dividend payment altogether, with the decision having nothing to do with the problems in the company; there may simply be some accounting incentives for it, for example. Otherwise, in the United States, bonds typically pay coupons on a semiannual basis while equities tend to pay dividends on a quarterly basis. Figure 2.10 is tailored to equities.

---

[6]Terms and conditions of certain preferred equities may impose strict guidelines on dividend policies that firms are expected to follow.

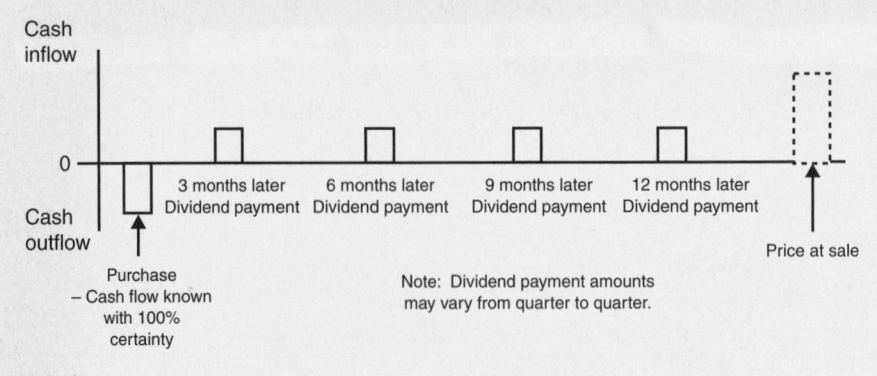

FIGURE 2.10 Cash flows of a typical equity.

We need to think not only about probabilities related to the nature and size of future dividends, but also about what to assume for the end price of an equity purchase. At least among the so-called *blue chip* (stocks of strong and well-established companies with reputations for paying dividends over a variety of market cycles) equities, investors tend to rest pretty comfortably with the assumption that regular and timely dividend payments will be made (just as with the debt instruments issued by blue chip corporations).

How can an investor attempt to divine an end price of an equity? There are formulas available to assist with answering this question, one of which is called the *expected growth in dividends formula*. As the name implies, a forecast of future dividends is required, and such a forecast typically is made with consideration of expectations of future earnings.

The expected growth in dividends approach to divining a future price for an equity is expressed as

$$\textit{Expected future price per share} = \frac{\textit{Expected dividend(s) per share}}{\textit{Cost of equity}\,(\%) - \textit{Expected growth rate of dividend(s)}\,(\%)}$$

While this formula may provide some rudimentary guidance on future price behavior, it falls short of the world of bonds where at least a final maturity price is prespecified.

Perhaps because of the more open-ended matter of determining what an equity's price ought to be, there tends to be less of a focus on using quantitative valuation methods with equities in favor of more qualitative measures.[7] For example, some equity analysts assign great value to determining an equity's *book value* and then forecasting an appropriate *multiple* for that book value. Book value is defined as the current value of assets on a company's balance sheet according to its accounting conventions, and the term "multiple" is simply a reference to how many times higher the book value could trade as an actual market price. For an equity with a $10 per share book value that an analyst believes should trade at a multiple of eight within the span of a year, the forecast is for a market value of $80 per share. The decision to assign a multiple of 8 instead of 4 or 20 may stem from anything ranging from an analyst's gut feeling to an extensive analysis of a company's overall standing relative to peer groups. Other valuation methods might include analysis of an equity's price relative to its earnings outlook, or even technical analysis, which involves charting an equity's past price behavior to extrapolate what future price patterns may actually look like.

Investors typically buy bonds for different reasons than why they buy equities. For example, an investor who is predisposed to a Treasury bond is likely to be someone who wants the predictability and safety that the Treasury bond represents. An investor who is predisposed to the equity of a given issuer (as opposed to the debt of that issuer) is likely to be someone who is comfortable with the risk and uncertainty of what its price will be in two years' time or even two months' time.

There are some pretty clear expectations about price patterns and behavior of bonds; in the equity arena, price boundaries are less well delineated. As two significant implications of this observation, equities tend to experience much greater price action (or volatility) relative to bonds, and the less constrained (and greater potential) for experiencing upside performance would be more likely linked with equities as opposed to bonds (at least as long as the longer-run economic backdrop is such that the underlying economy itself is growing). Both of these expectations hold up rather well on a historical basis.

---

[7] I do not mean to detract from the rigor of analysis that often accompanies a qualitative approach. The point is simply that a key forecast (or set of forecasts) is required (often pertaining to the expected behavior of future dividends and/or earnings), and this, by definition, requires cash flow assumptions to be made. This forecasting requirement is in contrast to the cash flow profile of a Treasury note where all expected distributions are known at time of purchase.

**Spot
Currencies**

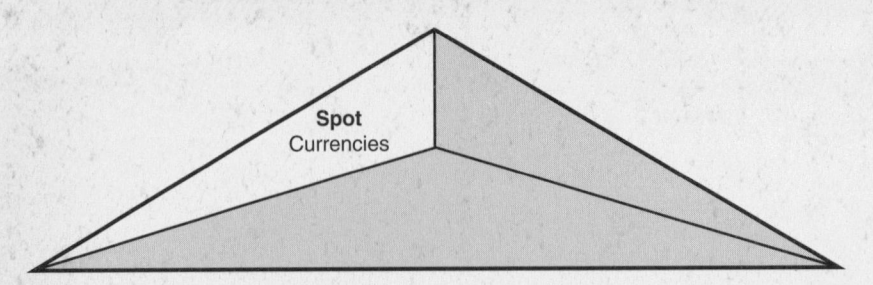

Currencies are considerably simpler than either equities or bonds when it comes to spot pricing. From a cash flow perspective, there is a cash outflow when a currency is purchased and a cash inflow when a currency is sold. There are no intervening cash flows. As with equities, there are no maturity dates, yet since there is typically one currency per country, shaping a view on a currency's prospects could well become much more involved than what is required for developing an outlook for a single company (as with forecasting future dividends). Chapter 3 explores important credit quality considerations for currencies.

SPOT SUMMARY

In summary, the spot price of an asset is nothing more than what the market says the price should be. There may very well be a difference between the market's price and our own views on an asset's true value. The fact that fixed income securities have an end price that is known at the time of purchase greatly facilitates the matter of arriving at an appropriate spot price of bonds. By contrast, the lack of a certain future value of an equity or unhedged currency gives rise to the use of various qualitative methods. For currencies, these methods may involve models centered on interest rate parity or purchasing power parity theories. In the case of equities these methods may involve models centered on forecasts of future dividends or earnings or even technical analysis.

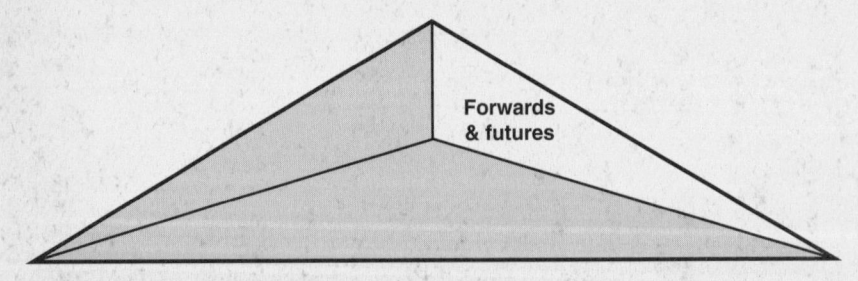

**Forwards
& futures**

A forward is one small step away from spot. As the term implies, a forward is an agreement to exchange a financial asset for cash at some point in the future—at some point beyond the time frame implied by the asset's typical settlement conventions.

In the spot market, a typical settlement period for a Treasury bill is one business day. A settlement for the same day that the trade is agreed on is called a *same-day* settlement or *cash* settlement. Any settlement agreement that extends beyond one business day is a *forward settlement*. If the number of days happens to be three, then in the vernacular of the bond markets this is referred to as *corporate settlement*. It takes this name because corporate bonds settle differently from Treasury instruments; they generally settle over three days instead of just one. If the future settlement date happens to be something other than cash, next day, or corporate, then it has no special name — it is simply referred to as being a forward settlement transaction of so many days from the *trade date*. The trade date is when a price, product, and quantity are agreed on, and the *settlement date* is when the product is exchanged for cash (or some other agreed-on exchange).

For a settlement date that goes beyond the day-to-day convention of the respective asset class, the spot price needs to be adjusted. To better understand why, let us consider a more extreme case where a settlement does not occur for one year.

Assume we desire to buy 10 ounces of gold for $400 per ounce, but we do not want to take physical delivery of the gold for one year. Perhaps we do not have the cash on hand today but anticipate having it in one year. Further, perhaps we believe that when we do have the cash in one year, the spot price of gold will be appreciably above $400 per ounce.

The person who is selling us those 10 ounces of gold may not like the fact that she has committed to selling something so far into the future for no up-front payment. Indeed, if our seller had received $4,000 under a regular settlement, then that $4,000 could have been invested in a one-year Treasury bill. But there is no $4,000 to invest over the one-year period because no exchange has taken place yet. This absence of an immediate payment represents an opportunity cost to our seller. Therefore, our seller is going to ask us to commit to a forward price of something above $400/ounce. How much above? Whatever the difference is between the total spot price of the gold and the opportunity cost of not having that total spot value over the course of one year. If the cost of money for one year were 5 percent, then the opportunity cost for our gold seller is $200:

$$\$200 = \$4,200 - \$4,000.$$
$$\$4,200 = \$4,000 \times (1 + 5\% \times 365/365).$$
$$\$4,000 = 10 \times \$400/\text{ounce}.$$

If the forward date were six months (183 days) instead of one year, then the opportunity cost for our gold seller would be $100:

$100 = $4,100 − $4,000.
$4,100 = $4,000 × (1 + 5% × 183/365).

Thus, the gold seller probably would want to sell the 10 ounces of gold for a total of $4,200 for a one-year settlement agreement and for $4,100 for a six-month settlement agreement.

The formula for a forward in the simple case of gold can be written as:

$$F = S(1 + RT)$$

where S = spot
R = opportunity cost
T = time

FUTURES

Now that we have reviewed the basic concepts underlying forwards, it is an easy matter to tie in the role of futures. Just like forwards, futures represent a vehicle for making a commitment today to purchase or sell something at a later date. The biggest difference between a forward and a future is how the cash flows work. With a forward agreement to buy 100 ounces of gold, for example, no cash is exchanged for the physical gold until the expiration day of the forward contract. With a futures contract on gold, it works a little differently.

Assume that the price of gold with a one-year futures contract is $440 an ounce and that an investor chooses to *go long* (purchase) a gold futures contract with the one-year futures price at that level. That future price of $440 becomes a line in the sand; it is the benchmark against which daily price changes in the value of gold will be measured over an entire year. At the end of one year, the investor can take delivery of the gold underlying the futures contract for $440 an ounce. However, it is important to note what happens between the time the futures contract is obtained and when it expires a year later.

Let us say that the futures contract is obtained on a Monday with gold at $440 an ounce. On Tuesday, the very next day, say the gold market closes at $441 an ounce. This additional $1 value of gold ($441 versus $440) goes into a special account of the investor (usually called a *margin account*[8]) that typically is maintained at the *exchange* (such as the Chicago Mercantile Exchange) where the futures contract was transacted. If she wanted to, our gold futures investor could immediately *unwind* (offset with an opposite trade) her futures contract (by selling the same contract) and instantly make a $1 profit. However, if our investor is a purchaser of gold and truly believes that a future price of $440 will be a bargain in one year's time, then she could very well decide to hold the contract to expiration. In this instance the $1 that goes into her account on Tuesday may not be something she considers to be a profit; rather, she may just consider it to be $1 less she will have to pay for gold in a year if the price remains at $441 an ounce.

Of course, the likelihood is fairly small that gold will remain at one price for an entire year. In fact, the gold investor expects that gold will keep climbing in price, though likely with some volatility along the way; the price of gold probably will not rise every single day, and over the course of a year it could very well end up lower than $440 an ounce.

Again, at least in the present case with gold, the biggest difference between a forward and a future is how the cash flows work between the time the trade is first executed and when it expires, that is, the daily mark-to-market dynamic with the futures contracts. The net effect of receiving a security at some later day but at an earlier agreed-on price is exactly the same for these two instrument types.

Chapter 6 will delve into more detail of when and why certain types of investors might prefer using futures instead of forwards.

Figure 2.11 shows the relationship between spots and forwards explicitly. Spot (S) is a key variable for calculating a forward (F) value. In fact, spot is so important that when $S = 0$, $F = 0$; a forward is nothing without some value for spot. Further, if there were no opportunity cost to money (meaning that money is borrowed and lent at an interest rate of zero), then $F = S$. And if there is no forward time horizon ($T = 0$; there is immediate settlement), then $F = S$. In short, a key difference between spots and forwards is the SRT term. RT is sometimes called *cost of carry* or simply *carry*.

For a forward settlement on a Treasury bill, the same logic applies that was just used for gold.

---

[8]If the market moves against a futures investor in a big way (as with a large decline in the price of gold in this example), the futures exchange might ask the investor to post margin. The investor is required to deposit money into the margin account to assure the exchange that she has the financial resources to make good on her commitments for future purchases at the agreed-on terms.

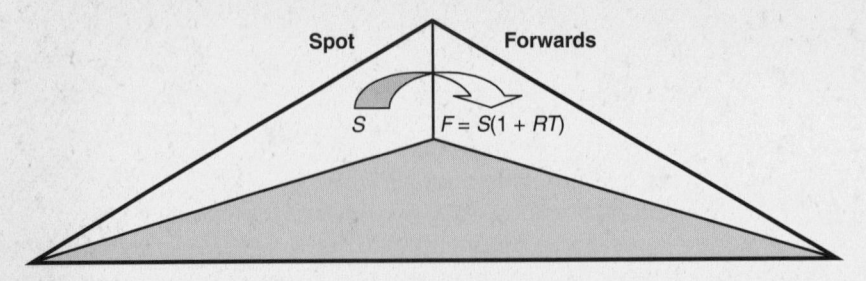

FIGURE 2.11 Relationship between spots and forwards.

For example, let us say we have a three-month Treasury bill with 90 days to maturity and with a dollar price of 98.7875 (from a *rate of discount* of 4.85 percent). Let us further assume that the prevailing forces of supply and demand for our Treasury bill in the *securities lending market* (or *repurchase (repo) market* for bonds), dictates a *financing rate* of 5.5 percent for a period of 30 days. A securities lending market is where specific financial instruments are borrowed (lent) by (to) investors over predetermined periods of time, and at an agreed-upon rate of financing. To calculate this Treasury bill's forward rate, we do the following calculation:

$$F = S(1 + RT)$$
$$99.2403 = 98.7875 + 98.7875 \times (1 + 5.5\% \times 30/360).$$

The difference between the cash price of 98.7875 dollars and the forward price of 99.2403 dollars, or 45.28 cents, is often referred to as the *carry*, the *forward drop*, or simply the *drop*.

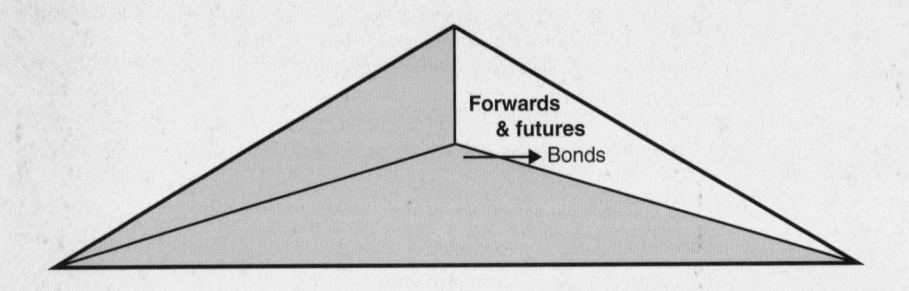

The calculation is pretty much the same to perform a forward price calculation with a coupon-bearing Treasury. Since coupon-bearing U.S. Treasuries pay coupons on a semiannual basis, and knowing that coupon payments key

Cash Flows

off of maturity dates, let us assume we have a Treasury that matures on November 15 in five years. Accordingly, this Treasury will pay a coupon every November 15 and May 15 until maturity. If today happens to be October 1 and we want to calculate a forward price for 30 days from now (October 31), our forward price formula will need to consider that the bond will be *accruing* (accumulating) coupon value over those 30 days. For coupon-bearing securities, prices often are referred to as being either *clean* or *dirty*.[9] If an investor is being quoted a bond's dirty price, the price includes any accrued coupon value; if it is quoted as clean, the price does not include any accrued coupon value. Figure 2.12 clarifies this point.

For a coupon-bearing bond, S must be defined in terms of both price and coupon dynamics. In particular, this added dimension of the coupon component gives rise to the need for inserting an additional rate in the forward calculation. This second rate is current yield.

In the case of bonds, current yield is defined as a bond's coupon divided by its current price, and it provides a measure of annual percentage coupon return. As shown in Table 2.1, for a security whose price is par, its yield-to-maturity

Coupon value

In the period between coupon payments, a coupon's value accretes on a daily basis and is called "accrued interest."

Coupon payment is made

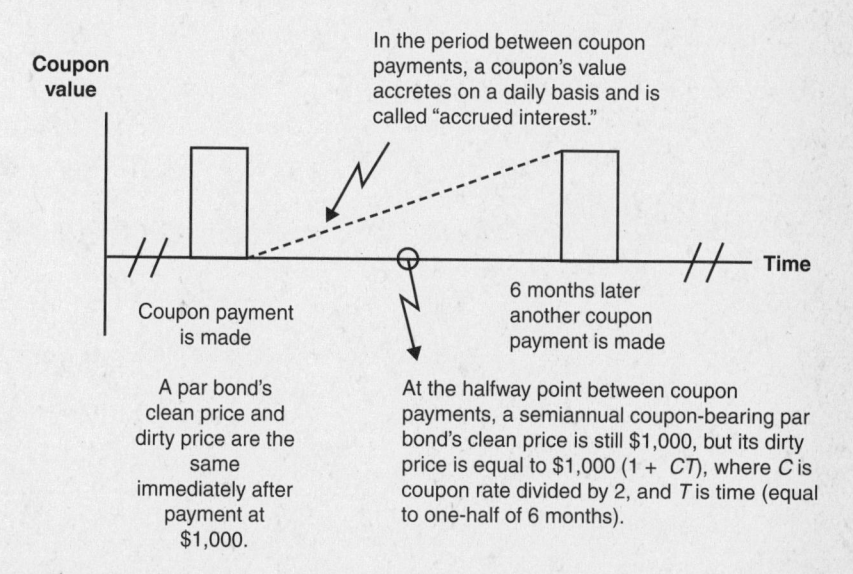

6 months later another coupon payment is made

A par bond's clean price and dirty price are the same immediately after payment at $1,000.

At the halfway point between coupon payments, a semiannual coupon-bearing par bond's clean price is still $1,000, but its dirty price is equal to $1,000 (1 + CT), where C is coupon rate divided by 2, and T is time (equal to one-half of 6 months).

FIGURE 2.12 Accrued interest, dirty prices, and clean prices.

---

[9]The clean price is also referred to as the flat price, and the dirty price is also referred to as the full price.

TABLE 2.1

Comparisons of Yield-to-Maturity and Current Yield for a Semiannual 6% Coupon 2-Year Bond

Price	Yield-to-Maturity (%)	Current Yield (%)
102	4.94	5.88
100	6.00	6.00
98	7.08	6.12

and current yield are identical. Further, current yield does not have nearly the price sensitivity as yield to maturity. Again, this is explained by current yield's focus on just the coupon return component of a bond. Since current yield does not require any assumptions pertaining to the ultimate maturity of the security in question, it is readily applied to a variety of nonfixed income securities.

Let us pause here to consider the simple case of a six-month forward on a five-year par bond. Assume that the forward begins one day after a coupon has been paid and ends the day a coupon is to be paid. Figure 2.13 illustrates the different roles of a risk-free rate (R) and current yield (Y_c).

As shown, one trajectory is generated with R and another with Y_c. Clearly, the purchaser of the forward ought not to be required to pay the seller's opportunity cost (calculated with R) on top of the full price (clean price plus accrued interest) of the underlying spot security. Accordingly, Y_c is subtracted from R, and the resulting price formula becomes:

$$F = S(1 + T(R - Y_c))$$

for a forward clean price calculation.

For a forward dirty price calculation, we have:

$$F_d = S_d(1 + T(R - Y_c)) + A_f,$$

where
  F_d = the full or dirty price of the forward (clean price plus accrued interest)
  S_d = the full or dirty price of the underlying spot (clean price plus accrued interest)
  A_f = the accrued interest on the forward at expiration of the forward

The equation bears a very close resemblance to the forward formula presented earlier as $F = S(1 + RT)$. Indeed, with the simplifying assumption that $T = 0$, F_d reduces to $S_d + A_f$. In other words, if settlement is immediate rather

Cash Flows

Price

Y_c trajectory (5%)

102.5 = 100 + 100 * 5% * 1/2

101.5 = 100 + 100 * 3% * 1/2

Of course, these particular prices may or may not actually prevail in 6 months' time...

100

R trajectory (3%)

101.5 − 102.5 = −1.0
100.0 − 1.0 = 99.0 = F,
where F is the clean forward price

Coupon payment date

6-month forward is purchased

Coupon payment date and forward expiration date

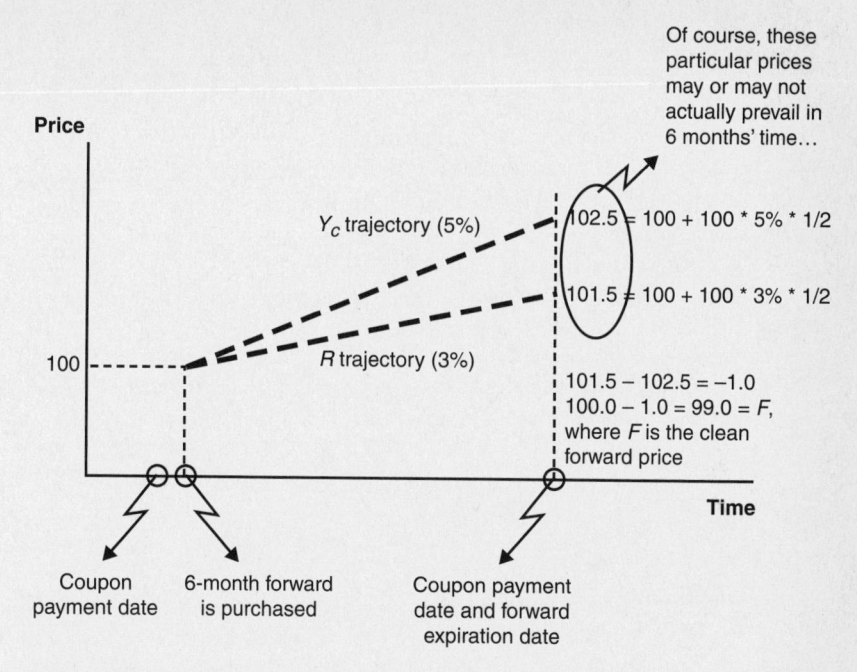

Time

FIGURE 2.13 Relationship between Y_c and R over time.

than sometime in the future, $F_d = S_d$ since A_f is nothing more than the accrued interest (if any) associated with an immediate purchase and settlement.

Inserting values from Figure 2.13 into the equation, we have:

$$F_d = 100 \, (1 + 1/2 \, (3\% - 5\%)) + 5\% \times 100 \times 1/2 = 101.5,$$

and 101.5 represents an annualized 3 percent rate of return (opportunity cost) for the seller of the forward.

Clearly it is the relationship between Y_c and R that determines if $F > S$, $F < S$, or $F = S$ (where F and S denote respective clean prices). We already know that when there are no intervening cash flows F is simply $S \, (1 + RT)$, and we would generally expect $F > S$ since we expect S, R, and T to be positive values. But for securities that pay intervening cash flows, S will be equal to F when $Y_c = R$; F will be less than S when $Y_c > R$; and F will be greater than S only when $R > Y_c$. In the vernacular of the marketplace, the case of $Y_c > R$ is termed positive carry and the case of $Y_c < R$ is termed negative carry. Since R is the short-term rate of financing and Y_c is a longer-term yield associated with a bond, positive carry generally prevails when the yield curve has a positive or upward slope, as it historically has exhibited.

For the case where the term of a forward lasts over a series of coupon payments, it may be easier to see why Y_c is subtracted from R. Since a forward involves the commitment to purchase a security at a future point in time, a forward "leaps" over a span of time defined as the difference between the date the forward is purchased and the date it expires. When the forward expires, its purchaser takes ownership of any underlying spot security and pays the previously agreed forward price. Figure 2.14 depicts this scenario. As shown, the forward leaps over the three separate coupon cash flows; the purchaser does not receive these cash flows since he does not actually take ownership of the underlying spot until the forward expires. And since the holder of the forward will not receive these intervening cash flows, he ought not to pay for them. As discussed, the spot price of a coupon-bearing bond embodies an expectation of the coupon actually being paid. Accordingly, when calculating the forward value of a security that generates cash flows, it is necessary to adjust for the value of any cash flows that are paid and reinvested over the life of the forward itself.

Bonds are unique relative to equities and currencies (and all other types of assets) since they are priced both in terms of dollar prices and in terms of yields (or yield spreads). Now, we must discuss how a forward yield of a bond is calculated. To do this, let us use a real-world scenario. Let us assume that an investor is trying to decide between (a) buying two consecutive six-month Treasury bills and (b) buying one 12-month Treasury bill. Both investments involve a 12-month horizon, and we assume that our investor intends to hold any purchased securities until they mature. Should our investor pick strategy (a) or strategy (b)? To answer this, the investor prob-

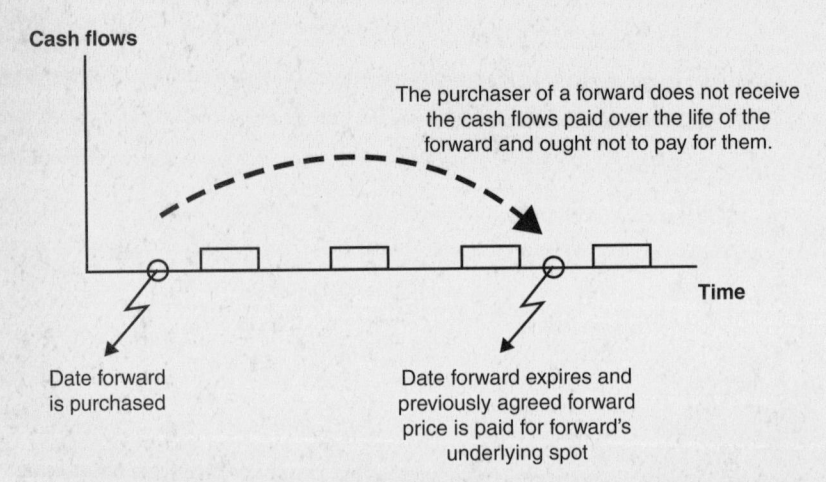

FIGURE 2.14 Relationship between forwards and ownership of intervening cash flows.

ably will want some indication of when and how strategy (a) will break even relative to strategy (b). That is, when and how does the investor become indifferent between strategy (a) and (b) in terms of their respective returns? Calculating a single forward rate can help us to answer this question.

To ignore, just for a moment, the consideration of compounding, assume that the yield on a one-year Treasury bill is 5 percent and that the yield on a six-month Treasury bill is 4.75 percent. Since we want to know what the yield on the second six-month Treasury bill will have to be to earn an equivalent of 5 percent, we can simply solve for x with

$$5\% = (4.75\% + x)/2.$$

Rearranging, we have

$$x = 10\% - 4.75\% = 5.25\%.$$

Therefore, to be indifferent between two successive six-month Treasury bills or one 12-month Treasury bill, the second six-month Treasury bill would have to yield at least 5.25 percent. Sometimes this yield is referred to as a hurdle rate, because a reinvestment at a rate less than this will not be as rewarding as a 12-month Treasury bill. Now let's see how the calculation looks with a more formal forward calculation where compounding is considered.

$$F_{6,6} = \left[\left[\frac{(1 + Y_2/2)^2}{(1 + Y_1/2)^1}\right] - 1\right] \times 2$$

$$F_{6,6} = \left[\left[\frac{(1 + 0.05/2)^2}{(1 + 0.0475/2)^1}\right] - 1\right] \times 2$$

$$= 5.25\%$$

The formula for $F_{6,6}$ (the first 6 refers to the maturity of the future Treasury bill in months and the second 6 tells us the forward expiration date in months) tells us the following: For investors to be indifferent between buying two consecutive six-month Treasury bills or one 12-month Treasury bill, they will need to buy the second six-month Treasury bill at a minimum yield of 5.25 percent. Will six-month Treasury bill yields be at 5.25 percent in six months' time? Who knows? But investors may have a particular view on the matter. For example, if *monetary authorities* (central bank officials) are in an easing mode with monetary policy and short-term interest rates are expected to fall (such that a six-month Treasury bill yield of less than 5.25 percent looks likely), then a 12-month Treasury bill investment would appear to be the better bet. Yet, the world is an uncertain place, and the forward rate simply helps with thinking about what the world would have to look like in the future to be indifferent between two (or more) investments.

To take this a step further, let us consider the scenario where investors would have to be indifferent between buying four six-month Treasury bills or one two-year coupon-bearing Treasury bond. We already know that the first six-month Treasury bill is yielding 4.75 percent, and that the forward rate on the second six-month Treasury bill is 5.25 percent. Thus, we still need to calculate a 12-month and an 18-month forward rate on a six-month Treasury bill. If we assume spot rates for 18 and 24 months are 5.30 percent and 5.50 percent, respectively, then our calculations are:

$$F_{6,12} = \left[\left[\frac{(1 + 0.053/2)^3}{(1 + 0.05/2)^2}\right] - 1\right] \times 2$$

$$= 5.90\%, and$$

$$F_{6,18} = \left[\left[\frac{(1 + 0.055/2)^4}{(1 + 0.053/2)^3}\right] - 1\right] \times 2$$

$$= 6.10\%.$$

For investors to be indifferent between buying a two-year Treasury bond at 5.5 percent and successive six-month Treasury bills (assuming that the coupon cash flows of the two-year Treasury bond are reinvested at 5.5 percent every six months), the successive six-month Treasury bills must yield a minimum of:

5.25 percent 6 months after initial trade
5.90 percent 12 months after initial trade
6.10 percent 18 months after initial trade

Note that 4.75% × .25 + 5.25%×.25 + 5.9%×.25 + 6.1%×.25 = 5.5%.

Again, 5.5 percent is the yield-to-maturity of an existing two-year Treasury bond.

Each successive calculation of a forward rate explicitly incorporates the yield of the previous calculation. To emphasize this point, Figure 2.15 repeats the three calculations.

In brief, in stark contrast to the nominal yield calculations earlier in this chapter, where the same yield value was used in each and every denominator where a new cash flow was being *discounted* (reduced to a present value), with forward yield calculations a new and different yield is used for every cash flow. This looping effect, sometimes called *bootstrapping*, differentiates a forward yield calculation from a nominal yield calculation.

Cash Flows

$$F_{6,6} = \left[\left[\frac{(1+0.05/2)^2}{(1+0.0475/2)^1}\right]-1\right] \times 2$$

$$= 5.25\%$$

$$F_{6,12} = \left[\left[\frac{(1+0.053/2)^3}{(1+0.05/2)^2}\right]-1\right] \times 2$$

$$= 5.90\%, \text{ and}$$

$$F_{6,18} = \left[\left[\frac{(1+0.055/2)^4}{(1+0.053/2)^3}\right]-1\right] \times 2$$

$$= 6.10\%.$$

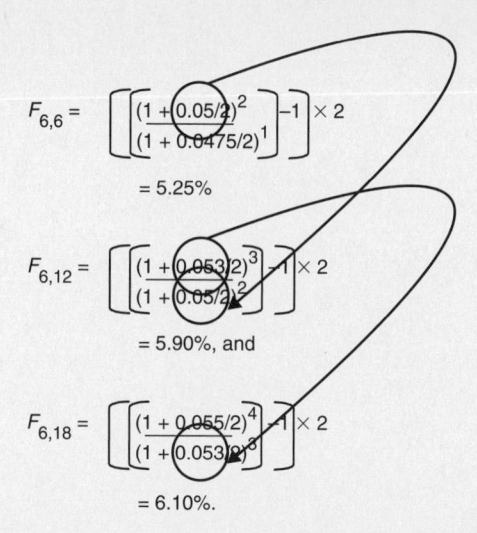

FIGURE 2.15 Bootstrapping methodology for building forward rates.

Because a single forward yield can be said to embody all of the forward yields preceding it (stemming from the bootstrapping effect), forward yields sometimes are said to embody an entire yield curve. The previous equations show why this is the case.

Table 2.2 constructs three different forward yield curves relative to three spot curves. Observe that forward rates trade above spot rates when the spot rate curve is normal or upward sloping; forward rates trade below spot rate when the spot rate curve is inverted; and the spot curve is equal to the forward curve when the spot rate curve is flat.

The section on bonds and spot discussed nominal yield spreads. In the context of spot yield spreads, there is obviously no point in calculating the spread of a benchmark against itself. That is, if a Treasury yield is the benchmark yield for calculating yield spreads, a Treasury should not be spread against itself; the result will always be zero. However, a Treasury forward spread can be calculated as the forward yield difference between two Treasuries. Why might such a thing be done?

Again, when a nominal yield spread is calculated, a single yield point on a par bond curve (as with a 10-year Treasury yield) is subtracted from the same maturity yield of the security being compared. In sum, two independent and comparable points from two nominal yield curves are being compared. In the vernacular of the marketplace, this spread might be referred to as "the spread to the 10-year Treasury." However, with a forward curve, if the underlying spot curve has any shape to it at all (meaning if it is anything other than flat), the shape of the forward curve will differ from the shape of the par bond curve. Further, the creation of a forward curve involves a

TABLE 2.2 Table Forward Rates under Various Spot Rate Scenarios

Forward Expiration	Scenario A Spot Forward	Scenario B Spot Forward	Scenario C Spot Forward
6 Month	8.00 /8.00	8.00 /8.00	8.00 /8.00
12 Month	8.25 /8.50	7.75 /7.50	8.00 /8.00
18 Month	8.50 /9.00	7.50 /7.00	8.00 /8.00
24 Month	8.75 /9.50	7.25 /6.50	8.00 /8.00
30 Month	9.00 /10.00	7.00 /6.00	8.00 /8.00

Scenario A: Normal slope spot curve shape (upward sloping)
Scenario B: Inverted slope spot curve
Scenario C: Flat spot curve

process whereby successive yields are dependent on previous yield calculations; a single forward yield value explicitly incorporates some portion of an entire par bond yield curve. As such, when a forward yield spread is calculated between two forward yields, it is not entirely accurate to think of it as being a spread between two independent points as can be said in a nominal yield spread calculation. By its very construction, the forward yield embodies the yields all along the relevant portion of a spot curve.

Figure 2.16 presents this discussion graphically. As shown, the benchmark reference value for a nominal yield spread calculation is simply taken from a single point on the curve. The benchmark reference value for a forward yield spread calculation is mathematically derived from points all along the relevant par bond curve.

If a par bond Treasury curve is used to construct a Treasury forward curve, then a zero spread value will result when one of the forward yields of a par bond curve security is spread against its own forward yield level. However, when a non-par bond Treasury security has its forward yield spread calculated in reference to forward yield of a par bond issue, the spread difference will likely be positive.[10] Therefore, one reason why a forward spread might be calculated between two Treasuries is that this spread gives a measure of the difference between the forward structure of the par bond Treasury curve versus non-par bond Treasury issues. This particular spreading of Treasury securities can be referred to as a measure of a given Treasury yield's *liquidity premium,* that is,

---

[10]One reason why non-par bond Treasury issues usually trade at higher forward yields is that non-par securities are *off-the-run* securities. An *on-the-run* Treasury is the most recently auctioned Treasury security; as such, typically it is the most liquid and most actively traded. When an on-the-run issue is replaced by some other newly auctioned Treasury, it becomes an off-the-run security and generally takes on some kind of liquidity premium. As it becomes increasingly off-the-run, its liquidity premium tends to grow.

Cash Flows 45

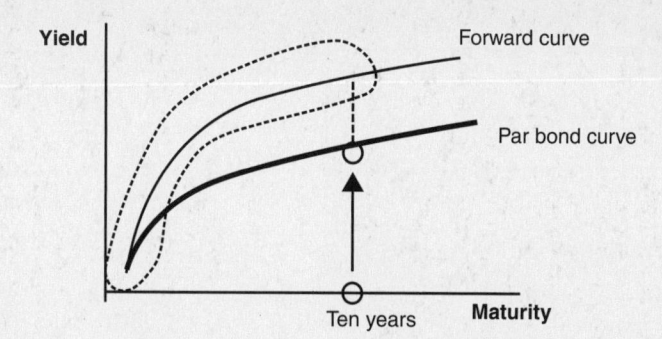

FIGURE 2.16 Distinctions between points on and point along par bond and forward curves.

the risk associated with trading in a non-par bond Treasury that may not always be as readily available in the market as a par bond issue.

To calculate a forward spread for a non-Treasury security (i.e., a security that is not regarded as risk free), a Treasury par bond curve typically is used as the reference curve to construct a forward curve. The resulting forward spread embodies both a measure of a non-Treasury liquidity premium and the non-Treasury credit risk.

We conclude this section with Figure 2.17.

BOND FUTURES

Two formulaic modifications are required when going from a bond's forward price calculation to its futures price calculation. The first key difference is the incorporation of a bond's *conversion factor*. Unlike gold, which is a standard commodity type, bonds come in many flavors. Some bonds have shorter maturities than others, higher coupons than others, or fewer bells and whistles than others, even among Treasury issues (which are the most actively traded of bond futures). Therefore, a conversion factor is an attempt to apply a standardized variable to the calculation of all candidates' spot prices.[11] As shown in the equation on page 46, the clean forward price

---

[11] A conversion factor is simply a modified forward price for a bond that is eligible to be an underlying security within a futures contract. As with any bond price, the necessary variables are price (or yield), coupon, maturity date, and settlement date. However, the settlement date is assumed to be first day of the month that the contract is set to expire; the maturity date is assumed to be the first day of the month that the bond is set to mature rounded down to the nearest quarter (March, June, September, or December); and the yield is assumed to be 8 percent regardless of what it may actually be. The dirty price that results is then divided by 100 and rounded up at the fourth decimal place.

A par bond curve of spot yields ... is used to construct a forward yield curve.

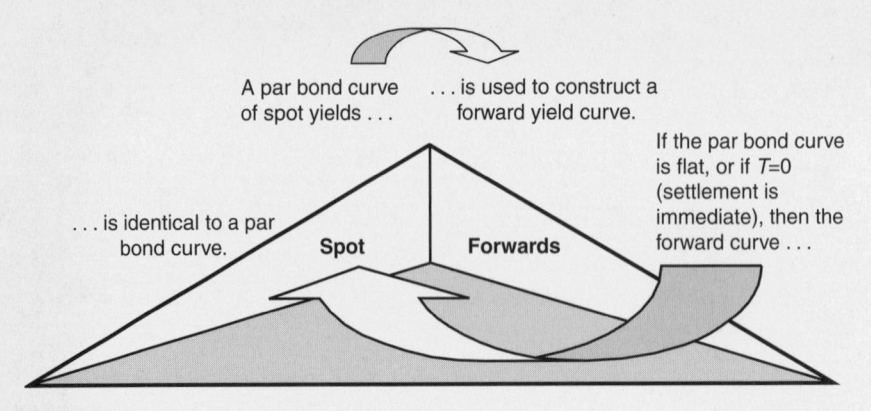

... is identical to a par bond curve.

Spot Forwards

If the par bond curve is flat, or if T=0 (settlement is immediate), then the forward curve ...

FIGURE 2.17 Spot versus forward yield curves.

of a contract-eligible bond is simply divided by its relevant conversion factor. When the one bond is flagged as the relevant underlying spot security for the futures contract (via a process described in Chapter 4), its conversion-adjusted forward price becomes the contract's price.

The second formula modification required when going from a forward price calculation to a futures price calculation concerns the fact that a bond futures contract comes with *delivery options*. That is, when a bond futures contract comes to its expiration month, investors who are short the contract face a number of choices. Recall that at the expiration of a forward or future, some predetermined amount of an asset is exchanged for cash. Investors who are long the forward or future pay cash and *accept delivery* (take ownership) of the asset. Investors who are short the forward or future receive cash and *make delivery* (convey ownership) of the asset. With a bond futures contract, the delivery process can take place on any business day of the designated delivery month, and investors who are short the contract can choose when delivery is made during that month. This choice (along with others embedded in the forward contract) has value, as does any asymmetrical decision-making consideration, and it ought to be incorporated into a bond future's price calculation. Chapter 4 discusses the other choices embedded in a bond futures contract and how these options can be valued.

A bond futures price can be defined as:

$$F_d = [S(1 + T(R - Y_c)) + A_f - O_d]/CF$$

where O_d = the embedded delivery options
CF = the conversion factor

Cash Flows

A minus sign appears in front of O_d since the delivery options are of benefit to investors who are short the bond future. Again, more on all this in Chapter 4.

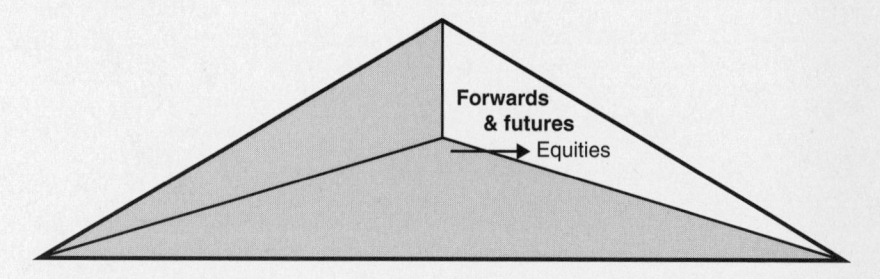

To calculate the forward price of an equity, let us consider IBM at $80.25 a share. If IBM were not to pay dividends as a matter of corporate policy, then to calculate a one-year forward price, we would simply multiply the number of shares being purchased by $80.25 and adjust this by the cost of money for one year. The formula would be $F = S(1 + RT)$, exactly as with gold or Treasury bills. However, IBM's equity *does* pay a dividend, so the forward price for IBM must reflect the fact that these dividends are received over the coming year. The formula really does not look that different from what we use for a coupon-bearing bond; in fact, except for one variable, it is the same. It is

$$F = S(1 + T(R - Y_d))$$

where Y_d = dividend yield calculated as the sum of expected dividends in the coming year divided by the underlying equity's market price.

Precisely how dividends are treated in a forward calculation depends on such considerations as who the owner of record is at the time that the intention of declaring a dividend is formally made by the issuer. There is not a straight-line accretion calculation with equities as there is with coupon-bearing bonds, and conventions can vary across markets. Nonetheless, in cases where the dividend is declared and the owner of record is determined, and this all transpires over a forward's life span, the accrued dividend factor is easily accommodated.

CASH-SETTLED EQUITY FUTURES

As with bonds, there are also equity futures. However, unlike bond futures, which have physical settlement, equity index futures are cash-settled. Physical settlement of a futures contract means that an actual underlying instrument (spot) is delivered by investors who are short the contract to investors who are long the contract, and investors who are long pay for the instrument. When a futures contract is cash-settled, the changing cash value of the underlying instrument is all that is exchanged, and this is done via the daily marking-to-market mechanism. In the case of the Standard & Poor's (S&P) 500 futures contract, which is composed of 500 individual stocks, the aggregated cash value of these underlying securities is referenced with daily marks-to-market.

Just as dividend yields may be calculated for individual equities, they also may be calculated for equity indices. Accordingly, the formula for an equity index future may be expressed as

$$F = S(1 + T(R - Y_d))$$

where S and Y_d = market capitalization values (stock price times outstanding shares) for the equity prices and dividend yields of the companies within the index.

Since dividends for most index futures generally are ignored, there is typically no price adjustment required for reinvestment cash flow considerations.

Equity futures contracts typically have prices that are rich to (above) their underlying spot index. One rationale for this is that it would cost investors a lot of money in commissions to purchase each of the 500 equities in the S&P 500 individually. Since the S&P future embodies an instantaneous portfolio of securities, it commands a premium to its underlying portfolio of spot instruments. Another consideration is that the futures contract also must reflect relevant costs of carry.

Finally, just as there are delivery options embedded in bond futures contracts that may be exercised by investors who are short the bond future, unique choices unilaterally accrue to investors who are short certain equity index futures contracts. Again, just as with bond futures, the S&P 500 equity future provides investors who are short the contract with choices as to when a delivery is made during the contract's delivery month, and these choices have value. Contributing to the delivery option's value is the fact that investors who are short the future can pick the delivery day during the delivery month. Depending on the marketplace, futures often continue to trade after the underlying spot market has closed (and may even reopen again in after-hours trading).

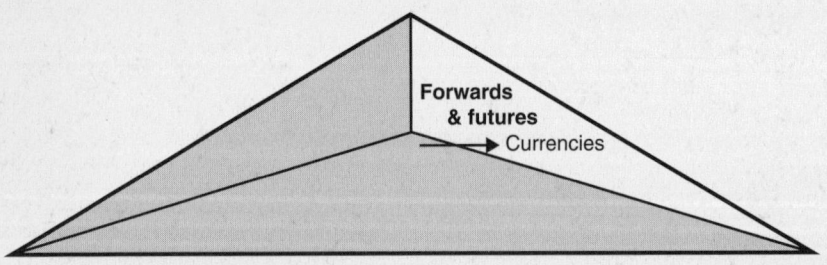

Forwards & futures → Currencies

The calculation for the forward value of an exchange rate is again a mere variation on a theme that we have already seen, and may be expressed as

$$F = S(1 + T(R_h - R_o))$$

where R_h = the home country risk-free rate
        R_o = the other currency's risk-free rate

For example, if the dollar-euro exchange rate is 0.8613, the three-month dollar Libor rate (London Inter-bank Offer Rate, or the relevant rate among banks exchanging euro dollars) is 3.76 percent, and the three-month euro Libor rate is 4.49 percent, then the three-month forward dollar-euro exchange rate would be calculated as 0.8597. Observe the change in the dollar versus the euro (of 0.0016) in this time span; this is entirely consistent with the notion of interest rate parity introduced in Chapter 1. That is, for a transaction executed on a fully hedged basis, the interest rate gain by investing in the higher-yielding euro market is offset by the currency loss of exchanging euros for dollars at the relevant forward rate.

If a Eurorate (not the rate on the euro currency, but the rate on a Libor-type rate) differential between a given Eurodollar rate and any other euro rate is positive, then the nondollar currency is said to be a *premium currency*. If the Eurorate differential between a given Eurodollar rate and any other Eurorate is negative, then the nondollar currency is said to be a *discount currency*. Table 2.3 shows that at one point, both the pound sterling and Canadian dollar were discount currencies to the U.S. dollar. Subtracting Canadian and sterling Eurorates from respective Eurodollar rates gives negative values.

There is an active forward market in foreign exchange, and it is commonly used for hedging purposes. When investors engage in a forward transaction, they generally buy or sell a given exchange rate forward. In the last example, the investor sells forward Canadian dollars for U.S dollars. A for-

TABLE 2.3   Rates from May 1991

Country	3 Month (%)	6 Month (%)	12 Month (%)
United States	6.0625	6.1875	6.2650
Canada	9.1875	9.2500	9.3750
United Kingdom	11.5625	11.3750	11.2500

ward contract commits investors to buy or sell a predetermined amount of one currency for another currency at a predetermined exchange rate. Thus, a forward is really nothing more than a mutual agreement to exchange one commodity for another at a predetermined date and price.

Can investors who want to own Canadian Treasury bills use the forward market to hedge the currency risk? Absolutely!

The Canadian Treasury bills will mature at par, so if the investors want to buy $1 million Canadian face value of Treasury bills, they ought to sell forward $1 million Canadian. Since the investment will be fully hedged, it is possible to state with certainty that the three-month Canadian Treasury bill will earn

$$5.670\% = \frac{(100/1.1600) - (97.90/1.1512)}{(97.90/1.1512)} \frac{(360)}{(87)}.$$

Where did the forward exchange rates come from for this calculation? From the currency section of a financial newspaper. These forward values are available for each business day and are expressed in points that are then combined with relevant spot rates. Table 2.4 provides point values for the Canadian dollar and the British pound.

The differential in Eurorates between the United States and Canada is 312.5 basis points (bps). With the following calculation, we can convert U.S./Canadian exchange rates and forward rates into bps.

$$316 \text{ basis points} = \frac{(1.1600 - 1.1512)}{1.1512} \times \frac{(360)}{87}$$

where

    1.1600 = the spot rate
    1.1512 = the spot rate adjusted for the proper amount of forward points

We assume that the Canadian Treasury bill matures in 87 days. Although 316 bps is not precisely equal to the 312.5 bp differential if calculated from

TABLE 2.4 Forward Points May 1991

Country	3 Month	6 Month	12 Month
Canada	90	170	290
United Kingdom	230	415	700

the yield table, consideration of transaction costs would make it difficult to structure a worthwhile arbitrage around the 3.5 bp differential.

Finally, note that the return of 5.670 percent is 15 bps above the return that could be earned on the three-month U.S. Treasury bill. Therefore, given a choice between a three-month Canadian Treasury bill fully hedged into U.S dollars earning 5.670 percent and a three-month U.S. Treasury bill earning 5.520 percent, the fully hedged Canadian Treasury bill appears to be the better investment.

Rather than compare returns of the above strategy with U.S Treasury bills, many investors will do the trade only if returns exceed the relevant Eurodollar rate. In this instance, the fully hedged return would have had to exceed the three-month Eurodollar rate. Why? Investors who purchase a Canadian Treasury bill accept a sovereign credit risk, that is, the risk the government of Canada may default on its debt. However, when the three-month Canadian Treasury bill is combined with a forward contract, another credit risk appears. In particular, if investors learn in three months that the counterparty to the forward contract will not honor the forward contract, investors may or may not be concerned. If the Canadian dollar appreciates over three months, then investors probably would welcome the fact that they were not locked in at the forward rate. However, if the Canadian dollar depreciates over the three months, then investors could well suffer a dramatic loss. The counterparty risk of a forward contract is not a sovereign credit risk. Forward contract risks generally are viewed as a counterparty credit risk. We can accept this view since banks are the most active players in the currency forwards marketplace. Though perhaps obvious, an intermediate step between an unhedged position and a fully hedged strategy is a partially hedged investment. With a partial hedge, investors are exposed to at least some upside potential with a trade yet with some downside protection as well.

OPPORTUNITIES WITH CURRENCY FUTURES

Most currency futures are rather straightforward in terms of their delivery characteristics, where delivery often is made on a single day at the end of the futures expiration. However, the fact that gaps may exist between the trading hours of the futures contracts and the underlying spot securities can give rise to some strategic value.

SUMMARY ON FORWARDS AND FUTURES

This section examined the similarities of forward and future cash flow types across bonds, equities, and currencies, and discussed the nature of the interrelationship between forwards and futures. Parenthetically, there is a scenario where the marginal differences between a forward and future actually could allow for a material preference to be expressed for one over the other. Namely, since futures necessitate a daily marking-to-market with a margin account set aside expressly for this purpose, investors who short bond futures contracts (or contracts that enjoy a strong correlation with interest rates) versus bond forward contracts can benefit in an environment of rising interest rates. In particular, as rates rise, the short futures position will receive margin since the future's price is decreasing, and this greater margin can be reinvested at the higher levels of interest. And if rates fall, the short futures position will have to post margin, but this financing can be done at a lower relative cost due to lower levels of interest. Thus, investors who go long bond futures contracts versus forward contracts are similarly at a disadvantage.

There can be any number of incentives for doing a trade with a particular preference for doing it with a forward or future. Some reasons might include:

- Investors' desire to leapfrog over what may be perceived to be a near-term period of market choppiness into a predetermined forward trade date and price
- Investors' belief that current market prices generally look attractive now, but they may have no immediate cash on hand (or perhaps may expect cash to be on hand soon) to commit right away to a purchase
- Investors' hope to gain a few extra basis points of total return by actively exploiting opportunities presented by the repo market via the lending of particular securities. This is discussed further in Chapter 4.

Table 2.5 presents forward formulas for each of the big three.

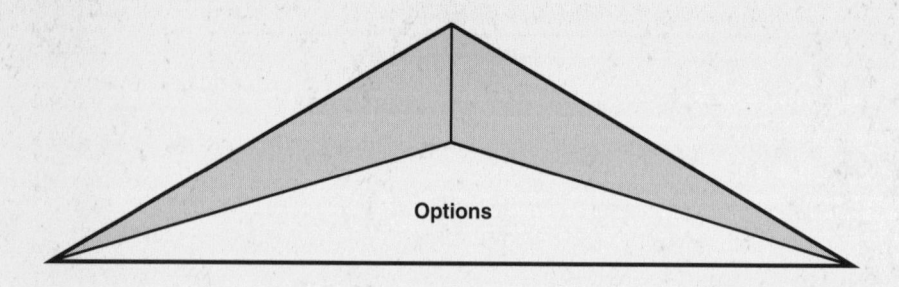

Options

We now move to the third leg of the cash flow triangle, options.

Continuing with the idea that each leg of the triangle builds on the other, the options leg builds on the forward market (which, in turn, was built on

TABLE 2.5 Forward Formulas for Each of the Big Three

Product	Formula	
	No Cash Flows	Cash Flows
Bonds	$S(1 + RT)$	$S(1 + T(R - Y_c))$
Equities	$S(1 + RT)$	$S(1 + T(R - Y_c))$
Currencies	$S(1 + T(R_h - R_o))$	

the spot market). Therefore, of the five variables generally used to price an option, we already know three: spot (S), a financing rate (R), and time (T). The two additional variables needed are *strike price* and *volatility*. Strike price is the reference price of profitability for an option, and an option is said to have intrinsic value when the difference between a strike price and an actual market price is a favorable one. Volatility is a statistical measure of a stock price's dispersion.

Let us begin our explanation with an option that has just expired. If our option has expired, several of the five variables cited simply fall away. For example, time is no longer a relevant variable. Moreover, since there is no time, there is nothing to be financed over time, so the finance rate variable is also zero. And finally, there is no volatility to be concerned about because, again, the game is over. Accordingly, the value of the option is now:

Call option value is equal to $S - K$

where
  S = the spot value of the underlying security
  K = the option's strike price

The call option value increases as S becomes larger relative to K. Thus, investors purchase call options when they believe the value of the underlying spot will increase. Accordingly, if the value of S happens to be 102 at expiration with the strike price set at 100 at the time the option was purchased, then the call's value is 102 minus 100 = 2.

A *put option* value is equal to $K - S$. Notice the reversal of positions of S and K relative to a call option's value. The put option value increases as S becomes smaller relative to K. Thus, investors purchase put options when they believe that the value of the underlying spot will decrease.

Now let us look at a scenario for a call's value prior to expiration. In this instance, all five variables cited come into play.

The first thing to do is make a substitution. Namely, we need to replace the S in the equation with an F. T, time, now has value. And since T is relevant, so too is the cost to finance S over a period of time; this is reflected by R and is embedded along with T within F. And finally, a value for volatility, V, is also a vital consideration now. Thus, we might now write an equation for a call's value to be

$$\text{Call value} = F - K + V.$$

Just to be absolutely clear on this point, when we write V as in the last equation, this variable is to be interpreted as the *value* of volatility in price terms (not as a volatility measure expressed as an annualized standard deviation).[12] Since there is a number of option pricing formulas in existence today, we need not define a price value of volatility in terms of each and every one of those option valuation calculations. Quite simply, for our purposes, it is sufficient to note that the variables required to calculate a price value for volatility include R, T, and σ, where σ is the annualized standard deviation of S.[13]

On an intuitive level, it would be logical to accept that the price value of volatility is zero when $T = 0$, because T being zero means that the option's life has come to an end; variability in price (via σ) has no meaning. However, if R is zero, it is still possible for volatility to have a price value. The fact that there may be no value to borrowing or lending money does not automatically translate into a spot having no volatility (unless, of course, the underlying spot happens to be R itself, where R may be the rate on a Treasury bill).[14] Accordingly, a key difference between a forward and an option is the role of R; R being zero immediately transforms a forward into spot, but an option remains an option. Rather, the Achilles' heel of an option is σ; σ being zero immediately transforms an option into a forward. With $\sigma = 0$ there is no volatility, hence there is no meaning to a price value of volatility.

Finally, saying that one cash flow type becomes another cash flow type under various scenarios (i.e., $T = 0$, or $\sigma = 0$), does not mean that they somehow magically transform instantaneously into a new product; it simply highlights how their new price behavior ought to be expected to reflect the cash flow profile of the product that shares the same inputs.

---

[12]It is common in some over-the-counter options markets actually to quote options by their price as expressed in terms of volatility, for example, quoting a given currency option with a standard three-month maturity at 12 percent.

[13]The appendix of this chapter provides a full explanation of volatility definitions, including volatility's calculation as an annualized standard deviation of S.

[14]Perhaps the most recent real-world example of R being close to (or even below) zero would be Japan, where short-term rates traded to just under zero percent in January 2003.

Rewriting the above equation for a call option knowing that $F = S + SRT$, we have

$$\text{Call value} = S + SRT - K + V.$$

If only to help us reinforce the notions discussed thus far as they relate to the interrelationships of the triangle, let us consider a couple of what-if? scenarios. For example, what if volatility for whatever reason were to go to zero? In this instance, the last equation shrinks to

$$\text{Call value} = S + SRT - K.$$

And since we know that $F = S + SRT$, we can rewrite that equation into an even simpler form as:

$$\text{Call value} = F - K.$$

But since K is a fixed value that does not change from the time the option is first purchased, what the above expression really boils down into is a value for F. We are now back to the second leg of the triangle. To put this another way, a key difference between a forward and an option is that prior to expiration, the option requires a price value for V.

For our second what-if? scenario, let us assume that in addition to volatility being zero, for whatever reason there is also zero cost to borrow or lend (financing rates are zero). In this instance, call value $= S + SRT - K + V$ now shrinks to

$$\text{Call value} = S - K.$$

This is because with T and R equal to zero, the entire SRT term drops out, and of course V drops out because it is zero as well. With the recognition, once again, that K is a fixed value and does not do very much except provide us with a reference point relative to S, we now find ourselves back to the first leg of the triangle. Figure 2.18 presents these interrelationships graphically.

As another way to evaluate the progressive differences among spot, forwards, and options, consider the layering approach shown in Figure 2.19. The first or bottom layer is spot. If we then add a second layer called cost of carry, the combination of the first and second layers is a forward. And if we add a third layer called volatility (with strike price included, though "on the side," since it is a constant), the combination of the first, second, and third layers is an option.

Spot   **Forwards**

S $F = S(1 + RT)$

When either R or T is zero (as with a zero cost to financing, or when there is immediate settlement), $F = S$. Therefore, F is differentiated from S by cost of carry (SRT)

Call value $= F - K + V$
$= S(1 + RT) - K + V$

Options

When T is zero (as at the expiration of an option), the call option value becomes $S - K$. This happens because F becomes S (see formula for F) and V drops away; volatility has no value for a security that has ceased to trade (as at expiration). In sum, since K is a constant, S is the last remaining variable. If just V is zero, then the call option value prior to expiration is $F - K$.

Therefore, F is differentiated from an option by K and V, and S is differentiated from an option by K, V, and RT.

Special Note
Some market participants state that the value of an option is really composed of two parts: an intrinsic value and a time value. Intrinsic value is defined as $F - K$ prior to expiration (for a call option) and as $S - K$ at expiration; all else is time value, which, by definition, is zero when $T = 0$ (as at expiration).

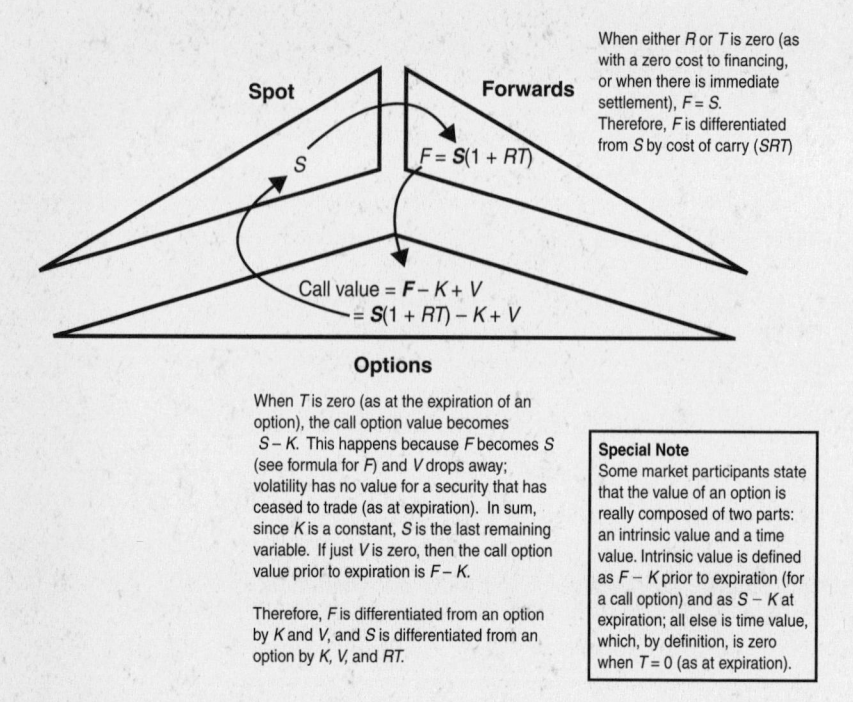

FIGURE 2.18 Key interrelationships among spot, forwards, and options.

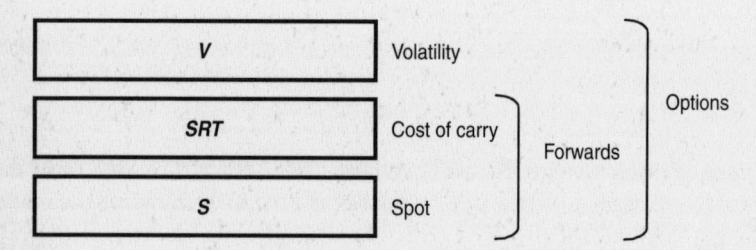

V	Volatility	
SRT	Cost of carry	Options
S	Spot	Forwards

FIGURE 2.19 Layers of distinguishing characteristics among spot, forwards, and options.

As part and parcel of the building-block approach to spot, forwards, and options, unless there is some unique consideration to be made, the presumption is that with an efficient marketplace, investors presumably would be indifferent across these three structures relative to a particular underlying security. In the context of spot versus forwards and futures, the decision to invest in forwards and futures rather than cash would perhaps be influenced by four things:

1. The notion that the forward or future is undervalued or overvalued relative to cash; that in the eyes of a particular investor, there is a material difference between the market value of the forward and its actual worth
2. Some kind of investor-specific cash flow or asset consideration where immediate funds are not desired to be committed; that the deferred exchange of cash for product provided by the forward or future is desirable
3. The view that something related to *SRT* is not being priced by the market in a way that is consistent with the investor's view of worth; again, a material difference between market value and actual worth
4. Some kind of institutional, regulatory, tax, or other extra-market incentive to trade in futures or forwards instead of cash

In the case of investing in an option rather than forwards and futures or cash, this decision would perhaps be influenced by four things:

1. The notion that the option is undervalued or overvalued relative to forwards or futures or cash; that in the eyes of a particular investor, there is a material difference between the market value of the forward and its actual worth
2. Some kind of investor-specific cash flow or asset consideration where the cash outlay of a strategy is desirable; note the difference between paying S versus $S - K$
3. The view that something related to V is not being priced by the market in a way that is consistent with the investor's view of worth; again, a material difference between market value and actual worth
4. Some kind of institutional, regulatory, tax, or other extra-market incentive to trade in options instead of futures or forwards or cash

It is hoped that these illustrations have helped to reinforce the idea of interlocking relationships around the cash flow triangle. Often people believe that these different cash flow types somehow trade within their own unique orbits and have lives unto themselves. This does not have to be the case at all.

As the concept of volatility is very important for option valuation, the appendix to this chapter is devoted to the various ways volatility is calculated. In fact, a principal driver of why various option valuation models exist is the objective of wanting to capture the dynamics of volatility in the best possible way. Differences among the various options models that exist today are found in existing texts on the subject.[15]

---

[15]See, for example, John C. Hull, *Options, Futures, and Other Derivatives* (Saddle-River. NJ: Prentice Hall, 1989).

Options
Bonds

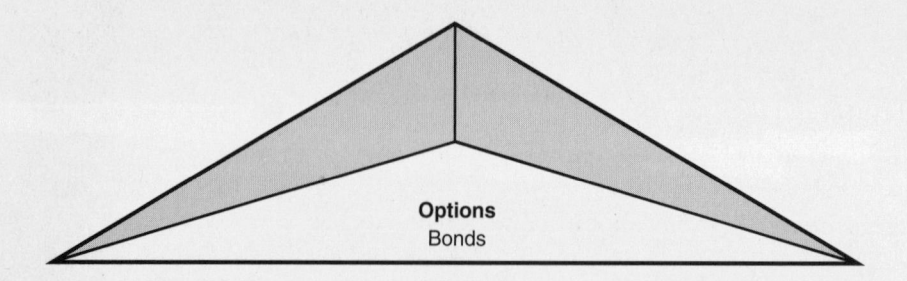

Because bonds are priced both in terms of dollar price and yield, an overview of various yield types is appropriate. Just as there are nominal yield spreads and forward yield spreads, there are also option-adjusted spreads (OASs).

Refer again to the cash flow triangle and the notion of forwards building on spots, and options, in turn, building on forwards. Recall that a spot spread is defined as being the difference (in basis points) between two spot yield levels (and being equivalent to a nominal yield spread when the spot curve is a par bond curve) and that a forward spread is the difference (in bps) between two forward yield levels derived from the entire relevant portion of respective spot curves (and where the forward curve is equivalent to a spot curve when the spot curve is flat). A nominal spread typically reflects a measure of one security's richness or cheapness relative to another. Thus, it can be of interest to investors as a way of comparing one security against another. Similarly, a forward spread also can be used by investors to compare two securities, particularly when it would be of interest to incorporate the information contained within a more complete yield curve (as a forward yield in fact does).

An OAS can be a helpful valuation tool for investors when a security has optionlike features. Chapter 4 examines such security types in detail. Here the objective is to introduce an OAS and show how it can be of assistance as a valuation tool for fixed income investors.

If a bond has an option embedded within it, a single security has characteristics of a spot, a forward, and an option all at the same time. We would expect to pay par for a coupon-bearing bond with an option embedded within it if it is purchased at time of issue; this "pay-in-full at trade date" feature is most certainly characteristic of spot. Yet the forward element of the bond is a "deferred" feature that is characteristic of options. In short, an OAS is intended to incorporate an explicit consideration of the option component within a bond (if it has such a component) and to express this as a yield spread value. The spread is expressed in basis points, as with all types of yield spreads.

Recall the formula for calculating a call option's value for a bond, equity, or currency.

$$O_c = F - K + V.$$

Table 2.6 compares and contrasts how the formula would be modified for calculating an OAS as opposed to a call option on a bond.

Consistent with earlier discussions on the interrelationships among spot, forwards, and options, if the value of volatility is zero (or if the par bond curve is flat), then an OAS is the same thing as a forward spread. This is the case because a zero volatility value is tantamount to asserting that just one forward curve is of relevance: today's forward curve. Readers who are familiar with the binominal option model's "tree" can think of the tree collapsing into a single branch when the volatility value is zero; the single branch represents the single prevailing path from today's spot value to some later forward value. Sometimes investors deliberately calculate a *zero volatility spread* (or *ZV spread*) to see where a given security sits in relation to its nominal spread, whether the particular security is embedded with any optionality or not. Simply put, a ZV spread is an OAS calculated with the assumption of volatility being equal to zero. Similarly, if $T = 0$ (i.e., there is immediate settlement), then volatility has no purpose, and the OAS and forward spread are both equal to the nominal spread.

An OAS can be calculated for a Treasury bond where the Treasury bond is also the benchmark security. For Treasuries with no optionality, calculating an OAS is the same as calculating a ZV spread. For Treasuries with optionality, a true OAS is generated. To calculate an OAS for a non-Treasury security (i.e., a security that is not regarded as risk free in a credit or liquidity context), we have a choice; we can use a Treasury par bond curve as our reference curve for constructing a forward curve, or we can use a par bond curve of the non-Treasury security of interest. Simply put, if we use a Treasury par bond curve, the resulting OAS will embody measures of both the risk-free and non–risk-free components of the future shape in the forward curve as well as a measure of the embedded option's value. Again, the term "risk free" refers to considerations of credit risk and liquidity risk.

TABLE 2.6

Using $O_c = F - K + V$ to Calculate a Call Option on a Bond versus an OAS (assuming the embedded option is a call option)

For a Bond	For an OAS
• O_c is expressed as a dollar value (or some other currency value).	OAS is expressed in basis points.
• F is a forward price value.	F is a forward yield value (which, via bootstrapping, embodies a forward curve).
• K is a spot price reference value.	K is expressed as a spot yield value (typically equal to the coupon of the bond).
• V is the volatility price value.	Same.

Conversely, if we use a non-Treasury par bond curve, the resulting OAS embodies a measure of the non–risk-free component of the forward curve's future shape as well as a measure of the embedded option's value. A fixed income investor might very well desire both measures, and with the intent of regularly following the unique information contained within each to divine insight into the market's evolution and possibilities. For example, an investor might look at the historical ratio of the pure OAS embedded in a Treasury instrument in relation to the OAS of a non-Treasury bond and calculated with a non-Treasury par bond curve.

One very clear incentive for using a non-Treasury spot curve when generating an OAS is the rationale that the precise nature of the non-Treasury yield curve may not have the same slope characteristics of the Treasury par bond curve. For example, it is commonplace to observe that credit yield spreads widen as maturities lengthen among non-Treasury bonds. An example of this is shown in Figure 2.20. This nuance of curve evolution and makeup can have an important bearing on any OAS output that is generated and can be a very good reason not to use a Treasury par bond curve.

We conclude this section with two around-the-triangle reviews of the spreads presented thus far. Comments pertaining to OAS are relevant for a bond embedded with a short call option (see Figure 2.21).

And for our second triangle review, consider Figure 2.22. As presented, nominal spread is suggested as being the best spread for evaluating liquidity or credit values, forward spread is suggested as being the best spread to capture the information embedded in an entire yield curve, and OAS is suggested as being the best spread to capture the value of optionality. Accordingly, if there is no optionality in a bond or if volatility is zero, then only a forward and a nominal spread offer insight. And if volatility is zero and the term structure of interest rates is perfectly flat, only a nominal spread offers insight.

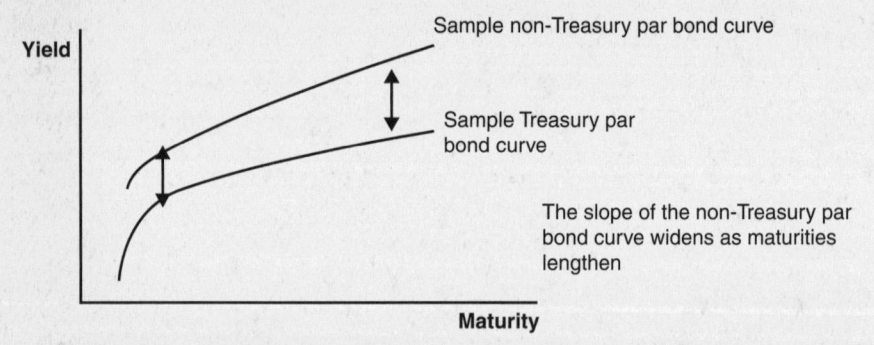

FIGURE 2.20 Credit yield spreads widen as maturities lengthen among non-Treasury bonds.

Cash Flows

- FS > 0 when par bond curves are upward sloping.
- FS < 0 when par bond curves are downward sloping.
- **FS = NS when par bond curves are flat.**

Nominal   Forward

Option-adjusted

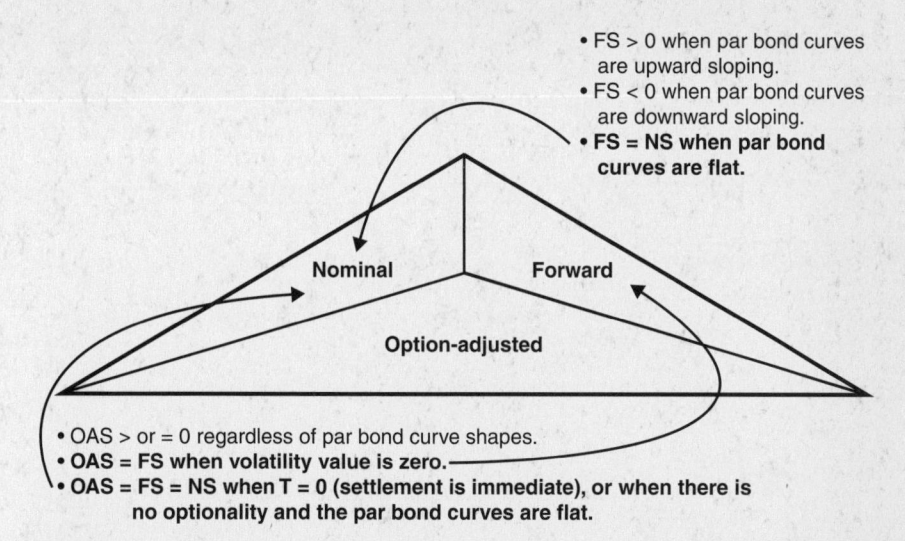

- OAS > or = 0 regardless of par bond curve shapes.
- OAS = FS when volatility value is zero.
- OAS = FS = NS when T = 0 (settlement is immediate), or when there is no optionality and the par bond curves are flat.

FIGURE 2.21 Nominal spreads (NS), forward spreads (FS), and option-adjusted spreads (OAS).

If the par bond curve is flat then there is no use for a forward spread analysis for bonds without optionality; the nominal spread will suffice.

Useful to identify liquidity and credit spread values

Nominal   Forward

Useful to identify an embedded curve value

Option-adjusted

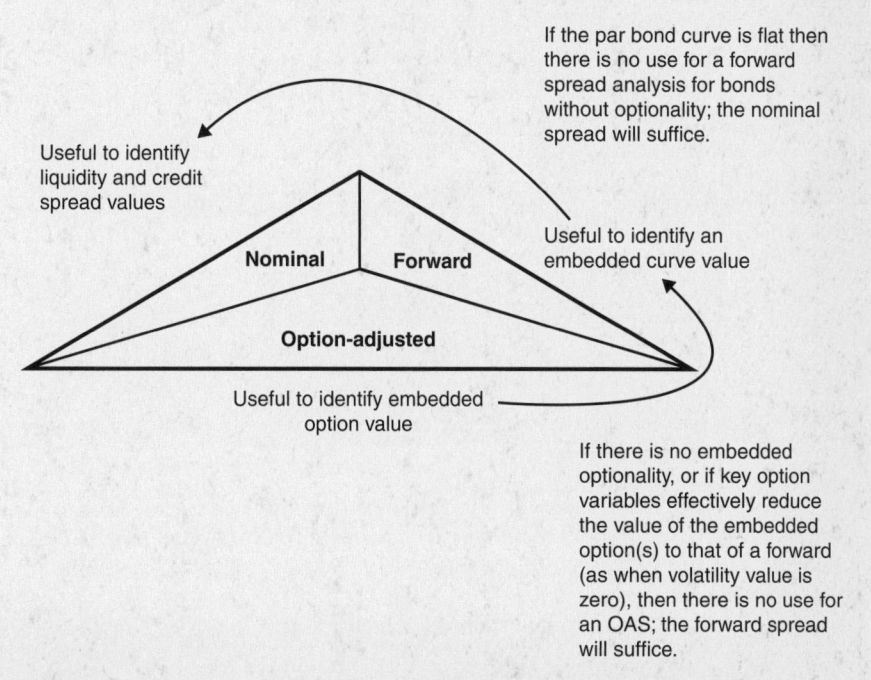

Useful to identify embedded option value

If there is no embedded optionality, or if key option variables effectively reduce the value of the embedded option(s) to that of a forward (as when volatility value is zero), then there is no use for an OAS; the forward spread will suffice.

FIGURE 2.22 Interrelationships among nominal, forward, and option-adjusted spreads.

A FINAL WORD

Sometimes forwards and futures and options are referred to as *derivatives*. For a consumer, bank checks and credit cards are derivatives of cash. That is, they are used in place of cash, but they are not the same as cash. By virtue of not being the same as cash, this may either be a positive or negative consideration. Being able to write a check for something when we have no cash with us is a positive thing, but writing a check for more money than we have in the bank is a negative thing. Similarly, forwards and futures and options as derivatives are easily traced back to a particular security type, and they can be used and misused by investors. In everyday usage, if something is referred to as being a derivative of something else, generally there is a common link. This is certainly the case here. Just as a plant is derived from a seed, earth, and water, spot is incorporated in both forward and future calculations as well as with option calculations. Thus, forwards and futures and options are all derivatives of spot; they incorporate spot as part of their valuation and composition, yet they also are different from spot.

It sometimes is said that derivatives provide investors with *leverage*. Again, in everyday usage, "leverage" can connote an objective of maximizing a given resource in as many ways as possible. If we think of cash as a resource, one way to maximize our use of it is to manage the way it works for us on a day-to-day basis. For example, when we pay for our groceries with a personal check instead of cash, the cash continues to earn interest in our interest-bearing checking account up until the time the check clears (perhaps even several days after we have eaten the groceries we purchased). We leveraged our cash by allowing its existence in a checking account to enable us to purchase food today and continue to earn interest on it for days afterward.

Similarly, when a forward is used to purchase a bond, no cash is paid up front; no cash is exchanged at all until the bond actually is received in the future. Since this frees up the use of our cash until it is actually required sometime later, the forward is said to be a leveraged transaction. However, whatever investors may do with their cash until such time that the forward expires, they have to ensure that they have the money when the expiration day arrives. The same is true for a futures contract that is held to expiration.

In contrast to the case with a forward or future, investors actually purchase an option with money paid at the time of purchase. However, this is still considered to be a leveraged transaction, for two reasons.

1. The option's price is not the price that would be paid for spot; the option's price (if it is a call option) is $F - K + V$, and for an at-the-money[16] option, $F - K + V$ is typically much less than S[17].
2. The presence of F within the option's price formula means that no exchange of cash for goods will take place until the option expires. In the case of a *futures option* where the option trades to an underlying futures contract as opposed to spot, there is an additional delay from when the option expires until the time that cash is exchanged for the spot security.

Leverage is usually the reason behind much of the criticism of derivatives voiced by market observers. A common complaint is that the very existence of derivatives allows (perhaps even encourages) irresponsible risk-taking by permitting investors to leverage a little cash into a lot of risk via security types that do not require the same initial cash outlay as spot. The implication is that when investors take on more risk than they should, they endanger themselves as well as possibly others who are party to their trading. Just as it is hard to argue for irresponsible consumers who spend the cash in their checking accounts before the grocery check has cleared, it is hard to argue for irresponsible investors who have no cash to honor a derivative transaction in the financial marketplace. Various safeguards exist to protect investors from themselves and others (as with credit and background checks as well as the use of margins, etc.). Indeed, larger financial institutions have entire risk management departments responsible for ensuring that trading guidelines are in place, are understood, and are followed. Even with the presence of these safeguards there are serious and adverse events that nonetheless can and do occur.

In sum, derivatives can most certainly be dangerous if misused, as can just about any financial instrument. Understanding the fundamental risks of any security ought to be prerequisite before, during, and after any purchase or sale.

---

[16] An *at-the-money* option is an option where K is equal to S. An *in-the-money* call option exists when S is greater than K, and an *out-of-the-money* call option exists when S is less than K. An in-the-money put option exists when S is less than K, and an out-of-the-money put option exists when S is greater than K.
[17] If time to expiration is a long period (many years), $F - K + V$ could be greater than S.

SUMMARY ON BONDS, EQUITIES, AND CURRENCIES

For bonds, equities, and currencies, the formula for an option's valuation is the same. For a call option it is $F - K + V$, and for a put option it is $K - F + V$. In either case, the worst-case scenario for an option's value is zero, since there is no such thing as a negative price. Although the variable labels are the same (F, K, and V), the inputs used to calculate these variables can differ appreciably. With regard to F, for example, F for a Treasury bill is as simple as $S(1 + RT)$ while for a currency it is $S(1 + T(R_b - R_o))$. And with regard to V, volatility value is a function of time, the standard deviation of the underlying spot, and R.

CHAPTER SUMMARY

This chapter outlined the principal differences and similarities among the three basic cash flow types in the market. Figure 2.23 reinforces the interrelationships among spot, forwards and futures, and options.

Chapter 3 adds the next layer of credit and shows how credit is greatly influenced by products (Chapter 1) and cash flows (Chapter 2).

Cash Flows

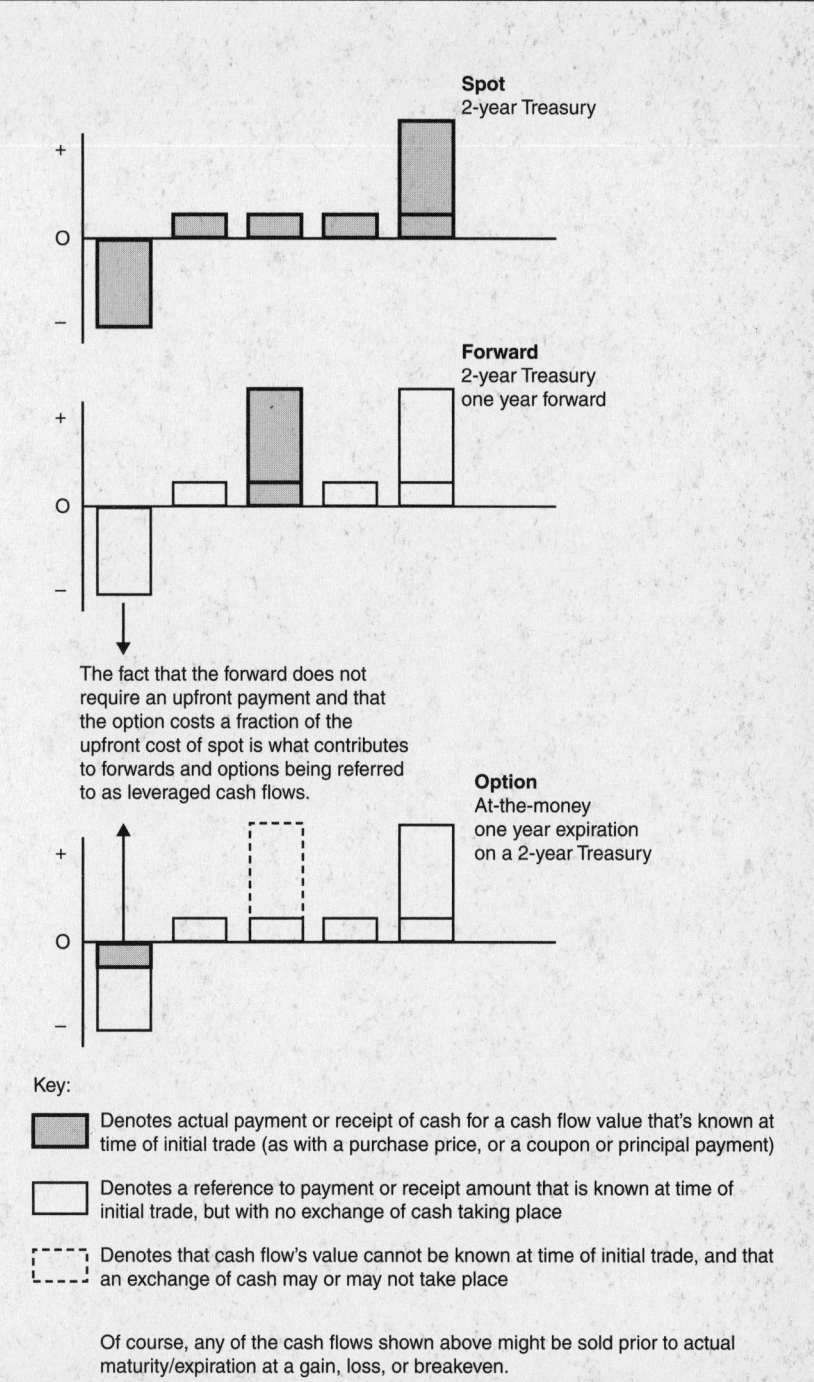

Spot
2-year Treasury

Forward
2-year Treasury
one year forward

The fact that the forward does not require an upfront payment and that the option costs a fraction of the upfront cost of spot is what contributes to forwards and options being referred to as leveraged cash flows.

Option
At-the-money
one year expiration
on a 2-year Treasury

Key:

▪ Denotes actual payment or receipt of cash for a cash flow value that's known at time of initial trade (as with a purchase price, or a coupon or principal payment)

☐ Denotes a reference to payment or receipt amount that is known at time of initial trade, but with no exchange of cash taking place

┆ ┆ Denotes that cash flow's value cannot be known at time of initial trade, and that an exchange of cash may or may not take place

Of course, any of the cash flows shown above might be sold prior to actual maturity/expiration at a gain, loss, or breakeven.

FIGURE 2.23 Evaluating spot, forwards, and options on the basis of cash flow profiles.

APPENDIX

Volatility

Volatility is perhaps the single most elusive variable in the marketplace. There are a variety of opinions about what constitutes the best methodology for calculating volatility on a given asset, and in the end there really is no right way to do it. A variety of texts have been published (and have yet to be published) on the topic of option pricing methodologies. The aim here is merely to flesh out a better understanding and appreciation for a rather fundamental and variable.

Historical Volatility and Implied Volatility

While volatility typically is characterized as a price phenomenon, in the world of bonds where yield is a key pricing variable, volatility may be quoted in price terms or in yield terms. Generally speaking, volatility on bond futures is expressed in price terms, while volatility on bond cash instruments is expressed in yield terms. And consistent with the properties of duration, whereby longer maturities/durations are associated with greater risk potential, a price volatility term structure tends to be upward sloping. This upward slope is consistent with incrementally greater price risks as maturity/duration extends. Conversely, in recognition of the inverse price/yield relationship that exists when pricing bonds, a yield volatility term structure tends to be downward sloping.

Essentially, volatility is measured with either historical methodology or implied methodology. Historical volatility usually is calculated by taking a series of daily data (perhaps three months' worth of daily closing prices of IBM stock, or maybe a year's worth of daily closes of the on-the-run 10-year Treasury's yield) and then calculating a rolling series of annualized standard deviations.

The classic statistical definition of a standard deviation is that it measures variation around a mean. Mean is a reference to average, and to calculate an average, we need to refer to a subset of data points. Using about 20 data points is a popular technique when daily observations are being tapped, because there are about 20 business days in a month. The formula for standard deviation is:

$$\sum_{t=1}^{T} \sqrt{\frac{(x_i - \overline{x})^2}{n-1}}$$

where Σ = summation
x_i = individual observations (i.e., daily or weekly)
$\bar{x}$ = mean or average of all observations
n = the number of observations

A standard deviation attempts to measure just how choppy a market is by comparing how extreme individual observations can become relative to their average.

Just as yields are expressed on an annualized basis, so too are volatilities. And just as there is no hard-and-fast rule for the number of data points that are used to calculate the mean, there is no industry convention for how annualizing is calculated. There is simply a reasonable amount of latitude that may be used to calculate. Many times the annualizing number is something close to 250, with the rationale that there are about 250 business days in the year. And why might we care only about business days? Perhaps because a variable cannot deviate from its mean if it is not trading, and the markets typically are closed over weekends and holidays. Yet U.S. Treasuries may be trading in Tokyo on what is Monday morning in Asia but on what is Sunday night in the United States. Such is the life of a global market.

Even if a market is closed over a weekend, this does not mean that the world stops and that market-moving news is somehow held back from being announced until the following Monday. Indeed, important meetings of the Group of Seven (G-7) or G-10 and others often occur over a weekend. Often an expectation of a weekend G-7 pronouncement gets priced into the market on the Friday ahead of the weekend, and this price behavior certainly is captured by an implied volatility calculation. And if a market-moving event transpires, then new prices at the market's open on Monday morning certainly become reflected within a historical volatility calculation that gets made on the following Tuesday. These are some of the considerations that frame the debate around annualizing conventions.

An annualizing term to the historical volatility formula is

$$\frac{365}{n}.$$

When combined with the formula for standard deviation, it provides

$$\sum_{t=1}^{T}\sqrt{\frac{(x_i - \bar{x})^2}{n-1}} \times \frac{365}{n}.$$

The term "rolling" refers to the idea that we want to capture an evolving picture of volatility over time. We achieve this by employing a moving-mean[1] (or moving-average) calculation.

Implied Volatility

To calculate implied volatility, we simply take an option pricing formula of our own choosing and plug in values for every variable in the equation except for standard deviation. By solving for "x" where x is standard deviation, we can calculate an implied volatility number. It is "implied" because it comes directly from the price being quoted in the market and embodies the market's view on the option's overall value.

Some investors feel that from time to time there actually may be more packed into an implied volatility number than just a simple standard deviation. That is, a standard deviation calculated as just described assumes that the relevant underlying price series is normally distributed. What if the market is on a marked trend upward or downward, without the kind of offsetting price dynamics consistent with a normally distributed pattern of observations? In statistical terms, *kurtosis* is a measure of the extent that data fall more closely around the mean of a series or more into the tails of a distribution profile relative to a normally distributed data set. For example, a kurtosis value that is less than that of a standard normal distribution may suggest that the distribution is wider around the mean and with a lower peak, while a kurtosis value greater than a normal distribution may suggest a higher peak with a narrower distribution around the mean and fatter tails. Indeed, there is a variety of literature on the topic of fat-tail distributions for various asset classes, and with important implications for pricing and valuation. Here it is important to note that there is no kurtosis variable in the formula for an option's fair market value. The only variable in any standard option formula pertaining to the distribution of a price series (where price may be price, yield, or an exchange rate) is standard deviation, and standard deviation in a form consistent with normally distributed variables. Having said this, two observations can be offered.

---

[1] A moving-mean or moving average calculation simply means that series of averages are calculated from one data set. For example, to calculate a 20-day moving average with a data set of 100 daily prices, one average is calculated using days 1 to 20, then a second average is calculated using days 2 to 21, then a third using 3 to 22, and so on. If standard deviations are then calculated that correspond with these moving averages, a rolling series of volatilities can be calculated. For pricing an option with a 20-day expiration, the last volatility data point of a 20-day moving average series would be an appropriate value to use as an input.

1. Any standard option-pricing model can be modified to allow for the pricing of options where the underlying price series is not normally distributed.
2. When an implied volatility value is calculated, it may well embody more value than what would be expected for an underlying price series that is normally distributed; it may embody some kurtosis value.

Perhaps for obvious reasons, historical volatility often is referred to as a backward-looking picture of market variation, while implied volatility is thought of as a forward-looking measure of market variation. Which one is right? Well, let us say that it is Monday morning and that on Friday a very important piece of news about the economy is scheduled to be released—maybe for the United States it is the monthly employment report—with the potential to move the market in a big way one direction or the other. Let us assume an investor was looking to buy a call option on the Dow Jones Industrial Average for expiration on Friday afternoon. To get a good idea of fair value for volatility, would the investor prefer to use a historical calculation going back 20 days (historical volatility) or an indication of what the market is pricing in today (implied volatility) as it looks ahead to Friday's event? A third possibility would involve looking at a series of historical volatilities taken from the same key week of previous months to identify any meaningful pattern. It is consistently this author's preference to rely upon implied volatility values.

To use historical volatility, a relevant question would be: How helpful is a picture of past data for determining what will happen in the week ahead? A more insightful use of historical volatility would be to look at data taken from those weeks in prior months when employment data were released. But if the goal of doing this is to learn from prior experience and derive a better idea of fair value on volatility this particular week, perhaps implied volatility already incorporates these experiences by reflecting the market-clearing price where buyers and sellers agree to trade the option. Perhaps in this regard we can employ the best of what historical and implied volatilities each have to offer. Namely, we can take implied volatility as an indication of what the market is saying is an appropriate value for volatility now, and for our own reality check we can evaluate just how consistent this volatility value is when stacked up against historical experience. In this way, perhaps we could use historical and implied volatilities in tandem to think about relative value. And since we are buying or selling options with a squaring off of our own views versus the market's embedded views, other factors may enter the picture when we are attempting to evaluate volatility values and the best possible vehicles for expressing market views.

The debate on volatility is not going to be resolved on the basis of which calculation methodology is right or which one is wrong. This is one of those areas within finance that is more of the art than the math. Over the longer run, historical and implied volatility series tend to do a pretty good job of moving with a fairly tight correlation. This is to be expected. Yet often what are of most relevance for someone actively trading options are the very short-term opportunities where speed and precision are paramount, and where implied volatility might be most appropriate.

Many investors are biased to using those inputs that are most relevant for a scenario whereby they would have to engineer (or reverse-engineer) a product in the marketplace. For example, if attempting to value a callable bond (which is composed of a bullet bond and a short call option), the inclination would be to price the call at a level of volatility consistent with where an investor actually would have to go to the market and buy a call with the relevant features required. This true market price would then be used to get an idea of where the callable would trade as a synthetic bullet instrument having stripped out the short call with a long one, and the investor then could compare this new value to an actual bullet security trading in the market. In the end, the investor might not actually synthetically create these products in the market if only because of the extra time and effort required to do so (unless, of course, doing so offered especially attractive arbitrage opportunities). Rather, the idea would be to go through the machinations on paper to determine if relative values were in line and what the appropriate strategy would be.

WHEN STANDARD DEVIATION IS ZERO

What happens when a standard deviation is zero in the context of the Black-Scholes model? Starting with the standard Black-Scholes option pricing formula for a call option, we have

$$C = SN(X) - Kr^{-t}N(X - \sigma\sqrt{t})$$

where $X \equiv \dfrac{\log(S/Kr^{-t})}{\sigma\sqrt{t}} + \dfrac{1}{2}\sigma\sqrt{t}$.

If there were absolutely no uncertainty related to the future value of an asset, then we have

$$C = SN\left(\frac{(\log(S/Kr^{-t}))}{\emptyset \times \sqrt{t}} + \frac{1}{2} \times \emptyset \times \sqrt{t}\right)$$

Cash Flows

$$-Kr^{-t} - N\left(\frac{\log(S/Kr^{-t})}{\emptyset \times \sqrt{t}} + \frac{1}{2} \times \emptyset \times \sqrt{t}\right) - \emptyset \times \sqrt{t}$$

$$= SN\left(\frac{\log(S/Kr^{-t})}{\emptyset}\right) - Kr^{-t} N\left(\frac{\log(S/Kr^{-t})}{\emptyset}\right).$$

Since anything divided by zero is zero, we have

$$C = SN(\emptyset) - Kr^{-t}N(\emptyset).$$

And since $N(\emptyset)$ simply means that the role of the normal distribution function has no meaningful influence on the value of S and K, we now have

$$C = S - Kr^{-t}.$$

Note that $S - Kr^{-t}$ is equivalent to $F - K$.

Thus, in the extreme case where there is zero market volatility (or, equivalently, where the future value of the underlying asset is known with certainty), the value of the call is driven primarily by the underlying asset's forward price. Specifically, it is the maximum of zero or the difference between the forward price and the strike price.

Again, rewriting $C = S - Kr^{-t}$, the purpose of r^{-t} is nothing more than to adjust K (the strike price) to a present value. An equivalent statement would be $C = Sr^t - K$, where Sr^t is the forward price of the underlying asset (or simply F). The strike price, K, is a constant (our marker to determine whether the option has intrinsic value), so when we let σ equal zero, the value of the option boils down to the relationship between the value of the forward and the strike price, or the maximum value between zero or $F - K$ (sometimes expressed as $C = \text{Max}(\emptyset, F - K)$.

And if we continue this story and let both σ = $\emptyset$ and $t = \emptyset$, we have

$$C = Sr^t - K,$$
$$\text{or}$$
$$= Sr^{\emptyset} - K.$$

A variable raised to the power of $\emptyset$ is equal to 1, so

$$C = S \times 1 - K$$
$$= S - K.$$

In the extreme case where there is zero market volatility and no time value (or, equivalently, we want today's value of the underlying asset), then the value of the call is driven primarily by the underlying asset's spot price. Specifically, it is the maximum of zero or the difference between the spot price and the strike price. Figure A2.1 places these relationships in the context of our triangle.

In summary, the Achilles' heel of an option is volatility; without it, an option becomes a forward, and without volatility and time, an option becomes spot.

$$C = SN(X) - Kr^{-t}N(X - \sigma\sqrt{t})$$

With both $\sigma = \emptyset$ and $t = \emptyset$,
$$C = Sr^t - K$$
$$= Sr^{\emptyset} - K$$
$$= \boxed{S} - K$$

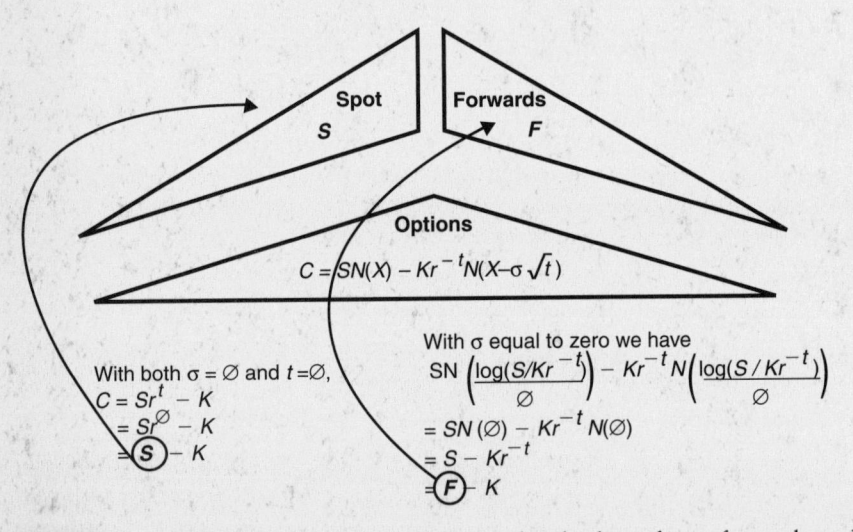

With σ equal to zero we have
$$SN\left(\frac{\log(S/Kr^{-t})}{\emptyset}\right) - Kr^{-t}N\left(\frac{\log(S/Kr^{-t})}{\emptyset}\right)$$
$$= SN(\emptyset) - Kr^{-t}N(\emptyset)$$
$$= S - Kr^{-t}$$
$$= \boxed{F} - K$$

FIGURE A2.1 Applying Black-Scholes to the interrelated values of spot, forwards, and options.

CHAPTER 3

Credit

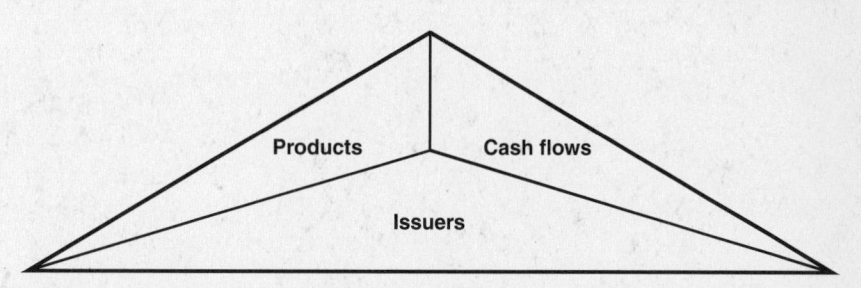

[Triangle diagram with "Products" and "Cash flows" labels on upper edges and "Issuers" at the base]

This chapter builds on the concepts presented in Chapters 1 and 2. Their importance is accented by their inclusion in the credit triangle. Simply put, credit considerations might be thought of as embodying the likelihood of issuers making good on the financial commitments (implied and explicit) that they have made. The less confident we are that an entity will be able to make good on its commitments, the more of a premium we are likely to require to compensate us for the added risk we are being asked to bear.

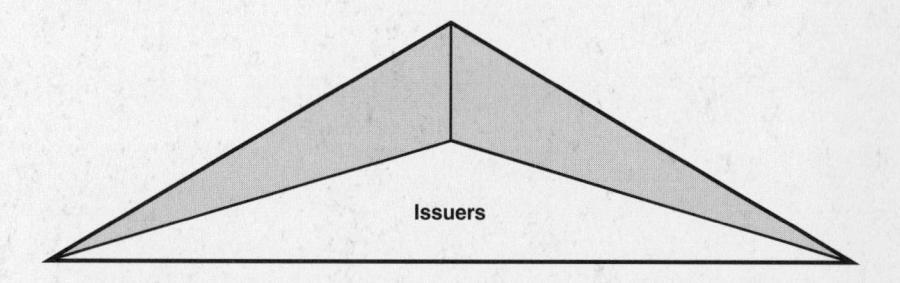

[Triangle diagram highlighting "Issuers" at the base]

There are hundreds and upon thousands of *issuers* (entities that raise funds by selling their debt or equity into the marketplace), and each with its own unique credit risk profile. To analyze these various credit risks, larger investors (e.g., large-scale fund managers) often have the benefit of an in-house credit research department. Smaller investors (as with individuals) may have to rely on what they can read in the financial press or pick up from the Internet or personal contacts. But even for larger investors, the task of

73

following the credit risk of so many issuers can be daunting. Thankfully, *rating agencies* (organizations that sell company-specific research) exist to provide a report card of sorts on many types of issuers around the globe. The most creditworthy of issuers carries a *rating* (a formally assigned opinion of a company or entity) of triple A, while at the lower end of the so-called investment grade ratings a security is labeled as BBB− or Baa3. An issuer with a rating below C or C1 is said to be in default.

Table 3.1 lists the various rating classifications provided by major rating agencies. Since it is difficult for one research analyst (or even a team of analysts) to stay apprised of all the credit stories in the marketplace at any time, analysts subscribe to the services of one or more of the rating agencies to assess an issuer's situation and outlook.

Because the rating agencies have been around for a while, databases have evolved with a wealth of historical data on *drift* and *default* experiences.

TABLE 3.1 Credit Ratings across Rating Agencies

Moody's	S&P	Fitch	D&P	
Aaa	AAA	AAA	AAA	Highest quality
Aa1	AA+	AA+	AA+	
Aa2	AA	AA	AA	High quality
Aa3	AA−	AA−	AA−	
A1	A+	A+	A+	
A2	A	A	A	Upper-medium quality
A3	A−	A−	A−	
Baa1	BBB+	BBB+	BBB+	
Baa2	BBB	BBB	BBB	Lower-medium quality
Baa3	BBB−	BBB−	BBB−	
Ba1	BB+	BB+	BB+	
Ba2	BB	BB	BB	Low quality
Ba3	BB−	BB−	BB−	
B1	B+	B+	B+	
B2	B	B	B	Highly speculative
B3	B−	B−	B−	
		CCC+		
Caa	CCC	CCC	CCC	Substantial risk
		CCC−		
Ca	CC	CC		
C	C	C		Extremely speculative
		C1		
			DDD	Default
			DD	
		D	D	

"Drift" means an entity's drifting from one rating classification to another — from an original credit rating of, say, single A down to a double B. "Default" simply means an entity's going from a nondefault rating into a default rating. Indeed, the rating agencies regularly generate probability distributions to allow investors to answer questions such as: What is the likelihood that based on historical experience a credit that is rated single A today will be downgraded to a single B or upgraded to a double A? In this way investors can begin to attempt to numerically quantify what credit risk is all about. For example, so-called credit derivatives are instruments that may be used to create or hedge an exposure to a given risk of upgrade or downgrade, and the drift and default tables are often used to value these types of products. Further, entities sell *credit rating insurance* to issuers, whereby a bond can be marketed as a triple-A risk instead of a single-A risk because the debenture comes with third-party protection against the risk of becoming a weaker security. Typically insurers insist on the issuer taking certain measures in exchange for the insurance, and these are discussed later in the chapter under the heading of "Credit: Cash Flows."

THE ELUSIVE NATURE OF CREDIT RISK

Despite whatever comfort we might have with better quantifying credit risks, we must guard against any complacency that might accompany these quantitative advances because in many respects the world of credit risk is a world of stories. That is, as much as we might attempt to quantify such a phenomenon as the likelihood of an upgrade or downgrade, there are any number of imponderables with a given issuer that can turn a bad situation into a favorable one or a favorable one into a disaster. Economic cycles, global competitive forces, regulatory dynamics, the unique makeup and style of an issuer's management team, and the potential to take over or be taken over — all of these considerations and others can combine to frustrate even the most thorough analysis of an issuer's financial statements. Credit risk is the third and last point on the risk triangle because of its elusive nature to be completely quantified.

What happens when a security is downgraded or upgraded by a rating agency? If it is downgraded, this new piece of adverse information must be reflected somehow in the security's value. Sometimes a security is not immediately downgraded or upgraded but is placed on *credit watch* or *credit review* by an agency (or agencies). This means that the rating agency is putting the issuer on notice that it is being watched closely and with an eye to changing the current rating in one way or another. At the end of some period of time, the relevant agency takes the issuer officially off of watch or review with its old rating intact or with a new rating assigned. Sometimes other information comes out that may argue for going the other way on a rating (e.g., an issuer originally going on watch or review for an upgrade might instead find itself coming off as a downgrade).

At essence, the role of the rating agencies is to employ best practices as envisioned and defined by them to assist with evaluating the creditworthiness of a variety of entities. To paraphrase the agencies' own words, they attempt to pass comment on the ability of an issuer to make good on its obligations.

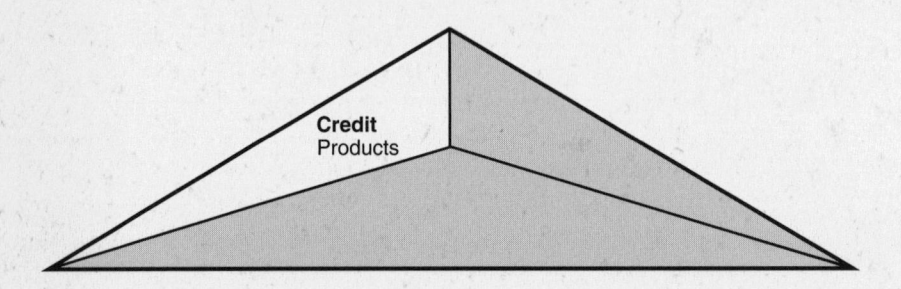

Credit
Products

Just as rating agencies rate the creditworthiness of companies, rating agencies often rate the creditworthiness of the products issued by those companies. The simple reason for this is because how a product is constructed most certainly has an influence on its overall credit risk. *Product construction* involves the mechanics of the underlying security (Chapter 1) and the cash flows associated with it (Chapter 2). To give an example involving the former, consider this case of bonds in the context of a spot profile.

Rating agencies often split the rating they assign to a particular issuer's short-term bonds and long-term bonds. When a *split maturity rating* is given, usually the short-term rating is higher than the long-term rating. A rationale for this might be the rating agency's view that shorter-term fundamentals look more favorable than longer-term fundamentals. For example, there may be the case that there is sufficient cash on hand to keep the company in good standing for the next one to two years, but there is a question as to whether sales forecasts will be strong enough to generate necessary cash beyond two years. Accordingly, short-term borrowings may be rated something like double A while longer-term borrowing might be rated single A. In sum, the stretched-out period of time associated with the company's longer-dated debt is deemed to involve a higher credit risk relative to its shorter-dated debt.

Now consider an example of bonds in the context of a spot versus forward profile. As Chapter 2 showed, an important variable distinguishing a spot and a forward is the length of time that passes from the *date of trade* (when a transaction of some type is agreed upon) to the date of actual exchange of cash for the security involved. With a spot trade, the exchange of cash for the security involved is immediate. With a forward-dated trade (which can include forwards, futures, and options), cash may not be exchanged for the underlying security for a very long time. Therefore, a credit risk consideration that uniquely arises with a forward trade is: Will the entity promising to provide an investor with an underlying security in the future still be around at that point in time to make good on the promise to provide it?[1] This particular type of risk is commonly referred to as *counterparty risk,* and it is considered to be a type of credit risk since the fundamental question is whether the other side to a trade is going to be able to make good on its financial representations.

When investors select the financial entity with which they will execute their trades, they want to be aware of its credit standing and its credit rating (if available). Further, investors will insist on knowing when its counterparty is merely serving as an intermediary on behalf of another financial entity, especially when that other financial entity carries a higher credit risk. Let us look at two examples: an *exchange transaction* (as with the New York Stock Exchange) and an *over-the-counter* (OTC) (off-exchange) transaction.

For the exchange transaction example, consider the case of investors wanting to go long a bond futures contract that expires in six months and that trades on the *Chicago Board of Trade* (CBOT, an option exchange). Instead of going directly to the CBOT, investors will typically make their purchases through their *broker* (the financial entity that handles their trades). If the investors intend to hold the futures contract to expiration and *take delivery* (accept ownership) on the bonds underlying the contract, then they are trusting that the CBOT will be in business in six months' time and that they will receive bonds in exchange for their cash value. In this instance, the counterparty risk is not with the investors' broker, it is with the CBOT; the broker was merely an intermediary between the investor and the CBOT. Incidentally, the CBOT (as with most exchanges) carries a triple-A rating.

For the OTC transaction example, consider the case of investors wanting to engage in a six-month forward transaction for yen versus U.S. dollars. Since forwards do not trade on exchanges (only futures do), the investors' counterparty is their broker or whomever the broker may decide

---

[1] It is also of concern that respective counterparties will honor spot transactions. Accordingly, when investors engage in market transactions of any kind, they want to be sure they are dealing with reputable entities. Longer-dated transactions (like forwards) simply tend to be of greater concern relative to spot transactions because they represent commitments that may be more difficult to *unwind* (offset) over time, and especially if a counterparty's credit standing does not improve.

to pass the trade along to if the broker is merely an intermediary. As of this writing, the yen carries a credit rating of double A.[2] If the broker (or another entity used by the broker) carries a credit risk of something less than double A, then the overall transaction is certainly not a double-A credit risk.

In sum, it is imperative for investors to understand not only the risks of the products and cash flows they are buying and selling, but the credit risks associated with each layer of their transactions: from the issuer, to the issuer's product(s), to the entity that is ultimately responsible for delivering the product.

Some larger investors (i.e., portfolio managers of large funds) engage in a process referred to as *netting* (pairing off) counterparty risk exposures. For example, just as an investor may have certain OTC forward-dated transactions with a particular broker where she is looking to pay cash for securities (as with buying bonds forward) in six months' time, she also may have certain OTC forward-dated transactions with the same broker where she is looking to receive cash for securities (as with selling equities forward). What is of interest is this: When all forward-dated transactions are placed side-by-side, under a scenario of the broker going out of business the very next day, would the overall situation be one where the investor would be left owing the broker or the other way around? This pairing off (netting) of trades with individual brokers (as well as across brokers) can provide useful insights to the counterparty credit exposures that an investor may have.

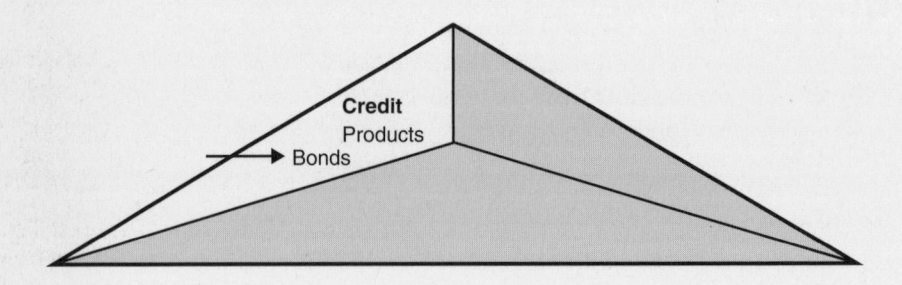

As discussed in the previous section, just because an issuer might be rated double B does not mean that certain types of its bonds might be rated higher or lower than that, or that the shorter-maturity bonds of an issuer might carry a credit rating that is higher relative to its longer-maturity securities. The credit standing of a given security is reflected in its yield level, where

---

[2] As of November 2002, the local currency rating on Japan's government bonds was A2 and the foreign currency rating was Aa1. Please see the section entitled "Credit: Products, Currencies" later in this chapter for a further explanation.

riskier securities have a higher yield (wider yield spread to Treasuries) relative to less-risky securities. The higher yield (wider spread) reflects the risk premium that investors demand to take on the additional credit risk of the instrument.

Bonds of issuers that have been upgraded or placed on positive watch generally will see their yield spread[3] narrow or, equivalently, their price increase. And securities of issuers that have been downgraded or placed on negative watch will generally see their yield spread widen or, equivalently, their price decline.

"Yield spread" is, quite simply, the difference between two yield levels expressed in basis points. Typically a Treasury yield is used as the benchmark for yield spread comparison exercises. Historically there are three reasons why non-Treasury security yields are quoted relative to Treasury securities.

1. Treasuries traditionally have constituted one of the most liquid segments of domestic bond markets. As such, they are thought to be pure in the sense that they are not biased in price or yield terms by any scarcity considerations.
2. Treasuries traditionally have been viewed as credit-free securities (i.e., securities that are generally immune from the kind of credit shocks that would result in an issuer being placed on watch or review or subject to an immediate change in the current credit rating).
3. Perhaps very much related to the first two points, Treasuries typically are perceived to be closely linked to any number of derivative products that are, in turn, considered to be relatively liquid instruments; consider that the existence and active use of Treasury futures, listed Treasury options, OTC Treasury options, and the repo and forward markets all collectively represent alternative venues for trafficking in a key market barometer.

When added on to a Treasury yield's level, a *credit spread* represents the incremental yield generated by being in a security that has less liquidity, more credit sensitivity, and fewer liquid derivative venues relative to a Treasury issue.

Why would an investor be interested in looking at a yield spread in the first place? Simply put, a yield spread provides a measure of *relative value* (a comparative indication of one security's value in relation to another via yield differences). A spread, by definition, is the difference between two yields, and as such it provides an indication of how one yield is evolving relative to another. For the reasons cited earlier, a Treasury yield often is used

---

[3] See Chapter 2 for another perspective on yield spread.

as a benchmark yield in the calculation of yield spreads. However, this practice is perhaps most common in the United States, where Treasuries are plentiful. Yet even in the United States there is the occasional debate of whether another yield benchmark could be more appropriate, as with the yields of federal agency securities. In Europe and Asia, it is a more common practice to look at relative value on the basis of where a security can be swapped or, equivalently, on the basis of its *swap spread* (the yield spread between a security's yield and its yield in relation to a reference swap curve).

A swap spread is also the difference between two yield levels, but instead of one of the yields consistently being a Treasury yield (as with a generic reference to a security's credit spread or yield spread), in a swap spread one of the benchmark yields is consistently Libor. A swap yield (or rate) is also known as a Libor yield (rate).

As discussed in Chapter 2, Libor is an acronym for London Inter-bank Offer Rate.[4] Specifically, Libor is the rate at which banks will lend one another U.S. dollars circulating outside of the U.S. marketplace. Dollars circulating outside of the U.S. are called *Eurodollars*. Hence, a Eurodollar yield (or equivalently, a Libor yield or a swap yield) is the yield at which banks will borrow or lend U.S. dollars that circulate outside of the United States. By the same token, a *Euroyen yield* is the rate at which banks will lend one another yen outside of the Japanese market. Similarly, a *Euribor rate* is the yield at which banks will lend one another euros outside of the European Currency Union.

Since Libor is viewed as a rate charged by banks to other banks, it is seen as embodying the *counterparty risk* (the risk that an entity with whom the investor is transacting is a reliable party to the trade) of a bank. Fair enough. To take this a step further, U.S. banks at the moment are perceived to collectively represent a double-A rating profile. Accordingly, since U.S. Treasuries are perceived to represent a triple-A rating, we would expect the yield spread of Libor minus Treasuries to be a positive value. Further, we would expect this value to narrow as investors grow more comfortable with the generic risk of U.S. banks and to widen when investors grow less comfortable with the generic risk of U.S. banks.

Swap markets (where swap transactions are made OTC) typically are seen as being fairly liquid and accessible, so at least in this regard they can take a run at Treasuries as being a meaningful relative value tool. This liquidity is fueled not only by the willingness and ability of *swap dealers* (entities that actively engage in swap transactions for investors) to traffic in a generic and standardized product type, but also by the ready access that

---

[4]Libor has the word "London" in it simply because the most liquid market in Eurodollars (U.S. dollars outside of the U.S. market) typically has been in London.

investors have to underlying derivatives. The Eurodollar futures contract is without question the most liquid and most actively traded futures contract in the world.

Although the swap market with all of its attendant product venues is a credit market (in the sense that it is not a triple-A Treasury market), it is a credit market for one rather narrow segment of all credit products. While correlations between the swap market (and its underlying link to banks and financial institutions) and other credit sectors (industrials, quasi-governmental bodies, etc.) can be quite strong at times (allowing for enticing hedge and product substitution considerations, as will be seen in Chapter 6), those correlations are also susceptible to breaking down, and precisely at moments when they are most needed to be strong.

For example, stemming from its strong correlation with various non-Treasury asset classes, prior to August 1998, many bond market investors actively used the swaps market as a reliable and efficacious hedge vehicle. But when credit markets began coming apart in August 1998, the swaps market was particularly hard hit relative to others. Instead of proving itself as a meaningful hedge as hoped, it evolved to a loss-worsening vehicle.

Chapter 6 examines how swaps products can be combined with other instruments to create new and different securities and shows how swap spreads sometimes are used as a synthetic alternative to equities to create a desired exposure to equity market volatility.

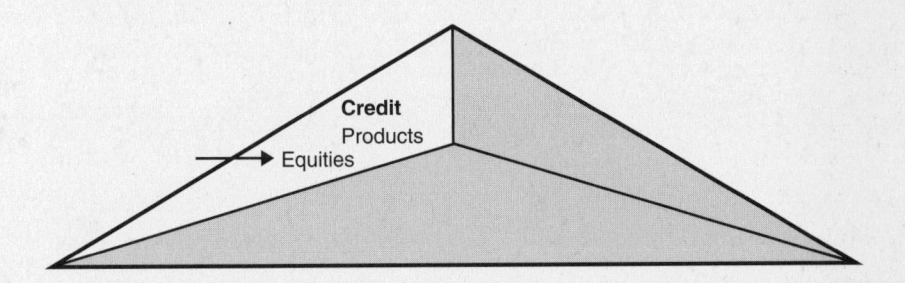

An adverse or favorable piece of news of a credit nature (whether from a credit agency or any other source) is certainly likely to have an effect on an equity's price. A negative piece of news (as with a sudden cash flow problem due to an unexpected decline in sales) is likely to have a price-depressing effect while a positive piece of news (as with an unexpected change in senior management with persons perceived to be good for the business) is likely to have a price-lifting effect.

With some equity-type products, such as preferred stock, there can be special provisions for worst-case scenarios. For example, a preferred stock's prospectus might state that in the event that a preferred issue is unable to make a scheduled dividend payment, then it will be required to resume payments, including those that are overdue, with interest added provided that it is able to get up and running once again. This type of dividend arrangement is referred to as *cumulative* protection.

While many investors rely on one or more of the rating agencies to provide them with useful information, out of fairness to the agencies and as a warning to investors, it is important to note that the agencies do not have a monopoly on credit risk data for three reasons.

1. Rating agencies are limited by the information provided to them by the companies they are covering and by what they can gather or infer from any sources available to them. If a company wants something withheld, there is generally a good chance that it will be withheld. Note that this is not to suggest that information is being held back exclusively with a devious intention; internal strategic planning is a vital and organic part of daily corporate existence for many companies, and the details of that process are rightfully a private matter.
2. Rating agencies limit themselves to what they will consider and discuss when it comes to a company's outlook. The agencies cannot be all things to all people, and generally they are quite clear about the methodologies they employ when a review is performed.
3. Rating agencies are comprised of individuals who commonly work in teams, and typically committees (or some equivalent body) review and pass ultimate judgment on formal outlooks that are made public. While a committee process has its merits, as with any process, it may have its shortcomings. For example, at times the rating agencies have been criticized for not moving more quickly to alert investors to adverse situations. While no doubt this criticism is sometimes misplaced—sometimes things happen suddenly and dramatically—there may be instances when the critique is justified.

For these reasons, many investors (and especially large fund managers) have their own research departments. Often these departments will subscribe to the services of one or more of the rating agencies, although they actively try to extend analysis beyond what the agencies are doing. In some cases these departments greatly rely on the research provided to them by the investment banks that are responsible for bringing new equities and bonds to the marketplace. In the case of an initial public offering (IPO), investors might put themselves in a position of relying principally and/or exclusively on the research of an investment bank.

As the term suggests, an IPO is the first time that a particular equity comes to the marketplace. If the company has been around for a while as a privately held venture, then it may be able to provide some financial and other information that can be shared with potential investors. But if the company is relatively new, as is often the case with IPOs, then perhaps not much hard data can be provided. In the absence of more substantive material, representations are often made about a new company's management profile or business model and so forth. These representations often are made on *road shows*, when the IPO company and its investment banker (often along with investment banking research analysts) visit investors to discuss the anticipated launching of the firm. Investors will want to ask many detailed questions to be as comfortable as possible with committing to a venture that is perhaps untested. Clearly, if investors are not completely satisfied with what they are hearing, they ought to pass on the deal and await the next one.

For additional discourse on the important role of credit ratings and their impact on equities, refer to "The Long-run Stock Returns Following Bond Ratings Changes" published in the *Journal of Finance* v. 56, n. 1 (February 2001), by Ilia D. Dichev at the University of Michigan Business School and Joseph D. Piotroski at the University of Chicago. They examine the long-run stock returns following ratings changes and find that stocks with upgrades outperform stocks with downgrades for up to one year following the rating announcement.

Their work also finds that the poor performance associated with downgrades is more pronounced for smaller companies with poor ratings and that rating changes are important predictors of future profitability. The average company shows a significant deterioration in return on equity in the year following the downgrade.

Finally, as we will see in Chapter 5, some investors make active use of a company's equity price data to anticipate future credit-related developments of a firm.

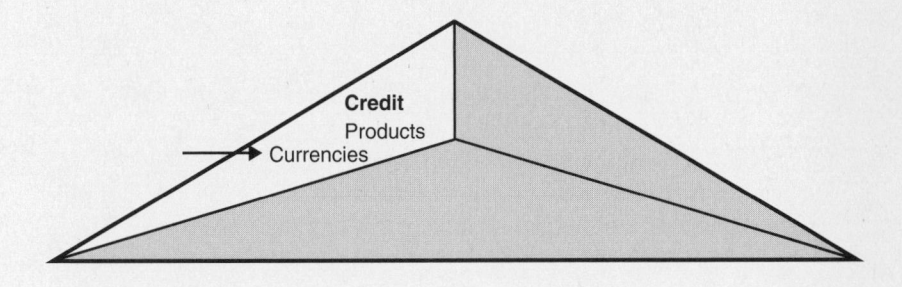

Credit
Products
Currencies

Generally speaking, the rating agencies (Moody's, Standard & Poor's, etc.) choose to assign sovereign ratings in terms of both a *local currency rating* (a rating on the local government) and a *foreign currency rating* (a rating on capital restrictions, if any). Why do the rating agencies frame their creditworthiness methodology around this particular financial variable (i.e., currency)? Presumably it is because they are confident that this particular instrument is up to the all-important role assigned to it. The purpose here is not to hype the role of currency—clearly it cannot possibly embody every nuance of a country's strengths and weaknesses—but with all due apologies to Winston Churchill, despite its shortcomings, currency may be the best overall variable there is for the task.

For most of the developed countries of the world, a local currency rating and foreign currency rating are the same. As we move across the credit risk spectrum from developed economies to less developed economies, splits between the local and foreign currency ratings become more prevalent. What exactly is meant by a local versus a foreign currency rating?

When assigning a local currency rating, the rating agency is attempting to capture sentiment about a country's ability (at the government level) to make timely payments on its obligations that are denominated in the local currency. Thus, this rating pertains to the ability of the U.S. government to make timely payments on U.S. Treasury obligations (Treasury bills, notes, and bonds) denominated in U.S. dollars. Just to highlight a historical footnote, not too long ago the U.S. government issued so-called *Carter Bonds*, which were U.S. Treasury bonds, denominated in deutsche marks. Their purpose was to allow U.S. Treasuries to be more appealing to offshore investors and to collect much-needed foreign currency reserves at the same time. During the Reagan administration, the issuance of yen-denominated Treasuries was considered, but it was not done.

Of course, not only is it of relevance that a given country can make timely payments on its obligations denominated in its own currency, but it is important that the local currency has *intrinsic value*. "Intrinsic value" does not mean that the currency is necessarily backed by something material or tangible (as when most major currencies of the world were on the gold standard and what kept a particular currency strong was the notion that there were bars of gold stacked up in support of it), but rather that there is the perception (and, one hopes, the reality) of political stability, a strong economic infrastructure, and so forth.

From one rather narrow perspective, a country always should be able to pay its obligations denominated in its local currency: when it has unfettered access to its printing presses. If having more of the local currency is as simple as making more of it, what is the problem? Such a casual stance toward debt management is not likely to go unnoticed, and in all likelihood rating agencies and investors will consider the action to be cheapening a country's overall economic integrity (not to mention the potential threat to inflation pressures). In short, while it may be theoretically (or even practically) possible for a country to print local currency on a regular basis simply to meet obligations without concomitantly working to implement more structural policies (i.e., improving roads and schools, or promoting more self-sustaining businesses for internal demand or external trade), as a long-run cornerstone of economic policy, it is perhaps not the most prudent of policies. This is certainly not to say that a country should not take on debt—perhaps even a lot of it; it simply is to say that prudence suggests that coupling debt with sound debt management is clearly the way to go. And what is sound debt management, or, equivalently, an appropriate amount of debt for a given country? With the blend of political, economic, regional, and other considerations that the rating agencies claim to evaluate, on the surface it would appear that no pat answer would suffice, but rather that a case-by-case approach is useful.

Meanwhile, a foreign currency rating applies to a country's ability to pay obligations in currencies other than its own. If the local currency was freely convertible into other currencies, then presumably securing a strong credit rating would not be an issue. However, many countries have in place (or have a history of putting in place) currency controls. Such restrictions on the free flow of currency can be troubling indeed. If a particular country were fearful of a *flight of capital*, whereby local currency were to quickly flee the country in search of safe havens offshore, then presumably one way to squash such an event would be to limit or even prohibit any exit of capital by effectively shutting down any venues of currency conversion—any non–black market venues, that is.

So can a country go into default?

Sure.

How?

First, if it does not have unfettered access to printing presses, a country cannot monetize itself out of an economic dilemma. For example, the European Central Bank is exactly that—a central bank for Europe. Thus, no one participating member country (i.e., Germany) can unilaterally print more euros for its own exclusive benefit. It is the same idea with the 50 states of the United States; if New York were to issue its own state bonds and not be able to generate sufficient revenues to pay its obligations, state authorities have no ability to just print dollars. Going another layer deeper, at the city level, the same applies. If New York City were to become at risk of default (as it was in the 1970s), the printing press does not exist as an option. However, if the federal government were to get involved, it becomes an entirely different matter.

A second way a country can go into default is if it has cheapened its currency to such a point that it is essentially deemed to be worthless. Again, such cheapening may be the result of political dynamics (e.g., a coup d'état), economic considerations (the loss or drastic curtailment, perhaps due to natural disaster, of an essential national industry or revenue-generating resource), an externally imposed event (a declaration of war or comparable action of hostility), or perhaps some other consideration.

We now need to consider a very real implication of the fact that businesses are, of course, domiciled within countries. The default of a sovereign nation is likely to have an adverse effect on any company located within that country.

While there may well be exceptions, generally it is expected that a company within a country is constrained in its credit rating potential by the uppermost credit rating assigned to the country where it is located. For this reason, it is rare to see a rating agency rate a company better than the overall rating assigned to the country in which it is domiciled. Thus, it sometimes is said that a country's foreign currency rating serves as a ceiling with respect to permissible ratings for companies within that country. That is, if a country's score were rated as AA−, then the best a company within that country could hope for in terms of a rating also would be AA−. At the core of this is the assumption that if a country fails at the sovereign level, then it is failing (or the larger failure will precipitate a failing) in the private sector as well. Yet a company within a country's borders may well be rated better than the country itself. Three scenarios for such an occurrence follow.

1. If the company is domiciled within the country but is a multinational company with a well-diversified geographical distribution of other related companies, and if the company's locally raised debt is not somehow confined to that one country alone (meaning that when the company issues debt within the country, it does so as a true multinational company and not as a stand-alone entity within the country), then it may well carry a credit rating superior to the country where it is located.
2. Strong company links to the outside world—links perhaps even stronger than those of the government itself—may help with a superior rating scenario. For example, if the company were an exporter of a particular commodity generally in strong demand (i.e., oil), a stand-alone status might be warranted.
3. The use of a creative financing arrangement might be sufficient to make the difference with a given rating decision. For example, in the 1970s the Argentine government issued special *Bonex bonds,* denominated in U.S. dollars. A principal reason for their sale was to facilitate a return of Argentine capital that had fled abroad. In addition to transferring foreign exchange risk to the U.S. dollar from the Argentinean peso, Bonex bonds were exempt from currency controls, were guaranteed by the government, and were freely tradable in Argentina and abroad. Bonex bonds were so successful that the so-called *Bonex clause* appeared in many contractual arrangements with Argentina in the

1970s and thereafter, stipulating that if access to dollars via traditional channels were to become limited, then there would be the obligation to obtain U.S. dollars via Bonex securities.

Just as a country's local currency and foreign currency ratings can have an important impact on national debt management policies (affecting such things as its cost of debt), these ratings can have enormous implications for the companies domiciled within the country. While there can be exceptions to a company's rating being capped by respective sovereign ratings, these exceptions are rare.

Sometimes the perception of the credit risk of a particular geographic region (or collection of countries) can have an impact (positive or negative) on a country's rating. For example, in the year immediately following perceptions of credit weakness in Asia (Asia's financial situation more or less began deteriorating in late 1997), it was clear to most market observers that Singapore was faring quite well relative to other regional countries. While the rating agencies explicitly recognized this greater relative strength of Singapore, because the region as a whole was still emerging from a very large shock to the financial markets (or so went many rating agency explanations at the time), Singapore continued to be rated below what it otherwise would have been rated if the region as a whole had been considered more resilient.

This illustration highlights the fact that credit rating is performed on a relative basis, not an absolute basis. As such, it can be predicted that there will never be a time in the marketplace where there is (are) no triple-A rated entity(s). A primary reason is that the perfect triple-A entity does not exist and realities of the true marketplace are what set the stage for relative (not absolute) strength and weakness in credit quality. After all, even the U.S. Treasury saw a portion of its securities placed in credit watch in 1996, when a budget impasse necessitated a federal government shutdown. Yet the U.S. government maintained the triple-A rating that it has enjoyed for many years and will likely continue to enjoy for years to come. Again, perhaps what is of relevance is that there is no such thing as a perfect triple-A country or company. Further, it ought to be noted that given the dramatic differences between a triple-A country like the United States, and any triple-A rated company, an investor would be ill-served to lump all triple-A securities into one basket regardless of entity type. That is, not all triple-A entities are created equal, and the same may be said of other credit classifications. In the case of the United States it is clearly a triple-A that is first among unequals.

Figure 3.1 presents a currency-issuer-rating triangle. There are important credit linkages among the three profiles shown. Clearly, a company must be based somewhere. Hence, a company's issuer rating is going to be influenced by the currency in which it transacts its daily business, and the local

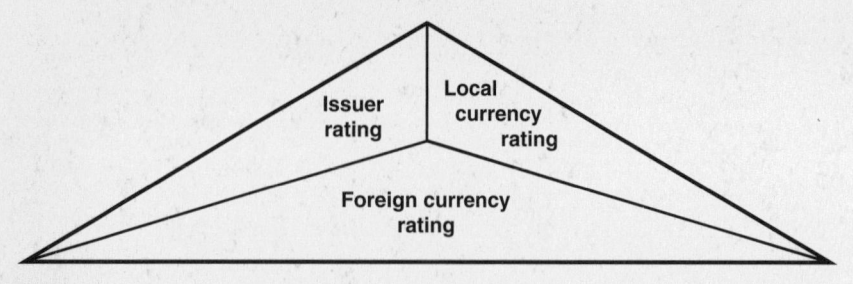

FIGURE 3.1 Currency rating triangle.

currency rating is thus a relevant consideration. However, this is not to say that the local currency rating serves as a ceiling for what any issuer rating might aspire to; a local government would have limited interest in restricting free access to its own currency. Yet the foreign currency rating, which evaluates the local government's stance on unfettered access to foreign currencies, can serve as ceiling to a local issuer's rating. However, there are several ways that an issuer's financial instruments might secure a rating above the relevant foreign currency rating. In almost every case where an issuer's rating rises above the local currency rating, the crucial factor is the issuer's being able to have access to some nonnational currency(s) in the event of a country-level default scenario.

While these various risk considerations are not of any immediate concern for G-7 and other well-developed markets, they can be quite important for *emerging market* (nondeveloped markets like those of certain parts of South America or Africa) securities, a segment of the global market that is large and growing.

For more of a discussion on the important role of currency ratings and their impact, see "Emerging Markets Instability: Do Sovereign Ratings Affect Country Risk and Stock Returns?", February 2001, by Graciela Kaminsky of George Washington University and Sergio Smukler of the World Bank. They find that the answer to the question posed in their title is "yes." As to specific case studies, consider the instance of Standard and Poor's decision in September 2002 to lower India's long-term soverign currency rating from BBB− to BB+ and to downgrade India's short-term local currency rating to B from a previous A-3. Consistent with previous adverse announcements by Standard and Poor's about India (dating back to at least October 2000), currency, equity, and bond markets reacted negatively to the news. A headline from the ENS Economic Bureau as provided by Indian Express Newspapers on October 11, 2000, read "S&P Downgrade Hits Rupee [currency], Bonds."

Credit
Cash flows
Spot
→ Bonds

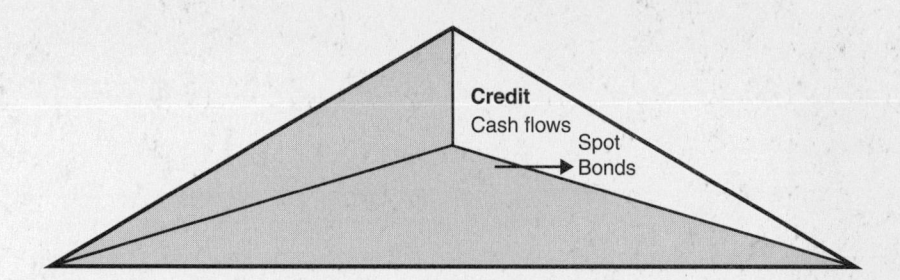

Earlier it was stated that rating agencies can assign credit ratings to companies as well as to the financial products of companies. When a credit rating is assigned at the company level, unless something dramatic happens in a positive or negative way, the rating typically sticks for a rather long time (sometimes many years). A company can do very little on a day-to-day basis to greatly influence its overall credit standing. Conversely, a company's financial products can be structured on a very short-term basis so as to satisfy rating agency criteria for receiving a rating that is higher than the overall company rating. In some instances a company may even seek to issue products with a rating below the company rating.

Generally speaking, all of the ways that a company might influence its financial product ratings are ultimately linked to cash flow considerations. This section presents those cash flow considerations in two categories as they relate to spot and bonds: collateralization and capital.

COLLATERALIZATION AND CAPITAL

Collateralization

Collateralization is one of the most basic and fundamental considerations when evaluating the credit risk of a bond (or any security). When a bank considers a loan to a homeowner or businessperson, one of the first things it is interested in learning is what the potential debtor has of value to collateralize against the loan. When it is a home loan, the home itself generally serves as the collateral. That is, if the homeowner is unable to make payments and ultimately defaults on the loan, then the bank often takes possession of the home and sells it. The proceeds from the sale go first to the bank to cover its costs and then any remaining funds will go to the homeowner. At the time a loan application is being reviewed, the bank also will want to review a homeowner's other assets (investments, retirement funds, etc.) as well as annual compensation.

With a business loan, the businessperson may have little capital in the business itself. The person may be renting the office space, and there may be little in the way of company assets aside from some office furniture and computer equipment. In such a case, the bank may ask the businessperson to provide some kind of nonbusiness collateralization, such as the deed to a property (a home or perhaps some land that is owned). If the business is profitable and simply in need of a short-term capital injection, the documented revenue streams may be sufficient to assure the bank of a business's creditworthiness. However, even if the business loan is granted and primarily on the basis of anticipated revenue, it is very likely that the rate of interest that is charged will be higher than what it could have been if collateral had been provided.

The issue of collateral is key to understanding another dimension of the difference between a bond and an equity. By virtue of a bondholder's having a more senior claim against the assets of an entity relative to a shareholder in the event of the entity's default, the bondholder is much closer to the issuer's collateral. Perhaps another way to put this would be as follows: While both a bond- and shareholder obviously hope for the ongoing viability and success of an issuer, a bondholder may be banking more on the ongoing value of the issuer's underlying assets while the shareholder is perhaps banking more on the ongoing profitability of the issuer's business. Generally speaking, the uncertainty of the former is typically less than the uncertainty of the latter. This fact may help to explain the greater price variability in mainstream equities versus mainstream bonds, as well as the greater risk-return profiles of equities versus bonds.

As a last comment on the role of collateralization and credit, let us consider *overcollateralization*.

As the term suggests, to overcollateralize a debt means to provide more dollar value of assets relative to the debt itself. For example, if a business loan is for $50,000 and $75,000 of assets is provided to collateralize it (perhaps the businessperson owns the office space), then the loan is overcollateralized. All else being equal, the businessperson should expect to pay a lower rate of interest relative to an *uncollateralized* loan.

Sometimes banks bundle together various loan profiles they have amassed and then *securitize* them. To securitize a bundle of loans simply means that the loans have been packaged into a single security to be sold to investors, generally in the form of a coupon-bearing bond. The coupons are paid out of the monthly interest payments provided by the various debtors, and the principal comes from the principal payments of the same loans. A bank might choose to securitize its loans to turn its liabilities into assets. When a bank has an outstanding loan, it is a liability; the person with the bank's money may or may not make good on the obligation. By bundling loans together and selling them as bonds, banks turn these liabilities into immediate cash. Banks can use this new cash to turn around and make more loans if they so choose, and repeat the process over and over again. There is a risk transfer whereby the risk of the loans being paid is shifted away from the banks and into the hands of the investors who purchase the bonds.

Banks make a variety of different types of loans, including home loans, auto loans, boat loans, and so forth. When these loans are securitized as bonds (and typically by respective categories of home, auto, etc.), they are sometimes referred to as *asset-backed securities*, because the loans are *backed-by* (collateralized by) the property underlying the loan (the home, the car, whatever). Typically a designated *servicer* of the asset-backed securities actually goes through the machinations of repossessing and selling assets when required.

Investors like to know the rating on the asset-backed securities they are being asked to purchase, just as they like to know the rating of any credit-sensitive securities they have been asked to buy. Going through the paperwork of the literally hundreds of persons whose individual loans might comprise a given asset-backed bond, all for the purpose of coming up with some aggregate credit risk profile, would be a rather daunting task (not to mention the legal considerations likely involved). A proposed solution for this, and one readily accepted by investors, is to overcollateralize the bond. By placing a face amount of loans into an asset-backed deal that is in excess of the bond's face value, investors are reasonably assured of a means to moderate their credit risk. Some latitude for loan defaults is allowed without an undue influence on the overall credit standing of the securitized venue. Moreover, the issuer is presumably happy with the lower coupon attached to a triple-A asset-backed security as this means more of an economic incentive to have its loans securitized in the first place.

Capital

Another way a company can secure a more favorable credit rating for one of its financial products would be to obtain third-party insurance. In such cases, a third-party says that it will guarantee the financial product's maintenance of a credit rating of a certain minimum level over the life of the product. In exchange for providing this guarantee, the issuer pays a fee (an insurance premium). The benefit of such an arrangement to the issuer could be a lower net cost of funds (since investors may demand less of a risk premium for buying a financial product that comes with guarantees) and the possibility of reaching more potential investors by structuring its product in such a way.

When an individual seeks to purchase a life insurance policy, insurance companies commonly insist on seeing the results of a physical exam prior to granting a policy. Upon seeing the results of that physical exam, the life insurance company might refuse to issue a policy, issue a policy but with higher premiums relative to what is charged to healthier customers, and/or issue a policy but only after receiving assurances that particular changes are made in the customer's lifestyle. For example, the potential customer may be a smoker, and an insurance company might insist that he quit before a policy is issued.

Similarly, before an investment bank chooses to *underwrite* (assist with) a particular firm's securities, it is likely to want to give the firm a complete physical. That is, it is likely to want to visit the premises and operations, look over financial statements, and interview key officers. Further, it ultimately may refuse to underwrite the firm's securities altogether, or it might insist that certain measures be taken prior to a policy being granted. Insisting on major policy changes may be difficult with well-established companies; often a simpler solution can be found. For example, the insurance company might simply ask the issuer to set aside an allocation of capital that it promises not to touch over the life of the security that is being guaranteed. In doing this the issuer is creating a *reserve*, a special account whose sole purpose is to provide a backup of dedicated financial resources in the event that they might be required to support or service the firm's financial product. Clearly it would be disadvantageous for the amount placed in the reserve to be equal to or greater than the amount being raised in the first place, so appropriate terms and conditions have to be agreed on. A currency deposit (which is hard cash, and which is spot[5]) is used to help secure a more desirable credit profile for an issuer's financial product.

Another way an issuer can attempt to achieve a more desirable credit profile for its financial products is with the creative use of another entity's capital structure. For example, if an issuer creates a financial product requiring certain inputs that can be obtained from an entity outside of the issuer's company (as with an interest rate swap provided by an investment bank), then the credit rating of that outside entity can contribute beneficially to the overall credit rating of the product being launched. It is then desirable, of course, that the outside entity's credit rating be above the issuer's rating and

---

[5]Just as futures and forwards and options are derivatives of spot when speaking of bonds and equities, cash has its derivatives. For example, the writing of a check is a variation of entering into a forward agreement. Unlike traditional forward agreements where goods are exchanged for cash at an agreed-on point in the future, goods typically are provided immediately and with actual receipt of cash coming several days later (when the check clears). In this fashion the use of a credit card is also a derivative of cash. Of course, another variation of the forward transaction is when payment is provided immediately for a delivery of goods that is not to be made until some point in the future.

that it remain above the issuer's rating. Many investment banks have in fact created triple-A rated subsidiaries or *special-purpose vehicles* (*SPVs* or special entities created to help isolate and secure certain market transactions; also known as a bankruptcy-remote entity and a derivatives product company) to assist with this type of creative product construction. Chapter 4 provides an explicit example of how the credit rating of a product can be directly influenced by the entities involved with creating it.

To link yield-related phenomena across the first three chapters of this text, consider Figure 3.2. Each successive layer that is added equates to a higher overall yield for this hypothetical bond.

As another perspective on the relationship between credit and the way securities are put together, consider Figure 3.3. As shown, credit risk most certainly can be ranked by security type, and investors should take this reality into consideration with each and every transaction.

Figure 3.3 is a conceptual guide to a hierarchy of relationships that can exist between security types and associated credit exposure. There is latitude for investors to place these or other security types in a different relation to one another.

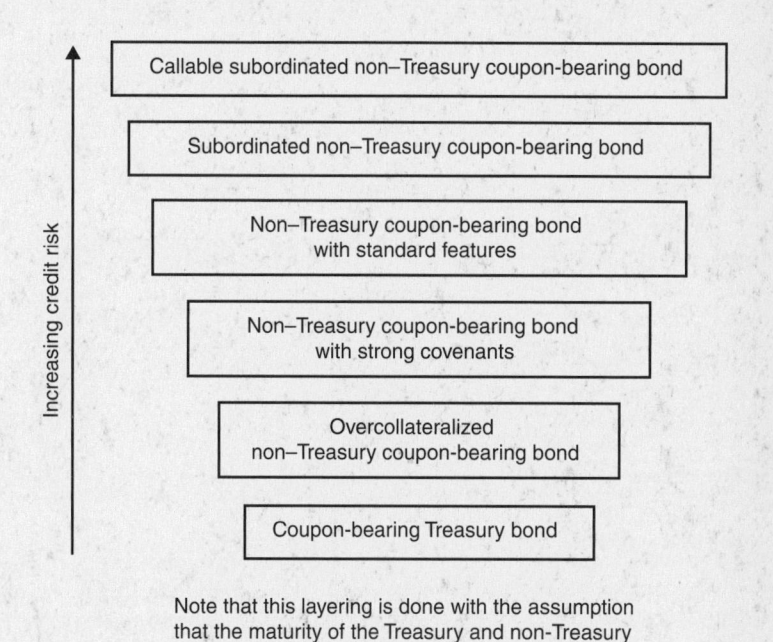

Increasing credit risk →

- Callable subordinated non–Treasury coupon-bearing bond
- Subordinated non–Treasury coupon-bearing bond
- Non–Treasury coupon-bearing bond with standard features
- Non–Treasury coupon-bearing bond with strong covenants
- Overcollateralized non–Treasury coupon-bearing bond
- Coupon-bearing Treasury bond

Note that this layering is done with the assumption that the maturity of the Treasury and non-Treasury securities is comparable and that the non-Treasury securities are all issued by a single entity profile.

FIGURE 3.2 Layering of credit-related risks within bonds.

Credit Risk Protection

- H Long-dated uncollateralized bullet
- G Long-dated uncollateralized bullet with protective covenants
- F Long-dated uncollateralized putable
- E Long-dated and collateralized
- D Short-dated bullet
- C Short-dated uncollateralized bullet with protective covenants
- B Short-dated uncollateralized putable
- A Short-dated and collateralized

Security Types: A B C D E F G H

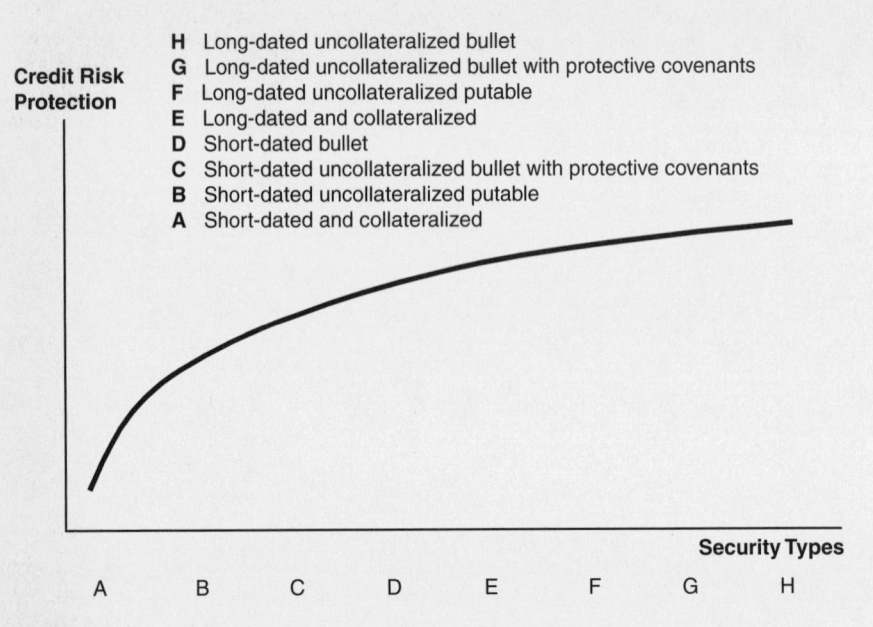

FIGURE 3.3 Conceptual linking of credit risk with security types.

Table 3.2 is taken from a survey performed by Standard & Poor's. Within the very real world of recovering value from investments that have gone bad, the table presents the relationship among various bonds and their associated success with recovering monies for investors.

TABLE 3.2 Average Recoveries

	Mean Recovery (%)	Median Recovery (%)	Standard Deviation (%)	Coefficient of Variation[a] (CV)	Count
All instruments	51.14	44.94	37.38	73.09	954
Bank debt	83.54	100.00	25.59	30.64	264
Senior secured notes	63.75	70.69	31.06	48.72	141
Senior notes	49.92	42.92	34.72	69.55	125
Senior subordinated notes	28.18	18.29	28.26	100.28	395
Junior subordinated notes	12.81	5.47	18.42	143.83	29

Source: Standard & Poor's, May 24, 2000, "Suddenly Structure Mattered: Insights into Recoveries of Defaulted Debt," Karen VandeCastle.

[a]Coefficient of variation: standard deviation/average recovery. Coefficient of variation (CV) normalizes standard deviation to the mean and reflects how much deviation occurs in the data set for each additional dollar, plus or minus the average recovery.

As shown, the uppermost senior structures (bank debt and senior secured notes) exhibit rather strong and favorable recovery statistics with mean and median recovery percentages ranging from 63 to 100 percent. At the opposite end of the spectrum (senior subordinated notes and junior subordinated notes), mean and median recovery percentages range from 5 to 28 percent. Clearly structure type matters (e.g., secured versus unsecured) as does the particular ranking of a security within the capital structure of its issuer (e.g., senior versus junior). Investors are well advised to take these factors into consideration when evaluating various investment opportunities. A security's standing in relation to the issuer's capital structure, and whether the security is secured or unsecured, collateralized or uncollateralized, and so on, can have an important material impact on its value in a worst-case scenario.

In a more recent study, Standard & Poor's reported a dramatic difference between debt with a sizable cushion versus debt with a less sizable cushion. *Debt cushion* is defined as the percentage of a company's debt that is inferior to a particular debt instrument. In other words, the larger the value of a debt cushion, the more senior the debt instrument being considered. Further, Standard & Poor's segmented its debt cushion analysis into debt without collateralized backing (unsecured) and debt with collateralized backing (secured). Accordingly, consideration is made of both the relative credit ranking of a debt instrument within a company's capital structure and its cash flow features. Table 3.3 summarizes the results and shows how a product's credit standing and structure of cash flows can have important bottom-line implications for investors.

TABLE 3.3 Weighted Average Discounted Recovery Rates, 1987–2001

Debt Cushion	No Collateral	Collateral
Less than 50%	33.8% (635)	67.5% (331)
Greater than 50%	71.5% (39)	86.5% (261)

Source: Standard & Poor's, January 24, 2002, "Ultimate Recovery Remains High," Kevin Kelhoffer.

The triangles in Figure 3.4 present a way to conceptualize this nature of credit dynamics in the context of products, cash flows, and capital. At each step a new consideration is added and with a positive effect on credit. Of course, numerous combinations of cash flow, capital, and product structures can be engineered.

96 PRODUCTS, CASH FLOWS, AND CREDIT

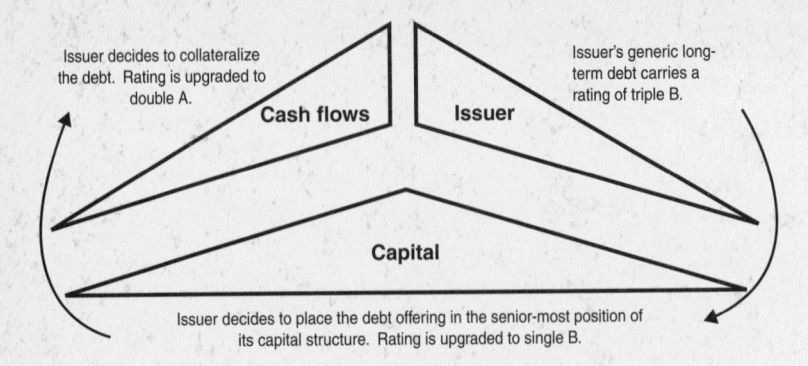

```
          Issuer decides to collateralize                    Issuer's generic long-
          the debt. Rating is upgraded to                    term debt carries a
                    double A.                                rating of triple B.
                              Cash flows      Issuer


                                        Capital

             Issuer decides to place the debt offering in the senior-most position of
                  its capital structure. Rating is upgraded to single B.
```

FIGURE 3.4 Incremental venues for increasing the credit quality of a bond.

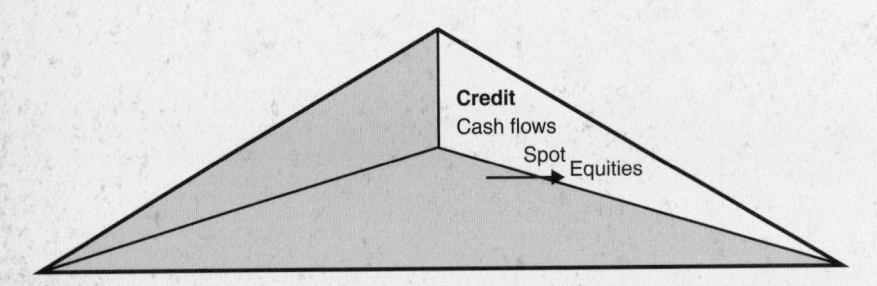

```
                              Credit
                              Cash flows
                                   Spot
                                        Equities
```

The ultimate consideration with credit risk is that an investor has some measure of assurance of receiving complete and timely cash flows. For a coupon-bearing bond, this means receiving coupons and principal when they are due and with payment in full. For equities, this can mean receiving dividends in a timely manner and/or simply being able to exchange cash for securities (or vice-versa) in an efficacious way. As stated, two clear differences between a bond and an equity are the senior standing embedded within the former in the event of a default and the fact that holders of equity truly own some portion of the underlying company.

Just as there are varying classifications of bonds in the context of credit risk (as with senior versus junior classes of bonds), the same is true of equities. Inevitably, with the evolution of several different layers of bond and equity types in the market, there emerges a gray area between where one type ends and another begins. While the philosophical aspect of this phenomenon is of interest, there are some rather practical considerations for portfolio managers. For example, fund managers in charge of bond funds will want to have defensible reasons for including products that some customers might believe are more equity related. A sensible rationale may be all that customers require to be assured that their money is being invested as advertised. To begin to put a sharper point to this discussion, let us take a specific product example.

A *perpetual bond* is a security that has no specified maturity date (like an equity). However, like a bond, a perpetual pays coupons,[6] has a final maturity value of par (whenever that final maturity may actually come), does not convey any voting rights, and in many cases is *callable* (may be retired at the discretion of the issuer). Therefore, by what criteria ought we decide that this (or any other hybrid type product) is a bond or equity? By voting rights? Maturity? How it is taxed? If it comes with the bells and whistles more commonly associated with an equity or bond (as with a callable feature)? If it pays a coupon as opposed to a dividend? If its price volatility is more like a longer-maturity bond than an equity? How far it is removed from a senior status in event of default? If it trades on an exchange (like most equities) as opposed to over-the-counter (like most bonds)? Parenthetically, at least in the experience of this author, perpetuals tend to be considered by most larger investment firms as more bondlike than equitylike, even though certain fixed income investors are prohibited from purchasing them due to in-house restrictions against equity purchases.

Meanwhile, other products variously referred to as equity or bonds (depending on one's particular perspective as issuer or investor or rating agency) include preferred stock and convertibles. Table 3.4 provides a high-level overview of various points of distinction that might be used for equities and bonds. Rather than trying to convince anyone that an equity or bond should always be seen by one and only one set of criteria, the aim here is to highlight the considerations to evaluate when attempting to make a case for a product that falls in between a pure equity and a pure bond. The ultimate categorization of equities, or bonds, or any other product types is best accomplished on the basis of a thoughtful review of the facts and circumstances. Markets evolve much too quickly and with too many innovations to continue to rely on historical methods that can be expected, out of fairness, only to provide answers of most relevance to a time that has passed.

CREDIT DERIVATIVES

Generally speaking, the development and use of innovative credit-linked instruments has been the purview of the fixed income arena. The bond market has long been devoted to the special considerations involved with segmenting and redistributing cash flows and applying this framework to credit represents both a natural and logical progression. The following section provides an overview of fixed income credit derivatives.

---

[6]Coupons of perpetuals generally are paid quarterly, and usually are linked to a level of some predetermined maturity of Libor plus or minus a yield spread (as with three-month Libor plus 25 basis points).

TABLE 3.4 Similarities and Differences between Equities and Bonds

	Common Equity	Bonds
Voting rights	√	
Maturity dates and values (par)		√
Taxation		
Price	Capital gains*	Capital gains
Dividends	Income[+]	
Coupons		Income
Covenants		√
Bells and whistles		√
Coupons		√
Dividends	√	
Yields	√	√
Price volatility	Generally higher than bonds	Generally lower than equities
Default status	Low	High
Exchange traded	√	
OTC		√

*A distinction exists between short- and long-term capital gains, with the latter being a lower rate.
[+]With dividends and coupons treated as income, the tax paid is dependent on the tax bracket of the investor.

Unlike a formula to derive the exact price of something like a Treasury bill, no such credit risk calculation tells us precisely how a security's price will evolve over time in response to credit-related phenomena. However, as a result of having collected decades' worth of credit-related statistics, Moody's and Standard & Poor's have assembled an impressive amount of statistical data that can be used as meaningful guidelines when assessing credit-related risks and opportunities. These statistics may be of value not only when evaluating investment exposures to particular issuers, but also when evaluating counterparties. Two other methods by which credit risk can be quantified are also presented: guidelines published by the Bank of International Settlements and the use of option pricing methods.

Table 3.5 provides just one of many statistical guides available with the benefit of Moody's and Standard & Poors' vast statistical data. It presents a perspective of default rates. As shown, the risk of default clearly increases as investors dip into lower-rated credits, and this is precisely as is to be expected. Beginning at less than 1 percent for both Moody's and S&P for triple-A securities under a five-year horizon, double digits are approached at Ba3/double-B minus, and values near 30 percent are reached at B3/B−.

Table 3.6 depicts historical *drift* experiences. "Drift" refers to the fact that ratings can edge higher or lower from year to year. As shown, a company that

TABLE 3.5 Default Rates at 1- and 5-Year Horizons by Agency (%)

Bond Rating		1-Year Default Rate		5-Year Default Rate	
S&P	Moody's	S&P	Moody's	S&P	Moody's
AAA	Aaa	0.00	0.00	0.15	0.22
AA+	Aa1	0.00	0.00	0.27	0.25
AA	Aa2	0.00	0.00	0.11	0.50
AA−	Aa3	0.00	0.07	0.40	0.45
A+	A1	0.03	0.00	0.48	0.75
A	A2	0.04	0.00	0.32	0.66
A−	A3	0.07	0.00	0.82	0.45
BBB+	Baa1	0.20	0.04	1.15	1.45
BBB	Baa2	0.19	0.08	1.36	1.29
BBB−	Baa3	0.30	0.31	3.21	2.79
BB+	Ba1	0.62	0.64	5.79	8.45
BB	Ba2	0.78	0.59	6.88	9.66
BB−	Ba3	1.19	2.55	12.23	20.76
B+	B1	2.42	3.56	16.18	25.56
B	B2	7.93	6.85	24.66	28.52
B−	B3	9.84	12.41	29.16	37.49
CCC	Caa1-C	20.39	18.31	41.29	38.30
Investment Grade		0.08	0.04	0.71	0.82
Speculative Grade		3.83	3.67	16.08	20.26

Source: Standard & Poor's, 1/23/03. Reprinted with permission from Moody's Investors Service.
Note: S&P data covers the period from 1981 to 1998. Moody's data covers the period from 1983 to 1998.

begins a year with a triple-A rating has an 85.44 percent likelihood of remaining a triple-A firm at the end of a year. Conversely, a single-B rated company has a 76.12 percent chance of remaining a single-B rated company. Further, while a triple-A rated company shows a zero percent chance of going into default over a year, a C-rated company has a 25.16 percent chance of default. While it may not be terribly surprising to learn that a triple-A rated company has an extremely low probability of defaulting over a year, Moody's data allow for the assignment of specific probabilities to credit-related events. While this may be valuable for getting an idea for how a portfolio of credits might behave over time, there are most certainly limitations to such data. For example, the data have been collected over strong and weak economic environments. All else being equal, more favorable drift statistics are expected for periods of economic strength than times of economic weakness. Nonetheless, generally speaking, the statistics provide a meaningful set of historical guidelines to help shape investment decision making. Such guidelines can be particularly useful with valuing complex credit derivatives.

TABLE 3.6 Moody's One-Year Transition Matrices

Corporate Average One-Year Rating Transition Matrix, 1980–1998
Rating to (%)

Initial Rating	Aaa	Aa	A	Baa	Ba	B	Caa—C	Default	WR*
Aaa	85.44	9.92	0.98	0.00	0.03	0.00	0.00	0.00	3.63
Aa	1.04	85.52	9.21	0.33	0.14	0.14	0.00	0.03	3.59
A	0.06	2.76	86.57	5.68	0.71	0.17	0.01	0.01	4.03
Baa	0.05	0.32	6.68	80.55	5.72	0.95	0.08	0.15	5.49
Ba	0.03	0.07	0.51	5.20	76.51	7.40	0.49	1.34	8.46
B	0.01	0.04	0.16	0.60	6.07	76.12	2.54	6.50	7.96
Caa—C	0.00	0.00	0.66	1.05	3.05	6.11	62.97	25.16	0.00

* WR: Withdrawn rating.
Source: Moody's Investor's Service, January 1999, "Historical Default Rates of Corporate Bond Issuers, 1920–1998."

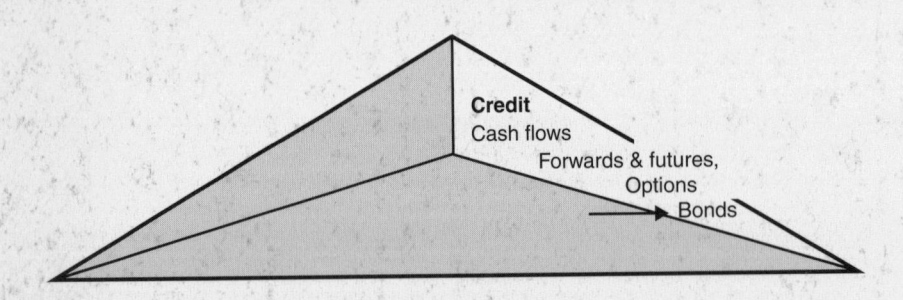

A *credit derivative* is simply a forward, future, or option that trades to an underlying spot credit-sensitive instrument or variable. For example, if investors purchase a 10-year bond of the XYZ corporation and the bond is rated single-A, they can purchase a credit spread option on the security such that their credit risk exposure is mitigated in the event of a deterioration in XYZ's credit standing—at least to the extent that this credit weakness translates into a widening credit spread. The pricing of a credit spread option certainly takes into consideration the kind of drift and default data presented, as would presumably any nonderivative credit-sensitive instrument (like a credit-sensitive bond). However, drift and default tables represent an aggregation of data at a very high level. Accordingly, the data are an amalgamation of statistics accumulated over several economic cycles, with no segmentation by industry-type, maturity of industry-type, or the average age of companies within an industry category. Thus, by slicing out these various profiles, a more meaningful picture may emerge pertaining to how a credit (or portfolio of credits) may evolve over time.

In addition to the simple case of buying or selling a credit spread put or call option on specific underlying bonds, credit derivatives, that account for a rather small percentage of the overall credit derivatives market, there are other types of credit derivative transactions. Any non-spot vehicle that can effectively absorb or transfer all or a portion of a security's (or portfolio's) credit risk can be appropriately labeled a credit derivative instrument. Consider the case of a *credit-linked note*.

A credit-linked note is a fixed income security with an embedded credit derivative. Simply put, if the reference credit defaults or goes into bankruptcy, the investor will not receive par at maturity but will receive an amount equivalent to the relevant recovery rate. In exchange for taking on this added risk, the investor is compensated by virtue of the credit-linked note having a higher coupon relative to a bond without the embedded derivative. Figure 3.5 shows how a credit-linked note can be created.

A credit-linked note is an example of a *credit absorbing* vehicle, and an investor in this product accepts exposure to any adverse move in credit standing. As a result of taking on this added risk, the investor is paid a higher coupon relative to what would be offered on a comparable security profile without the embedded credit risk.

In addition to these issuer-specific types of credit derivative products, other credit derivatives are broader in scope and have important implications for product correlations and market liquidity. For example, a simple *interest rate swap* can be thought of as a credit derivative vehicle. With an interest rate swap, an investor typically provides one type of cash flow in exchange for receiving some other type of cash flow. A common swap involves an investor exchanging a cash flow every six months that's linked

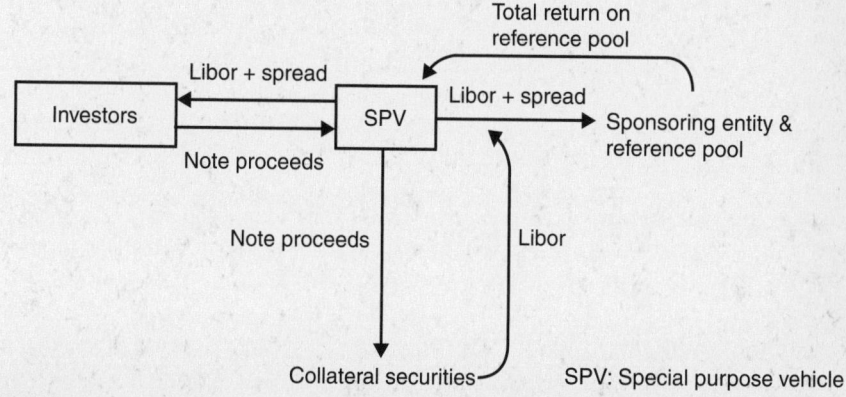

FIGURE 3.5 Schematic of a credit-linked note.

to a long-dated risk-free reference rate of interest (e.g., a five-year Treasury bond yield) in exchange for receiving a cash flow linked to a floating rate of interest (e.g., six-month Libor). In practice, the two parties to a swap typically net the relevant cash flows such that only one payment actually is made. Thus, if investors believe that credit spreads may widen, an interest rate swap may be just the ticket. Investors will want to set up the swap such that they are paying the risk-free rate (the Treasury rate) and receiving the credit rate (as with Libor).

Accordingly, swap investors will benefit under any one of these five scenarios:

1. The level of both the relevant Libor and Treasury rates rise, but Libor rises by more.
2. The level of both the relevant Libor and Treasury rates fall, but Libor falls by less.
3. The level of Libor rises while the Treasury rate stays the same.
4. The level of the Treasury falls while Libor stays the same.
5. The level of the Treasury falls while Libor rises.

Examples to correspond to each of these follow:

1. In a bear market environment (rising yields) that is exacerbated by economic weakness, as was the case in 1994, yield levels of all bonds will tend to rise, though the yields on credit-sensitive securities will tend to rise by more as they are perceived to have less protection for enduring hardship.
2. In a rallying market (falling yields) for Treasury bonds, non-Treasury products may lag behind Treasuries in performance. This stickiness of non-Treasury yields can contribute to a widening of spreads, as during 2002.
3. A unique event unfavorable to banking occurs, as with the news of Mexico's near default in August 1982.
4. A unique event favoring Treasuries occurs, as with the surprise news in 1998 that after 29 years of running deficits, the federal government was finding itself with a budget surplus.
5. Investors rush out of non-Treasury securities and rush into the safety of Treasury securities. This scenario is sometimes referred to as a flight to quality, and occurred in August 1998 when Russia defaulted on its sovereign debt.

Figure 3.6 presents the basic mechanics of an interest rate swap.

The above-referenced type of interest rate swap (Constant Maturity Treasury swap, or CMT swap) is a small part of the overall swaps market,

Credit

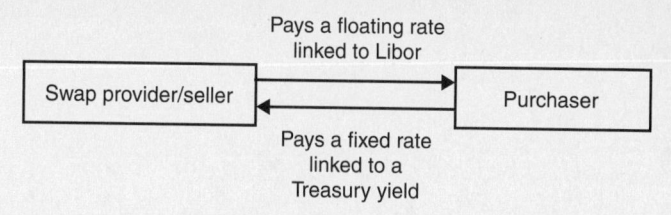

FIGURE 3.6 Interest rate swap schematic.

with the majority of swaps being fixed versus Libor without reference to Treasuries. It is this latter type of swap that is most commonly used for credit purposes.

Often credit spreads widen as yield levels rise. There are at least three reasons why this could be the case.

1. As yields rise, credit spreads may need to widen so as to keep pace on a relative basis; a credit spread of 20 basis points (bps) when the relevant Treasury yield is 6 percent amounts to 3.3 percent of the Treasury's yield (20bps/600bps), while 20 bps when the relevant Treasury yield is 8 percent amounts to 2.5 percent of the Treasury's yield.
2. As alluded to above, in times of economic weakness, when all bond yields have an upward bias, credit-sensitive securities can be especially vulnerable since they are perceived to be less insulated against the challenges of adverse times.
3. Demand for credit-sensitive products weakens since they are not expected to be strong performers, and this slack in the level of interest depresses price levels (and widens spreads).

A *total return swap* is another example of a credit swap transaction. A total return swap exists when an investor swaps the total return profile of one market index (or subset of a market index) for some other market index (or subset of a market index). For example, an investor may have a portfolio that matches the U.S. investment-grade (Baa-rated securities and higher) bond index of Morgan Stanley. Such a bond index would be expected to have U.S. Treasuries, mortgage-backed securities (MBS), federal agencies, asset-backed securities, and investment-grade corporate securities. Investors who are bearish on the near-term outlook for credit may want to enter into a total return swap where they agree to pay the total return on the corporate (or credit) portion of their portfolios in exchange for receiving the total return of the Treasury (or noncredit) portion of their portfolios. In short, the portfolio managers are entering into a forward contractual arrangement whereby any payout is based on the performance of underlying spot securities.

A *credit default swap* is still another example of a credit risk transfer vehicle. A credit default swap can be structured to trade to one or more underlying spot securities. In brief, if the underlying security (or basket of securities) goes into default, a payment is made that is typically equal to par minus any recovery value. Figure 3.7 presents an overview of the cash flows involved in a common credit default transaction (or financial guarantee).

Parenthetically, there are some investors who view credit default swaps and total return swaps as being close substitutes for bonds. That is, a swap is seen as comparable to buying a generic coupon-bearing bond and funding it at Libor on a rolling basis. The strategy can be summarized as follows:

$$\text{Fixed-coupon par bond} = \text{Par swap} + 3\text{- (or 6-) month Libor cash investment}.$$

At the end of the first quarterly (or semiannual) period, the floating part of the swap is again worth par and pays interest at the rate of Libor referenced at the start of the swap. This is precisely the case with the cash Libor investment; the cash investment precisely matches the floating part of the swap at each successive 3- (or 6-) month interval. Thus, the total return of a swap may be viewed as the return on a portfolio consisting of the swap and the cash investment in Libor; the return is equivalent to the total return of the fixed part of the swap considered to be economically equivalent to a bond.

There are many diverse considerations embedded within a credit derivative, not the least of which involve important legal and tax matters. From a legal perspective, an obvious though long-elusive requirement was for a clear and unambiguous definition of precisely when and how a default event is to be defined. The resolution of this particular issue was significantly aided with standardized documentation from the International Swaps and Derivatives Association (ISDA). In 1999 the ISDA presented a set of definitions that could be used in whole or in part by parties desiring to enter into complex credit-based transactions. However, even though the acceptance and

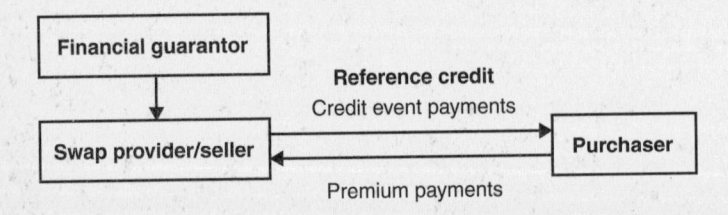

FIGURE 3.7 Financial guarantee schematic.

use of common terms and definitions is a large step in the right direction, different interpretations of those terms and definitions when viewed by various legal entities are likely. When interpretations are given, they often reflect the particular orientation and biases of the legal framework within the national boundaries of where the opinions are being rendered.

For example, in Western Europe, France is generally regarded as a debtor-friendly nation, while the United Kingdom is widely seen as a creditor-friendly country. Germany is sometimes viewed as being somewhere in the middle of France and the U.K. Thus, while the euro and other shared governmental policies within the European Community have gone a long way toward creating a single common approach to business practices, this is far from having been fully achieved. Presumably one way that this process of a more homogeneous legal infrastructure can be achieved is through the European courts. Court decisions made at the national level can be appealed to a higher European level (if not with original jurisdiction residing within certain designated European courts at the outset), and over time an accumulated framework of legal opinions on credit and related matters should trickle back down to the national level to guide interpretations on a country-by-country basis. This being said, as is often the experience in the United States, it is common to have participants in a default situation sit down and attempt to arrive at a particular solution among themselves. Again, and perhaps especially in this type of setting, which is somewhat distanced from more formal and constraining requirements of a judicially rooted approach, local customs and biases can play a more dominant role. Chapter 6 provides more detail on tax and legal implications for credit derivatives.

Finally, a popular instrument among credit derivatives is the *synthetic CDO*. CDO stands for collateralized debt obligation, and it is typically structured as a portfolio of spot securities with high credit risk. The securities generally include a mix of loans and bonds. A portfolio comprised predominantly of loans may be called a *CLO*, and a portfolio comprised predominantly of bonds may be called a *CBO*. Generally speaking, when a CDO, CLO, or CBO is structured, it is segmented into various tranches with varying risk profiles. The tranches typically are differentiated by the priority given to the payout of cash flows, and the higher the priority of a given class, the higher the credit rating it receives. It is not unusual for a CDO to have tranches rated from triple A down to single B or lower. These instruments are comprised of spot securities. A synthetic CDO necessarily involves an underlying CDO of spot securities, though it is also comprised of a credit-linked note and a credit default swap. Figure 3.8 presents a schematic overview of a synthetic CDO.

With a synthetic CLO, the issuer (commonly a bank) does not physically take loans off its books, but rather transfers the credit risk embedded within the loans by issuing a credit-linked note. The bank retains underlying spot

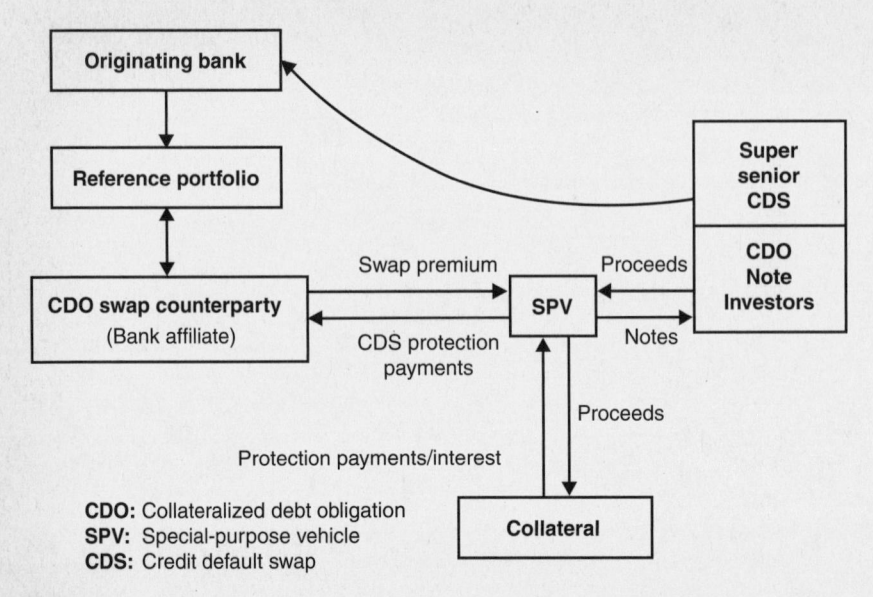

FIGURE 3.8 Schematic of a synthetic balance sheet structure.

CDO: Collateralized debt obligation
SPV: Special-purpose vehicle
CDS: Credit default swap

assets as loans. Since the credit risk in the loans is transferred to a special-purpose vehicle (*SPV*), a company specifically established to facilitate the creation of the CLO, it is the SPV that then transfers the credit risk to investors who are willing to take on the risk for the right price. As a result of having successfully transferred the credit risk off its books in this synthetic fashion, the bank is not required to hold as much capital in reserve. This freed-up capital can be directed in support of other business activities.

When the SPV sells the credit-linked notes, the proceeds of the sale do not revert back to the bank but are invested in low-risk securities (i.e., triple-A rated instruments). This conservative investment strategy is used to help ensure that repayment of principal is made in full to the holders of the credit-linked notes. The SPV originates a credit default swap, with the issuing bank as a counterparty. The bank pays a credit default swap insurance premium to the SPV under terms of the swap arrangement. Should a default occur with any of the loans at the originating bank, the bank would seek an insurance payment from the SPV. If this happens, investors in the SPV would suffer some type of loss. Just how much of a loss is experienced depends on the depth and breadth of default(s) actually experienced. If no default event occurs, investors in the SPV will receive gross returns equal to the triple-A rated investments and the default swap premium.

Aside from differences in how synthetic and nonsynthetic CDOs can be created, synthetic CDOs are not subject to the same legal and regulatory requirements as regular CDOs. For example, on the legal front, requirements with matters like making notice to obligors are less an issue since the issuer is retaining a synthetic CDO's underlying securities. On the regulatory front, and as already alluded to above, it has been held that for purposes of risk-based capital, an issuer of a synthetic CDO may treat the cash proceeds from the sale of credit-linked notes as cash that is designated as collateral. This then permits the reference assets—the loans carried on the books of the issuing bank—to be eligible for a zero percent risk classification to the extent that there is full collateralization. This treatment may be applied even when the cash collateral is transferred to the general operating funds of the bank and not deposited in a segregated account.

Table 3.7 shows credit derivatives in the context of their relationship to underlying securities. As shown, cost, the desired credit exposure or trans-

TABLE 3.7 Credit Derivative Profiles

Credit Derivative	Underlying Spot	Pros/Cons
Credit put/call options and forwards	Single reference security	Offers a tailor-made hedge, though may be expensive owing to its unique characteristics as created by buyer and seller
Credit default swap	Usually a portfolio of securities	Typically created with unique securities as defined by buyer and seller, so may be more expensive than a total rate of return swap
Total rate of return swap	Index (portfolio) of securities	Generally seen as less of a commodity than credit-linked notes, and may be more expensive as a result
Credit-linked notes	Single reference security or portfolio of securities	Often a more commoditized product relative to individual options and forwards, so may not be as expensive
Synthetic CDO	Portfolio of securities	Blend of a CDO, credit-linked note, and credit default swap in terms of cost, and may offer issuer certain legal and regulatory advantages
Interest rate swap	Reference credit rate (typically a Libor rate) relative to a non-credit-sensitive rate (typically a Treasury or sovereign rate)	Perhaps the least expensive of credit derivatives, but also considerably less targeted to a single issuer or issuer-type

fer of credit exposure, and various legal and regulatory considerations all can come into play in differing ways with these products. Chapter 6 presents more detail pertaining to the particular tax and legal issues involved.

The following chapters make reference to these products, and highlight ways in which other security types may be considered to be credit derivatives even if they are not conventionally thought of as such.

CHAPTER SUMMARY

This chapter examined how credit permeates all aspects of the financial markets; issuers, counterparties, and the unique packaging of various financial products are all of relevance to investors concerned about managing their overall credit exposures. While rating agencies can rate companies and their financial products, there are limitations to what rating agencies or anyone else can see and judge. Cash flows can be used to redistribute credit risk. Cash flows cannot eliminate credit risk, but they can help to channel it in innovative ways. And finally, a variety of innovations are constantly evolving in response to investors' needs for creating and transferring credit exposures.

As perhaps more of a conceptual way of summarizing the first three chapters, please refer to Figure 3.9. As shown, there can be creative ways

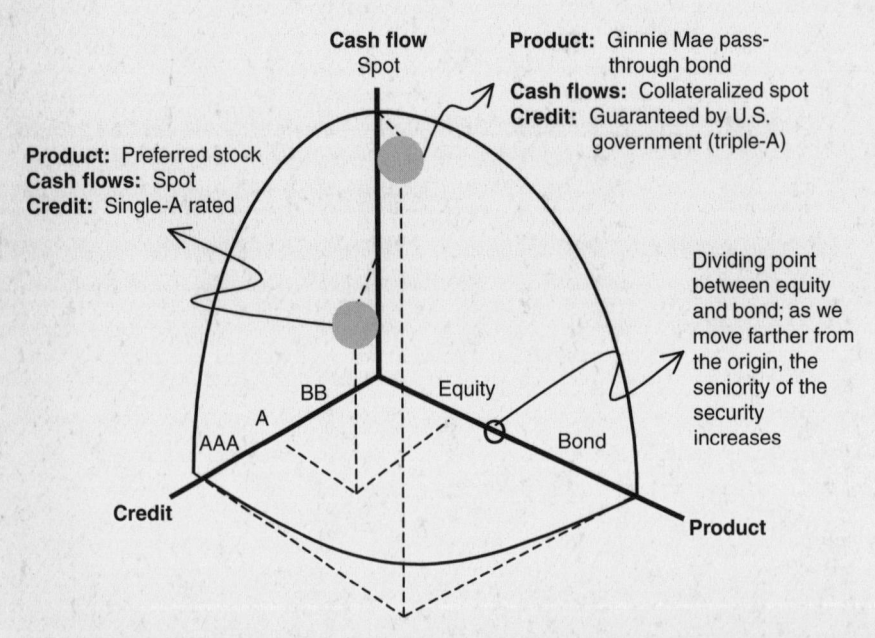

FIGURE 3.9 Conceptualizing risk relative to various cash flows and products.

of linking the first three triangles of products, cash flows, and credit. Consider how other products might be placed in such a three-dimensional context, not only as an academic exercise to reinforce an understanding of financial interrelationships, but also as a practical matter for how portfolios are constructed and managed.

Chapter 5 explores how credit and other risks can be quantified and managed.

PART TWO

Financial Engineering, Risk Management, and Market Environment

CHAPTER 4

Financial Engineering

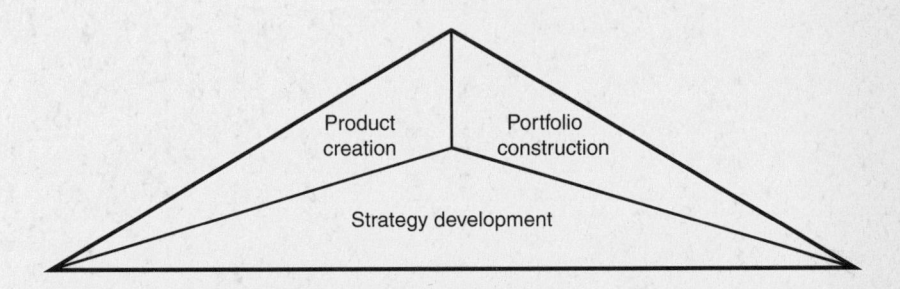

```
        Product          Portfolio
        creation         construction

              Strategy development
```

This chapter shows how combining different legs of the triangles presented in Chapters 1, 2, and 3 can facilitate the process of product creation, portfolio construction, and strategy development.

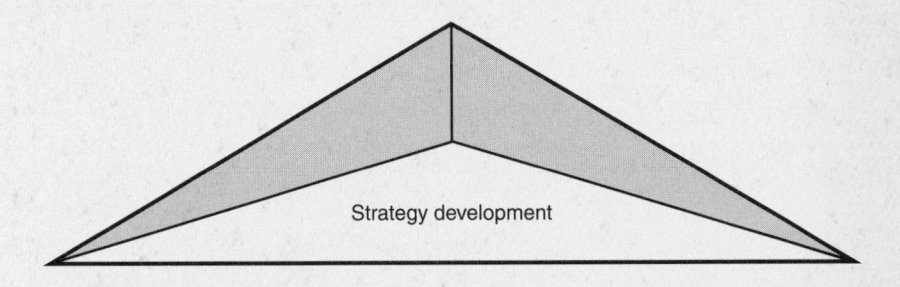

```
              Strategy development
```

This section presents three strategies: a basis trade from the bond market, a securities lending trade from the equity market, and a volatility trade from the currencies market.

Generally speaking, a basis trade (see Figure 4.1) is said to exist when one security type is purchased and a different security type is sold against it. Assume that an investor goes long spot and simultaneously sells a forward or futures contract against the long position. For a forward contract, this may be mathematically expressed as

$$\text{Basis trade} = S - F.$$

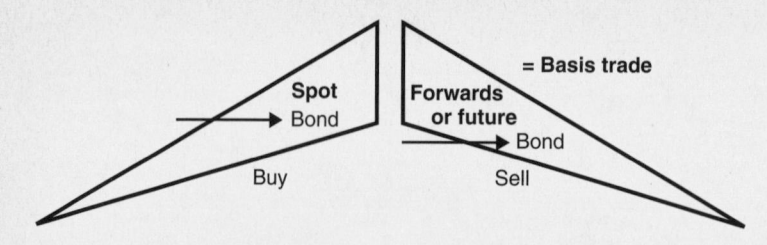

FIGURE 4.1 Combining spot and futures to create a basis trade.

Since we know that $F = S + SRT$ for an underlying spot with no cash flows, we can rewrite the above with simple substitution as

$$\text{Basis trade} = S - S - SRT.$$

The two spot terms cancel since one is a plus and the other is a minus, and we are left with

$$\text{Basis trade} = -SRT.$$

The minus sign in front of our SRT term simply reminds us that in this instance of going long the basis, we become short SRT (cost of carry). When we are short anything—an equity, a bond, or a bar of gold—we want the price of what we have shorted to go down. In this way the trade will be profitable.

Since basis refers to those instances where one security type (e.g., spot) is somehow paired off against another security type (e.g., futures), *basis risk* is said to be the risk of trading two (or more) different security types within a single strategy. The basis risk with the basis trade above is that prior to expiration of the futures contract, the value of SRT can move higher or lower. Again, since we want SRT to go lower, if it moves higher anytime prior to expiration of the futures contract (as with a higher level of spot), this may be of concern. However, if we are indifferent to market changes in the intervening time between trade date and expiration, then our basis risk is not as relevant as it would be for an investor with a shorter-term investment horizon.

If we know nothing else about SRT, we know that T (time) can go only toward zero. That is, as we move closer and closer to the expiration date, the value of T gets less and less. If we start the trade with 90 days to maturity, for example, after 30 days T will be 60/360, not 90/360. And at expiration, T is 0/360, or simply zero. Thus, it appears that we are virtually assured of earning whatever the value is of SRT at the time we go long the basis—that is, as long as we hold our basis trade to expiration.

Chapter 2 discussed how futures differ from forwards in that the latter involve a marking-to-market as well as margin accounts. To take this a step further, futures contract specifications can differ from one contract to another as well. For example, in the simple case of gold, gold is a standardized homogeneous product, and there is a lot of it around. Accordingly, when investors go long a gold futures contract and take delivery at expiration, they are reasonably assured of exactly what they will be receiving.

In the world of bond futures, things are a little different. While gold is homogeneous, bonds are not. Coupons and maturity dates differ across securities, outstanding supplies of bonds are uneven, and bond issuers embody varying credit exposures. Accordingly, even for a benchmark Treasury bond futures contract like the Chicago Board of Trade's (CBOT's) 10-year Treasury bond future, there is some uncertainty associated with the delivery process for trades that actually go to that point. Namely, the CBOT *delivery process* allows an investor who is short a futures contract to decide exactly which spot Treasury securities to deliver. However, the decision process is narrowed down by two considerations:

1. The bonds that are eligible for delivery are limited to a predetermined basket of securities to pick from.
2. There tends to be an economic incentive for delivering one or two specific bonds among the several that are eligible for delivery. In fact, the most economical bond to deliver has a special name, and it is *cheapest-to-deliver (CTD)*.[1] This ability to make a choice of which security to deliver has an associated value, and it is one of three different *delivery options* embedded in a CBOT bond futures contract. When a basis trade is held to the expiration of the futures contract and there is no change in CTD, we would expect the total return on the trade to be equivalent to cost-of-carry adjusted for the delivery options. Specifically, with a basis trade involving a coupon-bearing bond and a bond future, we have

$$S_d - F_d \times CF,$$

where
$S_d = P_d$ (dirty price at time of trade)
$F_d = S(1 + T(R - Y_c)) + A_f - O_d.$

---

[1]The formula to calculate which security is cheapest-to-deliver is nothing more than a basis trade expressed as an annualized total return; that is, $((F - S)/S) \times 360/T$, where F is calculated with the relevant conversion factor and T is time in days from trade date to expiration of the futures contract. The bond that generates the lowest rate of return is CTD.

With $CF=1$, the basis trade is

$$S_d - (S(1 + T(R - Y_c)) + A_f - O_d),$$
$$= -S_d T(R - Y_c) - A_f + O_d.$$

With our basis trade now equal to $-S_d T(R - Y_c) - A_f + O_d$ instead of simply $-SRT$, we have a more complex situation to evaluate. The overall value of the basis trade greatly depends on the relative values of R and Y_c, as shown in Table 4.1.

Even though the forward accrued interest term $(-A_f)$ and delivery options term (O_d) are unambiguous in terms of their respective values (where A_f is either negative or zero, and O_d is either positive or zero), the overall situation remains complex owing to the uncertainty of how all relevant variables ultimately interrelate with one another. For example, even if $-S_d T(R - Y_c)$ results in a negative value, its negative value combined with $-A_f$ may or may not be enough to outweigh the positive value of O_d. However, having said all this, we can make some observations regarding potential values as they march toward expiration. Quite simply, if $T=0$, as at the expiration of the basis trade, both O_d and $S_d T(R - Y_c)$ are zero as well. Accordingly, at expiration, a basis trade will always end up with a maximum possible return of $S_d T(R - Y_c)$. This return will be modified (if by much at all) by the value of A_f.

Thus, if going long the bond basis results in a negative price value (as is the result in the base case of no cash flows where carry is $-SRT$), a strategy of going long the basis results in a short position in carry. Being short carry generates a positive return as carry goes to zero. Conversely, if going long the basis results in a price value that is positive (as may be the case with a bond basis strategy where cash flows are now generated), then going long the basis results in a long position in carry. In this instance being long carry will generate a positive return as long as carry grows larger. Table 4.2 summarizes these different profiles.

As a guide to thinking about potential returns with a basis trade strategy, consider the following. For the base case of a basis trade involving an underlying spot without cash flows (as with gold), and where we are going long the basis (long S and short F), we end up with $-SRT$ (negative carry).

TABLE 4.1 Cost-of-Carry Value for Different Assumptions of R Relative to Y_c

$R > Y_c$	$R < Y_c$	$R = Y_c$
$-S_d T(R - Y_c) < 0$	$-S_d T(R - Y_c) > 0$	$-S_d T(R - Y_c) = 0$
Negative value	Positive value	Zero value

TABLE 4.2 Buying/Selling the Basis to Be Short Carry under Various Scenarios

$-SRT$	$-S_d T(R - Y_c) - A_f + O_d < 0$	$-S_d T(R - Y_c) - A_f + O_d > 0$
Buy the basis to be short carry	Buy the basis to be short carry	Sell the basis to be short carry

Figure 4.2 presents three scenarios for the value of carry as time to expiration approaches. As shown, if S and R are unchanged over the investment horizon, then carry shrinks in a linear fashion as time slowly erodes. By contrast, if S and R decline over time, then negative carry becomes even more negative, though is eventually forced to zero at expiration. And if S and R increase over time, then negative carry becomes less negative, though once again it inevitably goes to zero.

If we now expand the base case of a basis trade to involve a cash flow–paying product type, such as a coupon-bearing bond, let us assume we have a normal or upward–sloping yield curve and positive carry. Figure 4.3 presents three scenarios for the value of carry as expiration nears. Again, carry is $-S_d T(R - Y_c) - A_f$.

Overall we have a curious situation where our basis investor is looking for one part of the strategy to shrink in value (the carry that she is short) while at the same time being long something within the same strategy (the delivery options). However, as time passes both carry and the delivery options will shrink to zero because both are a function of time—that is, unless the delivery options take on intrinsic value.

If the intrinsic value of the delivery options is zero over the life of the strategy, then the return of the basis trade will simply be equal to the full value of the carry at the time the trade was originated. If intrinsic value is not zero, then the exercise of the delivery options will depend on the relationship

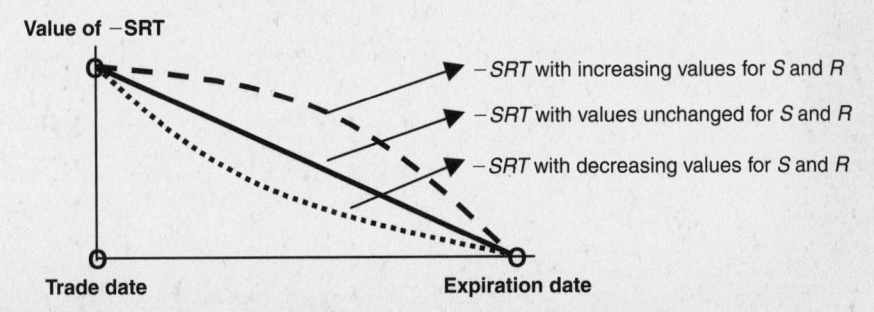

FIGURE 4.2 Three scenarios for the value of carry.

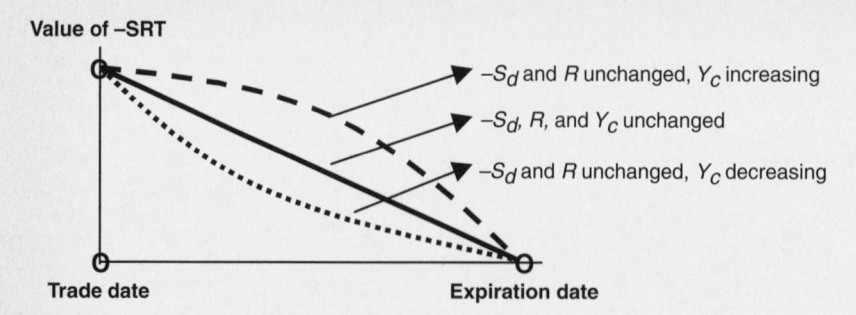

FIGURE 4.3 Three scenarios for the value of carry (expanded case).

between intrinsic value and the accrued value of carry. In other words, if exercising a delivery option means that the basis trade will cease to exist, then any carry value remaining in the basis trade is forfeited.

Figure 4.4 presents the relationship between the value of carry and the value of the delivery options as expiration approaches.

As long as S, R, Y_c, and σ are virtually unchanged over the life of the basis trade, then the value of carry will decline in a relatively linear fashion, as depicted. By contrast, the time decay pattern of O_d (as with options generally) is more curvilinear, as discussed in Chapter 5.

Of all the options said to be embedded in Treasury futures, the three most commonly cited are the quality option, the wildcard option, and the timing or cost-of-carry option. Regarding the quality option and the 10-year Treasury futures contract, any Treasury maturing in not less than 6½ years or more than 10 years from the date of delivery may be delivered into a long contract. Although only one deliverable bond is generally *CTD* at any one time, the *CTD* may change several times between a given trade date and delivery date. Unique profit opportunities are associated with each change in CTD, and investors are free to switch into more attractive cash/future combinations over time. The transitory behavior of the *CTD* has value to the holder of a short futures position, and the quality option quantifies this value.

As to the wildcard option, on each day between the first business day of the delivery month and the seventh business day before the end of the delivery month, the holder of a short bond futures position has until 9 P.M. Eastern Standard Time (EST) to notify the exchange of an intention to deliver. "Delivery" means that deliverable securities are provided in exchange for a cash payment. The investor who is short the futures contract sells the deliverable securities, and the investor who is long the futures contract buys those securities. To determine how much ought to be paid for the delivered securities, an invoice price is set at 3 P.M. EST. The invoice price is calculated from the future's settlement price at 3 P.M. EST on the day that a delivery notice is given. The

Financial Engineering **119**

This line represents the total return profile for the carry component of the basis trade as time approaches zero (date of contract expiration), and the threshold return that O_d must rise above in order to have a motive to exercise O_d prior to expiration of the basis trade

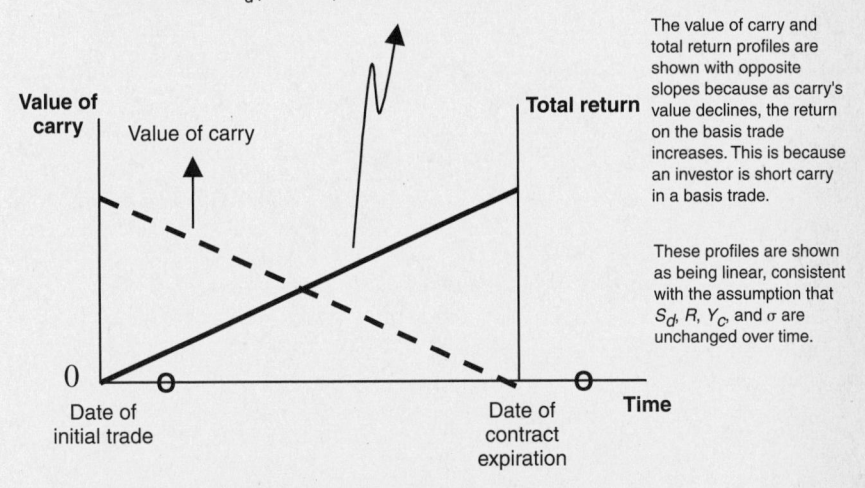

Value of carry   Value of carry

Total return — The value of carry and total return profiles are shown with opposite slopes because as carry's value declines, the return on the basis trade increases. This is because an investor is short carry in a basis trade.

These profiles are shown as being linear, consistent with the assumption that S_d, R, Y_c, and σ are unchanged over time.

Date of initial trade — Date of contract expiration — Time

If the delivery options do not take on intrinsic value over the life of the basis trade, then the value of O_d will trend steadily toward zero along with carry. However, if the delivery options take on intrinsic value (as via the quality option), then the option may be exercised prior to the expiration of the basis trade.

FIGURE 4.4 Values of carry ($-SRT$) and total return of carry as time approaches zero.

cash market does not close until 5 P.M. EST, so there is a two-hour window of opportunity when an investor holding a short future may profit from a decline in the cash market. In actuality, the market often does not really close at 5 P.M., remaining open for as long as there is a trader willing to make a market. Indeed, even if one is hard pressed to find a market maker in the United States after 5 P.M., it may not be difficult to find a market maker in Tokyo where the trading day is just getting under way. The wildcard option thus values the opportunity to profit from different trading hours for cash and futures.

Finally, the timing or cost-of-carry option attempts to quantify the optimal time to make delivery. If there is a positive cost-of-carry, then there is an incentive to put off delivery until the last possible delivery date. "Cost-of-carry" means the difference between the return earned on a cash security and the cost to finance that cash security in the repo market. If that difference is positive, then there is a positive cost-of-carry. Cost-of-carry is usually positive when the yield curve has a normal or positive shape. Conversely, if there is a negative cost-of-carry, then there is an incentive to make delivery on the first possible delivery date. Negative cost-of-carry exists if there is a negative difference between the return earned on a cash security and the cost to finance that cash security in the repo market. Cost-of-carry is usually negative when the yield curve has a negative or inverted shape. In sum, the cost-of-carry option may be viewed as an option on the slope of the yield curve. The timing option has its greatest value when the yield curve has a normal shape and the option is priced to the latest possible delivery date during the delivery month.[2]

The various delivery options generally, including the yield shift option or a new-auction option, can prove elusive to value and manage as some are mutually exclusive and others are interdependent. Other texts go into exhaustive detail; here it is sufficient to note that a short position in a futures contract avails an investor with multiple choices that have value.

Again, the value for the basis prior to expiration is less than what it would be at expiration since the delivery options would have no intrinsic value. This is because the positive value of O_d serves to minimize the negative value of carry. When O_d has a value greater than zero (as is certainly the case prior to expiration of the futures contract), the price of the futures contract will be below the forward price of the *CTD* (since a forward does not embody O_d). For this reason many investors will refer to how *futures trade cheap to spot* (trade at a price below spot owing to the delivery options in the futures). While this is true by definition, it is not intended to refer to relative value; the cheapness of futures to spot does not imply that the futures investor is getting some kind of bargain, but rather that bond futures are built differently from bond forwards and spot.

The following figures show potential scenarios for the value of O_d over time as well as the relationship of O_d to carry in a total return context. O_d is a function of all the usual variables associated with an option: S, R, T, K, and V. Figure 4.5 presents the scenario where S, R, and V are unchanged as time goes to zero.

Figure 4.6 shows the total return relationship between O_d and cost-of-carry ($-SRT$). Since an investor is short both O_d and carry, these contribute to the total return in a positive way as time passes.

In sum, and as illustrated in Figure 4.7, prior to expiration a basis trade includes elements of spot, futures, and options. The maximum profit of the strategy if held to expiration will be the carry's initial value, and it may be more

---

[2] Recall that in Chapter 2 we stated that options are unique relative to spot and forwards and futures since options embody the right (not the obligation) to do something; to exercise or not to exercise. In the context of the delivery options described here, the choices listed (what to deliver, when to deliver, and how to deliver) all have some kind of value prior to expiration. The values may be derived with traditional option pricing formulas or other methods. In sum, the term "delivery options" is intended to be descriptive both as verb (as in "to choose between delivering early or late in the delivery cycle") and as noun (as in "the calculated option price relevant for an expected CTD").

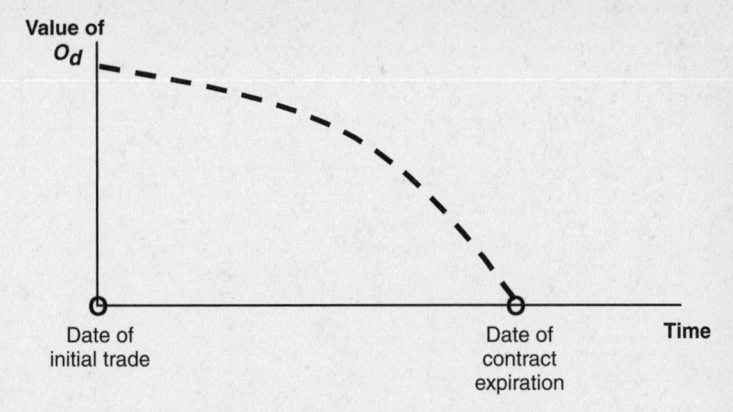

FIGURE 4.5 Delivery option value over time.

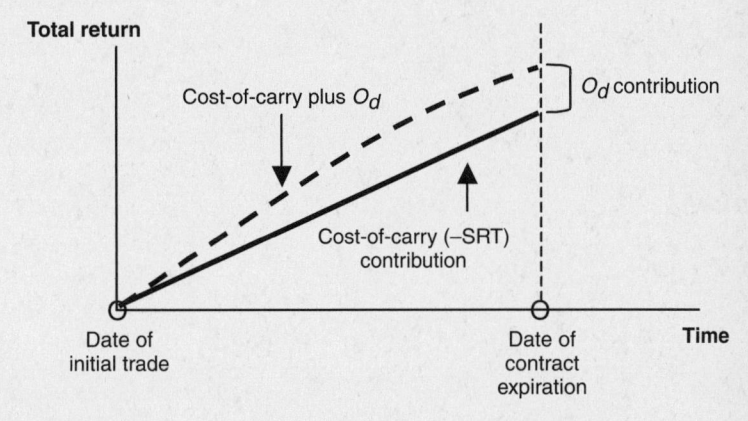

FIGURE 4.6 Total return relationship between O_d and cost-of-carry.

than that depending on the values of the various delivery options (and notably if there were a *beneficial change in CTD*[3]). As shown, a relatively straightforward strategy like a basis trade can combine all three of the fundamental cash flow elements. The triangle helps to show where key inter-relationships begin and end.

---

[3] A beneficial change in CTD via the quality option is simply this: If a new bond should happen to become CTD over the life of a futures contract, it could be profitable to change the S portion of the basis trade to a new underlying S. Deciding whether this would be profitable requires performing what-if calculations on the basket of bonds eligible to be switched with the spot that is currently used in the given basis trade.

Bond Basis = $-(S_d)T(R - Y_c) - A_f)(O_d)$

Spot: S

Futures: $F = S_d + S_d T(R - Y_c) - A_f$

O_d is a function of S, T, R, K, and σ

Options

When T equals zero, as at the expiration of the trade, then profit is the full value of carry that was originally shorted (assuming no beneficial change in CTD and, hence, no intrinsic value with O_d — only time value, which is worthless at expiration).

When R equals zero, then the value of carry is zero (noting that A_f may be zero or negative), and O_d remains alive until expiration of the strategy. The profit of the strategy depends on O_d's value when the trade was first initiated.

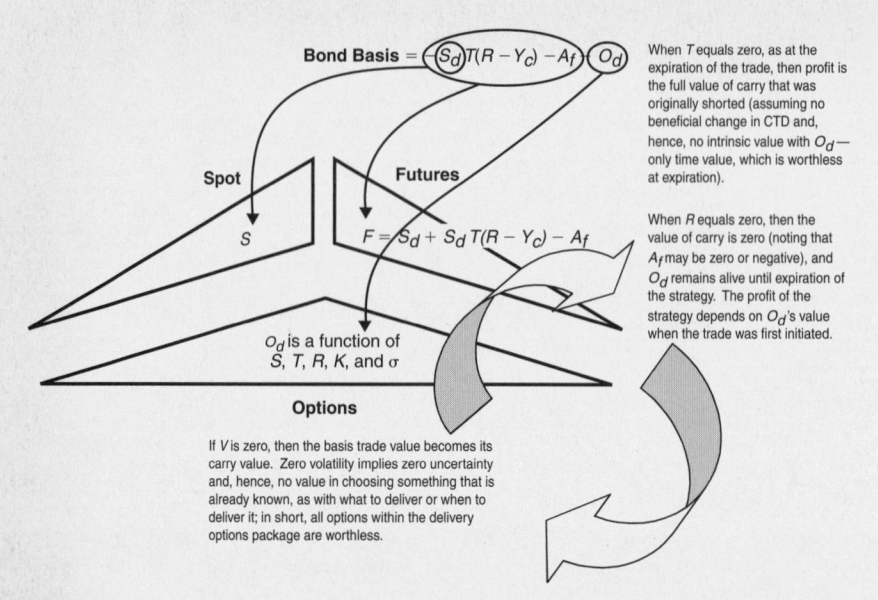

If V is zero, then the basis trade value becomes its carry value. Zero volatility implies zero uncertainty and, hence, no value in choosing something that is already known, as with what to deliver or when to deliver it; in short, all options within the delivery options package are worthless.

FIGURE 4.7 Bond basis.

Securities lending (see Figure 4.8) consists of four steps, which are presented in the context of a gold transaction.

1. One investor (Investor A) pays the prevailing spot price for an ounce of gold.
2. Investor A immediately lends her gold for a prespecified amount of time to Investor B in exchange for a loan of cash.
3. Investor A invests her loan of cash in a risk-free product (e.g., a Treasury bill).
4. When a prespecified amount of time has passed (perhaps a month), Investor A returns the loan of cash to Investor B, and Investor B returns the loan of gold to Investor A.

In sum, Investor A is happy because she lent something (the gold) and in exchange received a cash loan that she used to earn interest in a safe investment that otherwise would have just sat in her portfolio. Investor B, perhaps a trading desk at an investment bank that specializes in these types of transactions, is happy because of a satisfied need to borrow something needed (gold) in exchange for a temporary loan (of cash). We can only presume that both Investor A and B were happy with the overall terms of the loan transaction (namely the cash amounts paid and received); otherwise the fundamental laws of economics suggest that the transaction would not have been consummated in the first place.

Financial Engineering **123**

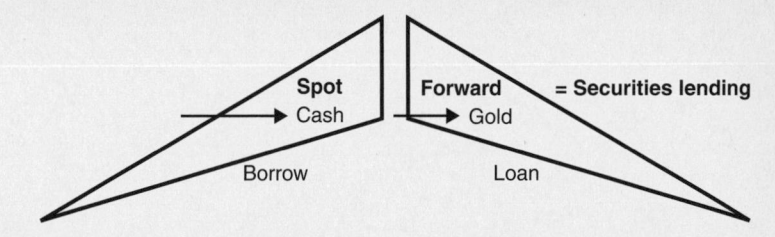

FIGURE 4.8 Use of spot and forward to create a securities lending strategy.

At this point readers may be asking what the real difference is between a regular buy/sell transaction and the cash-and-carry trade just described. After all, isn't there one investor providing a security in exchange for cash and another investor taking the security in exchange for cash? Yes. However, a key difference is the mind-set of the two investors at the start of the transaction. Namely, both investors agree at the outset that the cash and securities involved are to be returned at some prespecified date in the future. There also may be important differences in the tax treatment of a buy/sell versus a lend/borrow strategy. This type of borrowing and lending of securities and cash is commonplace, and is generally called *securities lending*. In the bond market, it is often referred to as engaging in a *repurchase agreement* (or *repo*, or *reverse repo*), as is discussed further in the next section.

Readers may have already surmised that a reverse repo (sometimes called a *cash-and-carry* trade) is really a variation of a forward transaction; it is a forward loan transaction where assets consisting of cash and securities guarantee the loan. Figure 4.9 illustrates this.

Why might investors be motivated to engage in a securities lending transaction as opposed to a simple forward transaction? From the perspective of the investor lending the equity (or gold, or bond, or whatever), the difference between securities lending rate and the risk-free rate may be a favorable one. That is, the rate of return on the safe investment that is made with the loan of money (in exchange for the loan of equity) could be advantageous. And from the perspective of the investor borrowing the equity, the ability to show the equity in a portfolio (if even for just a short period of time) allows him or her to show a position in the security that suits a particular strategy or objective.

Earlier in this chapter it was said that a bond future's CTD is determined by the lowest total return (which, incidentally, happens to be the same calculation for a total return for a basis trade). This total return value is sometimes called an *implied repo rate* (or *implied securities lending rate*), and it is applicable for basis trades on bonds and equities or any other security type. The reason is that the incentive for investors doing a basis trade rather than a securities lending trade may be the simple difference between how they are compensated for doing one trade over the other. Accordingly, an implied

Investor A agrees to accept a security from Investor B in 3 months, and at the 3-month forward price agreed at trade date.

Investor A provides Investor B with the forward price of the security in exchange for the security.

} The forward loan

Trade date — O —————— O ——————→
3 months later

Investor A lends Investor B the security that is to be returned in 3 months. In exchange, Investor B agrees to lend Investor A cash over the 3-month period. The amount of the cash lent is equal to the security's spot price.

Investor B returns Investor A's security, and Investor A returns Investor B's loan plus interest. The dollar amount of the interest is equal to the difference between the security's spot and forward prices of 3 months earlier.

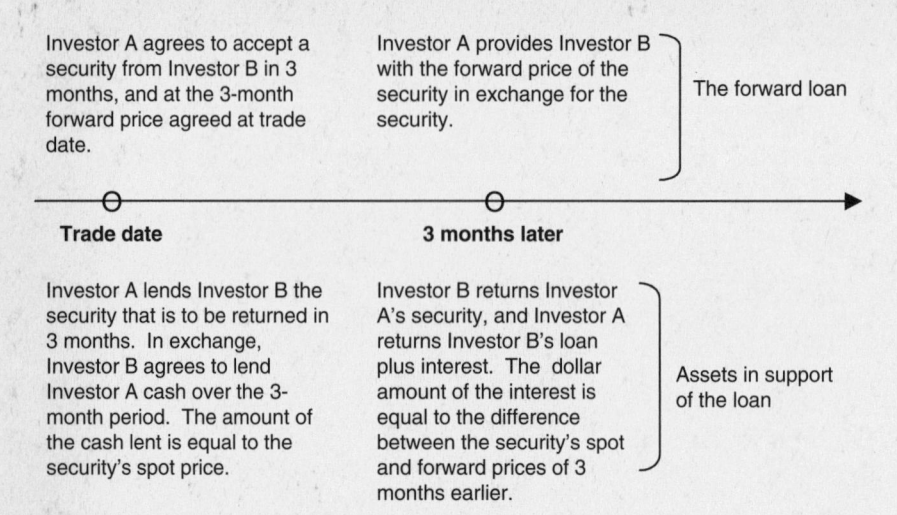

} Assets in support of the loan

FIGURE 4.9 Reverse repo as a variation of a forward transaction.

securities lending rate might be more appropriately called a breakeven securities lending rate for the simple reason that if the true securities lending rate were ever less than the breakeven securities lending rate, it would be desirable for investors to execute this arbitrage strategy:

- Buy the spot security underlying the futures contract.
- Go short an equal face amount of the futures contract.
- Finance the spot security in the securities lending market.

Since the spot security can be financed at the lending rate for less than the implied lending rate, the return earned on this strategy is an arbitraged profit, and the profit is equal to the difference in the true and implied lending rates.

Since cost-of-carry can be positive, zero, or even negative, a product that pays a dividend or a coupon will exhibit positive carry whenever the current yield of the product is above its financing rate. With bonds, this is typically the case when the yield curve has a positive or upward-sloping shape, as it usually does.

Repeating the formula for a call option, we have

$$O_c = F - K + V.$$

If investors believe volatility will soon move much higher than anyone expects, they may want to create a strategy that isolates volatility and benefits from its anticipated change as suggested by Figure 4.10. Why isolate volatility? Because our investors are not interested in F (or even X, but X is

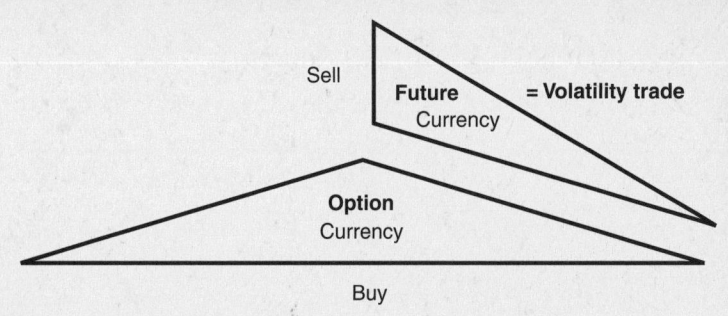

FIGURE 4.10 Use of futures and options to create a volatility strategy.

a constant); they are interested in V. How can volatility be isolated? If investors wish to buy volatility via an option, they will need to strip away the extraneous variables, namely F.

F is equal to S (1 + R) where S is spot and R is the risk-free rate. Therefore, to isolate volatility, we simply need to *go short* (*sell short*) an appropriate amount of S and R. Mathematically, we want to accomplish:

$$F - K + V - S(1 + R)$$
$$= S + SR - K + V - S - SR$$
$$= -K + V$$

In words, by going short some S and R, we can reduce a call option's value to K and V. We are not too concerned about K since it is a constant and does not change. The objective is to isolate V, and this can be done. Just how much of S and R do we need to go short? It depends on how far *in-* or *out-of-the-money* the option happens to be. A call option is said to be in-the-money if S is greater than K, *at-the-money* if S is equal to K, and out-of-the-money if S is less than K. For a put option, the formula is written as $Op = K - S + V$, and the put option is in-the-money if S is less than K, at-the-money if S is equal to K, and out-of-the-money if S is greater than K.

When a call or put option is at-the-money, the option has no *intrinsic value;* that is, there is no value to the difference between S and K since subtracting one from the other is zero. The only value to an at-the-money option is its *time value* RT and its *volatility value* V. If an at-the-money call option's spot value (S) moves just one dollar higher, then it immediately becomes an in-the-money option. And if it moves just one dollar lower, it immediately becomes an out-of-the-money option. Theoretically speaking, an option that is at-the-money has a 50/50 chance of moving higher or lower. It is just as likely to move up in price as it is likely to move down in price. When investors purchase an at-the-money option, they obviously believe that there is a greater than 50 percent chance that the market will go higher, but this is entirely their opinion. They may be right and they may be wrong. From a purely theoretical standpoint, it is always a 50/50 proposition for an at-the-money option.

The preceding discussion bears a clue for answering the question of how much of S and R we need to short to neutralize F and isolate V. The answer is approximately 50 percent. Under standard Black-Scholes assumption of log-normality, the delta of a call is greater than 50 percent and that of a put is less than 50 percent.

When an option contract is purchased, it is always in relation to some underlying reference (or *notional*) amount of spot. For example, a single option on the Standard & Poor's (S&P) 500 trades to an underlying S&P 500 futures contract with a reference amount of $250 times the current spot value of the index. In this instance, spot refers to a particular cash value of 500 stocks in the S&P index. However, when an investor purchases this option, she does not pay anything close to $250 times the current spot value of the index. Because the option has a strike price, the cost of a call option is $S(1 + R) - K + V$, not $S(1 + R) + V$. Therefore, if the S&P is at a level of 800 and an at-the-money option is being purchased, then the price to be paid is

$$\$250 \times 800 + \$250 \times 800 \times R - \$250 \times 800 + V,$$

which is considerably less than

$$\$250 \times 800 + \$250 \times 800 \times R + V.$$

This latter lower price is what many investors are referring to when they cite the leveraging features of derivatives.

The amount of S that our investor would go short would be the notional amount of the contract times 50 percent, or

$$\$250 \times 800 \times 50\%.$$

Since the short position is financed at some rate R, both S and R are *neutralized* or *hedged* (effectively offset) by going short. As is discussed more in Chapter 5 this type of hedge is commonly referred to as a *delta hedge*. Delta is the name given to hedging changes in S, as when an investor wants to isolate some other financial variable, such as V.

Going delta-neutral is not a strategy whereby investors can hedge it and forget it. Delta changes as spot changes, so a delta-neutral strategy requires investors to stay abreast of what delta is at all times to ensure proper hedge relationships between the option and spot. In point of fact, it can be very difficult indeed to dynamically hedge an option, a lesson many investors learned the hard way in the stock market crash of 1987.

Investors who truly want to speculate that volatility will rise typically will not buy a call or put option and delta hedge it, but will instead buy both a call option and a put option with at-the-money strike prices. Because both the call and put are at-the-money, the initial delta of the call at +0.5 offsets the initial delta of the put at −0.5. The delta of the call is positive because a call connotes a long position in the underlying; the delta of the put is negative because a put connotes a short position in the underlying. With the one delta canceling out the other, the initial position is delta neutral.

Note that it is the initial position that is delta neutral, since a market rally (sell off) would likely cause the delta of the call (put) to increase and thus create a mismatch between delta positions that will need to be adjusted via offsetting positions in spot.

Parenthetically, investors also can hedge R in an option trade. Just as the risk of a move in S is called delta risk, the risk of a move in R is called *rho risk*. One way that rho risk can be hedged is with Eurodollar futures. The incentive for hedging the rho risk may be to better expose the other remaining variables embedded in an options structure. For example, if investors believe that S will rise over the short term but that monetary policy also might become easier (and with concomitant pressures for lower interest rates), then eliminating or at least reducing the contribution of rho to an option's value could very well help. This could be achieved by shorting some Eurodollar futures (so as to benefit from a drop in R) of an amount equal to a delta-adjusted amount of the underlying notional value.

Though while the above methods allow for a way to capture volatility, they can prove to be quite difficult to implement successfully. Of good news to the investor desiring to isolate volatility is the advent of the volatility or variance swap. With a volatility swap, an investor gains if the benchmark rate of volatility is exceeded by the actual rate of volatility at a prespecified point in time. The payoff profile at expiration of the swap is simply

$$(\sigma_a - \sigma_i) \times N$$

where
    σ_a = is the actual volatility of the index over the life of the swap
    σ_i = is the volatility referenced by the swap
    N = the notional amount of the swap (in dollars or another currency) per unit of volatility

The above formula can also be modified to describe a variance swap, where variance is the square of volatility and we have

$$(\sigma_a^2 - \sigma_i) \times N$$

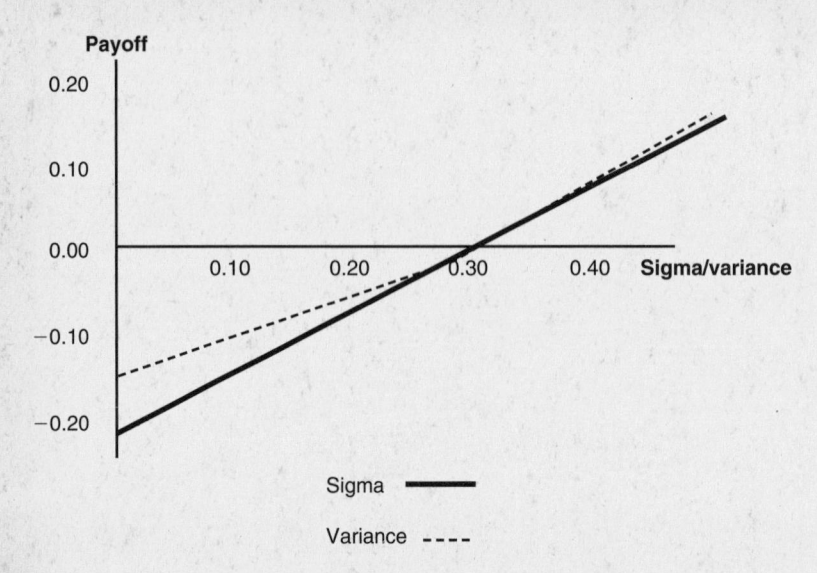

FIGURE 4.11 Payoff profiles for sigma (volatility) and variance.

A buyer of this swap receives N amount of payout for every unit increase in volatility (variance) above the volatility (variance) referenced by the swap (σ_{vol} or σ_{var}). σ_{vol} or σ_{var} is usually quoted as a percentage and N as an amount per 1 percent increase in volatility (for example, $1,000/0.5% volatility change, or $1,000 per 0.5% increase in volatility above the swap reference rate of volatility).

In Figure 4.11 we present an illustration of the difference in payoff profiles between a volatility and variance swap.

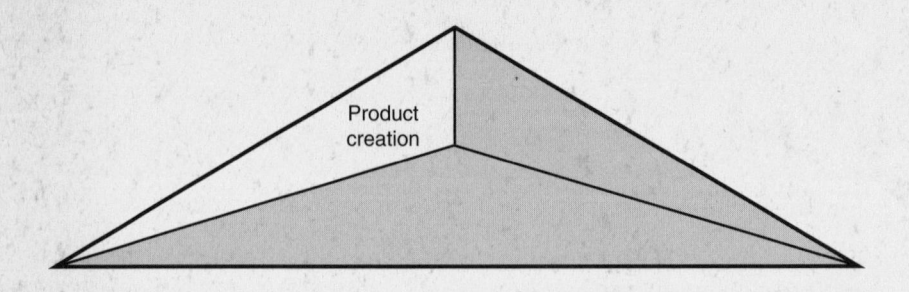

This section presents three instances of product creation that involve mixing and matching bonds, equities, and currencies with various cash flows:

1. Callable structures in the bond market (see Figure 4.12)
2. Preferred stock in the equity market
3. Currency-enhanced securities

First, a story.

A happy homeowner has just signed on the dotted line to take out a mortgage on her dream home. Although the bank probably did not say "Congratulations, you are now the owner of a new home, a mortgage, and a call option," our homeowner is, in fact, long a call option.

How? Well, if interest rates fall, our homeowner may have a rather powerful incentive to refinance her mortgage. That is, she can *pay off* (*prepay*) her existing mortgage with the proceeds generated by securing a new loan at a lower rate of interest. This lower rate of interest means lower monthly mortgage payments, and it is this consideration that gives rise to the value of the call option embedded within the mortgage agreement.

Now then, if our homeowner is long the call option, who is short the call option? After all, for every buyer there is a seller. Well, here the mortgage bank is short the call option. The mortgage bank is short the call option because it is not the entity who has the right to *exercise* (trade in) the option — it is our homeowner who took out the mortgage and who has the right to trade it in for a more favorable mortgage sometime in the future.

Now, let us assume that our mortgage bank decides, for whatever reason, that it no longer want to hold a large number of home mortgages. One option it has is to bundle together a *pool* (collection) of mortgages and sell them off to a federal agency, such as Fannie Mae or Freddie Mac. These federal agencies are in the business of helping people have access to affordable housing. When the mortgage bank bundles up these mortgages and sells them off, it is transferring over the short call options as well. Once received, Fannie Mae or Freddie Mac (or whatever entity purchased the mortgage bank's loans) has three choices of what to do with the loans.

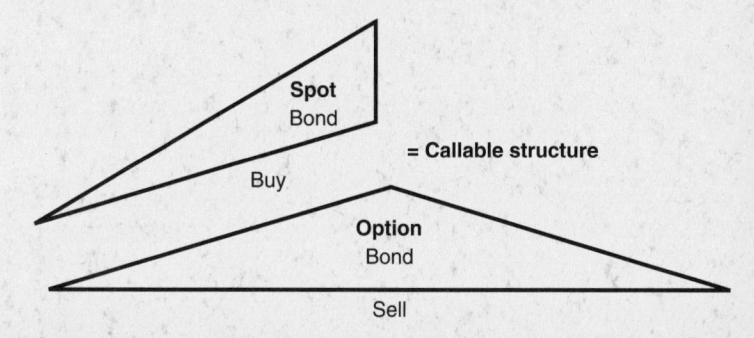

FIGURE 4.12 Use of spot and options to create a callable bond.

1. It may simply decide to keep them as outright investments.
2. It may decide to sell them. That is, it may decide to take a pool of home mortgages and sell them into the open market as tradable fixed income securities. When this is done, the organization that purchased the mortgages is transferring the embedded short options to other investors who purchase the home mortgages.
3. It may decide to keep the mortgages, but on a hedged basis. One way they could hedge the mortgages would be to issue *callable bonds* (a bond with a short call option).

How would issuing callable bonds help serve as a hedge against home mortgages? Recall that the creditor of a home mortgage (a bank, a mortgage company, or whatever) is holding a product that has a short call option embedded in it. It is a short call option because it is the homebuyer who has the right to make the choice of whether or not to refinance the mortgage when interest rates decline; the homebuyer is long the call option. A callable debenture (bond) consists of a bond with an embedded short call option. Anyone who purchases a callable bond subjects him- or herself to someone else deciding when and if the embedded option will be exercised. That "someone else" is the issuer of the callable bond, or in our story, Fannie Mae or Freddie Mac. Fannie Mae and Freddie Mac can attempt to hedge some of the short call risk embedded in their holdings of mortgage product by issuing some callable bonds against it.

Figure 4.13 borrows from the pictorial descriptions in Chapter 2 to present a callable bond.

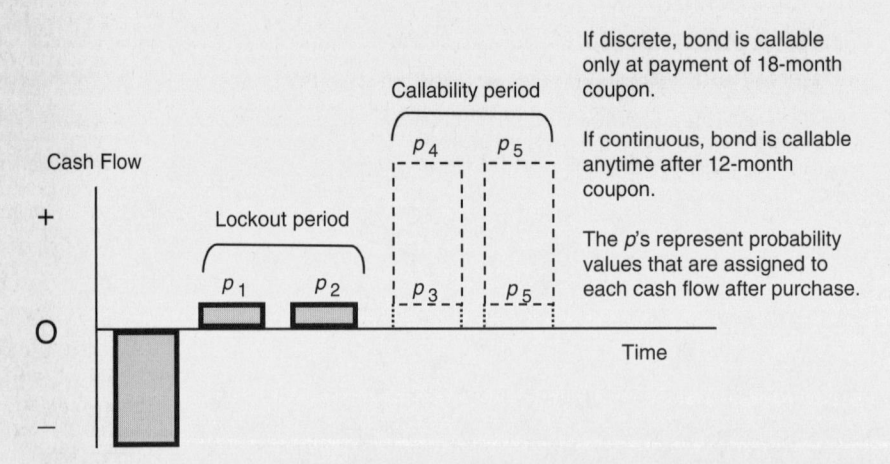

FIGURE 4.13 Conceptual presentation of a callable bond.

The callable shown in our diagram has a final maturity date two years from now and is *callable* one year from now. To say that it is callable one year from now is to say that for its first year it may not be called at all; it is protected from being called, and as such investors may be reasonably assured that they will receive promised cash flows on a full and timely basis. But once we cross into year 2 and the debenture is subject to being called by the issuer who is long the call option, there is uncertainty as to whether all the promised cash flows will be paid. This uncertainty stems not from any credit risk (particularly since mortgage securities tend to be collateralized), but rather from market risk; namely, will interest rates decline such that the call in the callable is exercised? If the call is exercised, the investors will receive par plus any accrued interest that is owed, and no other cash flows will be paid. Note that terms and conditions for how a call decision is made can vary from security to security. Some callables are *discrete,* meaning that the issue could be called only (if at all) at coupon payment dates; for *continuous* callables, the issue could be called (if at all) at any time once it has lost its callability protection.

Parenthetically, a two-year final maturity callable eligible to be called after one year is called a two-noncall-one. A 10-year final maturity callable that is eligible to be called after three years is called a 10-noncall-three, and so forth. Further, the period of time when a callable may not be called is referred to as the *lockout* period.

Figure 4.13 distinguishes between the cash flows during and after the period of call protection with solid and dashed lines, respectively. At the time a callable comes to market, there is truly a 50/50 chance of its being called. That is because it will come to market at today's prevailing yield level for a bond with an embedded call, and from a purely theoretical view, there is an equal likelihood for future yield levels to go higher or lower. Investors may believe that probabilities are, say, 80/20 or 30/70 for higher or lower rates, but options pricing theory is going to set the odds objectively at precisely 50/50.

Accordingly, to calculate a price for our callable at the time of issuance (where we know its price will be par), if we probability weight each cash flow that we are confident of receiving (due to call protection over the lockout period) at 100 percent, and probability weight the remaining uncertain (unprotected) cash flows at 50 percent, we would arrive at a price of par. This means $p_1=p_2=100\%$ and $p_3=p_4=p_5=50\%$. In doing this calculation we assume we have a discrete-call security, and since both principal and coupon are paid if the security is called, we adjust both of these cash flows at 50 percent at both the 18- and 24-month nodes. If the discrete callable is not called at the 18-month node, then the probability becomes 100 percent that it will trade to its final maturity date at the 24-month node, but at the start of the game (when the callable first comes to market), we can say only that there is a 50/50 chance of its surviving to 24 months.

Incremental yield is added when an investor purchases a callable, because she is forfeiting the choice of exercise to the issuer of the callable. If choice has value (and it does), then relinquishing choice ought to be recompensed (and it is). We denote the incremental yield from optionality as I_s, the incremental yield from credit risk as I_c, and the overall yield of a callable bond with credit risk as

Y = Yield of a comparable-maturity Treasury + $I_c + I_s$.

Next we present the same bond price formula from Chapter 2 but with one slight change. Namely, we have added a small p next to every cash flow, actual and potential. As stated, the p represents probability.

$$\text{Price} = \frac{C \times p_1}{(1 + Y/2)^1} + \frac{C \times p_2}{(1 + Y/2)^2}$$
$$+ \frac{C \times p_3 \& F \times p_4}{(1 + Y/2)^3} + \frac{(C \& F) \times p_5}{(1 + Y/2)^4} = \$1,000$$

where
- p_1 = probability of receiving first coupon
- p_2 = probability of receiving second coupon
- p_3 = probability of receiving third coupon
- p_4 = probability of receiving principal at 18 months
- p_5 = probability of receiving fourth coupon and principal at 24 months

Let's now price the callable under three assumed scenarios:

1. The callable is not called and survives to its maturity date:

$$p_1 = p_2 = p_3 = p_4 = p_5 = 100\%.$$

2. The callable is discrete and is called at 18 months:

$$p_1 = p_2 = p_3 = p_4 = 100\%.$$

3. The callable is discrete and may or may not be called at 18 months:

$$p_1 = p_2 = 100\%, \text{ and } p_3 = p_4 = p_5 = 50\%.$$

Assuming $Y=C=6\%$, what is the price under each of these three scenarios? "Par" is correct. At the start of a callable bond's life, $Y=C$ (as with a noncallable bond), and it is a 50/50 proposition as to whether the callable will in fact be called. Accordingly, any way we might choose to assign relevant probability weightings, price will come back as par, at least until time passes and Y is no longer equal to C.

Another way to express the price of a callable is as follows:

$$P_c = P_b - O_c,$$

where
  P_c = price of the callable
  P_b = price of a noncallable bond (bullet bond)
  O_c = call option

By expressing the price of a callable bond this way, two things become clear. First, we know from Chapter 2 that if price goes down then yield goes up, and the $-O_c$ means that the yield of a callable must be higher than a noncallable (P_b). Accordingly, Y and C for a callable are greater than for a noncallable. Second, it is clear that a callable comprises both a spot via P_b and an option (and, therefore, a forward) via O_c.

As demonstrated in Chapter 2, when calculating a bond's present value, the same single present yield is used to discount every one of its cash flows. Again, this allows for a quick and reasonably accurate way to calculate a bond's spot price. When calculating a bond's forward value in yield terms (as opposed to price terms), a separate and unique yield typically is required for every one of the cash flows. Each successive forward yield incorporates a chain of previous yields within its calculation. When these forward yields are plotted against time, they collectively comprise a forward yield curve, and this curve can be used to price *both* the bond *and* option components of a bond with embedded options. By bringing the spot component of the bond into the context of forwards and options, a new perspective of value can be provided. In particular, with the use of forward yields, we can calculate an option-adjusted spread (or OAS). Figure 4.14 uses the familiar triangle to highlight differences and similarities among three different measures of yield spread: nominal spreads, forward spreads, and option-adjusted spreads.

In our story we said that a second possibility was available to Fannie Mae and Freddie Mac regarding what they might do with the mortgages they purchased: Sell them to someone else. They might sell them in *whole loan* (an original mortgage loan as opposed to a participation with one or more lenders) form, or they could choose to repackage them in some way. One simple way they can be repackaged is by pooling together some of the mortgages into a single "portfolio" of mortgages that could be traded in the marketplace as a bundle of product packaged into a single security. This bundle would share some pricing features of a callable security. Callable bonds, like mortgages, embody a call option that is a short call option to the investor in these securities. Again, it is the homeowner who is long the call option.

- The difference in yield between a benchmark bond and a nonbenchmark bond.
- Spread is expressed in basis points.
- The two bonds have comparable maturity dates.

- Spread between a benchmark bond's spot yield and a (non)benchmark bond's forward yield.
- Spread is expressed in basis points.
- **When the spot curve is flat, the forward curve and spot curve are equal to one another, and a nominal spread is equal to a forward spread.**

Nominal   Forward

Option adjusted

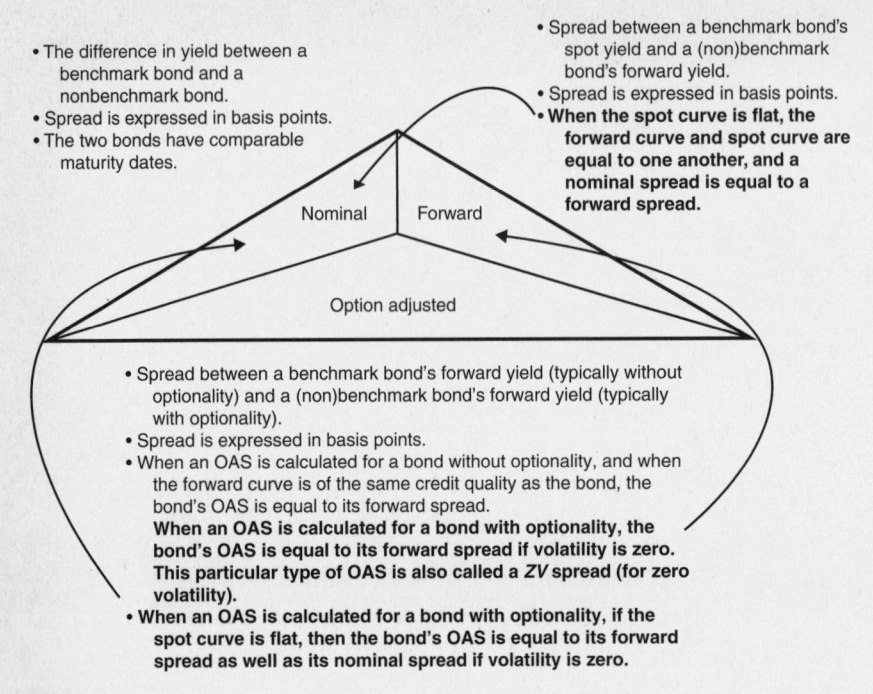

- Spread between a benchmark bond's forward yield (typically without optionality) and a (non)benchmark bond's forward yield (typically with optionality).
- Spread is expressed in basis points.
- When an OAS is calculated for a bond without optionality, and when the forward curve is of the same credit quality as the bond, the bond's OAS is equal to its forward spread.
  When an OAS is calculated for a bond with optionality, the bond's OAS is equal to its forward spread if volatility is zero. This particular type of OAS is also called a *ZV* spread (for zero volatility).
- When an OAS is calculated for a bond with optionality, if the spot curve is flat, then the bond's OAS is equal to its forward spread as well as its nominal spread if volatility is zero.

FIGURE 4.14 Nominal, forward, and option-adjusted spreads.

However, there can be very different option-related dynamics between a bundle of mortgages packaged into a single security (called a *mortgage-backed security*, or *MBS*) and a callable bond. Indeed, there are a variety of structure types between a callable bond and an MBS. The variations can be explained largely by option-related differences, as shown next.

VARIATIONS IN OPTIONALITY AMONG BOND PRODUCTS

An MBS is comprised of a portfolio of individual mortgages that are packaged together into a single security and sold to investors. The security is a coupon-bearing instrument, and it has a principal component as well. The funds used to pay the coupons of an MBS come directly from the monthly interest payments made by homeowners. The payments made by homeowners are passed through a servicing agent, who sends along appropriate payments directly to holders of the MBS. Accordingly, an MBS is sometimes called a *pass-through security* (or *pass-thru*), or an *asset-backed security* since its cash flows come from a bundle of assets (namely the home mortgages that are bundled together). An MBS also is sometimes called a securitized asset, for the same reason. All else being equal, investors like the idea of a bond that is physically backed by (supported by) assets that they can analyze and understand. In contrast with a more generic bond (*debenture*) that is backed by an issuer's overall credit rating or general financial standing, an asset-backed security provides investors with things they can "touch and feel"—not in a literal sense, but in the sense of bringing some form and definition to what they are buying.[4]

When homeowners make their monthly mortgage payment, a portion of that payment goes to paying the interest on the mortgage and a portion goes to paying the principal. In the early phase of the typically 30-year mortgage life, the largest portion of the monthly payment goes toward payment of interest. A growing portion of the monthly payment goes toward principal, and in the same way that interest payments are passed along to MBS holders as coupons, principal payments are passed along to MBS holders as principal. Herein lies a key difference between a traditional bond and a traditional pass-thru; the former pays 100 percent of its principal at maturity, while the latter pays out its principal over the life of the security as it is received and passed along to investors. Payments of principal and interest may not always be predictable; homeowners can refinance their mortgages if they want to, which involves paying down the principal remaining on their existing mortgage. This act of paying off a loan prior to its natural maturity (even if the purpose is to take on a new loan) is called *prepaying*, and *prepayments* can be attributable to many things, including a sudden decline in interest rates[5] (so that investors find it more cost-effective to obtain a new lower-cost loan), a natural disaster that destroys homes, changes in personal situations, and so forth.

Most MBSs are rated triple A. How is this possible unless every homeowner with a mortgage that is in the bundle has a personal credit rating that is comparable to a triple-A profile? One way to achieve this is by *overcollateralizing* (providing more collateralization than a 1:1 ratio of face value of security relative to underlying asset). The MBS is *collateralized* (backed by) mortgages. To *overcollateralize* an MBS, the originator of the MBS puts in more mortgages than the face value of the MBS. For example, if originators want to issue $10 million face amount of MBS that will be sold to investors, they put more than $10 million face amount of underlying mortgages into the

---

[4]Some larger investors do actively request and analyze detailed data underlying various asset-backed instruments.
[5]This decline in interest rates gives value to the long call option that homeowners have embedded in their mortgage agreement; the option (or choice) to refinance the mortgage at a lower rate has economic value that is realized only by refinancing the existing mortgage to secure new and lower monthly payments.

bundle that comprises the MBS. Accordingly, if some homeowners happen to default on their mortgages, the excess supply of mortgages in the bundle will help to cover that event. Another way that MBS products are able to secure a triple-A rating is by virtue of their being supported by federal agencies. The three major agencies of the United States involved with supporting mortgages include Ginnie Mae, Fannie Mae, and Freddie Mac.[6] The key purpose of these governmental organizations is to provide assurance and confidence in the market for MBSs and other mortgage products.

Table 4.3 summarizes key differences between an MBS and a callable bond.

The most dramatic differences between MBSs and callable bonds are that the options embedded with the former are continuous while the single option embedded in the latter tends to be discrete, and the multiple options within an MBS can be triggered by many more variables.

Figure 4.15 shows how an MBS's cash flows might look; none of the cash flow boxes is solid because none of them can be relied on with 100 percent certainty. While less-than-100% certainty might be due partly to the vagaries of what precisely is meant by saying that the federal agencies issuing these debt types are "supported by" the federal government, more of the uncertainty stems from the embedded optionality. Although it may very well be unlikely, it is theoretically possible that an investor holding a mortgage-backed security could receive some portion of a principal payment in one of the very first cash flows that is paid out. This would happen if a home-

TABLE 4.3 MBS versus Callable Bond Optionality

	Mortgage	Callable
Callability	Continuous	Discrete (sometimes continuous)
Call period	Immediately	Eligible after the passage of some time
Call trigger	Level of yields	Level of yields, other cost considerations
	Homeowner defaults	
	Homeowner sells property for any reason	
	Property is destroyed as by natural disaster	

---

[6]Ginnie Mae pass-thrus are guaranteed directly by the U.S. government regarding timely payment of interest and principal. Fannie Mae and Freddie Mac pass-thrus carry the guarantee of their respective agency only; however, both agencies can borrow from the Treasury, and it is not considered to be likely that the U.S. government would allow any of these agencies to default.

Financial Engineering

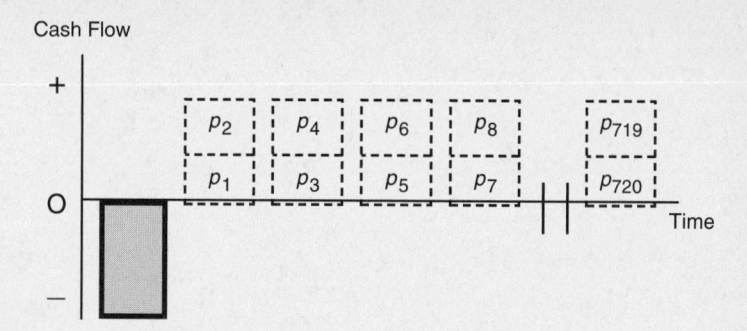

FIGURE 4.15 MBS cash flows over time.

owner decides or is forced to sell the home almost immediately after purchase and pays off the full principal of the loan. In line with what we would generally expect, principal payments will likely make their way more meaningfully into the mix of principal-coupon cash flows after some time passes (or, in the jargon of the marketplace, with some seasoning).

How can probabilities be assigned to the mortgage product's cash flows over time? While we can take the view that we adopted for our callable debenture—that at the start of the game every uncertain cash flow has a 50/50 chance of being paid—this type of evenly split tactic may not be very practical or realistic for mortgage products. For example, a typical home mortgage is a 30-year fixed-rate product. This type of product has been around for some time, and some useful data have been collected to allow for the evaluation of its cash flows over a variety of interest rate and economic environments. In short, various patterns can and do emerge with the nature of the cash flows. Indeed, a small cottage industry has grown up for the creation and maintenance of models that attempt to divine insight into the expected nature of mortgage product cash flows. It is sufficient here merely to note that no model produces a series of expected cash flows from year 1 to year 30 with a 50/50 likelihood attached to each and every payout. Happily, this conforms to what we would expect from more of an intuitive or common sense approach.

Given the importance of prepayment rates when valuing an MBS, several models have been developed to forecast prepayment patterns. Clearly, investors with a superior prepayment model are better equipped to identify fair market value.

In an attempt to impose a homogeneity across prepayment assumptions, certain market conventions have been adopted. These conventions facilitate trades in MBSs since respective buyers and sellers know exactly what assumptions are being used to value various securities.

One commonly used method to proxy prepayment speeds is the *constant prepayment rate* (CPR). A CPR is the ratio of the amount of mortgages prepaid in a given period to the total amount of mortgages in the pool at the beginning of the period. That is, the CPR is the percentage of the principal outstanding at the beginning of a period that will prepay over the following period. For example, if the CPR for a given security in a particular month is 10.5, then the annualized percentage of principal outstanding at the beginning of the month that will repay during the month is 10.5 percent. As the name implies, CPR assumes that prepayment rates are constant over the life of the MBS.

To move beyond the rather limiting assumption imposed by a CPR—that prepayments are made at a constant rate over the life of an MBS—the industry proposed an alternative measure, the *Public Securities Association (PSA) model*. The PSA model posits that any given MBS will prepay at an annualized rate of 0.2 percent in the first month that an MBS is outstanding, and prepayments will increase by 0.2 percent per month until month 30. After month 30, it is assumed that prepayments occur at a rate of 6 percent per year for all succeeding months.

Generally speaking, the PSA model provides a good description of prepayment patterns for the first several years in the life of an MBS and has proven to be a standard for comparing various MBSs. Figure 4.16 shows theoretical principal and coupon cash flows for a 9 percent Ginnie Mae MBS at 100 percent PSA. When an MBS is quoted at 100 percent PSA, this means that prepayment assumptions are right in line with the PSA model, above. An MBS quoted at 200 percent PSA assumes prepayment speeds that are twice the PSA model, and an MBS quoted at 50 percent PSA assumes a slower prepayment pattern.

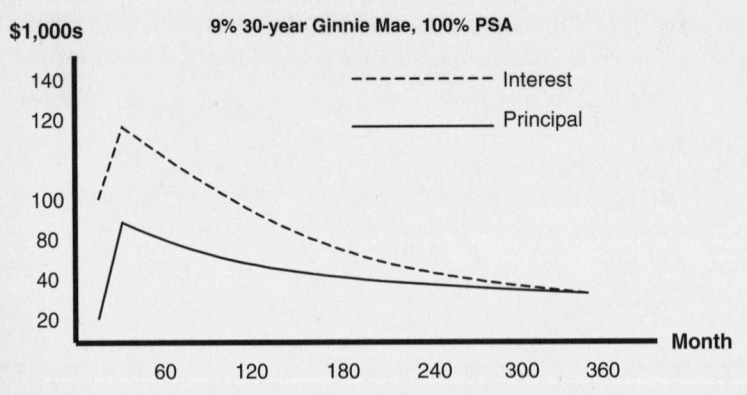

FIGURE 4.16 The relationship between pay-down of interest and principal for a pass-thru.

Another important concept linked to MBS is that of *average life*. As depicted in Figure 4.17, average life is the weighted average time to the return of a dollar of principal. It is often used as a measure of the investment life of an MBS and is typically compared against a Treasury with a final maturity that approximates the average life of the MBS. In short, it is a way to help fence in the nature of MBS cash flows to allow for some comparability with non-pass-thru type structures.

Since the principal or face value of an MBS is paid out over the life of the MBS and not in one lump sum at maturity, this is reflected in the price formula provided below. Accordingly, as shown, the MBS price formula has an F variable alongside every C variable. Further, every C and every F has its own unique probability value.

$$Price = \frac{C \times p_1 \& F \times p_2}{(1 + Y/2)^1} + \frac{C \times p_3 \& F \times p_4}{(1 + Y/2)^2} + \frac{C \times p_5 \& F \times p_6}{(1 + Y/2)^3} + \ldots = \$1,000$$

where
p_1 = probability-weighted first coupon
p_2 = probability-weighted first receipt of principal
p_3 = probability-weighted second coupon
p_4 = probability-weighted second receipt of principal,
 ... and so forth.

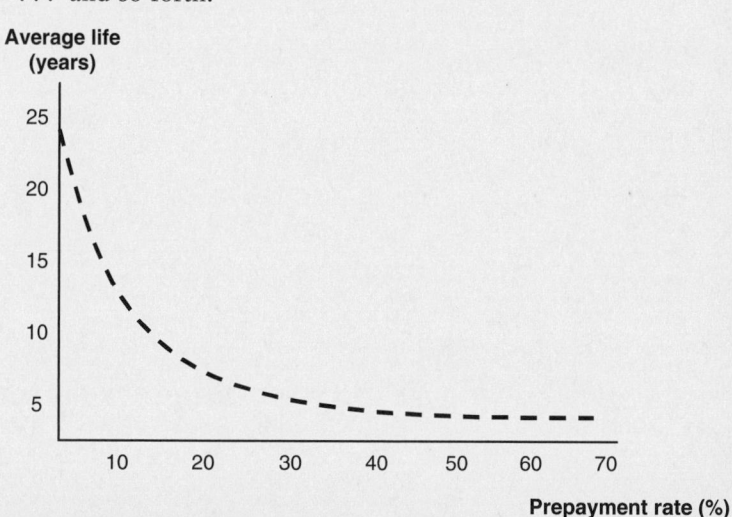

FIGURE 4.17 Average life vs. prepayment rate.

"Probability-weighted coupon" means the statistical likelihood of receiving a full coupon payment (equivalent to 100 percent of F times C). As principal is paid down from par, the reference amount of coupon payment declines as well (so that when principal is fully paid down, a coupon payment is equal to zero percent of F times C, or zero).

"Probability-weighted principal" means the statistical likelihood of receiving some portion of principal's payment.

As is the case with a callable debenture, the initial price of an MBS is par, and $Y=C$. However, unlike our callable debenture, there is no formal lockout period with an MBS. While we might informally postulate that probability values for F should be quite small in the early stages of an MBS's life (where maturities can run as long as 15 or 30 years), this is merely an educated guess. The same would be true for postulating that probability values for C should be quite large in the early stages of an MBS's life. Because an MBS is comprised of an entire portfolio of short call options (with each one linked to an individual mortgage), in contrast with the single short option embedded in a callable debenture, the modeling process for C and F is more complex; hence the existence and application of simplifying benchmark models, as with the CPR approach.

At this stage we have pretty much defined the two extremes of optionality with fixed income products in the U.S. marketplace. However, there are gradations of product within these two extremes. For example, there are PACs, or planned amortization class securities.

Much like a Thanksgiving turkey, an MBS can be carved up in a variety of ways. At Thanksgiving, some people like drumsticks and others prefer the thigh or breast. With bonds, some people like predictable cash flows while others like a higher yield that comes with products that behave in less predictable ways. To satisfy a variety of investor appetites, MBS pass-thrus can be sliced in a variety of ways. For example, *classes* of MBS can be created. Investors holding a Class A security might be given assurances that they will be given cash distributions that conform more to a debenture than a pass-thru. Investors in a Class B security would have slightly weaker assurances, those in a Class C security would have even weaker assurances, and so forth. As a trade-off to these levels of assurances, the class yield levels would be progressively higher.

A PAC is a prime example of a security type created from a pool of mortgages. What happens is that the cash flows of an MBS pool are combined such that separate bundles of securities are created. What essentially distinguishes one bundle from another is the priority given for one bundle to be assured of receiving full and timely cash flows versus another bundle.

For simplicity, let us assume a scenario where a pool of mortgages is assembled so as to create three tranches of cash flow types. In tranche 1, investors would be assured of being first in line to receive coupon cash flows generated by the underlying mortgages. In tranche 2, investors would be second in line to receive coupon cash flows generated by the underlying mortgages. If homeowners with mortgages in this pool decide to pay off their mortgage for whatever reason, then over time tranche 2 investors would not expect to receive the same complete flow of payouts relative to tranche 1 investors. If only for this reason, the tranche 2 investors should not expect to pay the same up-front price for their investment relative to what is paid by tranche 1 investors. They should pay less. Why? Because tranche 2 investors do not enjoy the same peace of mind as tranche 1 investors of being kept whole (or at least "more whole") over the investment horizon. And finally, we have tranche 3, which can be thought of as a "residual" or "clean-up" tranche. The tranche 3 investors would stand last in line to receive cash flows, only after tranche 1 and tranche 2 investors were paid. And consistent with the logic presented above for tranche 2, tranche 3 investors should not expect to pay the same up-front price for their investment as tranche 1 or 2 investors; they should pay less.

Note that tranche 1 investors are not by any means guaranteed of receiving all cash flows in a complete and timely matter; they only are the first in line as laying priority to complete and timely cash flows. In the unlikely event that every mortgage within the pool were to be paid off at precisely the same time, then each of the three tranches would simply cease to exist. This comment helps to reinforce the idea that tranche creation does not create new cash flows where none existed previously; tranche creation simply reallocates existing cash flows in such a way that at one end of a continuum is a security type that at least initially looks and feels like a more typical bond while at the other end is a security type that exhibits a price volatility in keeping with its more uncertain place in the pecking order of all-important cash flow receipts.

This illustration is a fairly simplified version of the many different ways in which products can be created out of mortgage pools. Generally speaking, PAC-type products are consistent with the tranche 1 scenario presented. Readers can refer to a variety of texts to explore this kind of product creation methodology in considerable detail. From PACs to TACs to A, B, C, and Z tranches (and much, much more), there is much to keep an avid mortgage investor occupied.

Figure 4.18 applies the PAC discussion to our cash flow diagram.

Notice that the cash flow boxes in the early part of the PAC's life are drawn in with solid lines. PACs typically come with preannounced lockout periods. Here, *lockout* refers to that period of time when the PAC is protected from not receiving complete and timely cash flow payments owing to option-related phenomena. The term of lockouts varies, though is generally 5 to 10 years. Again, the PAC is protected in this lockout period because it stands first in line to receive cash flows out of the mortgage pool. Many times a PAC is specified as being protected only within certain bandwidths of

> The *p*'s represent probability values that are assigned to each cash flow after purchase.

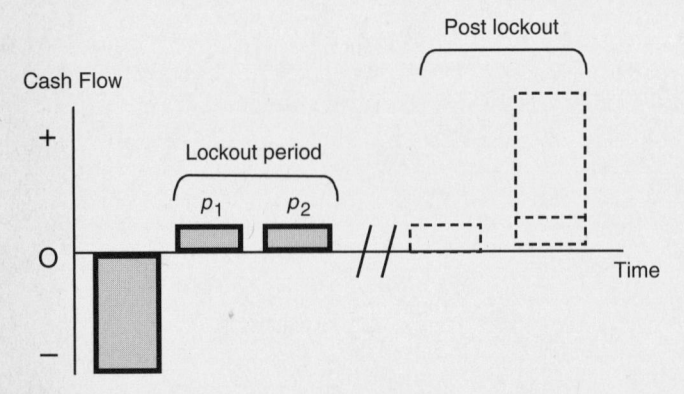

FIGURE 4.18 Applying the PAC discussion to the cash flow diagram.

option-related activity. Typically the activity of homeowners paying off their mortgages is referred to as *prepayment speed* (or *speed*). Moreover, a convention exists for how these speeds are quoted. Accordingly, often PAC bandwidths define an upper and lower bound within which speeds may vary without having any detrimental effect on the PAC's cash flows. The wider the bandwidth, the pricier the PAC compared to PACs with narrower bands. Once a particular PAC has experienced a prepayment speed that falls outside of its band, it is referred to as a "busted PAC." A PAC also is "busted" once its lockout period has passed. Not surprisingly, once "busted," a PAC's value tends to cheapen.

As perhaps the next logical step from a PAC, we have DUS, or delegated underwriting and servicing security. In brief, a DUS carries significant prepayment penalties, so borrowers do not have a great incentive to prepay their loans. Accordingly, a DUS can be thought of as having significant lockout protection.

The formula for a PAC or DUS or a variety of other products created from pass-thru might very well look like our last price formula, and it is repeated below. What would clearly differ, however, are the values we insert for probability. While large bond fund investors might perform a variety of complex analyses to calibrate precise probability values across cash flows, other investors might simply observe whether respective yield levels appear to be in line with one another. That is, we would expect a 10-noncall-five to trade at a yield below a 10-year DUS, a 10-year DUS to trade at a yield below a 10-year PAC with a lockout of five years, and so forth.

Financial Engineering

$$Price = \frac{C \times p_1 \& F \times p_2}{(1 + Y/2)^1} + \frac{C \times p_3 \& F \times p_4}{(1 + Y/2)^2}$$
$$+ \frac{C \times p_5 \& F \times p_6}{(1 + Y/2)^3} + \ldots = \$1,000$$

Figure 4.19 summarizes the yield relationship to the different callable bond structures presented in this section. Each successive layer represents a different and higher-yielding callable product.

For another perspective on the relationships among products, cash flows, and credit, consider Figure 4.20, which plots the price volatility of a triple-A-rated pass-thru against four 10-year final maturity bonds. One of the bonds is a bullet, while the other three are different types of callables. Each

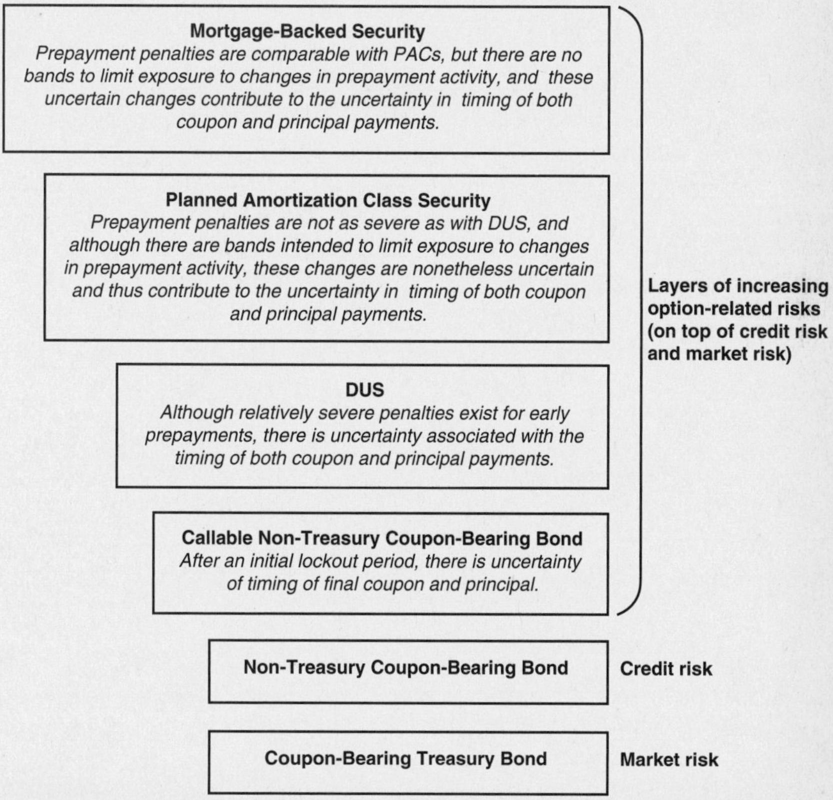

Mortgage-Backed Security
Prepayment penalties are comparable with PACs, but there are no bands to limit exposure to changes in prepayment activity, and these uncertain changes contribute to the uncertainty in timing of both coupon and principal payments.

Planned Amortization Class Security
Prepayment penalties are not as severe as with DUS, and although there are bands intended to limit exposure to changes in prepayment activity, these changes are nonetheless uncertain and thus contribute to the uncertainty in timing of both coupon and principal payments.

DUS
Although relatively severe penalties exist for early prepayments, there is uncertainty associated with the timing of both coupon and principal payments.

Callable Non-Treasury Coupon-Bearing Bond
After an initial lockout period, there is uncertainty of timing of final coupon and principal.

Layers of increasing option-related risks (on top of credit risk and market risk)

Non-Treasury Coupon-Bearing Bond — Credit risk

Coupon-Bearing Treasury Bond — Market risk

FIGURE 4.19 Summary of the yield relationship to callable bond structures.

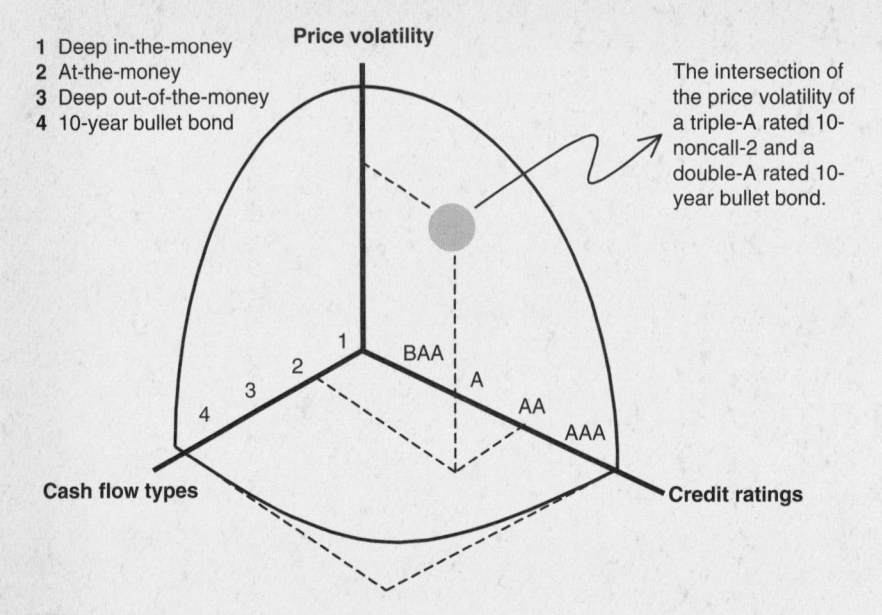

FIGURE 4.20 Mapping process.

of the callables is a 10-noncall-2, but each has a different status with regard to the relationship between F and K. Namely, one has $F = K$, the other has F much greater than K (deep in-the-money), and the last has F much less than K (deep out-of-the-money). The price volatility of an at-the-money 10-non-call-2 is the same as that for a generic double-A-rated corporate security. Accordingly, with all the shortcomings and limitations that a mapping process represents, it would appear that such a process might be used to find connectors between things like credit profiles and cash flow compositions. The particular relationship highlighted in the figure might be of special interest to an investor looking for an additional and creative way to identify value across various financial considerations inclusive of credit and structure types.

Parenthetically, a financing market exists for MBS securities as well. An exchange of an MBS for a loan of cash is referred to as a *dollar roll*. A dollar roll works very much like the securities lending example described earlier in this chapter, though obviously there are special accommodations for the unique coupon and price risk inherent in an MBS as opposed to a generic Treasury Bond.

A preferred stock is a security that combines characteristics of both bonds and equities (see Figure 4.21). Like bonds, a preferred stock usually has a predetermined maturity date, pays regular dividends, and does not convey voting rights. Like an equity, a preferred stock ranks rather low in

Financial Engineering

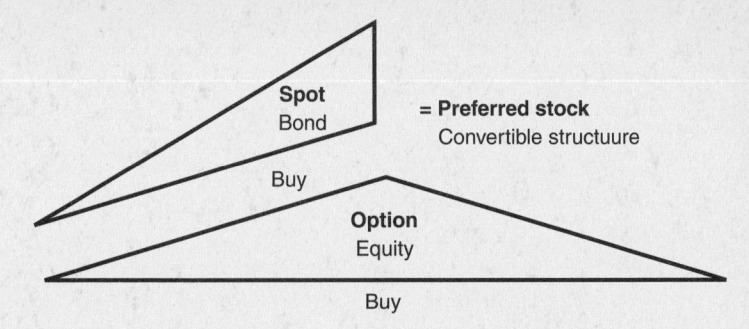

```
           Spot
           Bond           = Preferred stock
                          Convertible structuure
            Buy
          Option
          Equity
            Buy
```

FIGURE 4.21 Use of spot and options to create a convertible.

priority in the event of a default, but typically it ranks above common stock. The hybrid nature of preferred stock is supported by the fact that while some investment banks and investors warehouse these securities in their fixed income business, others manage them in their equity business.

One special type of preferred stock is known as a *convertible*. As the name suggests, the security can be converted from a preferred stock product into something else at the choice of the investor. The "something else" is usually shares of stock in the company that originally issued the preferred stock. A convertible typically is structured such that it is convertible at any time, the conversion right is held by the investor in the convertible, and the convertible sells at a premium to the underlying security. Investors accept the premium since convertibles tend to pay coupons that are much higher than the dividends of the underlying common stock.

Generally speaking, as the underlying common stock of a convertible declines, the convertible will trade more like a bond than an equity. That is, the price of the convertible will be more sensitive to changes in interest rates than to changes in the price of the underlying common stock. However, as the underlying stock price appreciates, the convertible will increasingly trade much more in-line with the price behavior of the underlying equity than with changes in interest rates.

Figure 4.22 shows a preferred stock's potential evolution from more of a bond product into more of an equity product.

A convertible's increasingly equitylike behavior is entirely consistent with the way a standard equity option would trade. That is, as the option trades more and more in-the-money, the more its price behavior moves into lockstep with the price behavior of the underlying equity's forward or spot price. Parenthetically, an option that can be exercised at any time is called an *American option*, while an option that can be exercised only at expiration is called a *European option*. In the case of a European option type structure, if the underlying equity price is above the convertible-equity conversion price as the convertible comes to maturity, then the conversion should be made; the option to receive equity in exchange for the convertible ought to be exercised. But if the underlying equity price is below the applicable conversion price, conversion should not be made; an investor is better off with taking the redemption value of the convertible.

To add another twist to this scenario, convertibles also can be issued with callable features. A callable feature entitles the issuer to force a given security into an early redemption. Thus, depending on its precise characteristics, the correct valuation of a convertible can be a complex undertaking.

The cash flow triangle shows how the price behavior of an in-the-money preferred stock can be seen as more spot- or forward-like, as well as more equity- or bond-like (see Figure 4.23).

The answer to the question of "What really is a convertible?" can very much depend on the particular time in the life of the convertible when the question is being posed. An understanding and appreciation of the factors driving the convertible around the triangle (pun very much intended) will greatly facilitate an investor's assessment of relative value and opportunity.

There are a few different ways to creatively influence the credit quality of a bond as illustrated by Figures 4.24 and 4.25. Within the world of fixed income, there are bonds with short call options embedded in them (callables) and bonds with long puts embedded in them (putables). Chapter 2 explained that a put option is generally thought of as providing downside price protection; as price falls, the value of a put option rises. Concomitantly, a credit call option suggests there is downside protection against the risks typically associated with a deteriorating credit story. These risks might include price-related dynamics as the market adjusts itself to a less favorable credit environment. Being long a credit call option will not prevent a credit rating agency from placing a company on credit watch or downgrading a company outright, but being long a credit call option might help to ameliorate the adverse price consequences typically associated with negative credit events.

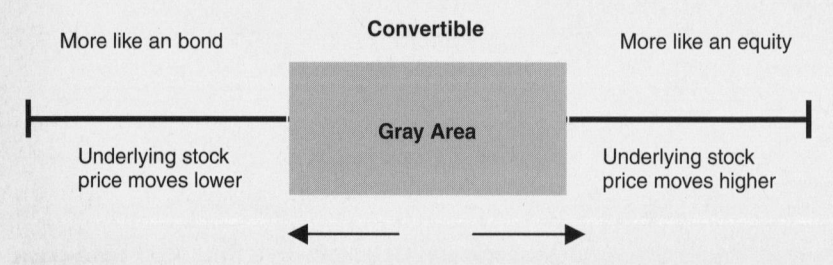

FIGURE 4.22 Transformation scenarios for a convertible bond.

Financial Engineering **147**

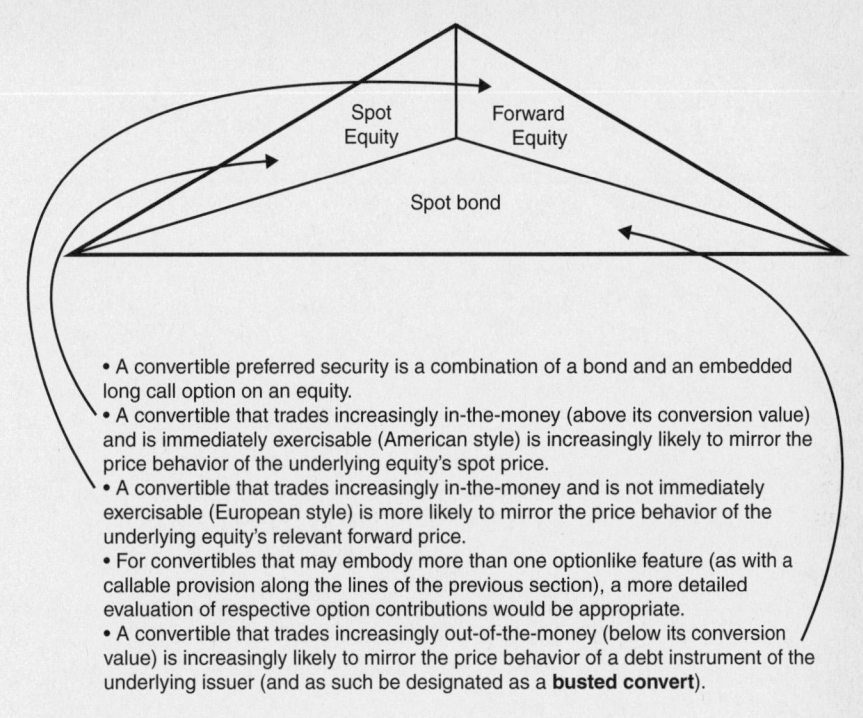

- A convertible preferred security is a combination of a bond and an embedded long call option on an equity.
- A convertible that trades increasingly in-the-money (above its conversion value) and is immediately exercisable (American style) is increasingly likely to mirror the price behavior of the underlying equity's spot price.
- A convertible that trades increasingly in-the-money and is not immediately exercisable (European style) is more likely to mirror the price behavior of the underlying equity's relevant forward price.
- For convertibles that may embody more than one optionlike feature (as with a callable provision along the lines of the previous section), a more detailed evaluation of respective option contributions would be appropriate.
- A convertible that trades increasingly out-of-the-money (below its conversion value) is increasingly likely to mirror the price behavior of a debt instrument of the underlying issuer (and as such be designated as a **busted convert**).

FIGURE 4.23 Cash flow triangle.

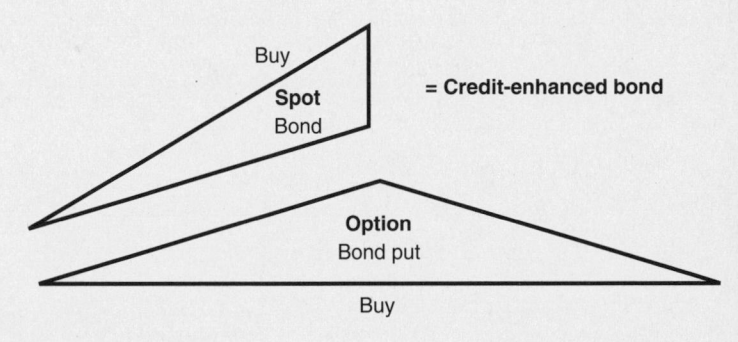

FIGURE 4.24 Use of spot and options to create a credit-enhanced bond.

As previously stated, a putable bond is composed of a bond and a long put option. The put option is most commonly viewed as being a put option on price; that is, if interest rates rise, causing price to fall, the put option presumably takes on value since it provides a support or floor level for prices.

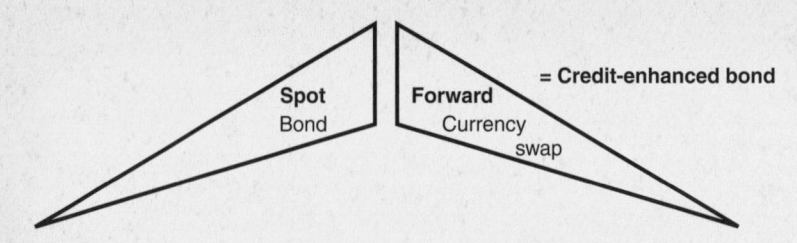

```
                Spot        Forward       = Credit-enhanced bond
                Bond        Currency
                            swap
```

FIGURE 4.25 Use of spot and forwards to create a credit-enhanced bond.

A putable bond differs from a callable bond in at least two fundamental respects.

1. With a putable bond, the embedded put is a long embedded put, and with a callable bond, the embedded call is a short embedded call.
2. As a direct consequence of number 1, the combination of being long a bond and long a put option, as with a putable bond, results in a payoff profile that much resembles a synthetic long call, while the combination of being long a bond and short a call option, as with a callable bond, results in a payoff profile that much resembles a synthetic short put.

The combination of a long call and a short put results in a payoff profile resembling a simple long position in a forward. The diagrams in Figure 4.26 show these various relationships.

All else being equal, except for being defensive on the market, put-call parity and efficient markets would suggest that we would be indifferent between the callable and the putable. That is, being short an embedded call or being long an embedded put are defensive or bearish strategies. However, if all else were not equal, and if credit risk were a particular matter of concern, then the put bond would take on a greater value relative to the callable. Since the putable bond has a payoff profile of a synthetic long call, downside price risk is limited while upside price potential is unlimited. If an adverse credit event were to occur, the putable bond still would provide price support on the downside.

The rationale for this downside support is simply that covenants for putable bonds (indeed, all covenants that this author is aware of) tend not to make any stipulations about the price support features of the put regarding segmenting market-related phenomena (as with changes in interest rates) versus any other phenomena (as with changes in credit risk). Accordingly, the put option embedded in a putable bond de facto provides a level of price support for any event that might otherwise push the price of a bond lower. This contrasts with a callable bond, where with its synthetic short put pro-

Financial Engineering

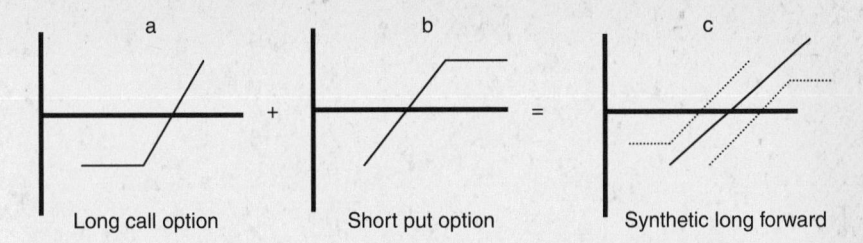

FIGURE 4.26 Use of a long call and a short put to create a synthetic long forward.

file, the price of the bond clearly does not receive any price support on the downside and indeed has its price appreciation limited on the upside.

In sum, while callable and putable bonds may be viewed primarily as interest rate risk bond products, they also can be viewed as being important credit products. In the case of a putable, downside credit risk protection (as with a downgrade) exists, and favorable credit-related appreciation (as with an upgrade) is limited. With a callable, favorable credit-related appreciation is also limited, as is downside credit risk protection.

A propitious choice of currency denomination also can have a favorable credit impact for a financial product. For example, it is no mere happenstance that the so-called Brady bonds of the 1990s were explicitly intended to assist Latin American countries with servicing their debt obligations, yet were denominated in U.S. dollars rather than pesos, or sucres, or colons, and so forth. Aside from any public relations benefit from having the bonds denominated in dollars, U.S. Treasury zero-coupon bonds and other high-grade instruments collateralize the principal and certain interest cash flows of these bonds. In sum, the involvement of the United States, including the international cachet of the U.S. dollar, greatly enhanced the real and perceived credit benefits of Brady bonds.

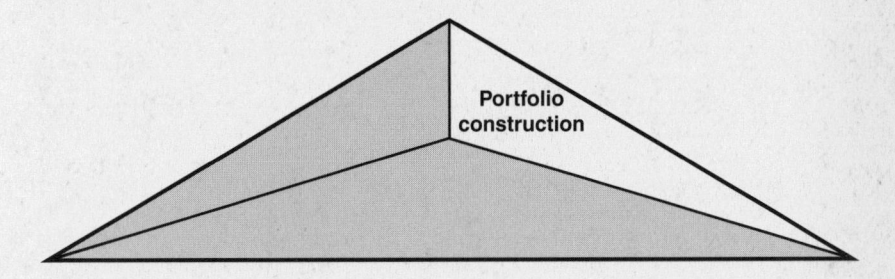

Obviously, a portfolio is an amalgamation of products, cash flows, and credit risks. There are hundreds of thousands of portfolios and investment funds in the world, typically managed with an orientation to a particular investment style. For example, funds occasionally are described as being either relative or absolute return oriented. A *relative return* fund, as the name suggests, is a fund whose performance is evaluated relative to a benchmark or index. For example, a relative return equity fund might be evaluated relative to the S&P 500 equity index. Accordingly, if a portfolio manager returns 20 percent in a given year, this may or may not be an impressive feat. If the S&P 500 returned 33 percent, then the portfolio manager's performance would not be very impressive at all. But if the S&P 500 returned 3 percent, then a 20 percent portfolio return would be very impressive indeed. Generally speaking, larger institutional fund managers manage relative return funds.

Conversely, an *absolute return* fund typically is managed without reference to a particular benchmark or index; the objective is not so much to provide a return that is impressive relative to a market benchmark (though that may be welcomed) as much as it is to provide an attractive return on an absolute basis. To achieve such a goal, it is expected that an absolute return fund would experience more return volatility relative to a relative return fund, but with larger longer-run aggregated returns in exchange for the higher year-over-year risk being taken. Generally speaking, smaller fund managers manage absolute return funds, as with *hedge funds* (special funds that are subject to special privileges and restrictions relative to more common investment funds).

Because of their more aggressive objectives, absolute return funds generally are more likely to bias their investments toward relatively more risky product, cash flow, and credit profiles in relation to relative return funds. That is, absolute return funds are more likely to invest in equity than bonds, more likely to invest in futures and options than spot, and more likely to dip into lower credit quality investments than higher credit quality securities.

ABSOLUTE RETURN INVESTING

The following list of fund-types are all, broadly speaking, absolute return-oriented styles.

Aggressive Growth

These funds typically invest in equities expected to experience acceleration in growth of earnings per share, have generally high P/E ratios and low or no dividends, and often are smaller-cap stocks. This category also includes sector specialist funds such as technology, banking, or biotechnology. There is a general bias toward being long the market.

Distressed Securities

These funds buy equity, debt, or trade claims at deep discounts of companies in or facing bankruptcy or reorganization. Profits are realized from the market's underappreciation of the true worth of these securities and from bargain prices precipitated by selling by institutional investors who cannot own below-investment-grade securities.

Emerging Markets

These funds invest in equity or debt of emerging (less mature) markets that tend to have high inflation and volatile growth.

Funds of Hedge Funds

These funds invest in a mix of hedge funds and other pooled investment vehicles. This blending of different funds aims to provide a more stable long-term investment return than any individual funds. Capital preservation is often an important consideration.

Income

These funds have a primary focus on yield or current income rather than on capital gains. These funds may use leverage buying bonds and perhaps other types of fixed income derivatives.

Macro

These funds seek to profit from changes in global economies, many times brought about by shifts in government policy that impact interest rates, currencies, stocks, and bond markets; though the funds may not be invested in all of these markets at the same time. Leverage and derivatives may be used to maximize the impact of market moves.

Market Neutral—Arbitrage

These funds attempt to hedge most market risk by taking offsetting positions, often in different securities of the same issuer. The funds may be long convertible bonds and short the underlying issuers equity, and may focus on obtaining returns with low or no correlation to both the equity and bond markets These relative value strategies include fixed income arbitrage, mortgage-backed securities, capital structure arbitrage, and closed-end fund arbitrage.

Market Neutral—Securities Hedging

These funds invest equally in long and short equity positions, and generally in the same sectors of the market. Market risk may be greatly reduced, but effective stock analysis and stock picking can be essential to obtaining meaningful results. Leverage may be used to enhance returns, and there is usually low or no correlation to the market.

Market Timing

These funds allocate assets among different asset classes depending on the fund's view of investment opportunities. Portfolio emphasis may swing widely between asset classes. Unpredictability of market movements and the difficulty of timing entry and exit from markets add to the volatility of this strategy.

Opportunistic

The investment theme for these funds changes from strategy to strategy as opportunities arise so as to profit from events such as IPOs, sudden price changes caused by unique events like earnings disappointments, hostile bids, and other kinds of event-driven opportunities.

Multistrategy

The investment approach for these funds consists of employing various strategies simultaneously to realize short- and long-term gains. Strategies may involve systems trading such as trend following or technical strategies.

Short Selling

The fund sells securities short in anticipation of being able to buy them again at a future date at a lower price due to the fund's assessment of the overvaluation of the securities the market, in anticipation of earnings disappointments often due to accounting irregularities, new competition, change of management, and so forth.

Special Situations

These funds invest in event-driven situations such as mergers, hostile takeovers, reorganizations, or leveraged buyouts. Strategies may involve simultaneous purchase of stock in companies being acquired and the sale of stock in its acquirer.

Value

These funds invest in securities perceived to be selling at deep discounts to their intrinsic or potential worth. Such securities may be out of favor or not actively followed by analysts. Long-term holding, patience, and strong discipline are often required until the ultimate desired value is achieved.

RELATIVE RETURN INVESTING

In the strictest possible sense, indexing means striving to match a portfolio's return to the return of a given index return exactly. While this might sound rather simple to do in theory—just buy every security that is in the index—there is the matter of costs associated with those purchases. Indices are typically constructed and maintained with some unrealistic assumptions about the ways of trading an actual portfolio. In the appendix of this chapter we highlight these unrealistic assumptions in the context of how portfolio managers may use them to achieve better fund performance. The point here is not to criticize the indices for not being more like real portfolios. The role of an index is to be an index and the role of a portfolio is to be a portfolio. The point merely is that the "simple" task of getting a portfolio to exactly explicate the performance of an index can be a challenge. Investors who prefer putting their money into indexed funds are essentially saying that they either do not believe in a portfolio's ability to do much better than what the index itself can do, or are satisfied with what the index consists of and what its potential is, and that is all that they want; nothing more and nothing less. In Table 4.4 we present a variety of fund management themes in the context of product types and relative return styles.

Now let us consider detailed descriptions of each of the fund categories cited above.

Total Return

Total return investing is typically when a *market index* of some kind comes into play as a sort of referee. For example, the S&P 500 is an equity market index; a variety of market indices exist for bonds as well. Accordingly, a mandate of a portfolio may be to generate a superior performance, and generally with that outperformance being defined as a better-than-index performance. Unlike indexed funds, where the goal is just to do as well as the relevant index, with total return funds portfolio managers may receive something more in their fee package when they outperform an index. The appendix of this chapter considers various ways that a portfolio manager might seek to engage in some opportunistic though risk-controlled (if properly managed) strategies that can help to add some total return potential to an index-oriented management philosophy.

TABLE 4.4 Fund Management Themes Used with Product Types

Fund Theme	Bonds	Equities	Currencies
Indexing	√	√	
Total return	√	√	
Growth		√	
Balanced	√	√	
Value		√	
Income	√		
Tax-free	√		
Yield enhancement	√		
Capital preservation	√		
International	√	√	√
Overlay			√
Relative return	√	√	
Absolute return		√	
Bull and/or bear		√	
Long and short		√	

Growth Fund

Typically a growth fund is a euphemism for a fund that is likely to take on greater risks (relative to, say, an income fund) so as to try to grow the capital base. In all likelihood, a growth fund strategy is not to stay strictly indexed, unless of course there is a meaningful growth-type index available (as perhaps a Nasdaq-type index might be, though even here a concern might be raised about more Internet-related components of this index as representing a disproportionate exposure to one particular sector). Generally speaking, equities, which demonstrate beta values greater than one, are likely to be strong growth fund candidates.

Capital Preservation Fund

Perhaps at the opposite end of the continuum from a growth-oriented fund would be a capital preservation fund. As the name clearly suggests, the idea with a capital preservation fund is more to maintain capital than to expose it, and typically with securities that tend not to exhibit much volatility. While it is certainly possible to find some equities within a capital preservation fund, they would likely exhibit betas of less than one. More typical components of a capital preservation fund would consist of relatively strong (highly rated) bonds.

Balanced Fund

A balanced fund usually is expected to represent a blend of equity and bond holdings. The idea is that by diversifying within one fund—such as taking a more aggressive/growth-oriented position in equities and a more conservative/preservation stance with bonds—this mix could result in an optimal best-of-both-worlds strategy for a given investor. Indeed, one school of thought holds that there is a "life cycle" blend of equities and bonds that is dynamic in nature. The general idea is that in the early stages of one's life, it is quite acceptable to be predisposed to equities rather than bonds; this would be a time in life when risk taking is more appropriate. In the middle stages of life, a shift to more of an equal holding of equities and bonds is more in keeping with hitting stride with income earnings as well as the need to ensure adequate resources for the coverage of present and future liabilities (as with a home mortgage and/or college educations). And then in the later stages of life, the notion is that the right strategy is more of a bias to bonds and capital preservation, if only so that the capital base that was once exposed (and properly so) is now more protected.

Income Fund

Income funds are closely linked to capital preservation funds in that both strive to limit capital exposure to an acceptable minimum. Income funds tend to prefer securities with higher coupons and dividends than capital preservation funds; in short, securities that generate as many "income"-like cash flows as possible. Again, equities probably would be limited to shares exhibiting a beta of less than one. Some utilities readily come to mind. Although higher coupons are paid only when greater credit risk is taken on, there are some rather aged (though still available) bonds with "large" coupons relative to their present credit risk profile. For example, a long-dated security may have been brought to market a while ago when prevailing yields were much higher and/or when the issuer's credit rating was worse than what it has evolved to become. Another possibility for income-oriented funds is to bias bond holding toward securities, which may embody more complex structures, as with callables. However, here as well capital preservation precautions must be maintained.

Tax-Free Funds

As discussed in some detail in Chapter 3, there can be entire segments within certain markets where designated securities are afforded some type of tax protection. If due only to the fact that these securities already enjoy a particular tax advantage, they are not typically sought after as higher-yielding securities. Tax-free yields tend to be lower relative to like-rated securities that are not tax-advantaged because of the tax-free advantage. While it should be expected that investors who might not be motivated by a tax-free opportunity might favor tax-free securities for a particular strategy (as when a total return-oriented portfolio manager believes that he may have spotted a mispriced relationship between taxables and nontaxables and wishes to capture it), tax-free securities are most likely to be found in "pure" tax-free funds and less likely to be found anywhere else.

Asset-Liability Management

Just as tax-free investment management can be thought of as a type of "tailored" management style (in this case tailored to tax-oriented strategies), asset-liability portfolio management might best be thought of as a "tailored" management style. Simply put, for an entity with fairly well-defined future liabilities (as with pensions or life insurance policies), it is highly desirable to put into place a matching (or nearly matching) series of asset streams to pair off against the anticipated liabilities. Perhaps not surprisingly, bonds are often a favored asset to use with asset-liability management owing to the fact that they have fairly well-defined characteristics when it comes to cash flow generation. Knowing when coupons and/or principal payments are likely to be made and in what amount can be tremendously helpful when trying to ensure that promises for timely payments on pension or life insurance policies are kept.

Insurance companies use actuarial tables and the like for the sole purpose of optimally deriving and applying any relevant statistical insights to better structure and manage life insurance–related commitments.

Yield Enhancement

Closely related to asset-liability management is the portfolio management approach of yield enhancement. In fact, it might be most helpful to describe yield enhancement as not so much a distinct investment style vis-à-vis asset-liability management, but rather as a management orientation as practiced by banks. A bank's "liabilities" can be thought of as its outstanding debt in the form of certificates of deposit or the bonds it has issued into the marketplace and so on. Just as a corporation must successfully pair off its pension liabilities with a predictable *asset stream* (a series of cash flows that generate payments of specific times into the future) and a life insurance company must successfully pair off its insurance liabilities with a reliable asset stream, so must a bank be able to generate a pool of bankable assets (so to speak). In the old-fashioned world of banking the idea was to be profitable simply by extending loans (the asset stream) that paid cash flows (coupons and principal) at rates in excess of wherever banks had to pay (the liability stream) to attract money (via certificates of deposit and the like) to be in a position to extend loans in the first place. In the world of more modern-day finance, a bank's assets might very well include some loans but increasingly also might include investments in market securities such as bonds and equities. Indeed, just as restrictions and guidelines typically exist for types of investments that an insurance company might engage in (as presented in Chapter 5), so too do such guidelines and restrictions exist for banks (also as presented in Chapter 5). These types of restrictions and guidelines exist on a global basis.

The reason why the term "yield enhancement" might be applied to banks in particular relates back to the notion of trying to assemble a collection of assets with an overall yield in excess of the yield that must be paid out on the bank's liabilities. There is typically a maturity element to a bank's asset and liability streams, and while it may be relatively straightforward to lock in a long-term loan or purchase a long-dated bond (both being assets), it may prove somewhat difficult to pair those off with a multiyear CD certificate of deposit or comparable product. This paradigm of a bank's generally running long-dated asset streams against short-dated liabilities gave rise to the notion of "gap management," or managing the differences between a bank's asset and liability streams. A number of consulting and software responses exist to assist banks with gap-management and other needs.

Value Investing

Value investing is often described as a process of separating "solid" companies from more speculative ones. A solid company might be defined in any number of ways, though criteria might include a long track record of steady earnings, an absence of large fluctuations in equity price, and/or perceptions of strong and experienced leadership at the helm. Value-oriented funds may not turn in the same kind of performance as more opportunistic portfolios when the market is soaring, though they would be expected to do better than opportunistic portfolios when markets are steady to weaker.

International Fund

An international fund is simply one that makes a deliberate effort to invest in securities denominated in currencies other than the home market currency. Thus, an international fund based in the United States might include securities denominated in yen, euros, Australian dollars, and so forth.

Overlay Fund

Many portfolio managers regard the currency decision as being separate and distinct from the decision-making process of picking individual equities or bonds. The rationale is that there are very different drivers behind currencies, bonds, and equities and that they are best treated in isolation or quasi-isolation. The notion that there are different drivers with currencies is perhaps reasonable, if only to the extent that they do exhibit very different risk/return profiles relative to equities and bonds. Yet as discussed in Chapter 2 under interest rate parity, there are meaningful links between key interest rate differentials and currency movements. Some portfolio managers make the strategic decision to concentrate exclusively on managing bonds or managing equities; they outsource the job of managing currencies or delegate it to someone who is more expert in that arena.

There are generally three types of currency management approaches: quantitative, fundamental, and blend. The quantitative approach involves a strict adhesion to mathematical models that attempt to signal appropriate times to buy or sell particular currencies. A fundamental approach claims to actively consider factors such as the state of a particular economy or capital flows or market sentiment. Note, however, that currency portfolio managers are not slaves to whatever the models might be saying; the models are intended to complement personal judgments, not override them. And finally, there are currency specialists who purport to use a particular mix of the two approaches.

This is not the place to decide if one approach is better than any other. The debate should be an internal one to the fund concerned, and directed to which particular approach would be most consistent with the investment philosophy of the portfolios—at least until it can be proven that one style alone is always and everywhere superior to all others.

Table 4.4 summarizes the fund types according to product profile. It is intended to be more conceptual than a carved-in-stone description of the way that investment funds use various financial products.

A Last Word

Historically investors have described themselves as being equity investors, bond investors, currency investors, or whatever. While these labels do have some value in describing the type of investing investors do, their prominence may give way to other more meaningful types of classifications. That is, perhaps instead of describing their investing profile by financial *products*, investors may describe their investing profile in terms of *credit* considerations. At one time in the not too distant past, the distinction between these two phenomena was not that great. For the United States and much of

Western Europe, for example, highly rated government debt dominated the bond landscape in these respective markets (if not globally), and equities commonly were seen as being the higher-risk investment. Today, however, there are many flavors of bond products, and investors are increasingly pushed to define exactly what criteria they will use to distinguish between a bond or an equity. Is the line in the sand whether or not the security carries voting rights? Is it a matter of where the security sits in the capital structure of the company balance sheet? Is it a consideration of how the security's risk/return profile compares to other product types?

In a world where bonds of certain governments actually go into default[7] and where some "equities" exhibit less price volatility and greater returns relative to same-issuer fixed income products, a more meaningful set of labels may be of help to distinguish one investment philosophy from another. For example, instead of investors describing themselves as oriented to a particular product profile (equities, bonds, currencies, etc.) they would describe themselves as oriented to a particular market risk profile (high, medium, low, or any other classifications of relevance). In turn, the market risk profile approach would encompass risks of product, cash flow, and credit.

Why would investors be interested in such a different way of looking at the marketplace? If investors focus on ultimately arriving at their destination and are indifferent to how they get there, then they will find great value in a market risk orientation to investing. If the "destination" is high capital exposure/shoot-for-the-stars, then a variety of investment products could fill the needs, products that cut across traditional lines separating bonds from equities (and other conventional product categories).

Issuers and investors, as well as regulators and rating agencies, will increasingly ask these questions and creative responses will need to be provided. For example, one approach might be construct and maintain a comparative total return table that would provide total return and risk profiles as sliced by credit risk as opposed to product labels. How do total returns of junior subordinated debt issued by a double-A-rated company stack up against the senior debt of a triple-B-rated company, for example, and how do these compare with a preferred stock? Much exciting work lies ahead.

CHAPTER SUMMARY

This chapter showed how combining various legs of the product and cash flow triangles can facilitate an understanding of how various strategies can

---

[7]Ecuador's Brady bonds, which were backed by U.S. Treasuries, nonetheless went into default in 1999.

be developed and how products can be created. How credit can be a key factor within the product creation process was considered. There are hundreds upon thousands of actual and potential products and strategies in the global markets at any given time. The purpose here is simply to provide a few examples of how that creative process might be organized in a straightforward and meaningful fashion. Finally, the chapter presented an overview of relative versus absolute return objectives and discussed a few portfolio types that might be found under the heading of relative (capital preservation) or absolute (long/short).

APPENDIX

Relative Return Investing Strategies

Many portfolio managers have their performance evaluated against a benchmark or index. The goal with such an exercise is generally either to match the portfolio's performance with the benchmark's or to beat the benchmark. Either objective is wrought with unique challenges. Indeed, it is the rare and quite the exceptional fund manager who can successfully outperform the market year in and year out and in a variety of market environments. For such investors who have identified a systemized way of investing, their success can be reflected in their fund's *alpha*.

In the finance industry the term "alpha" denotes returns generated in excess of a market index. For example, if the S&P 500 returns 10 percent and a stock portfolio returns 11.2 percent, then 120 basis points of alpha can be said to have been generated. Since alpha is typically used as a reference to excess returns, investors tend not to refer to negative alpha. In short, either alpha has been generated or it has not. Recognizing that returns and especially excess returns typically are generated in tandem with at least some measure of risk, the financial industry uses the term "sigma" to denote variability of returns or the notion that returns can be negative, just as they can be positive. It is certainly possible for a return to be negative yet also be a contributor to positive alpha. For example, if the return of the S&P 500 is 8 percent while the return of the stock portfolio is −7.5 percent then it can be said that 50 bps of alpha has been generated.

The notions of risk and reward, or sigma and alpha, are seen as inseparable and of great relevance when evaluating market opportunities. At many firms these functions are called trading and risk management respectively, and each area has detailed roles and responsibilities. For example, the trading function may be responsible for achieving the best possible execution of trades in the marketplace, while the risk management function may be responsible for overseeing the overall profile of a portfolio. Arguably, the more successful firms are those that have found ways to marry these two key areas in such a way that they are seen as complementary and reinforcing rather than competing and at odds.

This appendix highlights some strategies that can be used to eke out a few extra basis points of return for a benchmarked portfolio. Broadly speaking, such strategies may be categorized as:

- Stepping outside of benchmark definitions
- Leveraging a portfolio
- Capitalizing on changes within a benchmark's parameters

For the equity markets, benchmarks are fairly well known. For example, the Dow Jones Industrial Average (DJIA or Dow) is perhaps one of the best-known stock indexes in the world. Other indexes would include the Financial Times Stock Exchange Index (or FTSE, sometimes pronounced foot-see) in the United Kingdom and the Nikkei in Japan. Other indexes in the United States would include the Nasdaq, the Wilshire, and the Standard & Poor's (S&P) 100 or 500.

In the United States, where there is a choice of indexes, the index a portfolio manager uses is likely driven by the objectives of the particular portfolio being managed. If the portfolio is designed to outperform the broader market, then the Dow might be the best choice. And if smaller capitalized stocks are the niche (the so-called small caps), then perhaps the Nasdaq would be better. And if it is a specialized portfolio, such as one investing in utilities, then the Dow Jones Utility index might be the ticket.

Indexes are composed of a select number of stocks, a fact that can be a challenge to portfolio managers. For example, the Dow is composed of just 30 stocks. Considering that thousands of stocks trade on the New York Stock Exchange, an equity portfolio manager may not want to invest solely in the 30 stocks of the Dow. Yet if it is the portfolio manager's job to match the performance of the Dow, what could be easier than simply owning the 30 stocks in the index? Remember that there are transaction costs associated with the purchase and sale of any stocks. Just to keep up with the performance of the Dow *after costs* requires an outperformance of the Dow *before costs*. How might this outperformance be achieved? There are four basic ways.

1. Portfolio managers might own each of the 30 stocks in the Dow, but with weightings that differ from the Dow's. That is, they might hold more of those issues that they expect to do especially well (better than the index) while holding less of those issues that they expect may do less well (worse than the index).
2. Portfolio managers might choose to hold only a sample (perhaps none) of the stocks in the index, believing that better returns are to be found in other well-capitalized securities and/or in less-capitalized securities. Portfolio managers might make use of statistical tools (correlation coefficients) when building these types of portfolios.
3. Portfolio managers may decide to venture out beyond the world of equities exclusively and invest in asset types like fixed income instruments, precious metals, or others. Clearly, as a portfolio increasingly deviates from the makeup of the index, the portfolio may underperform the index,

and disgruntled investors may withdraw their funds stemming from disappointment that the portfolio strayed too far from its core mission.
4. When adjustments are made to the respective indexes, there may be unique opportunities to benefit from those adjustments. For example, when it is announced that a new equity is to be added to an index, it may enjoy a run-up in price as investors seek to own this newest member of a key market measure. Similarly, when it is announced that an equity currently in an index is to drop out of it, it may suffer a downturn in price as relative return investors unload it as an equity no longer required.

In the fixed income marketplace, it is estimated that at least three quarters of institutional portfolios are managed against some kind of benchmark. The benchmark might be of a simple homegrown variety (like the rolling total return performance of the on-the-run two-year Treasury) or of something rather complex with a variety of product types mixed together. Regrettably perhaps, unlike the stock market, where the Dow is one of a handful of well-recognized equity benchmarks on a global basis, a similarly recognized benchmark for the bond market has not really yet come into its own.

Given the importance that relative return managers place on understanding how well their portfolios are matched to their benchmarks, fixed income analytics have evolved to the point of slicing out the various factors that can contribute to mismatching. These factors would include things like mismatches to respective yield curve exposures in the portfolio versus the benchmark, differing blends of credit quality, different weightings on prepayment risks, and so on. Not surprisingly, these same slices of potential mismatches are also the criteria used for performance attribution. "Performance attribution" means an attempt to quantify what percentage of overall return can be explained by such variables as the yield curve dynamic, security selection, changes in volatility, and so forth.

Regarding a quantitative measure of a benchmark in relation to portfolio mismatching, sometimes the mismatch is normalized as a standard deviation that is expressed in basis points. In this instance, a mismatch of 25 bps (i.e., 25 bps of *total return* basis points) would suggest that with the assumption of a normally distributed mismatch (an assumption that may be most realistic for a longer-run scenario), there would be a 67 percent likelihood that the year-end total return of the portfolio would come within plus or minus 25 bps of the total return of the benchmark. The 67 percent likelihood number simply stems from the properties of a normal distribution. To this end, there would be a 95 percent likelihood that the year-end total return of the portfolio would come within plus or minus 50 bps of the total return of the benchmark and a 99 percent likelihood of plus or minus 75 bps.

Another way of thinking about the issue of outperforming an index is in the context of the *mismatch* between the benchmark and the portfolio that is created to follow or *track* (or even outperform) the benchmark. Sometimes this "mismatch" may be called a tracking error or a performance tracking measure. Simply put, the more a given portfolio looks like its respective benchmark, the lower its mismatch will be.

For portfolio managers concerned primarily with matching a benchmark, mismatches would be rather small. Yet for portfolio managers concerned with outperforming a benchmark, larger mismatches are common. Far and away the single greatest driver of portfolio returns is the duration decision. Indeed, this variable alone might account for as much as 80 to 90 percent of a portfolio's return performance. We are not left with much latitude to outperform once the duration decision is made, and especially once we make other decisions pertaining to credit quality, prepayment risk, and so forth.

In second place to duration in terms of return drivers is the way in which a given sector is distributed. For example, a portfolio of corporate issues may be duration-matched to a corporate index, but the portfolio distribution may look *bulleted* (clustered around a single duration) or *barbelled* (clustered around two duration values) while the index itself is actually *laddered* (spread out evenly across multiple durations).

A relative value bond fund manager could actively use the following strategies.

Jump Outside the Index

One way to beat an index may be to buy an undervalued asset that is not considered to be a part of the respective benchmark. For example, take Mortgage-backed securities (MBSs) as an asset class. For various reasons, most benchmark MBS indices do not include adjustable-rate mortgages (ARMs). Yet ARMs are clearly relevant to the MBS asset class. Accordingly, if a portfolio manager believes that ARMs will outperform relative to other MBS products that are included in an MBS index, then the actual duration-neutral outperformance of the ARMs will enhance the index's overall return. As another consideration, indexes typically do not include product types created from the collateral that is a part of the index. For example, Treasury STRIPS (Separately Traded Registered Interest and Principal Securities) are created from Treasury collateral, and CMOs (Collateralized Mortgage Obligations) are created from MBS collateral. Accordingly, if an investor believes that a particular STRIPS or CMO may assist with outperforming the benchmark because of its unique contributions to duration and convexity or because it is undervalued in some way, then these products may be purchased. Treasuries are typically among the lowest-yielding securities in the taxable fixed income marketplace, and a very large percentage of Treasuries have a maturity between one and five years. For this reason, many investors will try to substitute Treasuries in this maturity sector with agency debentures or highly rated corporate securities that offer a higher yield.

Product Mix

A related issue is the product mix of a portfolio relative to a benchmark. For example, a corporate portfolio may have exposures to all the sectors contained within the index (utilities, banks, industrials, etc.), but the percent weighting actually assigned to each of those sectors may differ according to how portfolio managers expect respective sectors to perform. Also at issue would be the aggregate statistics of the portfolio versus its index (including aggregate coupon, credit risk, cash flows/duration distribution, yield, etc.).

Reinvested Proceeds

All benchmarks presumably have some convention that is used to reinvest proceeds generated by the index. For example, coupons and prepayments are paid at various times intramonth, yet most major indices simply take these cash flows and buy more of the respective index at the *end* of the month—generally, the last business day. In short, they miss an opportunity to reinvest cash flows intramonth. Accordingly, portfolio managers who put those intramonth flows to work with reverse repos or money market products, or anything else, may add incremental returns. All else being equal, as a defensive market strategy portfolio managers might overweight holdings of higher coupon issues that pay their coupons early in the month.

Leverage Strategies

Various forms of leveraging a portfolio also may help enhance total returns. For example, in the repo market, it is possible to loan out Treasuries as well as spread products and earn incremental return. Of course, this is most appropriate for portfolio managers who are more inclined to buy and hold. The securities that tend to benefit the most from such opportunities are on-the-run Treasuries. The comparable trade in the MBS market is the dollar roll[1]. Although most commonly used as a lower-cost financing alternative for depository institutions, total return accounts can treat the "drop" of a reverse repo or dollar roll as fee income.

Credit Trades

Each index has its own rules for determining cut-off points on credit rankings. Many indexes use more than one rating agency like Moody's and Standard & Poor's to assist with delineating whether an issuer is "investment grade" or "high yield," but many times the rating agencies do not agree on what the appropriate rating should be for a given issue. This becomes especially important for "crossover" credits. "Crossover" means the cusp between a credit being "investment grade" or "noninvestment grade." Sometimes Moody's will have a credit rating in the investment grade category while S&P considers it noninvestment grade, and vice versa. For cases where there is a discrepancy, the general index rule is to defer to the rating decision of one agency to determine just what the "true" rating will be.

Generally, a crossover credit will trade at a yield that is higher than a credit that carries a pair of investment-grade ratings at the lowest rung of the investment-grade scales. Thus, if a credit is excluded from an index because it is a crossover, adding the issue to the portfolio might enhance the portfolio returns with its wider spread and return performance. For this to happen, the portfolio cannot use the same crossover decision rule as the benchmark, and obviously it helps if portfolio managers have a favorable outlook on the credit. Finally, the credit rating agency that is deferred to for crossovers within the investment-grade index (or portfolio) may not always be the credit rating agency that is deferred to for crossovers within the high-yield index (or portfolio).

Intramonth Credit Dynamics

Related to the last point is the matter of what might be done for an issue that is investment grade at the start of a month but is downgraded to non-

---

[1] A dollar roll might be defined as a reverse repo transaction with a few twists. For example, a reverse repo trade is generally regarded as a lending/borrowing transaction, whereas a dollar roll is regarded as an actual sale/repurchase of securities. Further, when a Treasury is lent with a reverse repo, the same security is returned when the trade is unwound. With a dollar roll, all that is required is that a "substantially identical" pass-through be returned. Finally, while a reverse repo may be as short as an overnight or as long as mutually agreed on, a dollar roll is generally executed on a month-over-month basis. The *drop* on a reverse repo or dollar is the difference between the sale and repurchase price.

investment grade or to crossover intramonth. If portfolio managers own the issue, they may choose to sell immediately if they believe that the issue's performance will only get worse in ensuing days[2]. If this is indeed what happens, the total return for those portfolio managers will be better than the total return as recorded in the index. The reason is that the index returns are typically calculated as month over month, and the index takes the pre-downgrade price at the start of the month and the devalued postdowngrade price at the end of the month.

If the portfolio managers do not own the downgraded issue, they may have the opportunity to buy at its distressed levels. Obviously, such a purchase is warranted only if the managers believe that the evolving credit story will be stable to improving and if the new credit rating is consistent with their investment parameters. This scenario might be especially interesting when there is a downgrade situation involving a preexisting pair of investment-grade ratings that changes into a crossover story.

As an opposite scenario, consider the instance of a credit that is upgraded from noninvestment grade at the start of the month to investment grade or crossover intramonth. Portfolio managers who own the issue and perceive the initial spread narrowing as "overdone" can sell and realize a greater total return relative to the index calculation, which will reference the issue's price only at month-end. And if the managers believe that the price of the upgraded issue will only improve to the end of the month, they may want to add it to their investment-grade portfolio before its inclusion in the index. Moreover, since many major indices make any adjustments at month-end, the upgraded issue will not be moved into the investment-grade index until the end of the month; beginning price at that time will be the already-appreciated price.

Marking Conventions

All indexes use some sort of convention when their daily marks are posted. It might be 3:00 P.M. New York time when the futures market closes for the day session, or it may be 5:00 P.M. New York time when the cash market closes for the day session. Any gaps in these windows generate an option for incremental return trading. Of course, regardless of marking convention, all marks eventually "catch up" as a previous day's close rolls into the next business day's subsequent open.

---

[2] Portfolio managers generally have some time—perhaps up to one quarter—to unload a security that has turned from investment grade to noninvestment grade. However, a number of indexed portfolio managers rebalance portfolios at each month-end; thus there may be opportunities to purchase distressed securities at that time.

Modeling Conventions

With nonbullet securities, measuring duration is less of a science and more of an art. There are as many different potential measures for option-adjusted duration as there are option methodologies to calculate them. In this respect, concepts such as duration buckets and linking duration risk to market return become rather important. While these differences would presumably be consistent—a model that has a tendency to skew the duration of a particular structure would be expected to skew that duration in the same way most of the time—this may nonetheless present a wedge between index and portfolio dynamics.

Option Strategies

Selling (writing) call options against the underlying cash portfolio may provide the opportunity to outperform with a combination of factors. Neither listed nor over-the-counter (OTC) options are included in any of the standard fixed income indexes today. Although short call positions are embedded in callables and MBS pass-thrus making these de facto buy/write positions, the use of listed or OTC products allows an investor to tailor-make a buy/write program ideally suited to a portfolio manager's outlook on rates and volatility. And, of course, the usual expirations for the listed and OTC structures are typically much shorter than those embedded in debentures and pass-thrus. This is of importance if only because of the role of time decay with a short option position; a good rule of thumb is that time decay erodes at the rate of the square root of an option's remaining life. For example, one-half of an option's remaining time decay will erode in the last one-quarter of the option's life. For an investor who is short an option, speedy time decay is generally a favorable event. Because there are appreciable risks to the use of options with strategy building, investors should consider all the implications before delving into such a program.

Maturity and Size Restrictions

Many indexes have rules related to a minimum maturity (generally one year) and a minimum size of initial offerings. Being cognizant of these rules may help to identify opportunities to buy unwanted issues (typically at a month-end) or selectively add security types that may not precisely conform to index specifications. As related to the minimum maturity consideration, one strategy might be to barbell into a two-year duration with a combination of a six-month money market product (or Treasury bill) and a three-year issue. This one trade may *step outside* of an index in two ways: (1) It invests in a product not in the index (less than one year to maturity), and (2) it creates a curve exposure not in the index (via the barbell).

Convexity Strategies

An MBS portfolio may very well be duration-matched to an index and matched on a cash flow and curve basis, but mismatched on convexity. That is, the portfolio may carry more or less convexity relative to the benchmark, and in this way the portfolio may be better positioned for a market move.

Trades at the Front of the Curve

Finally, there may be opportunities to construct strategies around selective additions to particular asset classes and especially at the front of the yield curve. A very large portion of the investment-grade portion of bond indices is comprised of low-credit-risk securities with short maturities (of less than five years). Accordingly, by investing in moderate-credit-risk securities with short maturities, extra yield and return may be generated.

Table A4.1 summarizes return-enhancing strategies for relative return portfolios broken out by product types. Again, the table is intended to be more conceptual than a carved-in-stone overview of what strategies can be implemented with the indicated product(s).

Conclusion

An index is simply one enemy among several for portfolio managers. For example, any and every debt issuer can be a potential enemy that can be analyzed and scrutinized for the purpose of trying to identify and capture

TABLE A4.1 Fund Strategies in Relation to Product Types

Strategy	Bonds	Equities	Currencies	
Product selection	√	√		
Sector mix	√	√		
Cash flow reinvestment	√	√		
Securities lending	√	√		
Securities going in/out	√	√		Cash flows
Index price marks vs. the market's prices	√	√		
Buy/writes	√	√	√	
Size changes	√			
Convexity				
Cross-over credits	√	⎫ Credit		
Credit changes	√	⎭		

something that others do not or cannot see. In the U.S. Treasury market, an investor's edge may come from correctly anticipating and benefiting from a fundamental shift in the Treasury's debt program away from issuing longer-dated securities in favor of shorter-dated securities. In the credit markets, an investor's edge may consist of picking up on a key change in a company's fundamentals before the rating agencies do and carefully anticipating an upgrade in a security's credit status. In fact, there are research efforts today where the objective is to correctly anticipate when a rating agency may react favorably or unfavorably to a particular credit rating and to assist with being favorably positioned prior to any actual announcement being made. But make no mistake about it. Correctly anticipating and benefiting from an issuer (the Treasury example) and/or an arbiter of issuers (the credit rating agency example) can be challenging indeed.

CHAPTER 5

Risk Management

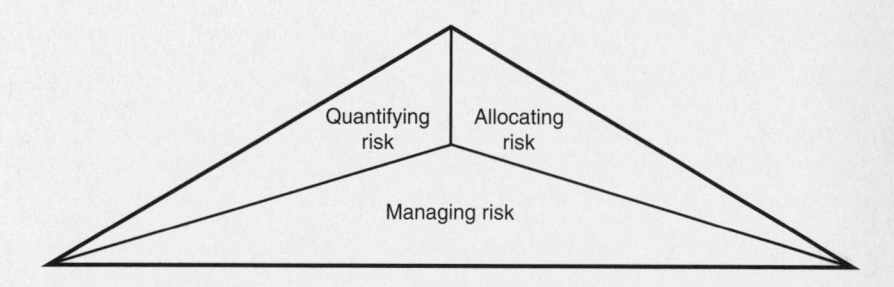

```
         Quantifying  | Allocating
            risk      |    risk
              Managing risk
```

This chapter examines ways that financial risks can be quantified, the means by which risk can be allocated within an asset class or portfolio, and the ways risk can be managed effectively.

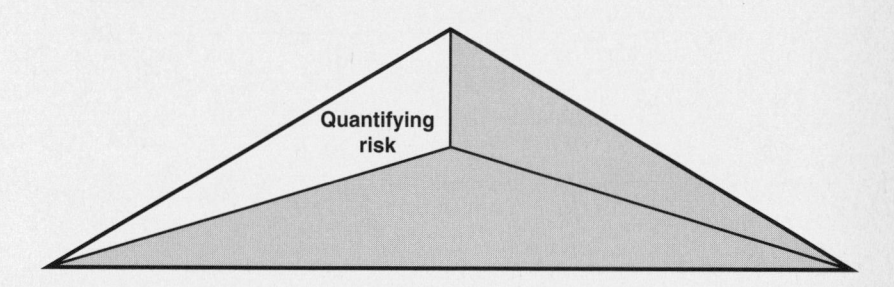

```
      Quantifying
         risk
```

Generally speaking, "risk" in the financial markets essentially comes down to a risk of adverse changes in price. What exactly is meant by the term "adverse" varies by investor and strategy. An absolute return investor could well have a higher tolerance for price variability than a relative return investor. And for an investor who is short the market, a dramatic fall in prices may not be seen as a risk event but as a boon to her portfolio. This chapter does not attempt to pass judgment on what amount of risk is good or bad; such a determination is a function of many things, many of which (like risk appetite or level of understanding of complex strategies) are entirely subject to particular contexts and individual competencies. Rather the text highlights a few commonly applied risk management tools beginning with

171

products in the context of spot, then proceeding to options, forwards and futures, and concluding with credit.

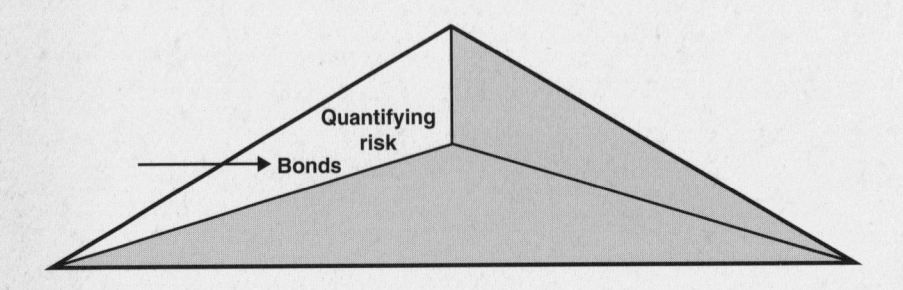

BOND PRICE RISK: DURATION AND CONVEXITY

In the fixed income world, interest rate risk is generally quantified in terms of duration and convexity. Table 5.1 provides total return calculations for three Treasury securities. Using a three-month investment horizon, it is clear that return profiles are markedly different across securities.

The 30-year Treasury STRIPS[1] offers the greatest potential return if yields fall. However, at the same time, the 30-year Treasury STRIPS could well suffer a dramatic loss if yields rise. At the other end of the spectrum, the six-month Treasury bill provides the lowest potential return if yields fall yet offers the greatest amount of protection if yields rise. In an attempt to quantify these different risk/return profiles, many fixed income investors evaluate the duration of respective securities.

Duration is a measure of a fixed income security's price sensitivity to a given change in yield. The larger a security's duration, the more sensitive that security's price will be to a change in yield. A desirable quality of duration is that it serves to standardize yield sensitivities across all cash fixed income securities. This can be of particular value when attempting to quantify differences across varying maturity dates, coupon values, and yields. The duration of a three-month Treasury bill, for example, can be evaluated on an apples-to-apples basis against a 30-year Treasury STRIPS or any other Treasury security.

The following equations provide duration calculations for a variety of securities.

---

[1] STRIPS is an acronym for Separately Traded Registered Interest and Principal Security. It is a bond that pays no coupon. Its only cash flow consists of what it pays at maturity.

Risk Management

TABLE 5.1 Total Return Calculations for Three Treasury Securities on a Bond-Equivalent Basis, 3-Month Horizon

Change in Yield Level (basis points)	Treasury Bill (1 year) (%)	7.75% Treasury Note (10 year) (%)	Treasury STRIPS (30 year) (%)
−100	8.943	36.800	75.040
−50	7.580	21.870	39.100
0	6.229	8.030	7.920
+50	4.883	−4.820	−19.130
+100	3.545	−16.750	−42.610

To calculate duration for a Treasury bill, we solve for:

$$\text{Duration} = \frac{P}{P} \frac{T_{sm}}{365}$$

where P = Price
T_{sm} = Time in days from settlement to maturity

The denominator of the second term is 365 because it is the market's convention to express duration on a *bond-equivalent basis*, and as presented in Chapter 2, a bond-equivalent calculation assumes a 365-day year and semiannual coupon payments.

To calculate duration for a Treasury STRIPS, we solve for:

$$\text{Duration} = \frac{P}{P} T_{sm}$$

where T_{sm} = Time from settlement to maturity in years.

It is a little more complex to calculate duration for a coupon security. One popular method is to solve for the first derivative of the price/yield equation with respect to yield using a Taylor series expansion. We use a price/yield equation as follows:

$$P_d = \frac{F \times C/2}{(1 + Y/2)^{T_{sc}/T_c}} + \frac{F \times C/2}{(1 + Y/2)^{T_{sc}/T_c}} + \dots \frac{F(1 + C/2)}{(1 + Y/2)^{N-1+T_{sc}/T_c}}$$

where P_d = Dirty price
F = Face value (par)

C = Coupon (annual %)
Y = Bond-equivalent yield
T_{sc} = Time in days from settlement to coupon payment
T_c = Time in days from last coupon payment (or issue date) to next coupon date

The solution for duration using calculus may be written as $(dP'/dY)P'$, where P' is dirty price. J. R. Hicks first proposed this method in 1939.

The price/yield equation can be greatly simplified with the Greek symbol sigma, Σ, which means summation. Rewriting the price/yield equation using sigma, we have:

$$P_d = \sum_{t=1}^{T} \frac{C'_t}{(1 + Y/2)^t}$$

where P_d = Dirty price
Σ = Summation
T = Total number of cash flows in the life of a security
C'_t = Cash flows over the life of a security (cash flows include coupons up to maturity, and coupons plus principal at maturity)
Y = Bond-equivalent yield
t = Time in days security is owned from one coupon period to the next divided by time in days from last coupon paid (or issue date) to next coupon date

Moving along then, another way to calculate duration is to solve for

$$\frac{\sum_{t=1}^{T} \frac{C'_t \times t}{(1 + Y/2)^t}}{\sum_{t=1}^{T} \frac{C'_t}{(1 + Y/2)^t}}$$

There is but a subtle difference between the formula for duration and the price/yield formula. In particular, the numerator of the duration formula is the same as the price/yield formula except that cash flows are a product of time (t). The denominator of the duration formula is exactly the same as the price/yield formula. Thus, it may be said that duration is a time-weighted average value of cash flows.

Frederick Macaulay first proposed the calculation above. *Macaulay's duration* assumes continuous compounding while Treasury coupon securities are generally compounded on an actual/actual (or discrete) basis. To adjust Macaulay's duration to allow for discrete compounding, we solve for:

$$D_{mod} = \frac{D_{mac}}{(1 + Y/2)}$$

where D_{mod} = Modified duration
D_{mac} = Macaulay's duration
Y = Bond-equivalent yield

This measure of duration is known as *modified duration* and is generally what is used in the marketplace. Hicks's method to calculate duration is consistent with the properties of modified duration. This text uses modified duration.

Table 5.2 calculates duration for a five-year Treasury note using Macaulay's methodology. The modified duration of this 5-year security is 4.0503 years.

For Treasury bills and Treasury STRIPS, Macaulay's duration is nothing more than time in years from settlement to maturity dates. For coupon securities, Macaulay's duration is the product of cash flows and time divided by cash flows where cash flows are in present value terms.

Using the equations and Treasury securities from above, we calculate Macaulay duration values to be:

1-year Treasury bill, 0.9205
7.75% 10-year Treasury note, 7.032
30-year Treasury STRIPS, 29.925

Modified durations on the same three Treasury securities are:

Treasury bill, 0.8927
Treasury note, 6.761
Treasury STRIPS, 28.786

The summation of column (D) gives us the value for the numerator of the duration formula, and the summation of column (C) gives us the value for the denominator of the duration formula. Note that the summation of column (C) is also the dirty price of this Treasury note.

$$D_{mac} = 833.5384/98.9690 = 8.4222 \text{ in half years}$$
$$8.4222/2 = 4.2111 \text{ in years}$$

TABLE 5.2 Calculating Duration

(A) C'_t	(B) t	(C) $C'_t/(1+Y/2)^t$	(D) (B) × (C)
3.8125	0.9344	3.6763	3.4352
3.8125	1.9344	3.6763	6.8399
3.8125	2.9344	3.4009	9.9796
3.8125	3.9344	3.2710	12.8694
3.8125	4.9344	3.1461	15.5240
3.8125	5.9344	3.0259	17.9571
3.8125	6.9344	2.9104	20.1817
3.8125	7.9344	2.7992	22.2102
3.8125	8.9344	2.6923	24.0544
103.8125	9.9344	70.5111	700.4868
Totals		98.9690	833.5384

Notes:
C'_t = Cash flows over the life of the security. Since this Treasury has a coupon of 7.625%, semiannual coupons are equal to 7.625/2 = 3.8125.
t = Time in days defined as the number of days the Treasury is held in a coupon period divided by the numbers of days from the last coupon paid (or issue date) to the next coupon payment. Since this Treasury was purchased 11 days after it was issued, the first coupon is discounted with t = 171/183 = 0.9344.
$C'_t/(1+Y/2)^t$ = Present value of a cash flow.
Y = Bond equivalent yield; 7.941%.

The convention is to express duration in years.

$$D_{mod} = D_{mac}/(1+Y/2)$$
$$= 4.2111/(1 + 0.039705)$$
$$= 4.0503$$

Modified duration values increase as we go from a Treasury bill to a coupon-bearing Treasury to a Treasury STRIPS, and this is consistent with our previously performed total returns analysis. That is, if duration is a measure of risk, it is not surprising that the Treasury bill has the lowest duration and the better relative performance when yields rise.

Table 5.3 contrasts true price values generated by a standard present value formula against estimated price values when a modified duration formula is used.

$$P_e = P_d \times (1 + D_{mod} \times \Delta Y)$$

where P_e = Price estimate
P_d = Dirty Price
D_{mod} = Modified duration
ΔY = Change in yield (100 basis points is written as 1.0)

Price differences widen between present value and modified duration calculations as changes in yield become more pronounced. Modified duration provides a less accurate price estimate as yield scenarios move farther away from the current market yield. Figure 5.1 highlights the differences between true and estimated prices.

While the price/yield relationship traced out by modified duration appears to be linear, the price/yield relationship traced out by present value appears to be curvilinear. As shown in Figure 5.1, actual bond prices do not change by a constant amount as yields change by fixed intervals.

Furthermore, the modified duration line is tangent to the present value line where there is zero change in yield. Thus modified duration can be derived from a present value equation by solving for the derivative of price with respect to yield.

Because modified duration posits a linear price/yield relationship while the true price/yield relationship for a fixed income security is curvilinear, modified duration provides an inexact estimate of price for a given change in yield. This estimate is less accurate as we move farther away from current market levels.

TABLE 5.3 True versus Estimated Price Values Generated by Present Value and Modified Duration, 7.75% 30-year Treasury Bond

Change in Yield Level (basis points)	Price plus Accrued Interest; Present Value Equation	Price plus Accrued Interest; Duration Equation	Difference
+400	76.1448	71.5735	4.5713
+300	81.0724	78.2050	2.8674
+200	86.4398	84.8365	1.6033
+100	92.2917	91.4681	0.8236
0	98.0996	98.0996	0.0000
−100	105.6525	104.7311	0.9214
−200	113.2777	111.3227	1.9550
−300	121.6210	117.9942	3.6268
−400	130.7582	124.6257	6.1325

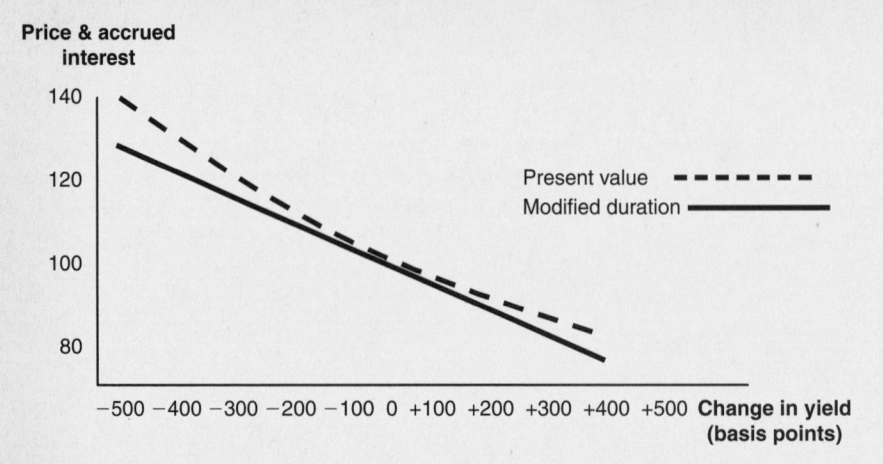

178 FINANCIAL ENGINEERING, RISK MANAGEMENT, AND MARKET ENVIRONMENT

FIGURE 5.1 A comparison of price/yield relationships, duration versus present value.

Figure 5.2 shows price/yield relationships implied by modified duration for two of the three Treasury securities. While the slope of Treasury bill's modified duration function is relatively flat, the slope of Treasury STRIPS is relatively steep. An equal change in yield for the Treasury bill and Treasury STRIPS will suggest very different changes in price. The price of a Treasury STRIPS will change by more, because the STRIPS has a greater modified duration. The STRIPS has greater price sensitivity for a given change in yield.

If modified duration is of limited value, how can we better approximate a security's price? Or, to put it differently, how can we better approximate the price/yield property of a fixed income security as implied by the present value formula? With *convexity* (the curvature of a price/yield relationship for a bond).

To solve for convexity, we could go a step further with either the Hicks or the Macaulay methodology. Using the Hicks method, we would solve for the second derivative of the price/yield equation with respect to yield using a Taylor series expansion. This is expressed mathematically as $(d^2P'/dY^2)P'$, where P' is the dirty price.

To express this in yet another way, we proceed using Macaulay's methodology and solve for

Risk Management

%ΔP axis, ΔY axis, with Treasury bill and Treasury STRIPS lines shown.

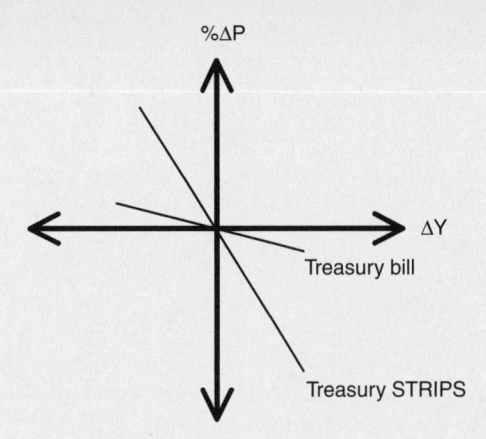

FIGURE 5.2 Price/yield relationships.

$$\frac{\sum_{t=1}^{T} \frac{C'_t \times t}{(1 + Y/2)^t} \times (t + 1)}{\sum_{t=1}^{T} \frac{C'_t}{(1 + Y/2)^t} \times 4 \times (1 + Y/2)^2}$$

Table 5.4 calculates convexity for a 7.625 percent 5-year Treasury note of 5/31/96. We calculate it to be 20.1036.

Estimating price using both modified duration and convexity requires solving for

$$P_e = P_d + P_d (D_{mod} \times \Delta Y + \text{Convexity} \times \Delta Y^2/2)$$

Let us now use the formula above to estimate prices. Table 5.5 shows how true versus estimated price differences are significantly reduced relative to when we used duration alone. Incorporating derivatives of a higher order beyond duration and convexity could reduce residual price differences between true and estimated values even further.

Figure 5.3 provides a graphical representation of how much closer the combination of duration and convexity can approximate a true present value.

The figure highlights the difference between estimated price/yield relationships using modified duration alone and modified duration with con-

TABLE 5.4 Calculating Convexity

(A) C'	(B) t	(C) $C'/(1+Y/2)^t$	(D) $(B) \times (C)$	(E) $(C) \times (B)^2$	(F) (D)
3.8125	0.9344	3.6763	3.4352	3.2100	6.6452
3.8125	1.9344	3.5359	6.8399	13.2313	20.0712
3.8125	2.9344	3.4009	9.9796	29.2843	39.2638
3.8125	3.9344	3.2710	12.8694	50.6338	63.5033
3.8125	4.9344	3.1461	15.5240	76.6022	92.1263
3.8125	5.9344	3.0259	17.9571	106.5652	124.5223
3.8125	6.9344	2.9104	20.1817	139.9487	160.1304
3.8125	7.9344	2.7992	22.2102	176.2255	198.4357
3.8125	8.9344	2.6923	24.0544	214.9121	238.9665
103.8125	9.9344	70.5111	700.4868	6958.9345	7659.4031
Totals		98.9690	833.5384	7769.5475	8603.0678

Notes:
C' = Cash flows over the life of the security. Since this Treasury has a coupon of 7.625%, semiannual coupons are equal to 7.625/2 =3.8125.
t = Time in days defined as the number of days the Treasury is held in a coupon period divided by the number of days from the last coupon paid (or issue date) to the next coupon payment. Since this Treasury was purchased 11 days after it was issued, the first coupon is discounted with t = 171/183 =0.9344.
$C'/(1+Y/2)$ = Present value of a cash flow.
Y = Bond-equivalent yield; 7.941%.
Columns (A) through (D) are exactly the same as in Table 5.3 where we calculated this Treasury's duration. The summation of column (F) gives us the numerator for our convexity formula. The denominator of our convexity formula is obtained by calculating the product of column (C) and $4 \times (1+Y/2)^2$. Thus,
Convexity = 8603.0678 / (98.9690 $\times$ 4 $\times$ (1+0.039705)^2)
= 20.1036

vexity; it helps to show that convexity is a desirable property. Convexity means that prices fall by *less* than that implied by modified duration when yields *rise* and that prices rise by *more* than that implied by modified duration when yields *fall*. We return to the concepts of modified duration and convexity later in this chapter when we discuss managing risk.

Risk Management

TABLE 5.5 True versus Estimated Price Values Generated by Present Value and Modified Duration and Convexity, 7.75% 30-year Treasury Bond

Change in Yield Level (basis points)	Price plus Accrued Interest, Present Value Equation	Price plus Accrued Interest, Duration and Convexity Equation	Difference
+ 400	76.1448	76.2541	(0.1090)
+ 300	81.0724	80.8378	0.2350
+ 200	86.4398	86.0067	0.4330
+ 100	92.2917	91.7606	0.5311
0	98.0996	98.0996	0.0000
− 100	105.6525	105.0237	0.6290
− 200	113.2777	112.5328	0.7449
− 300	121.6210	120.6270	0.9440
− 400	130.7582	129.3063	1.4519

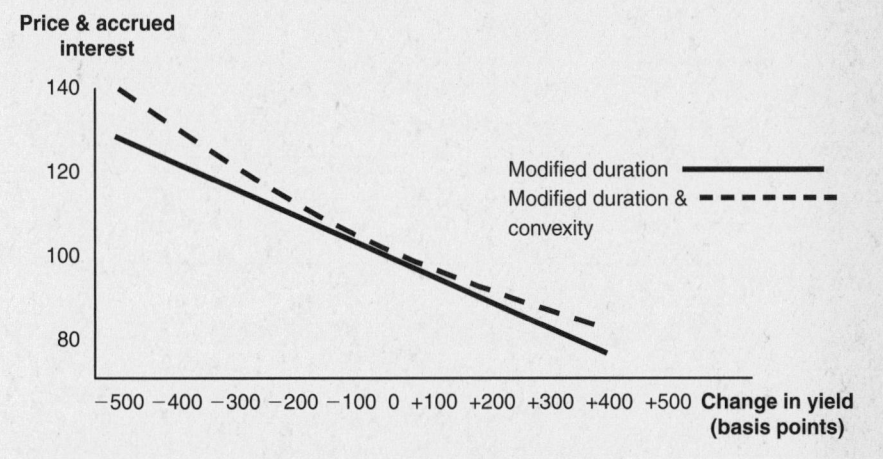

FIGURE 5.3 A comparison of price/yield relationships, duration versus duration and convexity.

To summarize, duration and convexity are important risk-measuring variables for bonds. While duration might be sufficient for scenarios where only small changes in yield are involved, both duration and convexity generally are required to capture the full effect of a price change in most fixed income securities.

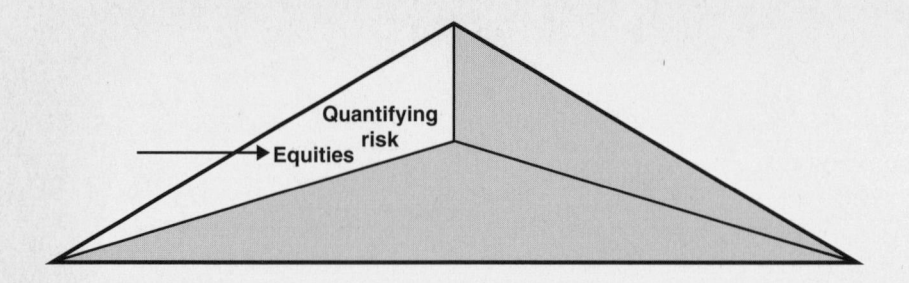

EQUITY PRICE RISK: BETA

The concepts of duration and convexity can be difficult to apply to equities. The single most difficult obstacle to overcome is the fact that equities do not have final maturity dates, although the issue that an equity's price is thus unconstrained in contrast to bonds (where at least we know it will mature at par if it is held until then) can be overcome.[2]

One variable that can come close to the concept of duration for equities is beta. Duration can be defined as measuring a bond's price sensitivity to a change in interest rates; beta can be defined as an equity's price sensitivity to a change in the S&P 500. As a rather simplistic way of testing this interrelationship, let us calculate beta for a five-year Treasury bond. But instead of calculating beta against the S&P 500, we calculate it against a generic U.S. bond index (comprising government, *mortgage-backed securities*, and investment-grade [triple-B and higher] corporate securities). Doing this, we arrive at a beta of 0.78.[3] Hence, in the same way that duration can give us a measure of a single bond's price sensitivity to interest rates, a beta calculation (which requires two series of data) can give us a measure of a bond's price sensitivity in relation to another series (e.g., bond index). Accordingly, two interest rate–sensitive series can be linked and quantified using a beta measure.

---

[2] One way to arrive at a sort of proxy of duration for an equity is to calculate a correlation for the equity versus a series of bonds sharing a comparable credit risk profile. If it is possible to identify a reasonable pairing of an equity to a bond that generates a correlation coefficient of close to 1.0, then it could be said that the equity has a quasi-duration measure that's roughly comparable to the duration of the bond it is paired against. All else being equal, such strong correlation coefficients are strongest for companies with a particular sensitivity to interest rates (as are finance companies or real estate ventures or firms with large debt burdens).
[3] A five-year Treasury was selected since it has a modified duration that is close to the modified duration of the generic index we used for this calculation. We used monthly data over a particular three-year period where there was an up, down, and steady pattern in the market overall.

Risk Management

As already stated, beta is a statistical measure of the expected increase in the value of one variable for a one-unit increase in the value of another variable. The formula[4] for beta is

$$\beta = \text{cov}(a,b) / \sigma^2(b)$$
$$\text{cov}(a,b) = \rho(a,b) \times \sigma(a) \times \sigma(b),$$

where σ^2 = Sigma squared (variance); standard deviation squared
ρ = Rho, correlation coefficient
σ = Sigma, standard deviation

Sigma is a standard variable in finance that quantifies the variability or volatility of a series. Its formula is simply

$$\sum_{t=1}^{T} \sqrt{\frac{(\bar{x} - x_t)^2}{n - 1}}$$

where $\bar{x}$ = Mean (average) of the series
x_t = Each of the individual observations within the series
n = Total number of observations in the series

A correlation coefficient is a statistical measure of the relationship between two variables. A correlation coefficient can range in value between positive 1 and negative 1. A positive correlation coefficient with a value near 1 suggests that the two variables are closely related and tend to move in tandem. A negative correlation coefficient with a value near 1 suggests that two variables are closely related and tend to move opposite one another. A correlation coefficient with a value near zero, regardless of its sign, suggests that the two variables have little in common and tend to behave independently of one another. Figure 5.4 provides a graphical representation of positive, negative, and zero correlations.

Figure 5.5 presents a conceptual perspective of beta in the context of equities. There are three categories: betas equal to 1, betas greater than 1, and betas less than 1. Each of the betas was calculated for individual equities relative to the S&P 500. A beta equal to 1 suggests that the individual equity has a price sensitivity in line with the S&P 500, a beta of greater than 1suggests an equity with a price sensitivity greater than the S&P 500, and a beta

---

[4]A beta can be calculated with an ordinary least squares (OLS) regression. Consistent with the central limit theorem, any OLS regression ought to have a minimum of about 30 observations per series. Further, an investor ought to be aware of the assumptions inherent in any OLS regression analysis. These assumptions, predominantly concerned with randomness, are provided in any basic statistics text.

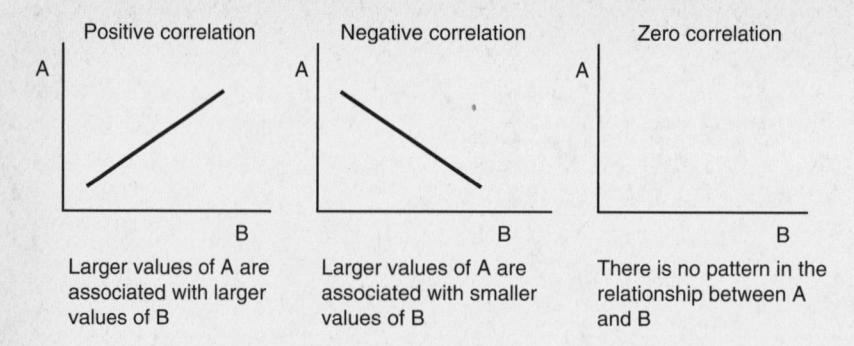

```
        Positive correlation              Negative correlation                Zero correlation
    A                                 A                                   A
           /                                \
          /                                  \
         /                                    \
              B                                   B                                  B
    Larger values of A are          Larger values of A are         There is no pattern in the
    associated with larger          associated with smaller        relationship between A
    values of B                     values of B                    and B
```

FIGURE 5.4 Positive, negative, and zero correlations.

of less than 1 suggests an equity with a price sensitivity that is less than the S&P 500. After calculating betas for individual equities and then grouping those individual companies into their respective industry categories, industry averages were calculated.[5] As shown, an industry with a particularly low beta value is water utilities, an industry with a particularly high beta value is semiconductors, and an industry type with a beta of unity is tires.

To the experienced market professional, there is nothing new or shocking to the results. Water utilities tend to be highly regulated businesses and are often thought fairly well insulated from credit risk since they are typically linked with government entities. Indeed, some investors believe that holding water utility equities is nearly equivalent in risk terms to holding utility bonds. Of course, this is not a hard-and-fast rule, and works best when evaluated on a case-by-case basis. At the very least, this low beta value suggests that water utility equity prices may be more sensitive to some other variable— perhaps interest rates. In support of this, many utilities do carry significant debt, and debt is most certainly sensitive to interest rate dynamics.

On the other end of the continuum are semiconductors at 2.06. Again, market professionals would not be surprised to see a technology-sector equity with a market risk factor appreciably above the market average. Quite simply, technology equities have been a volatile sector, as they are relatively new and untested—at least relative to, say, autos (sporting a beta of 0.95) or broadcasting (with a beta of 1.05).

And what can we say about tires? In good times and bad, people drive their cars and tires become worn. The industry sector is not considered to be particularly speculative, and the market players are generally well known.

In a sense, the S&P 500 serves as a line in the sand as a risk management tool. That is, we are picking a neutral market measure (the S&P 500)

---

[5] "Using Target Return on Equity and Cost of Equity," Parker Center, Cornell University, May 1999.

Risk Management

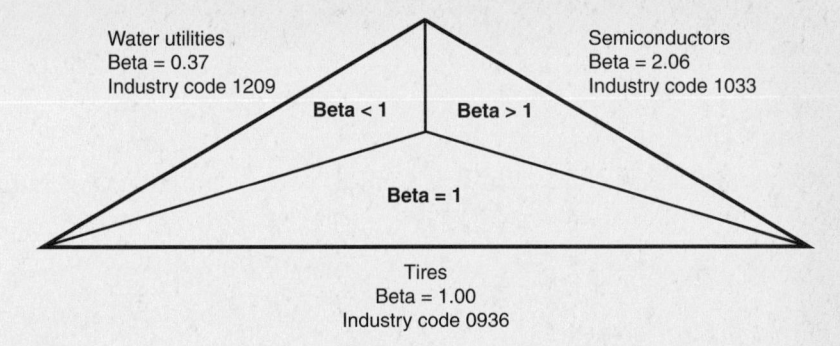

```
        Water utilities                          Semiconductors
        Beta = 0.37                              Beta = 2.06
        Industry code 1209                       Industry code 1033
                       Beta < 1   |   Beta > 1

                             Beta = 1

                              Tires
                            Beta = 1.00
                        Industry code 0936
```

FIGURE 5.5 Beta by industry types.

and are essentially saying: Equities with a risk profile above this norm (at least as measured by standard deviation) are riskier and equities below this norm are less risky. But such a high-level breakdown of risk has all the flaws of using a five-year Treasury duration as a line in the sand and saying that any bond with duration above the five-year Treasury's is riskier and anything below it is less risky. However, since equity betas are calculated using price, and to the extent that an equity's price can embody and reflect the risks inherent in a particular company (at least to the extent that those risks can be publicly communicated and, hence, incorporated into the company's valuation), then equity beta calculations can be said to be of some value as a relative risk measure. The hard work of absolute risk measurement (digging through a company's financial statements) can certainly result in unique insights as well.

Finally, just as beta or duration can be calculated for individual equities and bonds, betas and durations can be calculated for entire portfolios. For an equity portfolio, a beta can be derived using the daily price history of the portfolio and the daily price history of the S&P 500. For a bond portfolio, individual security durations can be aggregated into a single portfolio duration by simply weighting the individual durations by their market value contribution to the portfolio.

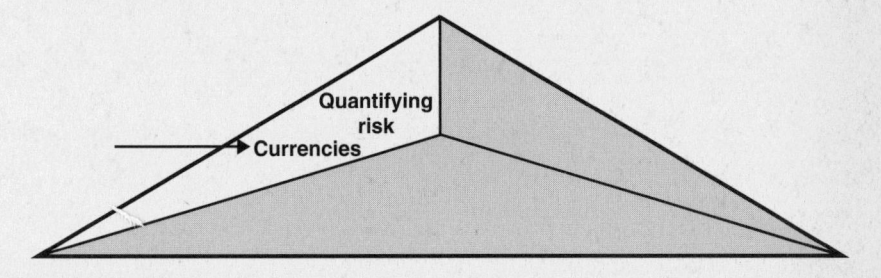

```
                        Quantifying
                           risk
              →→→    Currencies
```

As a first layer of currency types, there are countries with their own unique national currency. Examples include the United States as well as other Group of 10 (G-10) members. The next layer of currency types would include those countries that have adopted a G-10 currency as their own. An example of this would be Panama, which has adopted the U.S. dollar as its national currency. As perhaps one small step from this type of arrangement, there are other countries whose currency is linked to another at a fixed rate of exchange. A number of countries in western Africa, for example, have currencies that trade at a fixed ratio to the euro. Indeed, where arrangements such as these exist in the world, it is not at all uncommon for both the local currency and "sponsor" currency to be readily accepted in local markets since the fixed relationship is generally well known and embraced by respective economic agents.

Perhaps the next step from this type of relationship is where a currency is informally linked not to one sponsor currency, but to a basket of sponsor currencies. In most instances where this is practiced, the percentage weighting assigned to particular currencies within the basket has a direct relationship with the particular country's trading patterns. For the country that accounts for, say, 60 percent of the base country's exports, the weighting of the other country's currency within the basket would be 60 percent. Quite simply, the rationale for linking the weightings to trade flows is to help ensure a stable relationship between the overall purchasing power of a base currency relative to the primary sources of goods purchased with the base currency. A real-world example of this type of arrangement would be Sweden. The next step away from this type of setup is where a country has an official and publicly announced policy of tracking a basket of currencies but does not formally state which currencies are being tracked and/or with what percentages. Singapore is an example of a currency-type in this particular category.

Figure 5.6 provides a conceptual ranking (from low to high) of price risk that might be associated with various currency classifications.

One other way to think of price risk is in the context of planets and satellites. On this basis, four candidates for planets might include the U.S. dollar, the Japanese yen, the euro, and the United Kingdom's pound sterling. Orbiting around the U.S. dollar we might expect to see the Panamanian dollar, the Canadian dollar, and the Mexican peso. Orbiting around the yen we might expect to see the Hong Kong dollar, the Australian dollar, and the New Zealand dollar. Perhaps a useful guide with respect to determining respective orbits precisely would be respective correlation coefficients. That is, if the degree of comovement of a planet currency to a given satellite were quite strong and positively related, then we would expect a rather close orbit. As the correlation coefficient weakens, we would expect the distance from the relevant planet to increase. Figure 5.7 provides a sample of this particular concept.

Statistical consistency suggests that there is a relationship between the strength of a correlation coefficient and the volatility of a particular currency

Risk Management

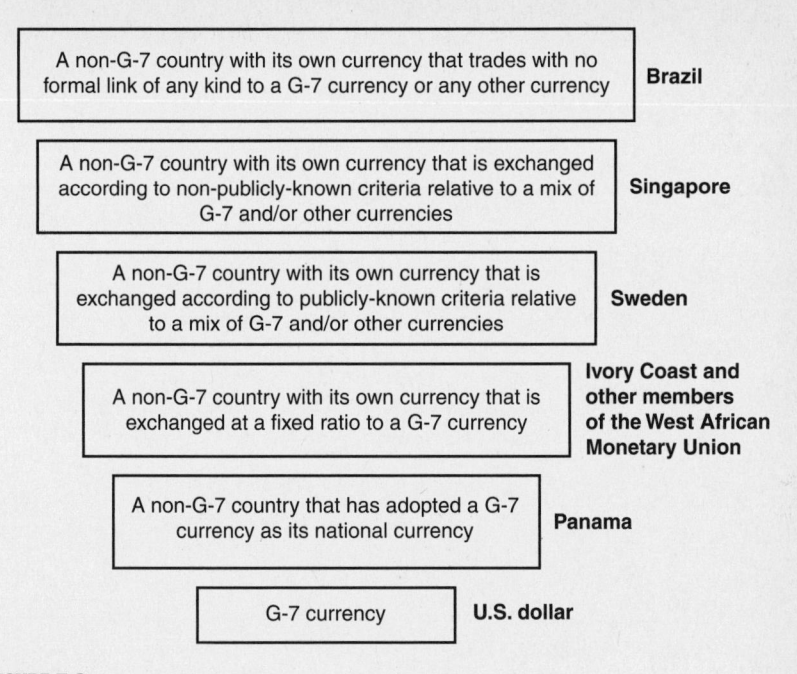

A non-G-7 country with its own currency that trades with no formal link of any kind to a G-7 currency or any other currency	Brazil
A non-G-7 country with its own currency that is exchanged according to non-publicly-known criteria relative to a mix of G-7 and/or other currencies	Singapore
A non-G-7 country with its own currency that is exchanged according to publicly-known criteria relative to a mix of G-7 and/or other currencies	Sweden
A non-G-7 country with its own currency that is exchanged at a fixed ratio to a G-7 currency	Ivory Coast and other members of the West African Monetary Union
A non-G-7 country that has adopted a G-7 currency as its national currency	Panama
G-7 currency	U.S. dollar

FIGURE 5.6 Price risk by currency classification.

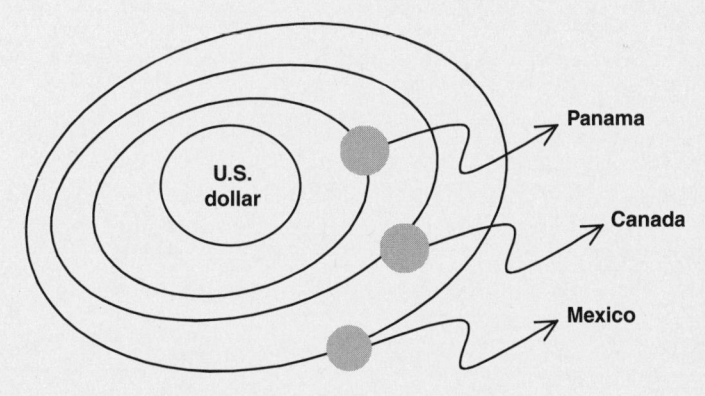

FIGURE 5.7 Price risk in the context of planets and satellites.

pairing. That is, correlation coefficients are expected to weaken as the volatility between two currencies (as measured by standard deviation) increases. Accordingly, and in contrast with what an investor might expect to see, Panama is shown as having a closer orbit to the U.S. dollar than Canada. The reason for this is that there is no volatility whatsoever between Panama's currency and the U.S. dollar; in fact, the volatility is zero. Why? Because Panama has adopted the U.S. dollar as its own national currency. However, this is not to say that commerce with Panama is not without potential currency risk. Namely, just as Panama decided to use the U.S. dollar as its national currency, it might decide tomorrow that it no longer wants the U.S. dollar as its national currency. With respect to Canada, the correlation between the U.S. dollar and Canadian dollar has historically been quite strong.

Something that a correlation coefficient cannot convey adequately is the degree to which a planet country (or grouping of planet countries) may or may not be willing to help bail out a satellite country in the event of a particularly stressful episode. An example of single-planet assistance would be the United States and Mexico in 1994–1995. An example of a collection of planets (and satellites, for that matter) supporting another entity would be International Monetary Fund loans to Russia and Eastern Europe in 1998. These more obvious examples (and certainly many others could be cited) reinforce the notion of credit risk within the global marketplace—credit risk that is, in this particular context, at a sovereign level.

And as one other consideration here, it may not necessarily be a positive phenomenon in every instance for a satellite currency to have a close orbit with a planet currency. Planet currencies do indeed experience their own volatility, and a reasonable expectation would be to see volatility among satellite currencies at least as great as that experienced by respective planet currencies, perhaps even greater as correlation coefficients weaken. The rationale for this expectation is simply that when times get tough and uncertain, currencies with a less obvious link to tried-and-true experiences are more likely to be hurt than helped in fast-moving uncertain markets.

As alluded to previously, currencies do not trade on a particular exchange, but are traded as nonlisted or over-the-counter products. Accordingly, no certificate is received, as with an equity purchase. In this sense, there is really nothing that we can touch or feel when we own currencies, except, of course, for the currency itself. Some kind of formal receipt or bank statement might be the closest currency investors get to their trades in the currency market.

How do we judge what a given currency's value should be? Again, just as an equity's value is expressed as being worth so many dollars (or euro or yen etc.), a dollar's value is expressed as being worth so many yen or euro or whatever other currency is of interest to us. A stronger dollar simply means that it takes fewer dollars to buy the same amount of another currency, a weaker dollar requires that more dollars must be spent to acquire the same amount of the other currency.

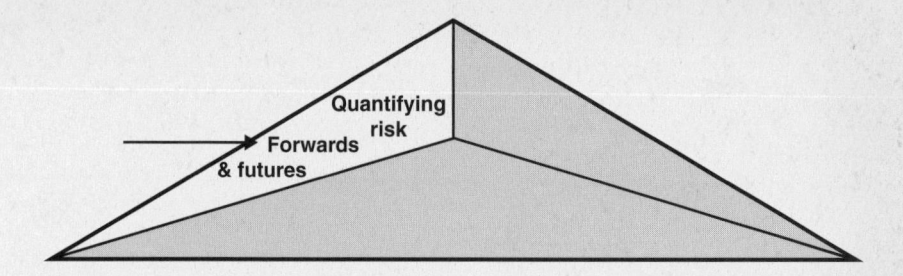

Recall from Chapter 2 that forwards and futures are essentially differentiated from spot by cost of carry (SRT). It is not difficult to show how spot-based risk measures such as duration and convexity can be extended from a spot to a forward context. Here we also discuss unique considerations pertaining to financing risk (via the R in SRT) for all products (though especially for bonds), and conclude by showing how forwards and futures can be used to hedge spot transactions.

Calculating a forward duration or convexity is simple enough. We already know from the duration and convexity formulas that required inputs include price, yield, and time; these are the same for forward calculations. However, an important difference between a spot and forward duration or convexity calculation is that we are now dealing with a security that has a forward settlement date instead of an immediate one. Accordingly, when a forward duration or convexity is calculated, an existing spot security's duration and convexity are truncated by the time between the trade date and the expiration date of the forward agreement. Figure 5.8 helps to illustrate this point. Although the figure is for duration, the same concept applies for convexity. Further, although the figure also describes a forward contract, the same concept applies for futures contracts.

Notice how the potential duration profiles of the forward agreement in Figure 5.8 are not always a horizontal line as for the duration profile at *; they may reflect a slight slope. This slope represents the price sensitivity contribution that a forward embodies relative to the underlying spot. The precise price sensitivity is linked directly to the carry component of the forward. Recalling that the basic formula for a bond forward is $F = S(1 + T(R-Y_c))$ (where S for a bond is the bond's price, and duration is a measure of a bond's price sensitivity), it is the carry component (the $ST(R-Y_c)$ component) that affects the price sensitivity (or duration) of a forward transaction. Note that because R and Y_c tend to be small values, carry also will tend to be a small value. Observe also that because carry is a function of time (T), the incremental duration contribution made by carry will shrink as the expiration date of the forward approaches, and eventually disappears altogether at the

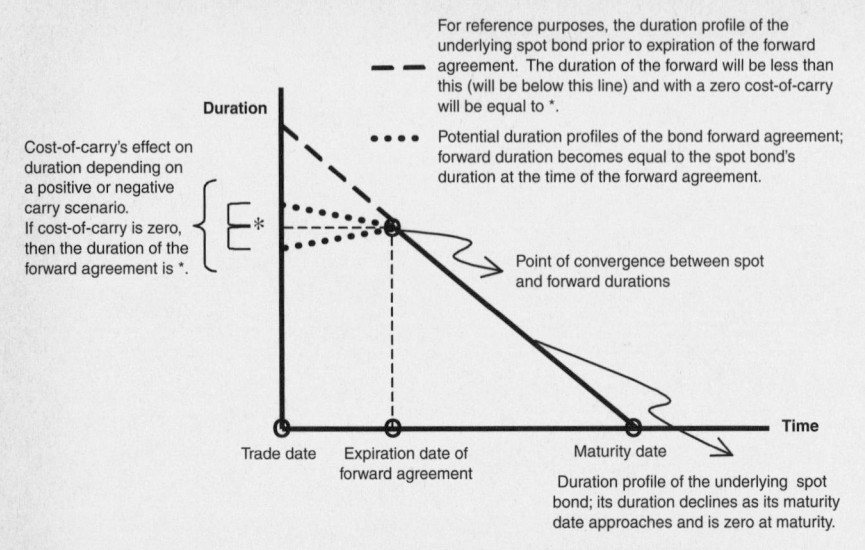

FIGURE 5.8 The relationship between cost-of-carry and duration.

forward's expiration. As a forward expiration date lengthens, carry will become larger (via a larger T value), and carry's positive or negative contribution to overall price sensitivity of the forward will increase. Whether the contribution to duration is positive or negative depends on whether carry is positive or negative. If carry is zero, then the duration of the forward over its life will be the duration of the underlying spot as calculated at the expiration date of the forward agreement. Indeed, as expirations lengthen, the importance of R and Y_c's contributions increases as well. Parenthetically, with longer-dated options as with LEAPS (*long-term equity anticipation securities*), unit changes in R can make as important a contribution to the value of the option as a unit change in the underlying spot.

In sum, and as shown in the figure, the duration of a forward is something less than the duration of its underlying spot. However, this lower level of market risk (via duration) should not be construed to be an overall reduction in risk with the strategy in general. That is, do not forget that a forward transaction means that payment is not exchanged for an asset until some time in the future; it is hoped that the counterparty to the trade will still be in business at that point in the future, but that is not 100 percent certain. Thus, the reduction in market risk (via duration) is accompanied by some element of credit risk (via delayed settlement).

Let us consider the forward duration value for an underlying security that does not yet exist. For example, consider the forward duration of a six-month Treasury bill 18 months forward. For relatively short financing horizons, the duration of a forward will not be much greater than the duration of the underlying spot security. Hence, the total forward duration of a six-month Treasury bill will not be much different from six months. However, it is appropriate to ask what yield the forward duration will be sensitive to if we assume that the risk-free rate is relatively constant; will it be sensitive to (a) changes in a generic 6-month Treasury bill spot yield, or (b) changes in the forward curve (which, by construction, embodies a six-month spot yield)? The answer is (b). Let us examine how and why this is the case.

Figure 5.9 shows that if this strategy is held to the expiration of the last remaining component, the investment horizon will stretch over two years: 18 months for the length of the forward contract and then an additional 6 months once the forward expires and is exchanged for the spot six-month Treasury bill.

Recall from Chapter 2 that we calculated an 18-month forward yield on a six-month Treasury bill to be 6.10 percent. Recall also that the step-by-step methodology used to arrive at that yield was such that a forward curve is embedded within the yield. This yield value of 6.10 percent is certainly not equal to the 4.75 percent spot yield value on a six-month Treasury bill referred to in Chapter 2, nor is it equal to the 5.5 percent spot yield value on the two-year Treasury bond cited there. In sum, despite the underlying security of this forward transaction being a spot six-month Treasury bill, and despite its having an investment horizon of two years, the relevant yield for duration/risk management purposes is neither one of these; it is the 18-month forward yield on an underlying six-month asset. Nonetheless, a fair question to pose might be: Is there a meaningful statistical correlation between an 18-month forward yield on an underlying six-month asset and the nominal yield

Forward yield is of relevance	Spot yield is of relevance	
Trade date Investor goes long an 18-month forward contract on an underlying 6-month Treasury bill.	**18 months later** Forward contract expires and is exchanged for spot 6-month Treasury bill. Convergence between spot and forward rates.	**24 months later** (6 months after forward expires) Treasury bill matures. **Investment horizon**

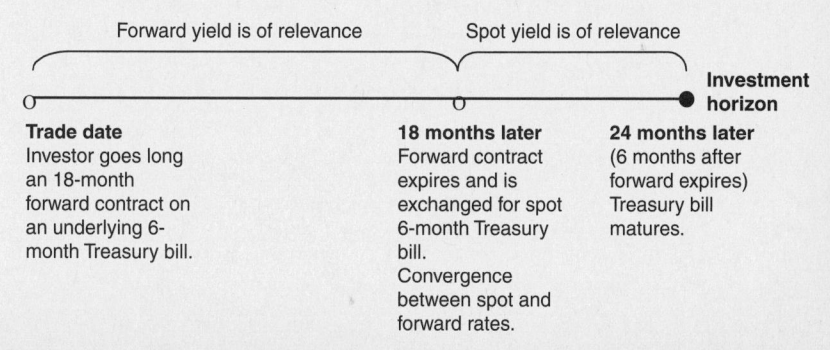

FIGURE 5.9   Convergence between forward and spot yields.

of a two-year spot Treasury? Not surprisingly, the short answer is "It depends." A number of statistical studies have been performed over the years to study the relationship between forward and spot yields and prices. Generally speaking, the conclusions tend to be that forward values over short-term horizons have strong correlations with spot values of short-life assets (as with Treasury bills or shorter-dated Treasury bonds). Accordingly, it would be a reasonably safe statistical bet that the correlation would be strong between a two-year Treasury and an 18-month forward yield on an underlying six-month asset. Why might this be of interest to a fixed-income investor? Consider the following.

Let us assume that an investor believes that market volatility will increase dramatically, but that for some reason she is precluded from executing a volatility strategy with options. Perhaps the firm she works for has internal or external constraints pertaining to the use of options. There is a Treasury bill futures market, and the underlying spot Treasury bill tends to have a three-month maturity. The futures are generally available in a string of rolling 3-month contracts that can extend beyond a year. However, futures on three-month Eurodollar instruments typically will extend well beyond the forward horizon of Treasury bill contracts. The price of these futures contracts is calculated as par minus the relevant forward yield of the underlying spot instrument. Thus, if the relevant forward yield of the underlying Treasury or Eurodollar spot is 6.0 percent then the price of the futures contract is $100 - 6 = 94$. A Treasury bill future typically involves a physical settlement if held to expiration (where a physical exchange of cash and Treasury bills takes place), while a Eurodollar future involves a cash settlement (where there is no physical exchange, but simply a last marking-to-market of final positions).

While there generally are no meaningful delivery options to speak of with Treasury bill or Eurodollar futures, there is one interesting price characteristic of these securities: Price changes are linked to a fixed predetermined amount. Accordingly, each time the forward yield changes by one-half basis point, the value of the futures contract changes by a fixed amount of $12.50 (or $25 per basis point). Why $25 per basis point? Simple. Earlier it was said that the Macaulay duration of a zero coupon security is equal to its maturity. The Macaulay duration of an underlying three-month asset is one-quarter of a year, or 0.25. Therefore, with a notional contract value of $1 million, 1 basis point change translates into $25. Figure 5.8 showed scenarios that might create a slight slope in the duration line of the forward as it approached the duration of the underlying spot asset; this slope represents carry's contribution to duration.

In short, as purely convenience for itself and its investors, the futures exchanges price the sensitivity of the underlying spot values of the Treasury bills and Eurodollars at their spot duration value (three months). This convenience can create a unique volatility-capturing strategy. By going long both Treasury bill futures and a spot two-year Treasury, we can attempt to replicate the payoff profile shown in Figure 5.10. If the Macaulay duration of the spot coupon-bearing two-year Treasury is 1.75 years, for every $1 million face amount of the two-year Treasury that is purchased, we go long seven Treasury bill futures with staggered expiration dates. Why seven? Because 0.25 times seven is 1.75. Why staggered? So that the futures contracts expire in line with the steady march to maturity of the spot two-year Treasury. Thus, all else being equal, if the correlation is a strong one between the spot yield on the two-year Treasury and the 21-month forward yield on the underlying three-month Treasury bill, our strategy should be close to delta-neutral. And as a result of being delta-neutral, we would expect our strategy to be profitable if there are volatile changes in the market, changes that would be captured by net exposure to volatility via our exposure to convexity.

Figure 5.11 presents another perspective of the above strategy in a total return context. As shown, return is zero for the volatility portion of this strategy if yields do not move (higher or lower) from their starting point. Yet even if the volatility portion of the strategy has a return of zero, it is possible that the coupon income (and the income from reinvesting the coupon cash flows) from the two-year Treasury will generate a positive overall return. Return

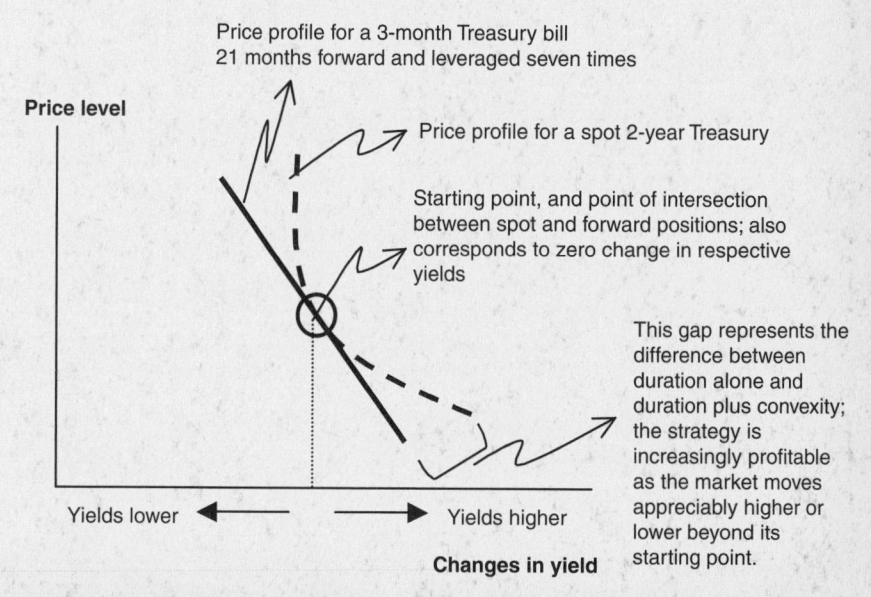

FIGURE 5.10 A convexity strategy.

Total return

This dip below zero (consistent with a slight negative return) represents transactions costs in the event that the market does not move dramatically one way or the other.

Yields lower ← → Yields higher

Changes in yield

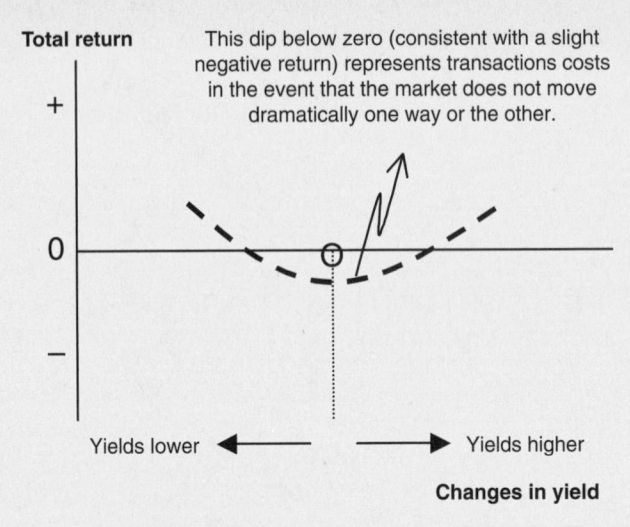

FIGURE 5.11 Return profile of the "gap."

can be positive when yields move appreciably from their starting point. If all else is not equal, returns easily can turn negative if the correlation is not a strong one between the spot yield on the two-year Treasury and the forward yield on the Treasury bill position. The yields might move in opposite directions, thus creating a situation where there is a loss from each leg of the overall strategy. As time passes, the convexity value of the two-year Treasury will shrink and the curvilinear profile will give way to the more linear profile of the nonconvex futures contracts. Further, as time passes, both lines will rotate counterclockwise into a flatter profile as consistent with having less and less of price sensitivity to changes in yield levels.

Finally, while R and T (and sometimes Y_c) are the two variables that distinguish spot from forward, there is not a great deal we can do about time; time is simply going to decay one day at a time. However, R is more complicated and deserves further comment.

It is a small miracle that R has not developed some kind of personality disorder. Within finance theory, R is varyingly referred to as a risk-free rate and a financing rate, and this text certainly alternates between both characterizations. The idea behind referring to it as a risk-free rate is to highlight that there is always an alternative investment vehicle. For example, the price for a forward purchase of gold requires consideration of both gold's spot value and cost-of-carry. Although not mentioned explicitly in Chapter 2, cost-of-carry can be thought of as an *opportunity cost*. It is a cost that the purchaser of a forward agreement must pay to the seller. The rationale for the cost is this: The forward seller of gold is agreeing not to be paid for the gold until sometime in the future. The seller's agreement to forgo an immediate receipt of cash ought to be compensated. It is. The compensation is in the form of the cost-of-carry embedded within the forward's formula. Again, the formula is $F = S(1 + RT) = S + SRT$, where SRT is cost-of-carry. Accordingly, SRT represents the dollar (or other currency) amount that the gold seller *could have earned* in a risk-free investment if he had received cash immediately, that is, if there were an immediate settlement rather than a forward settlement. R represents the risk-free rate he could have earned by investing the cash in something like a Treasury bill. Why a Treasury bill? Well, it is pretty much risk free. As a single cash flow security, it does not have reinvestment risk, it does not have credit risk, and if it is held to maturity, it does not pose any great price risks.

Why does R have to be risk free? Why can R not have some risk in it? Why could SRT not be an amount earned on a short-term instrument that has a single-A credit rating instead of the triple-A rating associated with Treasury instruments? The simplest answer is that we do not want to confuse the risks embedded within the underlying spot (e.g., an ounce of gold) with the risks associated with the underlying spot's cost-of-carry. In other words, within a forward transaction, cost-of-carry should be a sideshow to the main event. The best way to accomplish this is to reserve the cost-of-carry component for as risk free an investment vehicle as possible.

Why is R also referred to as a financing rate? Recall the discussion of the mechanics behind securities lending in Chapter 4. With such strategies (inclusive of repurchase agreements and reverse repos), securities are lent and borrowed at rates determined by the forces of supply and demand in their respective markets. Accordingly, these rates are financing rates. Moreover, they often are preferable to Treasury securities since the terms of securities lending strategies can be tailor-made to whatever the parties involved desire. If the desired trading horizon is precisely 26 days, then the agreement is structured to last 26 days and there is no need to find a Treasury bill with exactly 26 days to maturity. Are these types of financing rates also risk free? The marketplace generally regards them as such since these transactions are collateralized (supported) by actual securities. Refer again to Chapter 4 for a refresher.

Let us now peel away a few more layers to the R onion. When a financing strategy is used as with securities lending or repurchase agreements, the term of financing is obviously of interest. Sometimes an investor knows exactly how long the financing is for, and sometimes it is ambiguous. *Open* financing means that the financing will continue to be rolled over on a daily basis until the investor closes the trade. Accordingly, it is possible that each day's value for R will be different from the previous day's value. *Term* financing means that financing is for a set period of time (and may or may not be rolled over). In this case, R's value is set at the time of trade and remains constant over the agreed-on period of time. In some instances, an investor who knows that a strategy is for a fixed period of time may elect to leave the financing open rather than commit to a single term rate. Why? The investor may believe that the benefit of a daily compounding of interest from an open financing will be superior to a single term rate.

In the repurchase market, there is a benchmark financing rate referred to as *general collateral (GC)*. General collateral is the financing rate that applies to most Treasuries at any one point in time when a forward component of a trade comes into play. It is relevant for most off-the-run Treasuries, but it may not be most relevant for on-the-run Treasuries. On-the-run Treasuries tend to be traded more aggressively than off-the-run issues, and they are the most recent securities to come to market. One implication of this can be that they can be financed at rates appreciably lower than GC. When this happens, whether the issue is on-the-run or off-the-run, it is said to be *on special*, (or simply *special*). The issue is in such strong demand that investors are willing to lend cash at an extremely low rate of interest in exchange for a loan of the special security. As we saw, this low rate of interest on the cash portion of this exchange means that the investor being lent the cash can invest it in a higher-yielding risk-free security, such as a Treasury bill (and pocket the difference between the two rates).

Parenthetically, it is entirely possible to price a forward on a forward basis and price an option on a forward basis. For example, investors might be interested in purchasing a one-year forward contract on a five-year Treasury; however, they might not be interested in making that purchase today; they may not want the one-year forward contract until three months from now. Thus a forward-forward arrangement can be made. Similarly, investors might be interested in purchasing a six-month option on a five-year Treasury, but may not want the option to start until three months from now. Thus, a forward-option arrangement may be made. In sum, once one understands the principles underlying the triangles, any number of combinations and permutations can be considered.

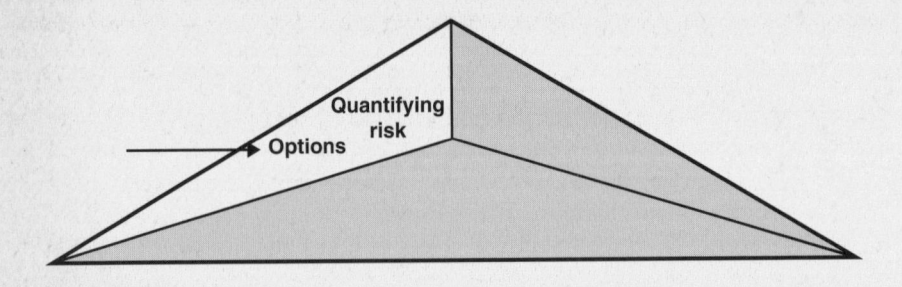

As explained in Chapter 2, there are five variables typically required to solve for an option's value: price of the underlying security, the risk-free rate, time to expiration, volatility, and the strike price. Except for strike price (since it typically does not vary), each of these variables has a risk measure associated with it. These risk measures are referred to as delta, rho, theta, and vega (sometimes collectively referred to as *the Greeks*), corresponding to changes in the price of the underlying, the risk-free rate, time to expiration, and volatility, respectively. Here we discuss these measures.

Chapter 4 introduced delta and rho as option-related variables that can be used for creating a strategy to capture and isolate changes in volatility. Delta and rho are also very helpful tools for understanding an option's price volatility. By slicing up the respective risks of an option into various categories, it is possible to better appreciate why an option behaves the way it does.

Again an option's five fundamental components are spot, time, risk-free rate, strike price, and volatility. Let us now examine each of these in the context of risk parameters.

From a risk management perspective, how the value of a financial variable changes in response to market dynamics is of great interest. For example, we know that the measure of an option's exposure to changes in spot is captured by delta and that changes in the risk-free rate are captured by rho. To complete the list, changes in time are captured by theta, and vega captures changes in volatility. Again, the value of a call option prior to expiration may be written as $O_c = S(1 + RT) - K + V$. There is no risk parameter associated with K since it remains constant over the life of the option. Since every term shown has a positive value associated with it, any increase in S, R, or V (noting that T can only shrink in value once the option is purchased) is thus associated with an increase in O_c.

For a put option, $O_p = K - S(1 + RT) + V$, so now it is only a positive change in V that can increase the value of O_p.

To see more precisely how delta, theta, and vega evolve in relation to their underlying risk variable, consider Figure 5.12.

As shown in Figure 5.12, appreciating the dynamics of option risk-characteristics can greatly facilitate understanding of strategy development. We complete this section on option risk dynamics with a pictorial of gamma risk (also known as convexity risk), which many option professionals view as being equally important to delta and vega and more important that theta or rho (see Figure 5.13).

The previous chapter discussed how these risks can be hedged for mainstream options. Before leaving this section let's discuss options embedded within products. Options can be embedded within products as with callable bonds and convertibles. By virtue of these options being embedded, they cannot be detached and traded separately. However, just because they cannot be detached does not mean that they cannot be hedged.

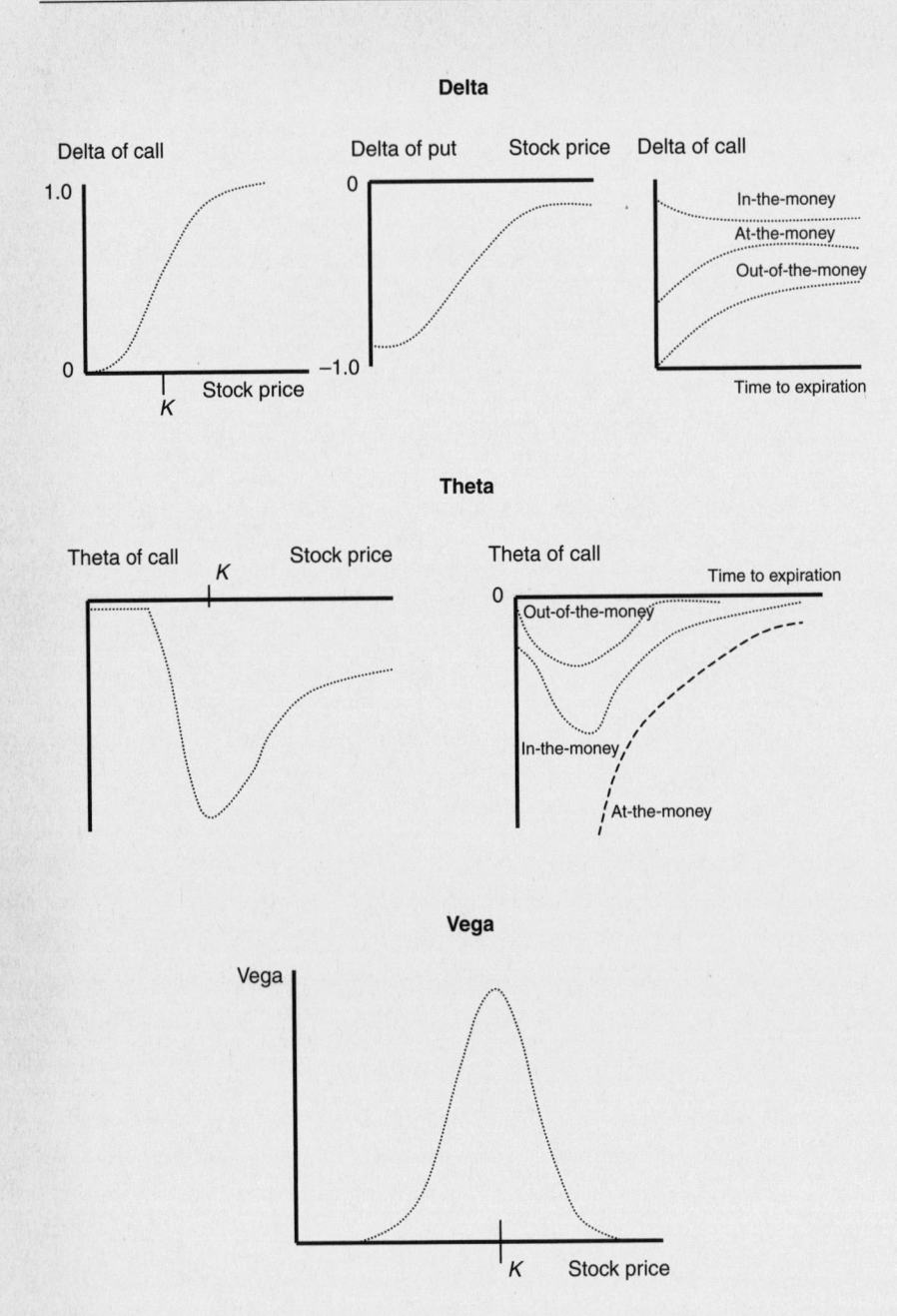

FIGURE 5.12 Price sensitivities of delta, theta, and vega.

Risk Management

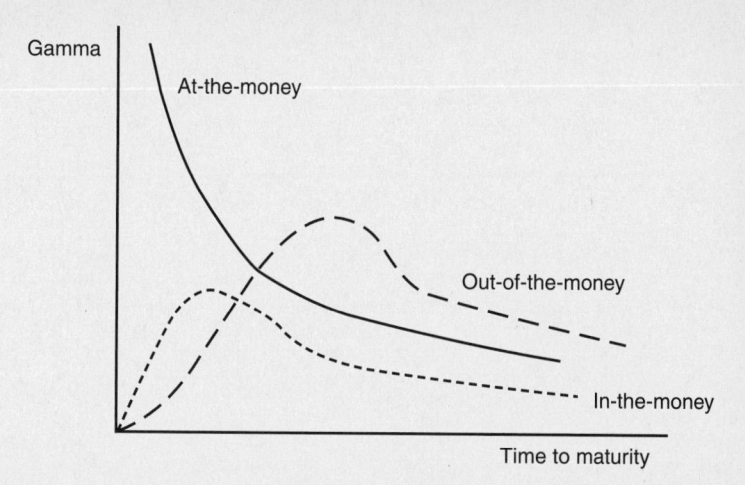

FIGURE 5.13 Gamma's relation to time for various price and strike combinations.

Remember that the price of a callable bond can be defined as

$$P_c = P_b - O_c,$$

where P_c = Price of the callable
P_b = Price of a noncallable bond
O_c = Price of the short call option embedded in the callable

Since callable bonds traditionally come with a lockout period, the option is in fact a deferred option or forward option. That is, the option does not become exercisable until some time has passed after initial trading. As an independent market exists for purchasing forward-dated options, it is entirely possible to purchase a forward option and cancel out the effect of a short option in a given callable. That market is the *swaps market*, and the purchase of a forward-dated option gives us

$$P_c = P_b - O_c + O_c = P_b$$

While investors do not often go through the various machinations of purchasing a callable along with a forward-dated call option to create a synthetic noncallable security, sometimes they go through the exercise on paper to help determine if a given callable is priced fairly in the market. They simply compare the synthetic bullet bond in price and credit terms with a true bullet bond.

As a final comment on callables and risk management, consider the relationship between OAS and volatility. We already know that an increase in volatility has the effect of increasing an option's value. In the case of a callable, a larger value of $-O_c$ translates into a smaller value for P_c. A smaller value for P_c presumably means a higher yield for P_c, given the inverse relationship between price and yield. However, when a higher (lower) volatility assumption is used with an OAS pricing model, a narrower (wider) OAS value results. When many investors hear this for the first time, they do a double take. After all, if an increase in volatility makes an option's price increase, why doesn't a callable bond's option-adjusted spread (as a yield-based measure) increase in tandem with the callable bond's decrease in price? The answer is found within the question. As a callable bond's price decreases, it is less likely to be *called away* (assigned maturity prior to the final stated maturity date) by the issuer since the callable is trading farther away from being in-the-money. Since the strike price of most callables is par (where the issuer has the incentive to call away the security when it trades above par, and to let the issue simply continue to trade when it is at prices below par), anything that has the effect of pulling the callable away from being in-the-money (as with a larger value of $-O_c$) also has the effect of reducing the call risk. Thus, OAS narrows as volatility rises.

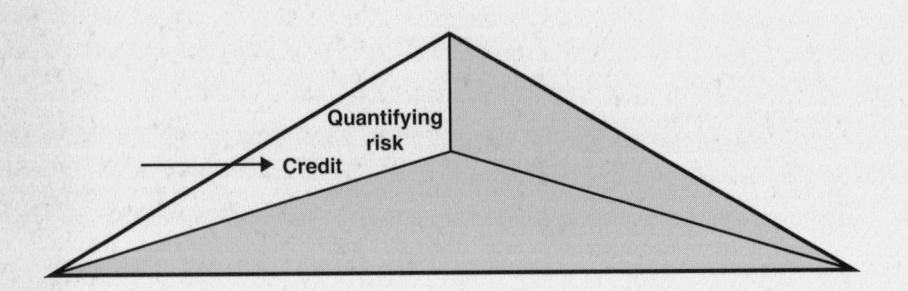

Borrowing from the drift and default matrices first presented in Chapter 3, a *credit cone* (showing hypothetical boundaries of upper and lower levels of potential credit exposures) might be created that would look something like that shown in Figure 5.14.

This type of presentation provides a very high-level overview of credit dynamics and may not be as meaningful as a more detailed analysis. For example, we may be interested to know if there are different forward-looking total return characteristics of a single-B company that:

Risk Management

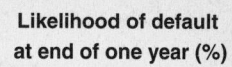

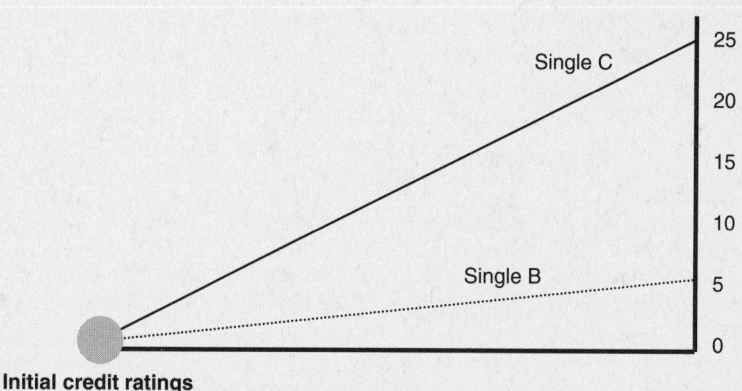

FIGURE 5.14 Credit cones for a generic single-B and single-C security.

- Just started business the year before, and as a single-B company, or
- Has been in business many years as a double-B company and was just recently downgraded to a single-B (a *fallen angel*), or
- Has been in business many years as a single-C company and was just recently upgraded to a single-B.

In sum, not all single-B companies arrive at single-B by virtue of having taken identical paths, and for this reason alone it should not be surprising that their actual market performance typically is differentiated.

For example, although we might think that a single-B fallen angel is more likely either to be upgraded after a period of time or at least to stay at its new lower notch for some time (especially as company management redoubles efforts to get things back on a good track), in fact the odds are less favorable for a single-B fallen angel to improve a year after a downgrade than a single-B company that was upgraded to a single-B status. However, the story often is different for time horizons beyond one year. For periods beyond one year, many single-B fallen angels successfully reposition themselves to become higher-rated companies. Again, the statistics available from the rating agencies makes this type of analysis possible.

There is another dimension to using credit-related statistical experience. Just as not all single-B companies are created in the same way, neither are all single-B products. A single-A rated company may issue debt that is rated double-B because it is a subordinated structure, just as a single-B rated company may issue debt that is rated double-B because it is a senior structure. Generally speaking, for a particular credit rating, senior structures of lower-rated companies do not fare as well as junior structures of higher-rated companies. In this context, "structure" refers to the priority of cash flows that are involved. The pattern of cash flows may be identical for both a senior and junior bond (with semiannual coupons and a 10-year maturity), but with very different probabilities assigned to the likelihood of actually receiving the cash flows. The lower likelihood associated with the junior structure means that its coupon and yield should be higher relative to a senior structure. Exactly how much higher will largely depend on investors' expectations of the additional cash flow risk that is being absorbed. Rating agency statistics can provide a historical or backward-looking perspective of credit risk dynamics. Credit derivatives provide a more forward-looking picture of credit risk expectations.

As explained in Chapter 3, a credit derivative is simply a forward, future, or option that trades to an underlying spot credit instrument or variable. While the pricing of the credit spread option certainly takes into consideration any historical data of relevance, it also should incorporate reasonable future expectations of the company's credit outlook. As such, the implied forward credit outlook can be mathematically *backed-out* (solved for with relevant equations) of this particular type of credit derivative. For example, just as an implied volatility can be derived using a standard options valuation formula, an implied credit volatility can be derived in the same way when a credit put or call is referenced and compared with a credit-free instrument (as with a comparable Treasury option). Once obtained, this implied credit outlook could be evaluated against personal sentiments or credit agency statistics.

In 1973 Black and Scholes published a famous article (which subsequently was built on by Merton and others) on how to price options, called "The Pricing of Options and Corporate Liabilities."[6] The reference to "liabilities" was to support the notion that a firm's equity value could be viewed as a call written on the assets of the firm, with the strike price (the point of default) equal to the debt outstanding at expiration. Since a firm's default risk typically increases as the value of its assets approach the book value (actual value in the marketplace) of the liabilities, there are three elements that go into determining an overall default probability.

1. The market value of the firm's assets
2. The assets' volatility or uncertainty of value
3. The capital structure of the firm as regards the nature of its various contractual obligations

---

[6] F. Black and M. Scholes, "The Pricing of Options and Corporate Liabilities," *Journal of Political Economy*, 81 (May–June 1973): 637–659.

Figure 5.15 illustrates these concepts. The dominant profile resembles that of a long call option.

Many variations of this methodology are used today, and other methodologies will be introduced. In many respects the understanding and quantification of credit risk remains very much in its early stages of development.

Credit risk is quantified every day in the credit premiums that investors assign to the securities they buy and sell. As these security types expand beyond traditional spot and forward cash flows and increasingly make their way into options and various hybrids, the price discovery process for credit generally will improve in clarity and usefulness. Yet the marketplace should most certainly not be the sole or final arbiter for quantifying credit risk. Aside from more obvious considerations pertaining to the market's own imperfections (occasions of unbalanced supply and demand, imperfect liquidity, the ever-changing nature of market benchmarks, and the omnipresent possibility of asymmetrical information), the market provides a beneficial though incomplete perspective of real and perceived risk and reward.

In sum, credit risk is most certainly a fluid risk and is clearly a consideration that will be unique in definition and relevance to the investor considering it. Its relevance is one of time and place, and as such it is incumbent on investors to weigh very carefully the role of credit risk within their overall approach to investing.

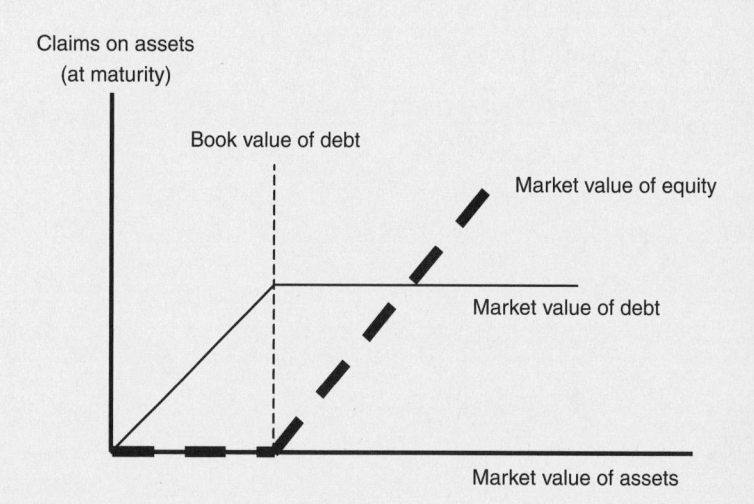

FIGURE 5.15 Equity as a call option on asset value.
Source: "Credit Ratings and Complementary Sources of Credit Quality Information," Arturo Estrella et al., Basel Committee on Banking Supervision, Bank for International Settlements, Basel, August 2000.

Allocating risk

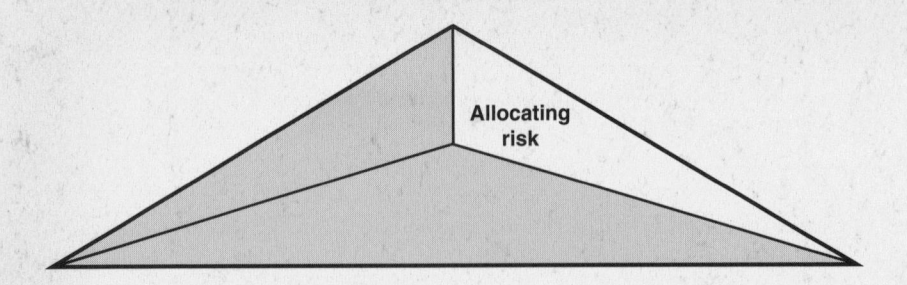

This section discusses various issues pertaining to how risk is allocated in the context of products, cash flows, and credit. By highlighting the relationships that exist across products and cash flows in particular, we see how many investors may have a false sense of portfolio diversification because they have failed to fully consider certain important cross-market linkages.

The very notion of allocating risk suggests that risk can somehow be compartmentalized and then doled out on the basis of some established criteria. Fair enough. Since an investor's capital is being put to risk when investment decisions are made, it is certainly appropriate to formally establish a set of guidelines to be followed when determining how capital is allocated. For an individual equity investor looking to do active trading, guidelines may consist simply of not having more than a certain amount of money invested in one particular stock at a time and of not allowing a loss to exceed some predetermined level. For a bond fund manager, guidelines may exist along the lines of the individual equity investor but with added limitations pertaining to credit risk, cash flow selection, maximum portfolio duration, and so forth. This section is not so much directed toward how risk management guidelines can be established (there are already many excellent texts on the subject), but toward providing a framework for appreciating the interrelated dynamics of the marketplace when approaching risk and decisions of how to allocate it. To accomplish this, we present a sampling of real-world interrelationships for products and for cash flows.

PRODUCT INTERRELATIONSHIPS

Consider the key interrelationship between interest rates and currencies (recalling our discussion of interest rate parity in Chapter 1) in the context of the euro's launch in January 1999. It can be said that prior to the melting of 11 currencies into one, there were 11 currency volatilities melted into one. Borrowing a concept from physics and the second law of thermodynamics—that matter is not created or destroyed, only transformed—what happened to those 11 nonzero volatilities that collapsed to allow for the euro's creation?

One explanation might be that heightened volatility emerged among the fewer remaining so-called global reserve currencies (namely the U.S. dollar, the yen, and the euro), and that heightened volatility emerged among interest rates between euro-member countries and the rest of the world. In fact, both of these things occurred following the euro's launch.

As a second example, consider the statistical methods between equities and bonds presented earlier in this chapter, namely, in the discussion of how the concepts of duration and beta can be linked with one another. Hypothetically speaking, once a basket of particular stocks is identified that behaves much like fixed income securities, a valid question becomes which bundle would an investor prefer to own: a basket of synthetic fixed income securities created with stocks or a basket of fixed income securities? The question is deceptively simple. When investors purchase any fixed income security, are they purchasing it because it is a fixed income security or because it embodies the desired characteristics of a fixed income security (i.e., pays periodic coupons, holds capital value etc.)? If it is because they want a fixed income security, then there is nothing more to discuss. Investors will buy the bundle of fixed income securities. However, if they desire the characteristics of a fixed income security, there is a great deal more to talk about. Namely, if it is possible to generate fixed income returns with non–fixed income products, why not do so? And if it is possible to *outperform* traditional fixed income products with non—fixed income securities and for comparable levels of risk, why ever buy another note or bond?

Again, if investors are constrained to hold only fixed income products, then the choice is clear; they hold only the true fixed income portfolio. If they want only to create a fixed income exposure to the marketplace and are indifferent as to how this is achieved, then there are choices to make. How can investors choose between a true and synthetic fixed income portfolio? Perhaps on the basis of historical risk/return profiles.

If the synthetic fixed income portfolio can outperform the true fixed income portfolio on a consistent basis at the same or a lower level of risk, then investors might seriously want to consider owning the synthetic portfolio. A compromise would perhaps be to own a mix of the true and synthetic portfolios.

For our third example, consider the TED spread, or Treasury versus Eurodollar spread. A common way of trading the TED spread is with futures contracts. For example, to buy the TED spread, investors buy three-month Treasury bill futures and sell three-month Eurodollar futures. They would purchase the TED spread if they believed that perceptions of market risk or volatility would increase. In short, buying the TED spread is a bet that the spread will widen. If perceptions of increased market risk become manifest in moves out of risky assets (namely, Eurodollar-denominated securities that are dominated by bank issues) and into safe assets (namely, U.S. Treasury securities), Treasury bill yields would be expected to edge lower relative to Eurodollar yields and the TED spread would widen. Examples of events that might contribute to perceptions of market uncertainty would include a weak stock market, banking sector weakness as reflected in savings and loan or bank failures, and a national or international calamity.

Accordingly, one way for investors to create a strategy that benefits from an expectation that equity market volatility will increase or decrease by more than generally expected is via a purchase or sale of a fixed income spread trade. Investors could view this as a viable alternative to delta-hedging an equity option to isolate the value of volatility (V) within the option.

Finally, here is an example of an interrelationship between products and credit risk. Studies have been done to demonstrate how S&P 500 futures contracts can be effective as a hedge against widening credit spreads in bonds. That is, it has been shown that over medium- to longer-run periods of time, bond credit spreads tend to narrow when the S&P 500 is rallying, and vice versa. Further, bond credit spreads tend to narrow when yield levels are declining. In sum, and in general, when the equity market is in a rallying mode, so too is the bond market. This is not altogether surprising since the respective equity and bonds of a given company generally would be expected to trade in line with one another; stronger when the company is doing well and weaker when the company is not doing as well.

CASH FLOW INTERRELATIONSHIPS

Chapter 2 described the three primary cash flows: spot, forwards and futures, and options. These three primary cash flows are interrelated by shared variables, and one or two rather simple assumptions may be all that's required to change one cash flow type into another. Let us now use the triangle approach to highlight these interrelationships by cash flows and their respective *payoff profiles*.

A payoff profile is a simple illustration of how the return of a particular cash flow type increases or decreases as its prices rises or falls. Consider Figure 5.16, an illustration for spot.

As shown, when the price of spot rises above its purchase price, a positive return is enjoyed. When the price of spot falls below its purchase price, there is a loss.

Figure 5.17 shows the payoff profile for a forward or future. As readers will notice, the profile looks very much like the profile for spot. It should. Since cost-of-carry is what separates spot from forwards and futures, the distance between the spot profile (replicated from Figure 5.16 and shown as a dashed line) and the forward/future profile is SRT (for a non–cash-flow paying security). As time passes and T approaches a value

Risk Management

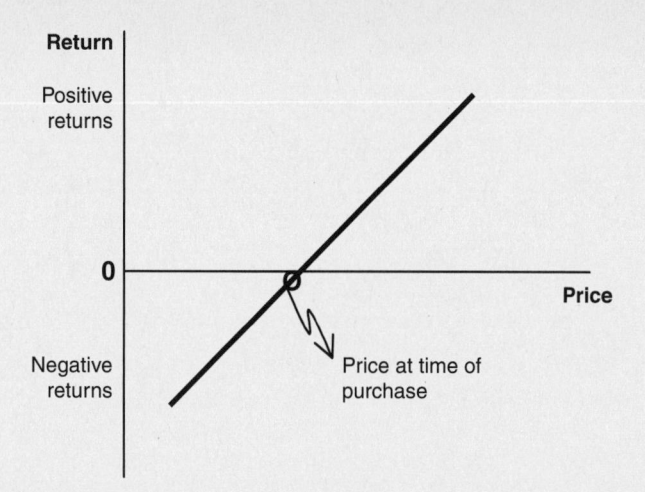

FIGURE 5.16 Payoff profile.

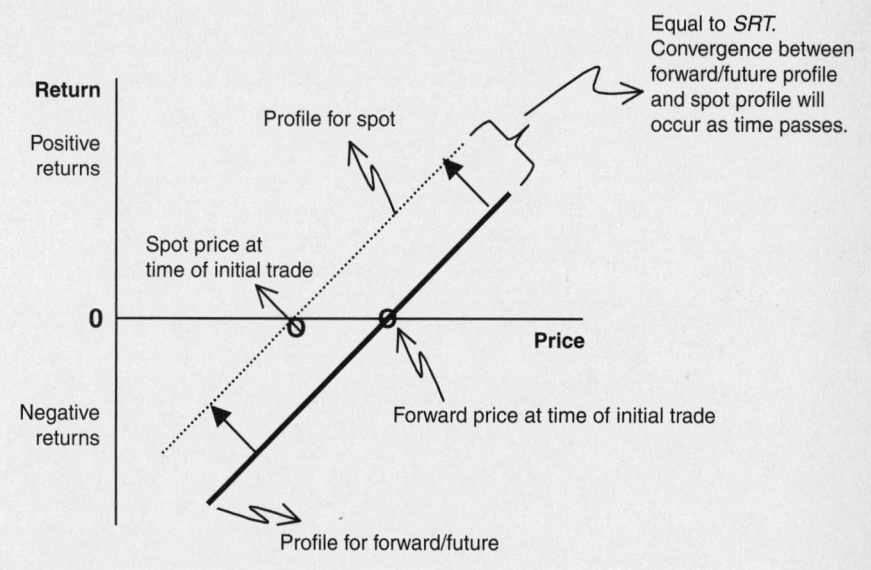

FIGURE 5.17 Payoff profile for a forward or future.

of zero, the forward/future profile gradually converges toward the spot profile and actually becomes the spot profile. As drawn it is assumed that R remains constant. However, if R should grow larger, the forward/future profile may edge slightly to the right, and vice versa if R should grow smaller (at least up until the forward/future expires and completely converges to spot).

Figure 5.18 shows the payoff profile for a call option. The earlier profile for spot is shown in a light dashed line and the same previous profile for a forward/future is shown in a dark dashed line. Observe how the label of "Price" on the x-axis has been changed to "Difference between forward price and strike price" (or $F - K$). An increasingly positive difference between F and K represents a larger in-the-money value for the option and the return grows larger. Conversely, if the difference between F and K remains constant or falls below zero (meaning that the price of the underlying security has fallen), then there is a negative return that at worst is limited to the price paid for the option. As drawn, it is assumed that R and V remain constant. However, if R or V should grow larger, the option profile may edge slightly to the right and vice versa if R or V should grow smaller (at least up until the option expires and completely converges to spot).

A put payoff profile is shown in Figure 5.19. The lines are consistent with the particular cash flows identified above.

With the benefit of these payoff profiles, let us now consider how combining cash flows can create new cash flow profiles. For example, let's create a forward agreement payoff profile using options. As shown in Figure 5.20, when we combine a short at-the-money put and a long at-the-money call option, we generate the same return profile as a forward or future.

Parenthetically, a putable bond has a payoff profile of a long call option, as it is a combination of being long a bullet (noncallable) bond and

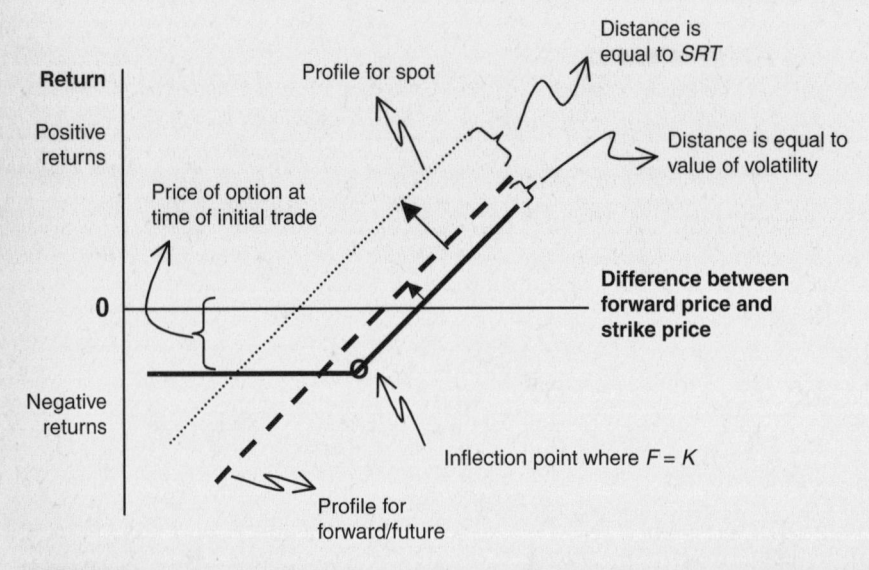

FIGURE 5.18 Call payoff profile.

Risk Management

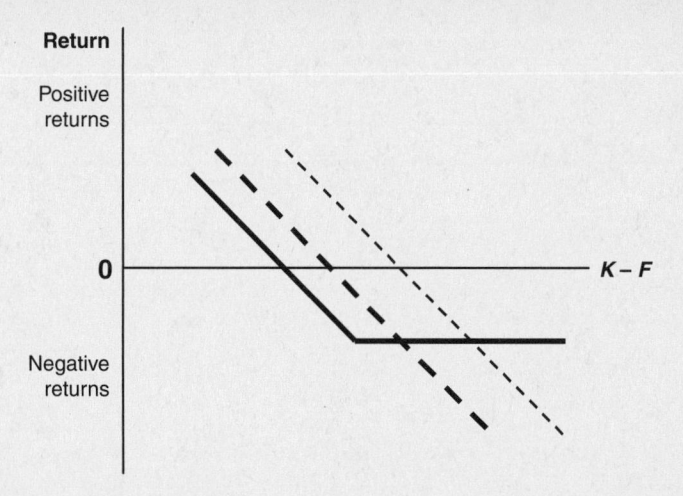

FIGURE 5.19 Put payoff profile.

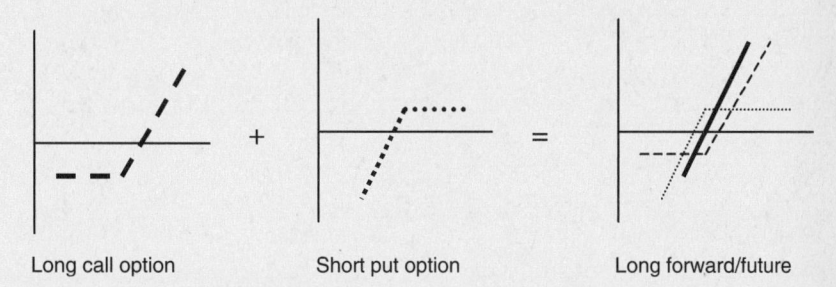

FIGURE 5.20 Combining cash flows.

Long call option + Short put option = Long forward/future

a long put option. A callable bond has a payoff profile of a short put option as it is a combination of being long a bullet bond and a short call option. Since a putable and a callable are both ways for an investor to benefit from steady or rising interest rates, it is unusual for investors to have both putables and callables in a single portfolio. Accordingly, it is important to recognize that certain pairings of callables and putables can result in a new cash flow profile that is comparable to a long forward/future.

Let us now look at a combination of a long spot position and a short forward/future position. This cash flow combination ought to sound familiar because it was first presented in Chapter 4 as a basis trade (see Figure 5.21).

Next let us consider how an active delta-hedging strategy with cash and forwards and/or futures can be used to replicate an option's payoff profile. Specifically, let us consider creating a synthetic option.

Long spot + **Short forward/future** = **Basis trade**

The distance between where these two payoff profiles cross the price line is equal to SRT, cost-of-carry.

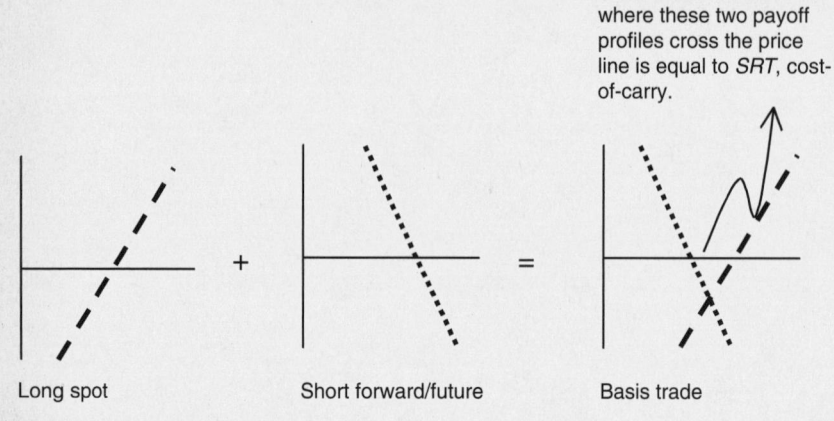

FIGURE 5.21 A basis trade.

Why might investors choose to create a synthetic option rather than buy or sell the real thing? One reason might be the perception that the option is trading rich (more expensive) to its fair market value. Since volatility is a key factor when determining an option's value, investors may create a synthetic option when they believe that the true option's implied volatility is too high—that is, when investors believe that the expected price dynamics of the underlying variable are not likely to be as great as that suggested by the true option's implied volatility. If the realized volatility is less than that implied by the true option, then a savings may be realized.

Thus, an advantage of creating an option with forwards and Treasury bills is that it may result in a lower cost option. However, a disadvantage of this strategy is that it requires constant monitoring. To see why, we need to revisit the concept of delta.

As previously discussed, delta is a measure of an option's exposure to the price dynamics of the underlying security. Delta is positive for a long call option because a call trades to a long position in the underlying security. Delta is negative for a long put option because a put trades to a short position in the underlying security. The absolute value of an option's delta becomes closer to 1 as it moves in-the-money and becomes closer to zero as it moves out-of-the-money. An option that is at-the-money tends to have a delta close to 0.5.

Let us say that investors desire an option with an initial delta of 0.5. If a true option is purchased, delta will automatically adjust to price changes in the underlying security. For example, if a call option is purchased on a share of General Electric (GE) equity, delta will automatically move closer to 1 as the share price rises. Conversely, delta will move closer to zero as the share price falls. Delta of a synthetic option must be monitored constantly because it will not automatically adjust itself to price changes in the underlying security.

If an initial delta of 0.5 is required for a synthetic call option, then investors will go long a forward to cover half (0.5) of the underlying security's face value, and Treasury bills will be purchased to cover 100 percent of the underlying security's forward value. We cover 100 percent of the security's forward value because this serves to place a "floor" under the strategy's profit/loss profile. If yields fall and the implied value for delta increases, a larger forward position will be required. If yields rise and the implied value for delta decreases, a smaller forward position will be required. The more volatile the underlying security, the more expensive it will become to manage the synthetic option. This is consistent with the fact that an increase in volatility serves to increase the value of a true option. The term *implied delta* means the value delta would be for a traditional option when valued using the objective strike price and expected volatility. Just how we draw a synthetic option's profit/loss profile depends on a variety of assumptions. For example, since the synthetic option is created with Treasury bills and forwards, are the Treasury bills financed in the repo market? If yes, this would serve to lever the synthetic strategy. It is an explicit assumption of traditional option pricing theory that the risk-free asset (the Treasury bill) is leveraged (i.e., the Treasury bill is financed in the repo market).

Repo financing on a synthetic option that is structured with a string of overnight repos is consistent with creating a synthetic American option, which may be exercised at any time. Conversely, the repo financing structured with a term repo is consistent with a European option, which may be exercised only at option maturity. Since there is no secondary market for repo transactions, and since investors may not have the interest or ability to execute an offsetting repo trade, a string of overnight repos may be the best strategy with synthetic options.

By going long a forward, we are entering into an agreement to purchase the underlying security at the forward price. Thus, if the actual market price lies anywhere above (below) the forward price at the expiration of the forward, then there is a profit (loss). There is a profit (loss) because we purchase the underlying security at a price below (above) the prevailing market price and in turn sell that underlying security at the higher (lower) market price. Of course, once the underlying security is purchased, investors may decide to hang onto the security rather than sell it immediately and realize any gains (losses). Investors may choose to hold onto the security for a while in hopes of improving returns.

A long option embodies the *right* to purchase the underlying security. This is in contrast to a long forward (or a long future) that embodies the *obligation* to purchase the underlying security. Thus, an important distinction to be made between a true option and an option created with Treasury bills and forwards is that the former does not commit investors to a forward purchase.

Although *secondary markets* (markets where securities may be bought or sold long after they are initially launched) may not be well developed for all types of forward transactions, an offsetting trade may be made easily if investors want to reverse the synthetic option strategy prior to expiration. For example, one month after entering into a three-month forward to purchase a 10-year Treasury, investors may decide to reverse the trade. To do this, investors would simply enter into a two-month forward to sell the 10-year Treasury. In short, these forward transactions would still *require* investors to buy and sell the 10-year Treasury at some future date. However, these offsetting transactions allow investors to "close out" the trade prior to the maturity of the original forward transaction. "Close out" appears in quotes because the term conveys a sense of finality. Although an offsetting trade is indeed executed for purposes of completing the strategy, the strategy is not really dead until the forwards mature in two months' time. And when we say that an *offsetting* forward transaction is executed, we mean only that an opposite trade is made on the same underlying security and for the same face value. The forward price of an offsetting trade could be higher, lower, or the same as the forward price of the original forward trade. The factor that determines the price on the offsetting forward is the same factor that determines the price on the original forward contract: cost-of-carry.

Figure 5.22 shows how combining forwards and Treasury bills creates a synthetic option profile. The profile shown is at the expiration of the synthetic option.

If the synthetic call option originally were designed to have a delta of 0.5, then the investors would go long a forward to cover half of the underlying security's face value and would purchase Treasury bills equal to 100 percent of the underlying security's forward value. One half of the underlying security's face value is the benchmark for the forward position because the target delta is 0.5. If the target delta were 0.75, then three quarters of the underlying security's face value would be the benchmark. If the price of the underlying security were to rise (fall), then the forward position would be increased (decreased) to increase (decrease) the implied delta. The term *implied delta* means the value for delta if our synthetic option were a true option.

The preceding example assumes that the synthetic option is intended to underwrite 100 percent of the underlying asset. For this reason our at-the-money synthetic option requires holding 50 percent of the underlying face value in our forward position. If our synthetic option were to move in-the-money with delta going from 0.5 to close to 1.0, we would progressively hold up to 100 percent of the underlying's face value in our forward position.

Risk Management

Treasury bill
Total return
At maturity of the Treasury bill

Treasury forward
Total return
At maturity of the Treasury bill

Synthetic option
Total return

This distance below a zero total return represents the transaction costs associated with the constant fine-tuning required for a synthetic option. In short, the floor return (generated by the fixed and known return on the Treasury bill) is lowered by the costs of delta hedging.

At maturity of the synthetic option

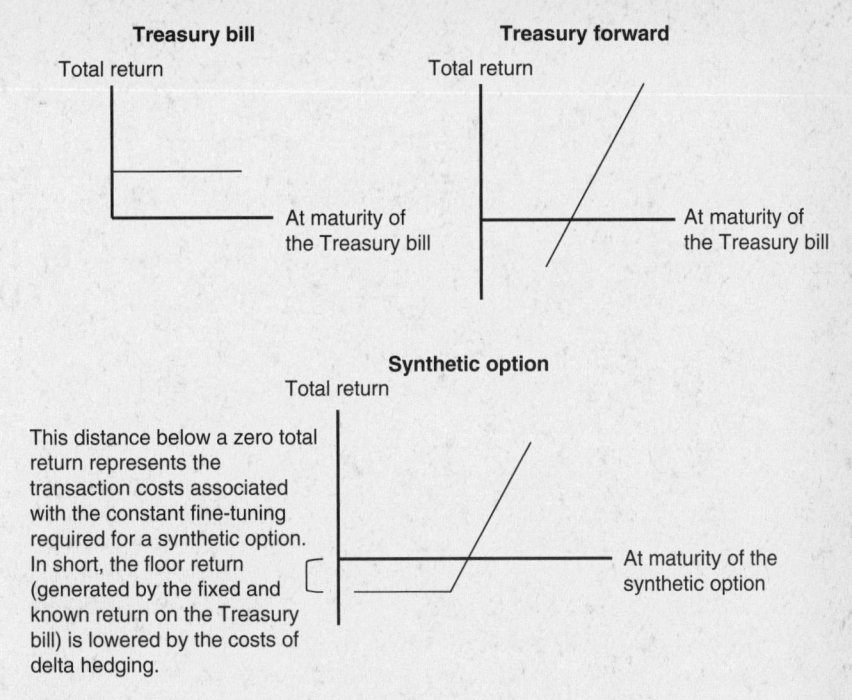

FIGURE 5.22 Synthetic option profile.

It is a simple matter to determine the appropriate size of the forward position for underwriting anything other than 100 percent of the underlying asset. For example, let us assume that we want to underwrite 50 percent of the underlying asset. In this instance, we would want to own 50 percent of the underlying's face value in Treasury bills and 25 percent of the underlying's forward value for an at-the-money option. The delta for an at-the-money option is 0.5, and 50 percent times 0.5 is equal to 25 percent. Thus, we want to own 25 percent of the underlying's forward value in our forward position.

Again, the delta of a synthetic option will not adjust itself continuously to price changes in the underlying security. Forward positions must be managed actively, and the transaction costs implied by bid/offer spreads on successive forward transactions are an important consideration. Thus, how well the synthetic option performs relative to the true option depends greatly on market volatility. The more transactions required to manage the synthetic option, the greater its cost. The horizontal piece of the profit/loss profile is drawn below zero to reflect expected cumulative transactions costs at expiration. Thus, expected volatility may very well be the most important criterion for investors to consider when evaluating a synthetic versus a true option strategy. That is, if investors believe that the true option is priced rich on a volatility basis, they may wish to create a synthetic option. If the realized volatility happens to be less than that implied by the true option, then the synthetic option may well have been the more appropriate vehicle for executing the option strategy.

Finally, the nature of discrete changes in delta may pose special challenges when investors want to achieve a delta of zero. For example, there may be a market level where investors would like to close out the synthetic option. Since it is unlikely investors can monitor the market constantly, they probably would leave market orders of where to buy or sell predetermined amounts of forwards or Treasury bills. However, just leaving a market order to be executed at a given level does not guarantee that the order will be filled at the prices specified. In a fast-moving market, it may well be impossible to fill a large order at the desired price. An implication is that a synthetic option may be closed out, yet at an undesirable forward price. Accordingly, the synthetic option may prove to be a less efficient investment vehicle than a true option. Thus, creating synthetic options may be a worthwhile consideration only when replicating option markets that are less efficient. That is, a synthetic strategy may prove to be more successful when structured against a specialized option-type product with a wide bid/ask spread as opposed to replicating an exchange-traded option.

Aside from using Treasury bills and forwards to create options, Treasury bills may be combined with Treasury note or bond futures, and Treasury bill futures may be combined with Treasury note or bond futures and/or forwards. However, investors need to consider the nuances of trading in these other products. For example, a Treasury bill future expires into a three-month cash bill; it does not expire at par. Further, Treasury futures have embedded delivery options.

Let us now take a step back for a moment and consider what has been presented thus far. Individual investors are capable of knowing the products and cash flows in their portfolio at any point in time. However, at the company level of investing (as with a large institutional fund management company or even an investment bank), it would be unusual for any single trader to have full knowledge of the products and cash flows held by other traders. Generally speaking, only the high-level managers of firms have full access to individual trading records. Something that clearly is of interest to high-level managers is how the firm's risk profile appears on an aggregated basis as well as on a trader-by-trader basis. In other words, assume for a moment that there is just one single firm-wide portfolio that is composed of dozens (or even hundreds) of individual portfolios. What would be the risk profile of that single firm-wide portfolio? In point of fact, it may not be as large as you might think. Why not? Because every portfolio manager may not be following the same trading strategies as everyone else, and/or the various strategies may be constructed with varying cash flows. Let us consider an example involving multiple traders, where each trader is limited to having one strategy in the portfolio at any given time.

Say that trader A has a volatility trade in her portfolio that was created by going long an at-the-money call option and an at-the-money put option. Trader A simply believes that volatility is going to increase more than generally expected. Say trader B has a future in his portfolio and believes that the underlying security will appreciate in price. Note that these trades may not at all appear to be contradictory on the surface. Volatility can increase even without a change in pattern of the underlying asset's price (as with a surprise announcement affecting all stocks, such as the sudden news that the federal government will shut down over an indefinite period owing to a deadlock with the Congress over certain key budget negotiations). Such a risk type is sometime referred to as *event risk*. The whole idea behind isolating volatility is to be indifferent to such asset price moves. From the presentations above, we know that a future can be created with a long at-the-money call option and a short at-the-money put option. Accordingly, when we sum across the portfolios of traders A and B we have

$$O_c + O_p + O_c - O_p = 2 \times O_c.$$

By combining one strategy that is indifferent to price moves with another that expects higher prices, the net effect is a strong bias to upward-moving prices. It should now be easy to appreciate how an aggregation of individual strategies can be a necessary and insightful exercise for firms with large trading operations.

Let us now take this entire discussion a step further. Assume that all of a firm's cash flows have been distilled into one of three categories: spot, forward and futures, and options. The aggregate spot position may reflect a net positive outlook for market prices; the net forward and future position also may reflect a net positive outlook though on a smaller scale; and the net option position may reflect a negative outlook on volatility. Could all of these net cash flows be melted into a single dollar (or other currency) value? Yes, if we can be permitted to make some assumptions to simplify the issue. For example, we already know from our various tours around the triangle that with some pretty basic assumptions, we can bring a forward/future or option back to spot. By doing this we could distill an entire firm's trading operation into a single number. Would such a number have limitations to meaningful interpretation? Absolutely yes. The fact that we could distill myriad products and cash flows into a single value does not mean that we can or should rely on it as a daily gauge of capital at risk. We can think of quantifying risk as an exercise that can fall along a continuum. At one end of the continuum we can let each strategy stand on its own as an individual transaction, and at the other end of the continuum we have the ability (though only with some strong assumptions) to reduce a complex network of strategies into a single value. What one firm will find most relevant and meaningful may not be the same as any other firm, and the optimal risk management profiles and methodologies may well come only with perseverance, creativity, and trial and error.

Credit Interrelationships

As discussed in some detail in Chapter 3, credit permeates all aspects of finance. Credit risk always will exist in its own right, and while it can take on a rather explicit shape in the form of different market products, it also can be transformed by an issuer's particular choice of cash flows. The decision of how far investors ought to extend their credit risk exposure is fundamental. All investors have some amount of capital in support of their trading activity, and a clear objective ought to be the continuous preservation of at least some portion of that capital so that the portfolio can live to invest another day. While investments with greater credit risks often provide greater returns as compensation for that added risk, riskier investments also can mean poor performance. Thus, it is essential for all investors to have clear guidelines for just how much credit risk is acceptable and in all of its forms.

Figure 5.23 provides a snapshot of some of the considerations that larger investors may want to include in a methodology for allocating credit risk. Generally speaking, a large firm will place ceilings or upper limits on the

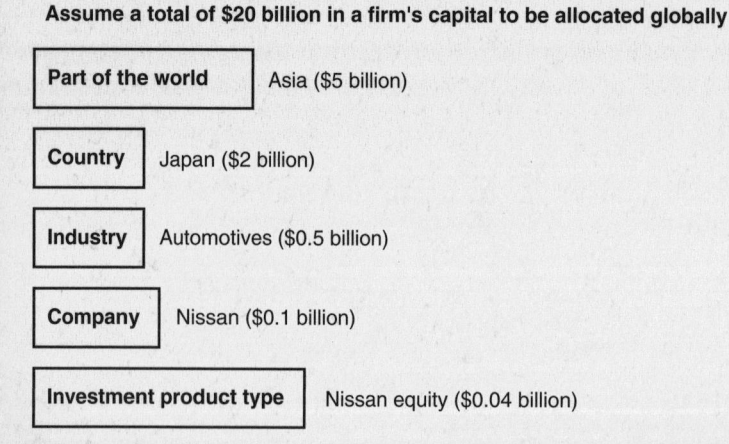

Assume a total of $20 billion in a firm's capital to be allocated globally

Part of the world	Asia ($5 billion)
Country	Japan ($2 billion)
Industry	Automotives ($0.5 billion)
Company	Nissan ($0.1 billion)
Investment product type	Nissan equity ($0.04 billion)

FIGURE 5.23 Allocating risk capital.

amount of investment funds that can be allocated to any one category, where category might be a part of the world, a particular country, or a specific company. While the map might be excessive for some investors, it could be woefully incomplete for others. For example, GE is a large company. Does the credit officer of a large bank limit investments to GE businesses with GE taken as a whole, or does she recognize that GE is made up of many diversified businesses that deserve to be given separate industry-specific risk allocations? Perhaps she creates a combination of the two different approaches and evaluates situations on more of a case-by-case basis.

As shown in Figure 5.22, the first layer of a top/down capital allocation process may be by "part of the world," followed by "country," and so on. At each successive step lower, the amount of capital available diminishes. Since Japan is not the only country in Asia, and since a company is unlikely to put all of its Asian-designated capital into just Japan, the amount of capital allocated to Japan will be something less than the amount of capital allocated to Asia generally. Similarly, since automotives is not the only industry in Japan, the amount of capital allocated to automotives will be something less than the amount of capital allocated to Japan, and so on.

Clearly, the credit risk allocation methodology that is ultimately selected by any investor will be greatly dependent on investment objectives, capital base, and financial resources. While there is no single right way of doing it, just as there is no single right way of investing, at least there are well-recognized quantitative and qualitative measures of credit risk that can be tailored to appropriate and meaningful applications.

Summary

In this section, we have discussed the interrelationships of risk in the context of products, cash flows, and credit. We now conclude with a discussion of ways that a firm's capital can be allocated to different business lines that involve the taking of various risks. Since capital guidelines and restrictions are also a way that certain financial companies are regulated (as with insurance firms and banks), we further explore the topic of capital allocation in Chapter 6.

Generally speaking, risk limits are expressed as *ceilings*—upper limits on how much capital may be committed to a particular venture (as with securities investments, the making of loans, the basic running of a particular business operation, etc.). For especially large companies, ceilings might exist for how much capital might be committed to a particular country or part of the world. For smaller investment companies, ceilings might exist simply for how much capital might be allocated to different types of securities.

Especially large companies have employees who serve as designated credit officers. Among other responsibilities, they are regularly requested to grant special requests for increased allocations of capital. For a business manager, capital represents the lifeblood of running a successful operation, so more capital often means the difference between having had a good year and a fantastic year. All else being equal, if a credit manager is loath to grant an outright increase in capital, he might otherwise be inclined to consider borrowing from another ceiling. For example, if there is a limit to how much capital can be allocated to Japan and Singapore, but the ceiling for Singapore is far from being reached, then a portion of Singapore's credit allocation might be approved for Japan's use on a temporary basis. A similar type arrangement might be made to allow for a greater investment in automotives versus steel, and so forth. At the investment product-type level, while investors might find themselves up against a particular equity ceiling in Japan, on a *net basis* (where long investments are permitted to cancel out short investments) they may find that their combined equity investments in Japan and Singapore are well below the combined equity ceilings of these two markets. Of course, for each of the examples we've cited here, the appropriate corporate officer will have to decide as to whether the requested capital allocation is in the overall interests of the company.

This hierarchy of how capital might be allocated across various categories did not explain for the process by which the allocation decisions were made. That is, how does a company decide that Asia will receive a 10 percent allocation of capital and that Western Europe will receive an allocation of 25 percent? How does a company determine the ceiling for investments in the equity of a particular issuer relative to that issuer's bonds?

To begin with, the answers to some of these types of questions may be much more qualitative than quantitative. For example, a company that is headquartered in Asia may be much more likely to have a higher capital allocation ceiling in Asia than in Europe or the United States simply because its people know the Asian marketplace much better. However, some global companies may try to employ a more quantitative approach, using regional and country scorings that carefully evaluate risk variables such as political and economic stability.

Once relevant geographic considerations (part of world and country) are completed as relates to capital allocation, quantitative measures might be more readily applied pertaining to how much capital may be committed. For industry, company, and product-type categories, rating agencies provide detailed information on these types of things. Further, investors themselves can devise various measures to quantify the risk of these classifications. For example, *RAROC* (*risk-adjusted return on capital*) is used for risk analysis and project evaluation where a higher net return is required for a riskier project than for a less risky project. The risk adjustment is performed by reducing the risky return at the project or instrument return level rather than by adjusting some type of capital charge. Another measure of risk relative to capital is *RORAC (return on risk-adjusted capital)*; it is similar to *RAROC* except that the rate of return is measured without a risk adjustment and the capital charge varies depending on the risk associated with the instrument or project. Finally, there is *RARORAC (risk-adjusted return on risk-adjusted capital)*, which is a combination of *RAROC* and *RORAC*; specific risk adjustments are made to the expected returns, and the capital charge is varied to reflect differing expectations of risk in different projects or securities. While this may seem like double counting, the adjustments on each side of the process usually cover different risks.

The specific types of risk that might be considered with a capital adjustment can be separated into *systematic risk* and *nonsystematic risk*. The former could be defined as the risk associated with movement in a market or market segment as opposed to distinct elements of risk associated with a specific security. Systematic risk cannot be diversified away; it only can be hedged. Within the context of the standard *capital asset pricing model (CAPM)*, exposure to systematic risk is measured by beta. *Nonsystematic risk* is the element of price risk that can be largely eliminated by diversification within an asset class. It may also be called *security-specific risk, idiosyncratic risk,* or *unsystematic risk,* and in *regression analysis* it is equal to the *standard error*.

Table 5.6 presents bonds, equities, and currencies in the context of systematic versus nonsystematic risk.

Let us now consider specific formulas that include capital- and risk-adjusted variables. We begin with an unadjusted return on capital measure, or simply *return on capital*:

$$\frac{Expected\ return\ on\ security}{Capital\ allocated\ to\ trade\ the\ security}; \text{or simply}$$

TABLE 5.6 Systematic vs. Nonsystematic Risks

	Systematic Risk	Nonsystematic Risk
Bonds	Market risk ➤ Interest rates ➤ Volatility	Credit risk
Equities	Market risk ➤ S&P 500/Dow	Credit risk
Currencies		Credit risk

$$\frac{Expected\ return}{Capital}.$$

For a risk-adjusted return on capital we need to adjust expected return downward to reflect the risks being taken with the investment being considered. Accordingly, *RAROC* can be stated as

$$\frac{Expected\ return\ -\ Expected\ expenses\ -\ Expected\ losses}{Capital}.$$

The numerator is smaller due to the deduction of expected expenses and losses; by virtue of a smaller numerator, we will have a smaller overall return.

For a return on risk-adjusted capital, we need to adjust capital upward to reflect the risks to be supported by the investment being considered. Accordingly, *RORAC* can be stated as

$$\frac{Expected\ return}{Capital\ to\ support\ market\ risk\ +\ Credit\ risk\ +\ Other\ risks\ -\ Correlations}.$$

"Correlations" (in the denominator) simply means to subtract any overlapping capital contributions among market risk, credit risk, and any other risks of interest or relevance so as not to engage in a double counting.

The denominator is larger due to the addition of various capital charges; by virtue of a larger denominator, we will have a smaller overall return.

And for a risk-adjusted return on risk-adjusted capital, we need to adjust both expected return and capital in the same way as we adjusted them above. Accordingly, *RARORAC* can be stated as

$$\frac{Expected\ return\ -\ Expected\ expenses\ -\ Expected\ losses}{Capital\ to\ support\ market\ risk\ +\ Credit\ risk\ +\ Other\ risks\ -\ Correlations}.$$

We now have both a larger denominator and a smaller denominator, thus rendering the value for *RARORAC* less than either *RAROC* or *RORAC*.

As long as there are risks to be measured, each of these return ratios—*RARORAC*, *RAROC*, and *RORAC*—will generate a value that is less than expected return divided by capital. And that is the point. A predetermined and clearly specified target (or hurdle) rate of return must be reached to justify any allocation of capital in support of that endeavor; the rate of return must be high enough to cover the costs and capital expenditures needed to support the particular proposal.

Parenthetically, there is also a *systemic risk*, which is defined as the risk associated with the general health or structure of a financial system. It is almost invariably discussed in terms of the system's inability to handle large quantities of market, credit, or settlement risk.

By what methodology does someone calculate precise values for "expected expenses," "expected losses," or "capital to support market risk and credit risk and other risks"? The most simple and yet most accurate answer to this question is that it varies by firm. Obviously enough, each firm has different objectives, different levels of risk tolerance, and different areas of expertise when it comes to markets and risk management. Accordingly, some risk calculations (if they even exist at all in some firms) may appear to be simplistic or naïve, while other risk calculations may appear to be overly complex or confusing. One organization that has made tremendous efforts to both create risk measurements and educate about their relevance has been the Bank for International Settlements (BIS) headquartered in Switzerland. As banking certainly tends to be a regulated industry, we take up the matter of reporting requirements and related methodologies in Chapter 6.

No matter how quantitative or objective the capital allocation process may appear, it undoubtedly reflects at least some underlying linkages to some qualitative and subjective biases. These biases may be geographic (as in where the company is headquartered), industry-specific (if the company is an investment bank as opposed to a hedge fund), or even shaped by the personality of the company's key managers. Whatever the biases, the capital allocation process is often a fluid one, and perhaps ought to be for certain industry types so as to keep up with market opportunities as they arise.

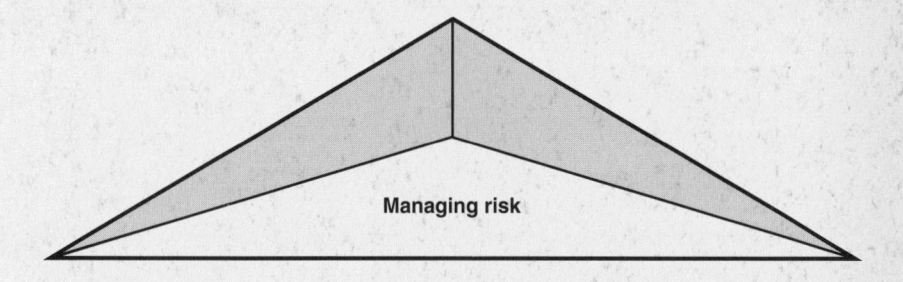

Managing risk

Now that we have discussed how risks can be quantified and allocated, we turn to how risks can be managed on a day-to-day basis. For some investors, it all begins with one fundamental consideration: probability. Accordingly, investment-related decisions are made on the basis of how a particular choice appears relative to available data, and those data typically are based on previous experiences. However, such an orientation can be made even more meaningful when it can be combined with a forward-looking approach, as with scenario analysis. Once a probability assessment is made, decisions inevitably follow. Finally, we examine a few basic approaches to hedging products and cash flows.

At its very essence, the managing of risk consists of probability, time, and cash flows. Figure 5.24 helps to illustrate this in the context of three different securities: a Treasury bill, a 30-year single-A rated corporate bond, and a share of equity. Probability is labeled as "uncertainty" to be consistent with lower uncertainties (greater probabilities) residing closer to the origin. As shown, a one-month Treasury bill sits pretty close to the origin since its credit is that of the U.S. government, it has but one cash flow (principal at maturity), and if held to maturity its total return is known with certainty at time of purchase. At the other extreme we have an equity, which is last in line from a credit perspective, and there is little certainty as to its future price value.

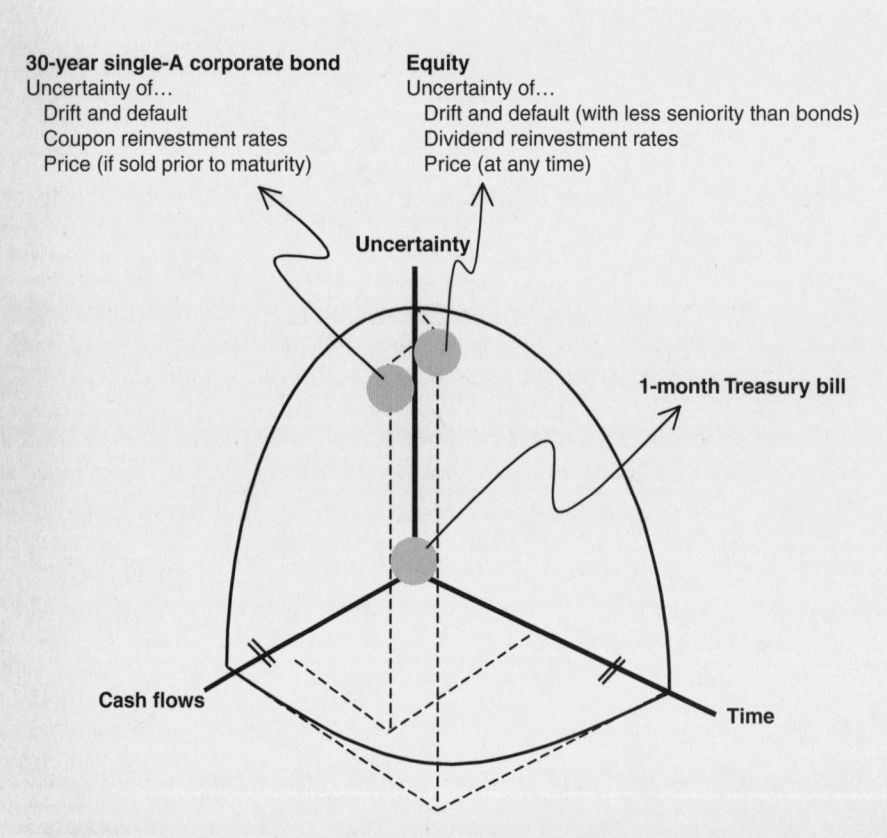

30-year single-A corporate bond
Uncertainty of...
   Drift and default
   Coupon reinvestment rates
   Price (if sold prior to maturity)

Equity
Uncertainty of...
   Drift and default (with less seniority than bonds)
   Dividend reinvestment rates
   Price (at any time)

FIGURE 5.24 A conceptual mapping of uncertainties.

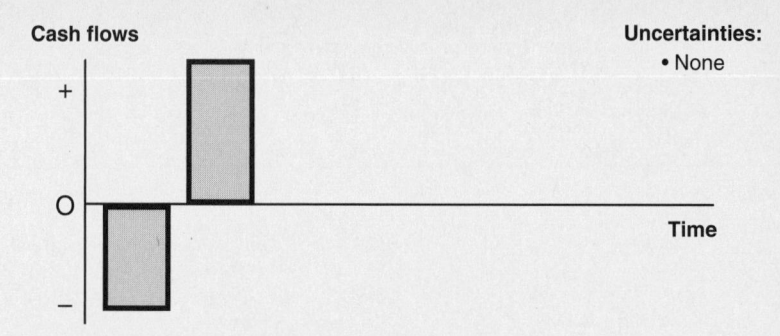

FIGURE 5.25 Six-month Treasury bill.

To further illustrate the relationships among probability, time, and cash flows, the next figures use a layering approach. We begin with something that's 100 percent certain, possesses one single cash flow, and ceases to exist after 180 days: a six-month Treasury bill (see Figure 5.25).

As shown in Figure 5.25 it can be said with 100 percent certainty (to the extent that anything can be 100 percent certain in life or in finance) that there is no credit risk, no reinvestment risk, and no price risk (if the Treasury bill is held to maturity). Accordingly, it can be said with 100 percent certainty at the time of purchase exactly what the total return of the Treasury bill will be in six months' time.

Figure 5.26 considers a two-year Treasury. Again there is no credit risk and no price risk (if the Treasury bill is held to maturity), but we can no longer say that there is 100 percent certainty of knowing total return at time of purchase. The reason is reinvestment risk; we do not know the rates of reinvestment for the coupon cash flows that are received between purchase and maturity dates. While this might seem to be a minor point, keep in mind that for a 20-year bond, well over one-half of its lifetime total return can easily come from its reinvested coupon income.[7]

Now let us change our two-year Treasury into a two-year double-B rated corporate bond. The incremental risk of credit is highlighted Figure 5.27.

What can we say about the three cases presented thus far? While we do not have enough information to comment on specific total return values, we certainly can make some general observations. If we let p_{tb} represent the

---

[7]For a 20-year bond with an 8 percent coupon, a reinvestment rate of 10 percent could lead to the reinvestment of coupon cash flows contributing more than 60 percent to the security's overall total return at maturity.

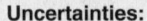

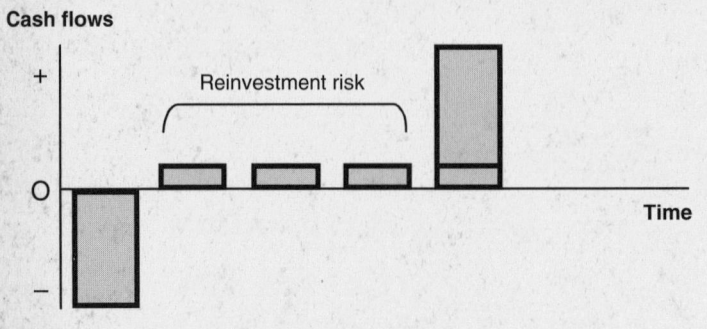

FIGURE 5.26 Two-year Treasury bond.

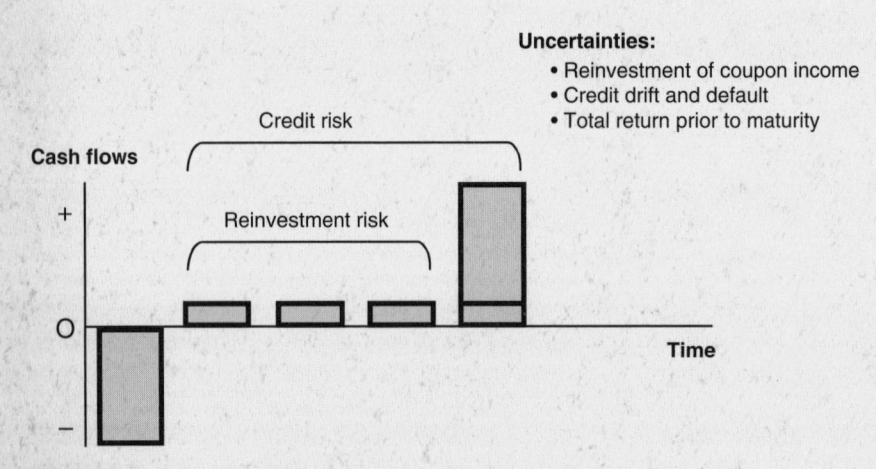

FIGURE 5.27 Two-year double-B corporate bond.

probability of knowing a Treasury bill's total return at time of purchase (holding it to maturity), $p_{tb} = 100$ percent. If we let p_{2yt} represent the probability of knowing a two-year Treasury's total return at time of purchase, at the very least we know that p_{2yt} is less than p_{tb}. In fact, it has to be less than p_{tb} since the two-year Treasury bond embodies more risk (via the added risk of reinvesting coupons). It then stands to reason that p_{2c} (representing a two-year corporate bond) must be less than p_{2t}. Putting these side-by-side, we have $p_{tb} > p_{2t} > p_{2c}$.

Risk Management

Earlier it was stated that managing risk could be seen in the context of cash flows, probability, and time. In the last two examples, time was held constant at two years. Not surprisingly, uncertainty only increases with time. Investors who think it is difficult to forecast what reinvestment rates might be over the next two years should try to imagine how tough it is to forecast reinvestment rates for the next 20 years. Rating agencies make distinctions between a company's short-term debt ratings and its long-term debt ratings. When the two ratings differ, typically the longer-term rating is lower. Accordingly, we can safely say that $p_{2t} > p_{20t}$ and that $p_{2c} > p_{20c}$.

If we can safely say that $p_{2t} > p_{20t}$ and $p_{2c} > p_{20c}$, can we say that $p_{20t} > p_{2c}$? No, at least not on the basis of what we have seen thus far. The uncertainty related to the reinvestment risk of a 20-year Treasury may be greater than the uncertainty related to the credit risk of a double-B corporate bond, but we are comparing apples (reinvestment risk) with oranges (credit risk). But hey, apples and oranges are both fruits that grow on trees, so let us not be so quick to end the conversation here. In fact, consider Figure 5.28. As shown, price volatilities between corporate and Treasury coupon-bearing securities appear to cross with seven-year Treasuries and five-year triple-B rated corporates.

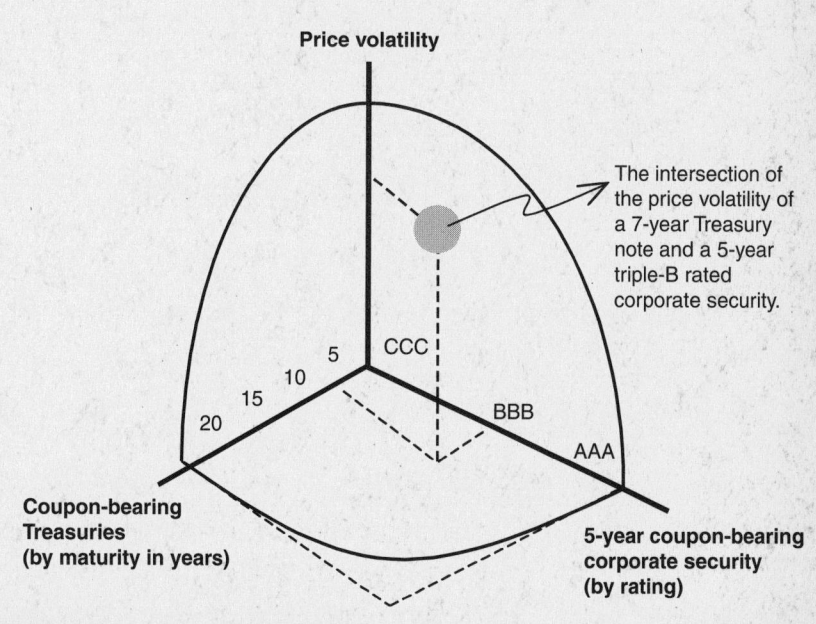

FIGURE 5.28 A conceptual mapping of risk profiles.

226 FINANCIAL ENGINEERING, RISK MANAGEMENT, AND MARKET ENVIRONMENT

Having now addressed uncertainties associated with credit and reinvestment of cash flows, let us now consider uncertainties related to timing and payment of coupon and principal as with pass-through securities. As shown in Figure 5.29, credit risk fades as a concern with pass-through securities, though risks associated with the timing and amounts of cash flows step into the picture. We use the same key for designating cash flow characteristics as we used in Chapter 2.

The cash flows of an equity can be illustrated as in Figure 5.30.

As the figure confirms, there is a much greater degree of uncertainty related to an equity's cash flow profile than to that of a bond. Accordingly, it ought not come as any surprise that the price risk of equities (typically measured in terms of price volatility) is generally greater than that of bonds. Further, and consistent with risk-reward trade-offs, historically a basket of

■ Denotes actual payment or receipt of cash for a cash flow value that's known at time of initial trade (as with a purchase price or a coupon or principal payment).

▯ Denotes that a cash flow's value cannot be known at time of initial trade and that an exchange of cash may or may not take place.

Of course, a product may be be sold prior to actual maturity/expiration at a gain, loss, or break even.

Uncertainties:
- Reinvestment of coupon income
- Timing and amounts of coupon and principal payments
- Total return prior to maturity

Cash flows   Prepayment risk; cash flows may include coupon and principal

Reinvestment risk

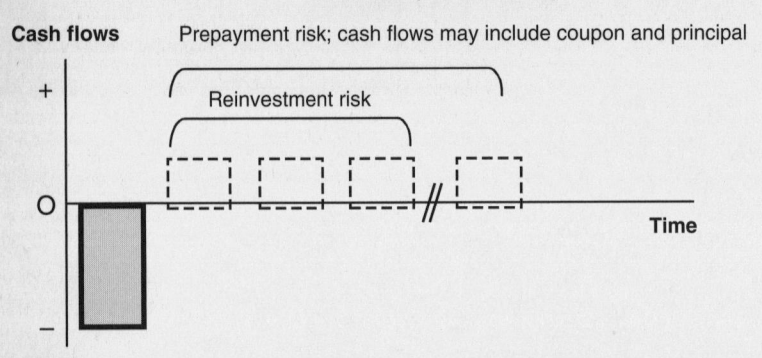

Time

FIGURE 5.29   15-year pass-thru security.

Risk Management

Uncertainties:
- Reinvestment of dividends
- Amount of dividends
- Credit drift and default
- Total return prior to end of investment horizon
- Price at any time

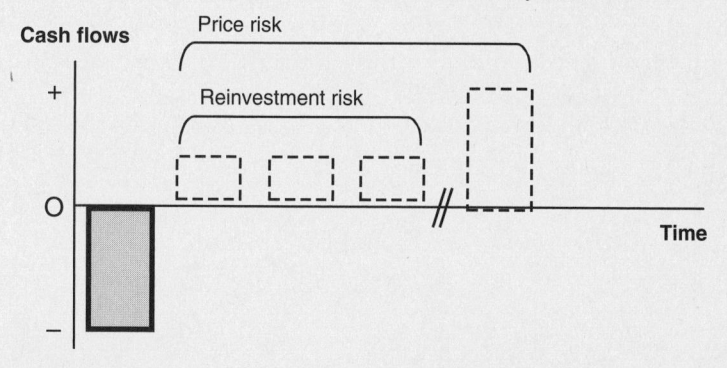

FIGURE 5.30 Equity.

diversified equities will generate higher returns relative to a basket of diversified bonds over long stretches of time (say five years or more).

Next we describe a hierarchy or ranking of probabilities for cash flows. The three principal types of cash flows are spot, forwards and futures, and options. At first pass it may be tempting to assert that a derivative of a spot (i.e., its forward or option) at the very least embodies all the risks embedded within the underlying spot. This is not necessarily the case. For example, with a spot purchase of a coupon-bearing bond, there is a reinvestment risk with the coupons that are paid over time. If an 8 percent coupon-bearing bond is purchased at par and held to maturity, its total return will be less than 8 percent if coupons are reinvested at rates under 8 percent. However, with a forward on an 8 percent coupon-bearing bond, the holder of a forward contract receives no coupons, so there are no coupons to be reinvested. To be sure, the value of all relevant coupons is embedded in a forward contract's price at time of purchase, and it is this *locking in* of the coupon's value (inclusive of reinvested income) that allows the holder of the forward contract to dispense with the reinvestment risk associated with the underlying spot. The same is true for an option on the underlying spot. Figure 5.31 repeats the illustrations for spot, forwards and futures, and options from Chapter 2.

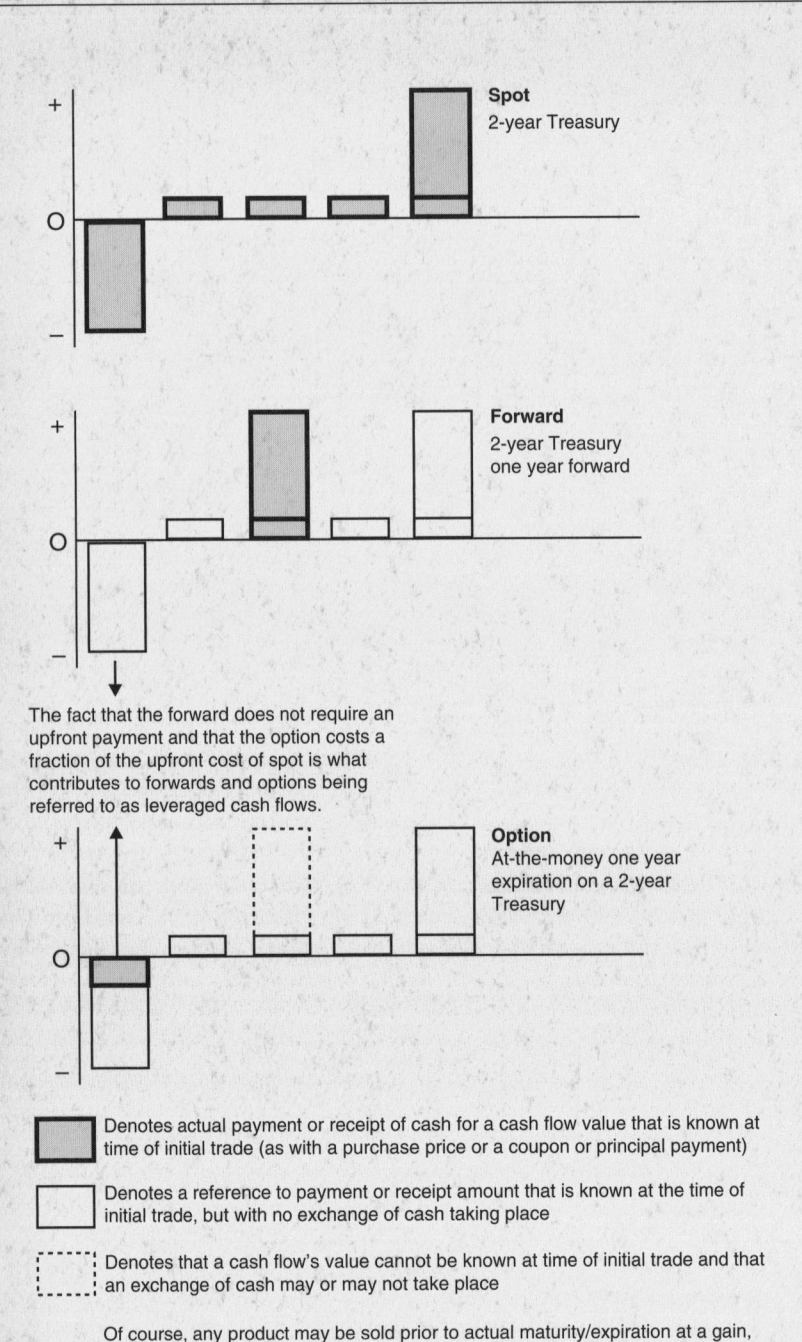

228   FINANCIAL ENGINEERING, RISK MANAGEMENT, AND MARKET ENVIRONMENT

Spot
2-year Treasury

Forward
2-year Treasury one year forward

The fact that the forward does not require an upfront payment and that the option costs a fraction of the upfront cost of spot is what contributes to forwards and options being referred to as leveraged cash flows.

Option
At-the-money one year expiration on a 2-year Treasury

■ Denotes actual payment or receipt of cash for a cash flow value that is known at time of initial trade (as with a purchase price or a coupon or principal payment)

□ Denotes a reference to payment or receipt amount that is known at the time of initial trade, but with no exchange of cash taking place

⌐ ⌐ Denotes that a cash flow's value cannot be known at time of initial trade and that an exchange of cash may or may not take place

Of course, any product may be sold prior to actual maturity/expiration at a gain, loss, or break even.

FIGURE 5.31   Spot, forwards and futures, and options.

However, although a forward or option might save an investor from directly confronting the matter of actually reinvesting coupon cash flows,[8] other unique risks do surface with forwards and options. To see how, simply consider the following variables and formulas below.

S = Spot
$F = S(1 + RT)$, Forward (for non–cash-flow paying securities)
$O_c = F - X + V$, Option (call)

As shown, F is differentiated from S with RT (cost-of-carry), and O_c is differentiated from F with V (volatility value). Since both cost-of-carry and volatility value are functions of time (T), they will shrink in value until they have a value of zero at the expiration of the forward or option. Thus, if the investment horizon of relevance is the expiration date, then there may be no risk to speak of for either carry or volatility, since both are zero at that juncture. However, if the horizon of relevance is a point in time prior to expiration, then carry and volatility values will likely be non-zero. And since their precise value cannot be known with certainty at the time a forward or option contract is purchased, it is not possible to know total return at time of purchase.

In the base case scenario involving a Treasury bill, we know its total return at time of purchase if the Treasury bill is held to maturity. In this simple case, the probability of knowing the Treasury bill's total return at time of purchase is 100 percent ($p_{tb} = 100\%$). It is 100 percent since there is no reinvestment risk of coupon payments and no credit risk, and we know that the Treasury bill will mature at par. If the Treasury bill is not held to maturity, the probability of knowing its total return at time of purchase is less than 100 percent. However, we can say that any uncertainty associated with a 12-month-maturity Treasury bill will be less than the uncertainty associated with a 12-month coupon-bearing Treasury. Why? Because the 12-month coupon-bearing Treasury carries reinvestment risk.

Accordingly, if not held to maturity, we can say that $p_{tb} > p_{1t}$ (where p_{1t} is the probability of knowing total return at time of purchase for a one-year

---

[8]While a forward or option on a bond might "save an investor from directly confronting the matter of actually reinvesting coupon cash flows," this may or may not be desirable. If reinvestment rates become more favorable relative to when the forward contract was purchased, then it is an undesirable development. However, reinvestment rates could become less favorable, and in any event, it is not something that holders of a forward contract can control in the way they can if they were holding the underlying bond.

coupon-bearing Treasury, and p_{tb} involves the same type of probability estimate for a 12-month Treasury bill). Further, with the added component of carry with a forward, we could say that $p_{tb} > p_{1t} > p_{1tf}$ (where p_{1tf} is the probability of knowing total return at time of purchase for a forward contract on a one-year coupon-bearing Treasury). And with the added components of both carry and volatility values embedded in an option, we could say that $p_{tb} > p_{1t} > p_{1tf} > p_{1to}$ (where p_{1to} is the probability of knowing total return at time of purchase for an option on a one-year coupon-bearing Treasury).

We conclude this section with a series of charts that provide another perspective of the varying risk characteristics of equities, bonds, and currencies.

Beginning with bonds, Figure 5.32 presents a price cone for a five-year-maturity coupon-bearing Treasury bond. The cone was created by shocking the Treasury with interest rate changes of both plus and minus 300 basis points at the end of each year from origination to maturity. As shown, as the maturity date draws near, the pull to par becomes quite strong.

Figure 5.33 is a price cone for both the previous five-year Treasury and a one-year Treasury bill. Among other considerations, the cone of the Treasury bill relationship to price is not centered symmetrically around par. The simple reason for this is that unlike the five-year Treasury, the Treasury bill is a discount instrument and thus has no coupon. Accordingly, this price cone helps to demonstrate the price dynamics of a zero coupon security.

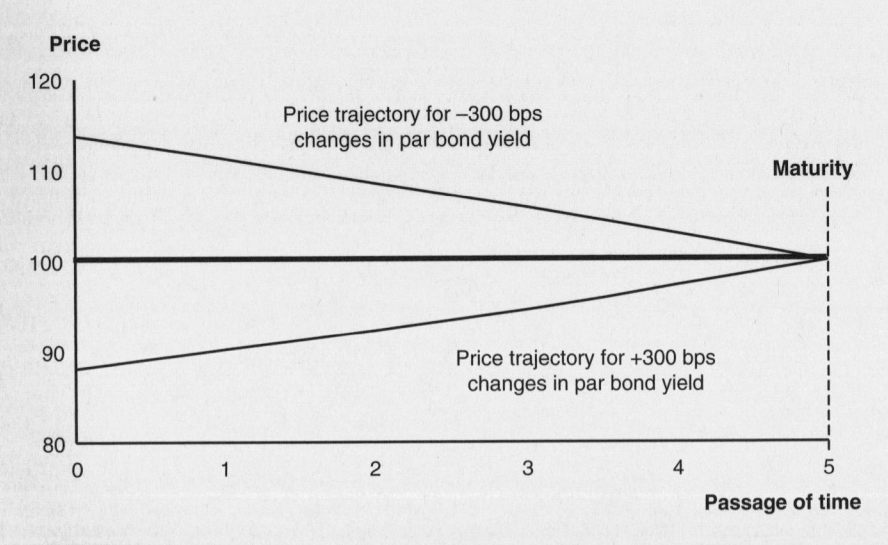

FIGURE 5.32 Price cone for a 5-year-maturity coupon-bearing Treasury.

Risk Management

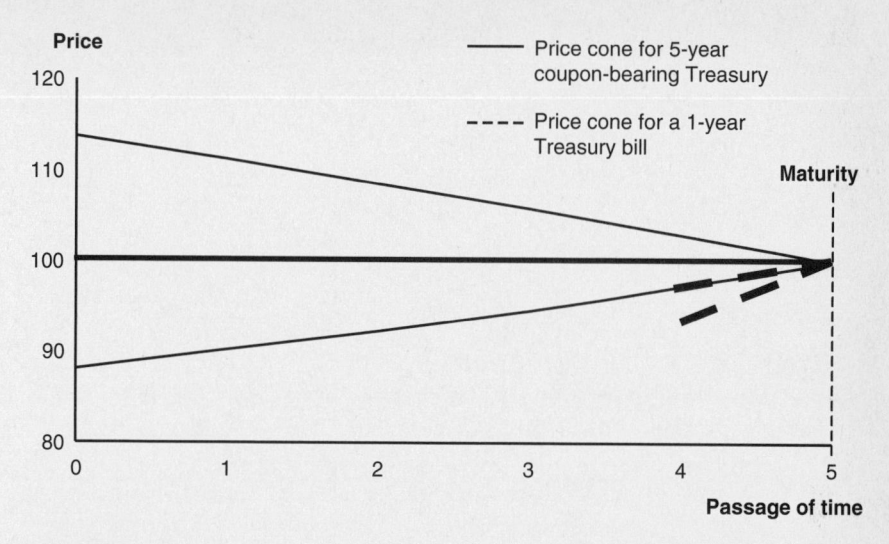

FIGURE 5.33 Price cone for a 5-year Treasury and 1-year Treasury bill.

Transitioning now from bonds to equities, consider Figure 5.34. As a rather dramatic contrast with the figure for bonds, there is no predetermined maturity date and, related to this, no convergence toward par with the passage of time. In fact, quite the contrary; the future price possibilities for an equity are open-ended, both on the upside and the downside. However, and as depicted, a soft floor exists at the point where the book value of assets becomes relevant. As one implication of this greater ambiguity, a variety of methodologies may be used to generate some kind of forecast of what future price levels might become. These methods include price forecasts based on an equity's valuation relative to other equities within its peer group, analyses of where the equity ought to trade relative to key performance ratios inclusive of its multiple of price to book value (total assets minus intangible assets and liabilities such as debt) or price-earnings (P/E) ratio (current stock price divided by current earnings per share adjusted for stock splits), and the application of technical analysis (analysis that seeks to detect and interpret patterns in past security prices).

Figure 5.35 shows currencies. Not too surprisingly, the figure more closely resembles the profile for equities than that for bonds, and this is explained by the more open-ended nature of potential future price values. As with equities, a soft floor is inserted where an embedded credit call might be said to exist that reflects some value of a country's economic and political capital. Again, a variety of methodologies might be used to forecast a

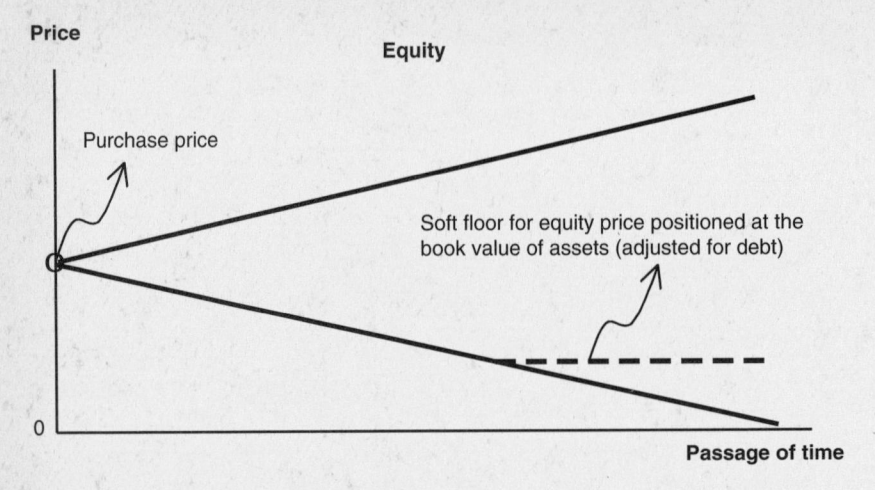

FIGURE 5.34 Price cone for an equity.

future exchange rate value, including consideration of interest rate parity or purchasing power parity models. Another way a cone might be created is with reference to a given exchange rate's implied volatility. In short, a forward series of implied volatilities could be used to generate an upper and lower bound of potential exchange rate values over time. In fact, this method of generating cones could be used for any financial instrument where an implied volatility is available.

For another perspective of evaluating the different issues involved with price and total return calculations across cash flows and products, consider Table 5.7.

In the table, there are two "Yes" indications for bonds, one for equities, and none for currencies. As a very general statement about the total return profile of investment-grade bonds versus equities and currencies, over the long run, the total returns of bonds tends to be less volatile relative to the returns of equities, and the total returns of equities tends to be less volatile relative to the returns of currencies. This pattern can be linked directly to the frequency and variety of cash flows generated by a given product (where frequency and variety relate to cash flow diversification) and to the relative predictability of all the cash flows.

Finally, the exercise of defining upper and/or lower bounds to financial variables of interest can be applied in a number of creative and meaningful ways. Its usefulness stems from assisting an investor with thinking about the parameters of what a best- and worst-case scenario actually might look like.

Risk Management

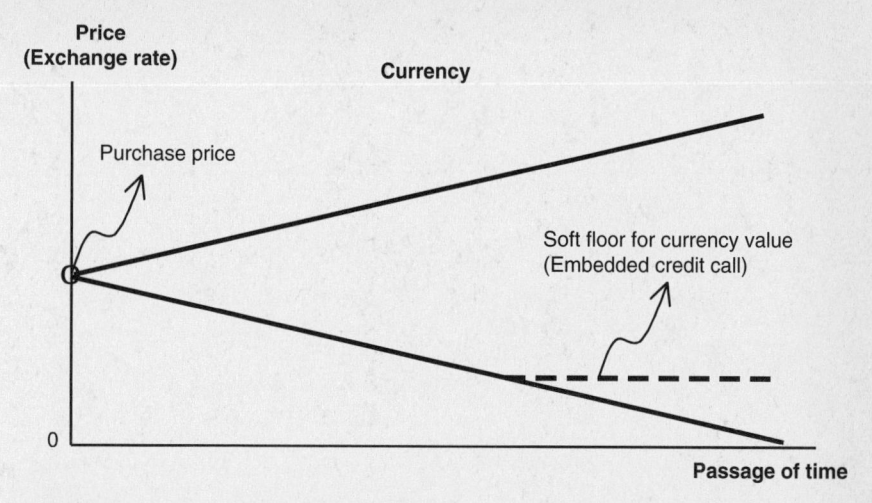

**Price
(Exchange rate)**

Purchase price

Currency

Soft floor for currency value
(Embedded credit call)

Passage of time

FIGURE 5.35 Price cone for currencies.

TABLE 5.7 Comparison of Total Return Components for a One-Year Horizon

	Products		
	Bonds	Equities	Currencies
Cash flow End price	Yes	No	No
Cash flows	Yes	Yes	N/A
Reinvestment of cash flows	No	No	N/A

To provide an example outside of the broader strokes of product types, consider the effect of different prepayment speeds on the outstanding balance of principal for an MBS. Figure 5.36 embodies a set of scenarios to be considered.

As shown, prepayment speeds can have a very important impact indeed on the valuation of an MBS, and these speeds can vary from month to month. Just as these types of illustrations can be useful with evaluating the risk of a particular security, they also can be used to evaluate the risk profile of entire portfolios. Another popular way to conceptualize the risks of a portfolio is with scenario analysis.

"Scenario analysis" refers to evaluating a particular strategy and/or portfolio construction by running it through all of its paces, all the while taking

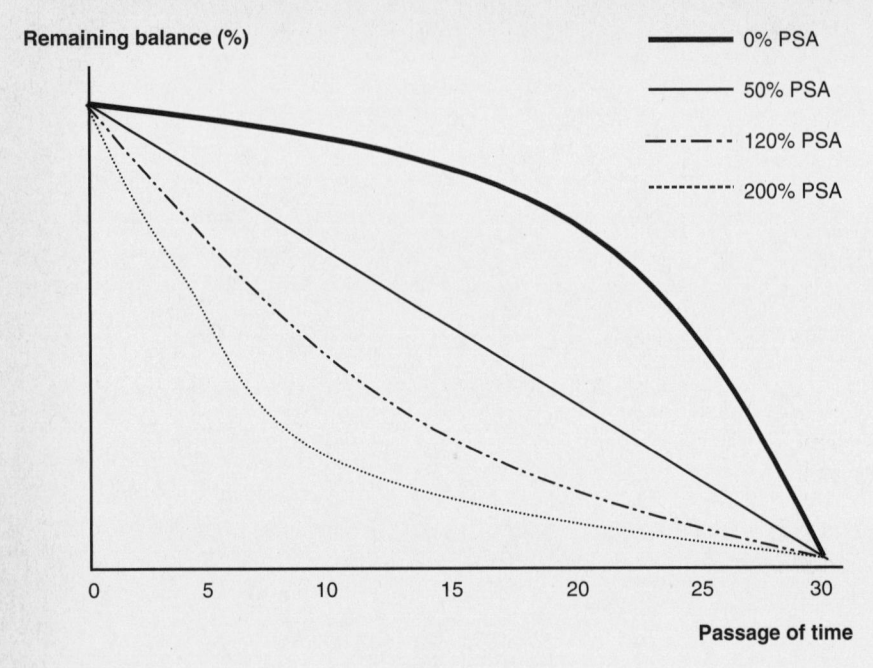

FIGURE 5.36 Outstanding principal balances for a generic "current coupon" 30-year pass-thru.

note of how total return evolves. For example, for a proposed bond portfolio construction, a portfolio manager might be interested in observing how total returns look on a six-month horizon if the yield curve stays relatively unchanged, if the yield curve flattens, or if the yield curve inverts. The total returns for these different scenarios then can be compared to the prevailing six-month forward yield curves and to the portfolio manager's own personal forecast (should she have one), and the proposed portfolio construction then can be evaluated accordingly. A variety of instrument types can be layered onto this core portfolio, including futures and options, so as to incorporate the latter. Additional scenarios (or "stress tests" as they are sometimes called) also might be performed that include different assumptions for volatility.

Scenario analysis can help give investors a working idea of the risks and rewards embedded in a particular strategy or portfolio structure *before* the plan is actually put into place. Of course, regardless of the number of what-if scenarios applied, the actual experience may or may not correspond exactly to any one of the scenarios. In this regard the value of scenario analysis lies in helping to identify boundary conditions.

In a more macro context of risk, consider the challenge of linking environmental dynamics with financial products. Let us assume that a company is headquartered in country X with a rather large and important subsidiary in country Y. Further, assume that the currencies in country X and Y are different and that the company repatriates its profits on an annual basis to its home base. It would be rather straightforward to envision a scenario whereby the subsidiary in country Y has a very profitable year but where those profits would quickly diminish after the relevant exchange rate were applied. This reflects a situation where the currency of country Y depreciated in a significant way relative to the currency of country X.

If the company had elected at the start of the year to hedge its currency exposures on an ongoing basis when and where practical, likely its profitability would have been at least partially protected. Accordingly, this strategy is often called an *economic hedge*. The motivation for the strategy would be to protect against a macro-oriented business level exposure (as opposed to a more micro-oriented portfolio- or product-level exposure). Other examples include an energy-sensitive industry, such as an airline, using oil futures to hedge or otherwise protect against high fuel costs, or a rate-sensitive industry, as with banking, using interest rate futures to hedge or protect against adverse moves in rates.

Summary

Probability plays a central role in attempts to characterize an investment's total return. In the absence of uncertainties, probability is 100 percent. As layers of risks are added, a 100 percent probability is whittled down to something other than complete certainty. In the classic finance context of a trade-off between risk and reward, riskier investments will generate higher returns over a long run relative to less risky investments, assuming there is some diversification within respective portfolios.

As another perspective on the inter-relationship between probability and products, consider Figure 5.37. With probability on one axis and time on the other, it shows profiles of a sample bond, equity, and currency.

As shown, a product's price is known with 100 percent certainty at the time it is purchased, and there is a relatively high degree of certainty that its price will not change dramatically within a short time after purchase. However, as time from purchase date marches onward, the certainty of what the price may do steadily declines. However, in the case of bonds, which have known prices at maturity, the pull to par eventually becomes a dominant factor and the probability related to price begins to increase (and reaches 100 percent at maturity for a Treasury security). The lower equity and currency profiles are consistent with the higher uncertainty (lower probability) associated with these products relative to bonds. (The standard deviation of price tends to be lowest for bonds, higher for equities, and higher again for currencies.)

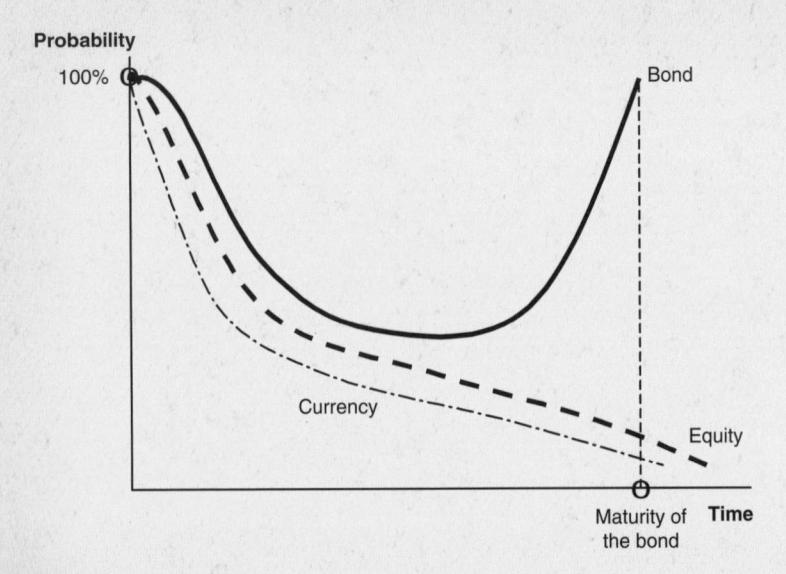

FIGURE 5.37 Probability profiles of a sample bond, equity, and currency.

CHAPTER SUMMARY

As we have seen time and again, we do not need to venture very far in the world of finance and investments to come face-to-face with a variety of risk considerations. If all we care about is a safe investment with a six-month horizon, then we can certainly go out and buy a six-month Treasury bill. There is no credit risk, reinvestment risk, or price risk (as long as we hold the Treasury bill to maturity). But what if we have a 12-month horizon? Do we then buy a 12-month Treasury bill, or do we consider the purchase of two consecutive six-month bills? What do we think of the price risk of a six-month Treasury bill in six months? In sum, there is risk embedded in many of the most fundamental of investment decisions, even if these risks are not explicitly recognized as such. When investors purchase a 12-month Treasury bill, they are implicitly (if not explicitly) stating a preference over the purchase of:

a. Two consecutive six-month Treasury bills
b. Four consecutive three-month Treasury bills
c. Two consecutive three-month Treasury bills, followed by the purchase of a six-month Treasury bill
d. A six-month Treasury bill, followed by the purchase of two consecutive three-month Treasury bills, or
e. A three-month Treasury bill, followed by the purchase of a six-month Treasury bill, followed by the purchase of another three-month Treasury bill

Risk Management

Although the risks among these various scenarios may be minimal with Treasury bills, the point here is to highlight how the decision to pursue strategy option a necessarily means not pursuing strategy b (or c or d, etc.). There are consequences for every investment decision that is taken as well as for each one that is deferred.

In addition to the various risk classifications presented in this chapter, there is also something called as *event risk*. Simply put, event risk may be thought of as any sudden unanticipated shock to the marketplace. It is not prudent for most portfolio managers to structure their entire portfolio around an event that may or may not occur. However, it can be instructive for portfolio managers to know what their total return profiles might look like in the event of a market shock. Scenario analysis can assist with this. Further, it also may be instructive for portfolio managers to know how products have behaved historically when subject to shocks. One way to conceptualize this would be with a charting of relevant variables as in Figure 5.38.

In sum, risk is elusive; that is why it is called risk. Simply dismissing it is irresponsible. By thinking of creative ways in which to better understand, classify, and manage risk, investors will be better equipped to handle the vagaries of risk when they arise.

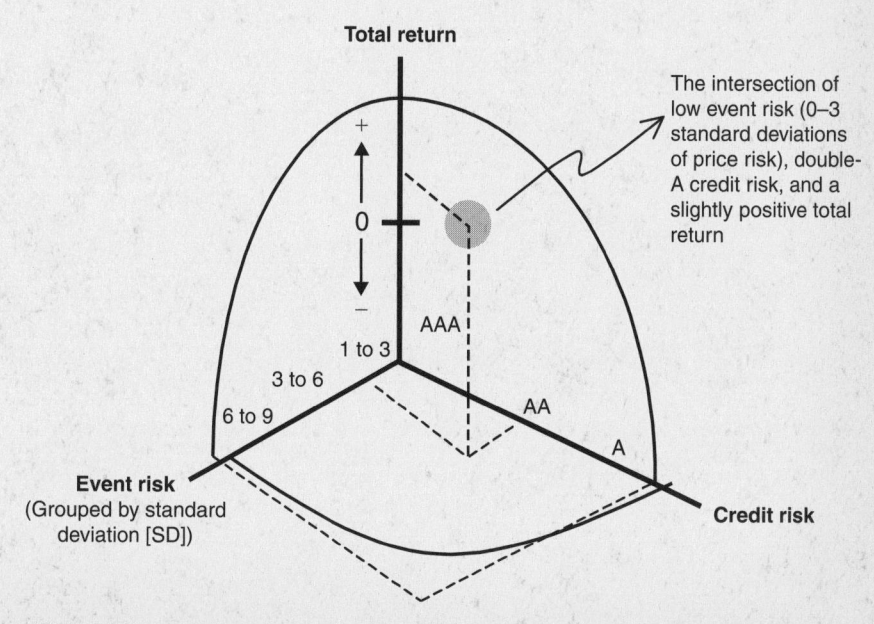

FIGURE 5.38 Another conceptual mapping of risk profiles.

APPENDIX

Benchmark Risk

At first pass, having the words "benchmark" and "risk" together may seem incongruous. After all, isn't the role of a benchmark to provide some kind of a neutral measure, some kind of pure yardstick by which to gauge relative market performance? While that certainly is the ideal role of a benchmark, with the dynamic nature of the marketplace generally, it often is an ideal that is difficult to live up to.

For example, for decades U.S. Treasuries were seen as the appropriate benchmark for divining relative value among bonds. In the late 1990s, with the advent of unexpected and persistent federal budget surpluses, this status began to look a little shaky. With Treasuries on a relative decline, investors began to ask if there might be another benchmark security type that could replace Treasuries as an arbiter of value. A particular financial instrument does not become a benchmark by formal decree; it is much more by what the market deems to be of relevance in a very practical way. That is, the marketplace naturally gravitates toward obvious solutions that work rather than pursue solutions that may be more theoretically pure though less practical. Indeed, during the 1970s in the United States, longer-dated corporate securities were used as market benchmarks, largely because they were more prevalent at that time than the burgeoning federal budget deficits that dominated the 1980s. In the late 1990s and into 2000, a debate was waged as to whether federal agency debt might represent a more appropriate market benchmark in light of the agencies' net growth of issuance contrasting against a net contraction in Treasuries. Indeed, the likes of Fannie Mae and Freddie Mac introduced a regular cycle to key maturities in their debt management program to provide a market alternative to Treasuries. Over the period of debate the federal agencies were greatly increasing their borrowing programs relative to the U.S. government.

Another vehicle that sometimes is named as a benchmark possibility is the swap yield. Proponents of this variable do not hold it up as a paragon of market solutions, since it (like any one single variable that would be selected) has its own strengths and weaknesses. As benchmark candidates, swap yields have these points going for them (listed in no particular order).

- Swap yields have a tried-and-true history of assisting with relative value identification in European markets.
- Many markets around the globe (and notably within Asia) have for a long time run federal budgets that have at least been neutral if not in surplus,

and in the absence of being able to defer to swap yields would have no other benchmark candidates in common with other markets globally.
- As is perhaps now obvious in light of the two preceding points, if swap yields were adopted in the U.S. market as a benchmark prototype, they could easily translate into every market around the world.
- Considering the possibility (at least as of this writing) of the U.S. federal government cutting its ties to federal agencies by no longer agreeing to back their debt implicitly, with the stroke of a pen the agencies could very well become much more like non-Treasury instruments than Treasury instruments. In this regard, if agencies were to become much more creditlike anyway, then why not just revert to swap yields? This question and others serve to highlight how the fluidity of the marketplace often affects the role and value of market benchmarks, and investors are well advised to stay abreast of benchmark-related topics, especially if the portfolio performance of interest to them is a performance relative to a benchmark measure.

As pointed out in the appendix to Chapter 4, a benchmark may best be thought of as a moving target rather than a static one. While this is obvious in the context of fast-moving markets, in some instances it can be just as important when nothing really happens, as with fixed income securities.

While it may seem obvious to say that the value of a fixed income instrument is going to be influenced by changes in interest rates, a variety of things can impact the nature of those changes. Clearly, if a 10-year-maturity Fannie Mae bullet is being quoted relative to the yield of the 10-year Treasury, then the rise and fall in yield of the Treasury presumably will translate into the rise and fall of the yield on the Fannie Mae issue. However, if a new 10-year Treasury happens to come to market (as of this writing, a 10-year Treasury comes to market every quarter) and becomes the new issue against which the Fannie Mae security is quoted, then the yield spread of the Fannie Mae relative to the Treasury may change. Its change would not be attributable to anything new or different with Fannie Mae as a credit risk, nor, for that matter, to anything new or different with the Treasury as a credit risk, but solely because a benchmark Treasury rate has "rolled" into a new benchmark rate.

Another type of interest rate risk, and clearly a broader definition of the "roll risk" just described, is "roll-down" risk. "Roll down" is a term used to describe the fact that the yield curve typically has a slope to it, and as time passes, a 10-year security is going to roll down into a 9-year maturity, then an 8-year maturity, and so on. This phenomenon is called "roll down" because the typical shape of the yield curve slopes upward, with yields at shorter maturities being lower than yields for longer maturities. Thus, rolling down the yield curve into shorter maturities generally would mean rolling down into lower yield levels. However, this may not always be the case. Indeed, even if the overall curve tends to have a normal upward slope to it, there may be special cases where there is "roll-up." For example, if a widely anticipated newly issued Treasury were to come to market and with strong demand, it may very well find itself "on special" and trading with a lower yield, even though it has a maturity that is slightly longer than the shorter-maturity Treasury that it is replacing.

In sum, benchmarks can be misleading if thought of only as static and unchanging arbiters of relative value. They are fluid and dynamic, and if they are indeed the enemy to be beaten for a value-oriented investor, then taking the time to understand and appreciate the nature of a particular index would be time well spent indeed.

CHAPTER 6

Market Environment

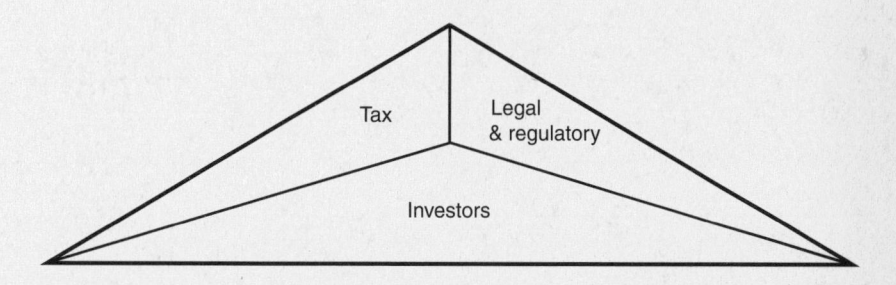

Tax · Legal & regulatory · Investors

This chapter continues with a more macro orientation toward investments, examining tax, legal and regulatory, and investor-related issues. Specific cases of how products and cash flows are affected by these macro dynamics, and more general cases of how investment decision making is affected are presented.

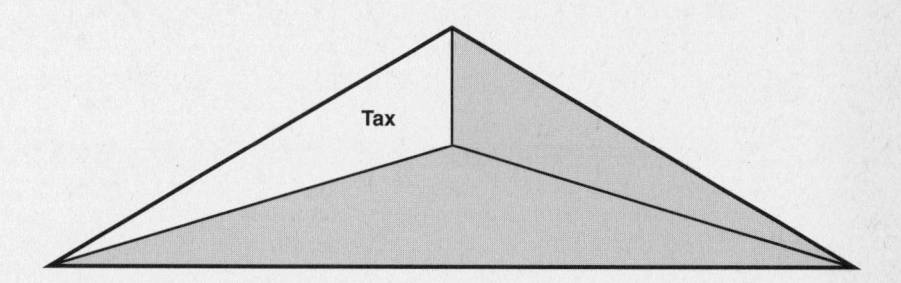

Tax

Although perhaps all to easy to dispense with in the excitement of investing, paying taxes is, regrettably, a fact of life—unless one is investing on behalf of not-for-profit entities. Taxes can make a very large impact on an investor's realized total returns. The goal of this chapter is to highlight how consideration of taxes can have a very important impact on an investor's decision making.

In the United States, as in most other developed financial markets, equities and bonds can be subject to a variety of different tax structures. There is the capital gains tax, which is differentiated into a short-term rate (for holding periods of less than one year) and a long-term rate (for holding periods of more than one year). As an incentive to investors to hold on to their

241

investments and minimize short-term profit-taking strategies, the long-term *capital gains* (gain on the amount of principal invested) tax rate is less than the short-term capital gains tax rate. Then there are some cash flows, such as coupons, that are subject to tax not at a capital gains rate but at a rate consistent with an investor's *ordinary income* (non-investment-related) tax bracket. Further, some fixed income instruments are taxed only at a city, state, or federal level, or at some combination of these. For example, Treasury bonds are exempt from federal tax (but not state and local tax[1]), while selected bonds of federal agencies are subject to federal tax but not state and local tax. And finally, there are even types of investment vehicles that benefit from certain tax advantages. Examples of these would include *401(k)s* (retirement accounts), *529s* (college savings accounts), and *individual retirement accounts* (IRAs). Aside from being subject to differential tax treatment, these products also may impose severe penalties if investors do not follow prescribed rules pertaining to their usage.

Although it seems obvious to say that the way a security is taxed can greatly affect its contribution to a portfolio's total return, tax effects are often overlooked. For example, in the case of mutual funds, it is not the fund manager who is taxed, but the individuals who invest in the fund. Accordingly, each year fund investors receive a statement from their fund company that reports the tax effect of the fund's various investments; the investor is required to report any tax liability to appropriate tax authorities. Since tax liabilities are passed through to investors and are not directly borne by fund managers, investors will want to be aware of a fund's tax history prior to investing in it. A particular fund's returns might look impressive on a before-tax basis but rather disappointing on an after-tax basis, especially if the fund manager is aggressively engaged in tax-disadvantaged strategies in the pursuit of superior returns. As the result of a recent ruling by the Securities and Exchange Commission (SEC), today funds are required to report both before- and after-tax returns, and there's sound reasoning for this requirement.

Specific examples of how taxes might transform a bond from one that looks desirable on the basis of its yield to be relatively unattractive on the basis of its after-tax total return follow. In particular, let us focus on the bonds of various federal agencies. Table 6.1 presents an overview of how various federal agency bonds are taxed at the federal, state, and local levels.

As shown in Table 6.1, there are discrepancies among the agencies in the terms of their tax treatment. For example, while Fannie Mae and Freddie Mac are not exempt at the state and local levels, the Federal Home Loan Bank and Tennessee Valley Authority are.

---

[1]Not all states and localities impose taxes.

Market Environment

TABLE 6.1 Taxable Status of U.S. Federal Agency Bonds

Issuer	Tax Exempt Federal Level	Tax Exempt State & Local Level
Federal Home Loan Banks	No	Yes
Federal Farm Credit Bank	No	Yes
Federal Home Loan Mortgage Corporation (Freddie Mac)	No	No
Federal National Mortgage Association (Fannie Mae)	No	No
Tennessee Valley Authority	No	Yes
Agency for International Development	No	No
Financing Corporation	No	Yes
International Bank for Reconstruction and Development	No	No
Resolution Funding Corporation	No	Yes
Private Export Funding Corporation	No	No

Tax laws are subject to frequent changes, and investors ought to consult with their tax adviser prior to investing in any of these securities.

Table 6.2 provides tax-adjusted total return scenarios whereby an investor (for our purposes here, an investor taxed at the applicable corporate tax rates) can compare one agency to another or to another fixed income sector. The assumptions are provided so that readers can see exactly how numbers were generated.

As shown in Table 6.2, at first pass, the nominal spread differences of the agencies to the single-A rated corporate security appear rather meaningful. Yield differences between the agencies and the cheaper corporate security range from 38 basis points (bps) with the five-year maturities, to 45 bps with the 10-year maturities, and to 59 bps with the 20-year maturities. Yet when we calculate tax-adjusted total returns, the spreads that are there when stated as nominal yield differences dissipate when expressed as total return. Indeed, they invert. The total return advantage for state and local exempt agencies (Federal Home Loan Bank and Tennessee Valley Authority [TVA] in these instances) relative to the single-A corporate security is 12 bps for five-year maturities and 2 bps for 20-year maturities. Since the analysis assumes constant spreads over the one-year investment horizon, any outlook on the relative performance of these securities is certainly of relevance.

The choice of an 8 percent benchmark for state and local tax rates (combined) is lower than the national average. If we were to single out New York, for example, the state and New York City rates would combine to just over 10%. Massachusetts at the state level alone is at a rate of more than 10 percent. Using a combined state and local tax assumption of 9 per-

TABLE 6.2 Tax-Adjusted Total Returns of Agency vs. Corporate Securities, One Year Horizon

5-Year Maturities	Nominal Spread (bps)	Nominal Yield (%)	After-Tax Return (%) (1)	(2)	(3)
Fannie Mae	2	5.66	4.47	3.91	3.34
FHLB	21	5.66	4.81	4.25	3.68
Single-A corporate bond	59	6.04	4.77	4.17	3.56
10-year Maturities					
Fannie Mae	30.5	5.89	4.65	4.06	3.47
FHLB	30.5	5.89	5.00	4.41	3.83
Single-A corporate bond	76	6.34	5.01	4.37	3.74
20-year Maturities					
Fannie Mae	25	6.17	4.87	4.26	3.64
TVA	25	6.17	5.24	4.63	4.01
Single-A corporate bond	84	6.76	5.34	4.66	3.99

(1) Represents after-tax rates of return; rates after federal tax rate of 15% and a state and local tax rate of 8%.
(2) Represents a federal tax rate of 25% and a state and local rate of 8%.
(3) Represents a federal tax rate of 35% and a state and local rate of 8%.
Assumptions: It is assumed that securities are purchased and sold at par and are held over a one-year horizon. This par assumption allows us to ignore consideration of capital gains and losses, though when we do incorporate these scenarios, our results are consistent with the overall results shown. We also assume that at the time of the security's purchase, the present value of future tax payments are set aside, quarterly for federal corporate tax and a one-time filing for state and local corporation tax. All cash flows are discounted at the respective security's yield-to-maturity. Finally, our choice of 8% as a benchmark rate for state and local tax is less than the average of the highest and lowest rates across the country. One motivation for using a lower-than-average rate is to attempt to incorporate at least some consideration of how federal tax payments are deductible when filing state and local returns.

cent, the total return advantage of an agency to a single-A corporate security widens to 30 bps at the highest federal tax rate for five-year maturities, to 28 bps for 10-year maturities, and up to 22 bps for 20-year maturities. Clearly, for buy-and-hold-oriented investors, these total return differentials may appreciably enhance overall performance over the life of a security.

While we have touched on many issues here related to tax considerations, there are others. For example, there is the matter of relative performance when capital gains enter the picture. In all likelihood, the price of a given security at year-end will not be what it was at the time of initial trade. However, under some basic what-if scenarios, the relative performance stories above generally hold with both capital gain and loss scenarios (assuming duration-neutral positions for like changes in yield levels, constant spreads).

In addition to applying a tax analysis to notes and bonds, we also can apply it to shorter-dated money market instruments like discount notes. Applying a methodology similar to the one used in the note and bond analysis, we examined three- and six-month discount notes against like-maturity corporate securities.

As shown in Table 6.3, yield differences between discount notes and a short-dated corporate security range from 26 bps with three-month instruments to 38 bps with six-month instruments. Since the state and local tax exemptions that apply to agency bonds also apply to discount notes, on a tax-adjusted basis we would expect initial yield advantages to dissipate into total return advantages favoring different issues. In the analysis, the total return advantage for the state and local exempt agencies (Federal Home

TABLE 6.3 Tax-Adjusted Total Returns for Agencies versus Corporates, Annualized

	Spread (bps)	Yield (%)	After-Tax Return (%) (1)	(2)	(3)
3-month instruments					
FHLMC discount note	48	5.51	4.31	3.80	3.30
FHLB discount note	48	5.51	4.68	4.24	3.74
Corporate Baa1-rated	Libor+10bps	5.77	4.51	3.98	3.45
6-month instruments					
FHLMC discount note	34	5.53	4.32	3.81	3.80
FHLB discount note	32	5.51	4.68	4.13	3.58
Corporate Baa-rated	Libor+20bps	5.89	4.60	4.06	3.52

(1) Represents after-tax rates of return based on a federal tax of 15% and a state and local tax rate of 8%.
(2) Represents federal tax rate of 25% and a state and local tax rate of 8%.
(3) Represents federal tax rate of 35% and a state and local tax rate of 8%.
Assumptions: It is assumed that securities are purchased at a discount and are held to maturity. This par assumption allows us to ignore consideration of capital gains and losses, though when we do incorporate these scenarios, our results are consistent with the overall results presented. We also assume that at the time of a security's purchase, the present value of future tax payments are set aside, quarterly for federal corporate tax and a one-time filing for a state and local corporation tax. All cash flows are discounted at the respective security's yield-to-maturity. Finally, our choice of 8% as a benchmark rate for state and local tax is near the average national rate. Note, however, that tax rates vary considerably from state to state, and consultation with a tax adviser is recommended.

Loan Bank and Farm credit, for instance) relative to the corporate security is 26 bps for three-month instruments and 7 bps for six-month instruments. This assumes a combined state and local tax rate of 8 percent and a federal corporate tax rate of 25 percent. To reiterate, because the analysis assumes constant spreads over the investment horizon, any outlook on the relative performance of these securities, though relevant, is not fully considered here for purposes of keeping the analysis cleaner. And again, investors should consult with appropriate tax advisers when evaluating these opportunities.

As a final statement about tax-related considerations, note that tax treatments may well influence the type of structure that one agency might prefer offering over another. Consider Federal Home Loan Bank (FHLB) (exempt from state and local taxes) and Fannie Mae (not exempt from state and local taxes) debt issuance. In contrast to Fannie Mae, the FHLB is predisposed to offering callable product with lockouts of under one year. Although Fannie Mae and the FHLB have different funding objectives that mirror their different mandates, it is nonetheless striking that the overwhelming bias of Fannie Mae is to bring its callables with lockouts longer than one year (at 62 percent), while the FHLB brought the majority (76 percent) of its callables with lockouts of 12 months and under. This phenomenon is consistent with the FHLB wanting to appeal to yield-oriented investors, such as banks, that are able to take advantage of the preferential tax opportunity provided by the FHLB's shorter lockouts and higher yield spreads.[2]

This type of tax adjustment total return methodology certainly appeals to individual investors as well as investors at corporations not generally subject to unique industry-specific categories of tax law. Investment divisions in corporate goods sectors (e.g., manufacturing) would find a stronger motivation for this approach than, say, corporate services sectors (e.g., insurance).

All else being equal, if it were possible for tax policy to be applied within the marketplace such that no heterogeneous distortions could emerge, then it is plausible that the market would continue along in much the way that it would have done in the absence of any kind of tax policy. The reality, however, is that the temptation to use tax as a policy variable (namely a nonhomogenous application of taxes) is a powerful one, and as such it can give rise to market opportunities.

As with regulations, tax policy can be used to deter or promote certain types of market behavior. It also can be the case that the tax is put into place because it is anticipated to be a good revenue source. Again, for our purposes we simply want to advance the notion that tax policies influence how market decisions are made, for issuers as well as for investors.

---

[2] The higher yield spread is the result, all else being equal, of the difference in structure of the FHLB callable product compared to the Fannie Mae product.

Like other bonds, municipal bonds have credit risk, market risk, and so forth. In some instances the nature of the credit risk may be very different from that of corporate securities (as with a municipality's ability to generate tax revenues as opposed to profits in a more traditional business sense), and may be quite similar to corporate securities in other instances (as when a hospital issues revenue bonds that must be supported by successful ongoing operations).

As an incentive for states and municipalities to have access to lower-cost funding sources, municipal securities typically are offered with some kind of tax free-status attached.

Since investors know going into the investment that they will be tax-protected to at least some degree, they get a lower yield and coupon on their investment. This lower coupon payment directly translates into a lower cost of funding for the municipal entity. Often investors in municipal securities monitor the ratio of municipal yield levels to fully taxable yield levels, as one measure of gauging relative value on a broad basis between these two asset classes. Ultimately, the investment decision of whether or not to invest in municipal securities comes down to the matter of tax incentives.

Tax matters may not be the most terribly exciting of considerations when it comes to strategy development, but they can be tremendously important when it comes to the calculation of total returns and, hence, the making of appropriate choices among investment opportunities.

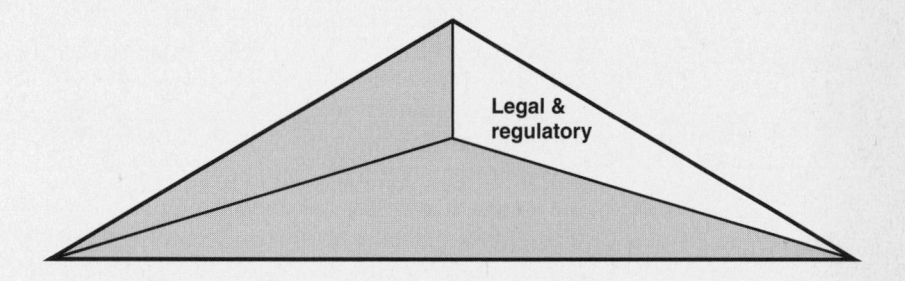

Legal & regulatory

The legal environment of a given market is an extremely important consideration. Yet the paradox is that although it is so important, it is also taken for granted, so much so that it is often conveniently put out of mind as something requiring any significant deliberation. Certainly one of the criteria used by the rating agencies when assigning currency ratings is some assessment of the strength, independence, and effectiveness of judicial infrastructure. To provide a picture or relevant legal considerations in the marketplace, let us use the triangle of product, cash flow, and credit as our point of reference.

As to equities, a battery of registrations is typically required for a company to have its shares listed on an exchange. Filings typically must be made not only with the exchange itself, but with governmental agencies as well. Among the more rigorous of registration requirements, significant details of present and past dealings may be demanded of the company's board of directors and officers, and restrictions may be placed on when and how the equity is retained or sold by company insiders. Clearly it is to a potential investor's advantage to know what protections do not exist and especially when the investment involves an IPO and particularly when the IPO is being brought in a market that is foreign to an investor's.

For currencies, transactions occur in an over-the-counter (OTC) market. The only rules and regulations typically encountered include considerations of types and amounts of cash transfers and if exchanges of different currencies are being done at the officially set exchange rate or at some black market rate (as relevant, of course, only for those countries that do not allow for a freely floating market-determined exchange rate).

Bonds also are an OTC market, yet various rules and guidelines exist at national and local levels to help ensure fairness in buying and selling securities. For both currencies and bonds, investors are well advised to be aware of a given market's best practices, especially if it is not the investors' home market.

As the structure of financial instruments grows more complex, legal considerations may become more complex as well. For example, if a bundle of existing bonds were packaged together as a single portfolio of securities, and if the securities were originally brought to market as U.S. dollar-denominated issues, what special legal considerations might arise, and especially if the currency exposure were transferred into euros via a currency swap? Let us consider this a piece at a time. First, we consider the bundled aspects of the bonds.

When investors purchase a single security, typically the investors must pursue any actions that might be required should the security experience difficulty. For example, if investors were to buy high-yield bonds, they would have to pursue remedial action if that security became distressed or defaulted. By contrast, if a bundle of high-yield securities were formally packaged and sold as a single product, individual investors would not be as likely to be the ones to bear the responsibility for seeking remedial action if one or more of the securities within the bundle experienced difficulty. Typically when this type of structured product is created, the entity arranging the structure makes provisions for how distressed/default situations are to be handled and charges an up-front and/or ongoing management/servicing fee. Clearly, it is imperative that investors understand that they have delegated an appreciable amount of authority and control to someone else as pertains to legal prerogatives. Investors should make necessary inquiries to be reasonably assured that the entity(s) handling the legal end of things is reputable.

The swapped component of this example introduces yet another layer of potential legal considerations. Many types of swaps might be executed, including currency swaps, interest rate swaps, basis swaps, and index swaps. A common element to all of these swaps is the embedded promise to make good on all cash flows provided over the life of the swap. This is pretty consistent with the promise embedded in a bond that pays coupons. Yet if a swap is combined with a bond (as might be done to convert the original currency exposure of the bond into something else), two levels of legal considerations are brought into play. First, if an industrial company issued the bond, there would be remedial action with this entity in a distressed/default situation. Second, if a currency swap were then to overlay the industrial company bond, it is doubtful that the industrial company would be providing investors with the currency swap as well. Typically, investment banks would provide the currency swap. Accordingly, investors must know the rules of the game as they relate to a distressed/default situation of the underlying bond (the industrial company), and of the investment bank providing an essential overlay to that underlying bond (as with the currency swap). But we do not have to go all the way down to the distressed/default end of the continuum to appreciate key legal dynamics of adding structural dimensions to standard product types. For example, investment banks can be upgraded and downgraded by the rating agencies, just as everything else can. Continuing with the industrial company example, let us say that both the industrial company's bond and the investment bank providing the currency swap were initially rated as double-A and that the investment bank subsequently was downgraded to a triple-B entity. This event would have the effect of lowering the credit profile of the combined products to single A, due to no fault on the bond issuer's part. Once again it is instructive to make a distinction between investors buying the bond and the currency swap as a prepackaged bundle or purchasing them separately. The prepackaged bundle approach implies the presence of someone doing the structuring on behalf of someone else and charging some kind of fee (typically embedded in the product's overall price) for that service. What must be made clear in this model is who will be responsible for what; where does accountability ultimately lie?

For example, let us say that issuer A approaches investment bank B about structuring one of its bonds with a currency swap so as to expand its marketing and investor profile overseas. Let us also say that investment bank B structures this bundled transaction, yet does so with the currency swap component coming from investment bank C. Assuming that the deal was successfully put together and sold in the marketplace, who is responsible for what if investment bank C is downgraded (forcing a downgrade of the transaction and a concomitant decline in its price)?

Should investment bank C be expected to provide an injection of capital to the business unit underwriting the swap so as to improve the credit quality of the products issued by that entity? Should the issuer set aside moneys in a reserve fund to appease the rating agencies so that investors are facing a better implied outlook on their investment? Is there any role or responsibility for investment bank B?

It is too late to ask these questions after a downgrade has been experienced. These matters should be clearly laid out with a *prospectus* and ought to be fully addressed before a purchase is made. A prospectus is a document that accompanies a security when it comes to market. It ought to provide relevant details pertaining to legal protections. Within bond prospectuses these types of provisions are commonly referred to as covenants.

While convenants may be welcome in some instances (as with some consumers who might not otherwise be familiar with the unique risks associated with investing in hedge funds), they may not be so welcome in other instances (as with hedge funds that want their offerings to be more accessible to small investors).

Simply put, covenants help to bring greater precision to how exactly a borrower intends to act once it receives its borrowings and/or how the borrower intends to respond to particular events (anticipated or otherwise) while its debt is outstanding. There are generally three types of covenants to consider.

1. Some covenants attempt to guide the nature of an issuer's future pledges against assets. Limitations on liens, sometimes called a negative pledge, prohibit a company from granting a lien on an asset in favor of future debtholders unless the lien also would benefit existing debtholders.
2. Some covenants attempt to guide the nature of an issuer's future indebtedness. For example, an issuer might be restricted from additional debt that it (or its subsidiaries) can take on or guarantee.
3. Some covenants limit certain payments, such as payments of dividends and/or *equity buybacks* (when a company purchases shares of its own stock in the open market) where a significant *decapitalization* (when a company's overall level of capital is decreased) could occur.

While some people believe that covenants really just serve the interests of investors, issuers certainly stand to benefit. Generally the market tends to prefer certainty to uncertainty. When a company's present and future actions are codified (not necessarily in detail, but certainly in meaningful ways regarding financial operations), this information is valuable to investors. At the same time, this road map is presumably of assistance to the company's management. Further, to the extent that the covenants provide for certain measures in the event of severe financial difficulties, investors would be less likely to demand a premium for the uncertainty associated with such difficulties (as with default). In sum, as investors are likely to reward greater certainty with a lower credit premium on the securities they purchase, issuers presumably would welcome that greater certainty. It is a balance of interests. At the same time that investors desire reasonable assurances, they certainly ought not want to limit a company's ability to move nimbly in response to market opportunities and exigencies as they occur.

Table 6.4 lists of the various types of covenants that can exist. It is not enough that a particular prospectus might contain one particular covenant type or another if the covenants are structured in such a way that they are in some way (as with another contradicting convenant) rendered ineffectual. For example, an entity may be able to point to a limitation of indebtedness. This means that the issuer pledges to limit the amount of additional debt it

TABLE 6.4 Various Covenant Types

Covenant Type	Description
Change of control	In its most basic of forms, restricts any one or more related entities from acquiring over 50% of the voting shares in the borrower or its parent group.
Cross default	Intended to place the debt on equal footing with covenants embedded within any other company debt in the event of a company-wide default.
Debt	Limitations on indebtedness. May be defined in any number of ways. For example, definitions of what constitutes maximum levels of additional "borrowings" may be strictly articulated.
Debt coverage	Promises related to sustaining ability to make good on debt obligations. May be defined in any number of ways. For example, definitions of what constitutes minimum levels of "profit" may be strictly articulated.
Disposal restriction	Limitations on when and how assets may be sold.
Negative pledge	A restriction on the issuer regarding commitments of assets that can be made on future borrowings. An exemption might be permitted in the case of new companies being acquired.
Pari passu	A common companion to the negative pledge, the pari passu provision restricts the issuer in subordinating a borrowing in deference to future creditors.
Payment limitations	Can include restrictions on the company's future payments on non-debt instruments (as with dividend payments on equities), or on the type of investments it might be permitted to make.

brings on itself; typically it is considered a positive move for investors. But if this limitation allows for a holding company to have, say, more than 50 percent of debt relative to servicing capabilities (a rather generous "limitation"), then the value of the covenant is cheapened. Differences between the spirit and the letter of a covenant may be difficult to distinguish, but taking the time to dig into the details can be well rewarded, either by avoiding a risky security that does not offer desirable protection, or by purchasing a risky security that does embody meaningful protections (and especially when it experiences an unexpected turn of events).

As we dip into lower-rated and riskier credits among bonds, the relative importance of covenants and their precise terms take on heightened significance. Generally speaking, investors do not get too concerned when evaluating precise terms and conditions of differences between junior and senior subordinated debt when the issuing entity carries an investment-grade rating overall. But when the credit actually is much closer to having to test the boundaries or realities of becoming distressed, then precise terms and conditions should move into sharp focus.

In the final analysis, whether there were good covenants in place or not, if there are no assets to be seized and sold or exchanged in the event of a worst-case scenario of default, then even covenants intended to be strong are not worth very much. For this reason, just as valid a part of any *due diligence* process that is followed when purchasing a bond is its fundamental business profile. For some holding companies, for example, assets may not consist of much more than office furniture. And if we are dealing with an entity with appreciable off-shore activities, then it would be time well spent to trace through just how difficult it could be to lay claim to those assets if necessary; some off-shore foreign legal considerations of favor to the issuer could come into play.

Covenants sometimes can be too restrictive. There may well be instances where a fine line sits in between conservative-oriented bondholders on the one side and more aggressive risk-oriented bondholders on the other side. And if the issuer's management is inclined to be aggressive, then overly restrictive covenants may be harmful to debt-management objectives oriented to the longer term. In other words, it may very well prove to be prudent for a given issuer to take on more debt at a particular moment since it might add to a war chest for making meaningful acquisitions, acquisitions that could well add appreciably to cash flow and profitability over time.

Generally, however, the perception among investors at large is that covenants could always be stronger. Many issuers have conceded this point as well. Why are bond covenants not stronger? There are three reasons.

1. Most local market orientations around the world tend to be equity biased. That is, investors tend to be more interested in and focused on

equity phenomena, more likely to know where the price of Coca-Cola's stock is trading than the yield of its notes and bonds.
2. It often is easier for an institutional investor to be a large equityholder but not necessarily a large bondholder (if only due to the fact that while there typically are just one or two equity types in the marketplace that trade on an exchange at any given point in time, there can be numerous notes, bonds, and money market instruments trading in the OTC market at any time). Accordingly, it may be relatively easier for equityholders to band together to express or press particular views.
3. There is a considerable gray area pertaining to covenants, ranging from what different types exist, to whether or not it is always desirable to have certain types. Not too surprisingly, generally it is thought that bondholders are not necessarily receiving all the protections that they might otherwise be entitled to have or could expect to have if they were somehow better organized.

Let us not lose sight of the fact that covenants are created out of words, even if they look like mathematical formulas. When reviewing a prospectus, it is not enough simply to note that a certain key turn of phrase is present. What is all-important is how the key phrase is presented within its particular context as well as how it might be strengthened or abrogated by other key phrases. For example, a prospectus may mention the issuer's intent to limit just how much future debt it takes on, but if those "limits" prove to be well above typical industry averages, then perhaps no real guidelines exist.

As with many things in life, the devil is in the details. It is necessary though not sufficient to know the types of covenants contained within a given debenture. It is imperative to know how the covenants are represented and how they sit relative to the overall package of proposed covenants. While it is probably rare that a particular covenant or set of covenants would inspire a rating agency to offer a credit rating a notch above what it would have otherwise been assigned, it certainly can be argued that the absence of key covenants can mean a far messier situation for a given issuer if things were to begin falling apart. To put this another way, covenants are perhaps best thought of as a type of safety net for when bad things happen to good bonds, rather than being thought of as booster rockets designed to help push a security into some kind of super-performance potential.

One fundamental consideration always will carry the day when it comes to bonds, and even the most creative of covenants cannot supersede this: There is no substitute for an issuer's ability to generate sufficient timely cash flows to make good on its obligations. But in the event that something goes awry, wouldn't it be comforting to know that there are some protections underlying the security?

This last point sheds some light on why investors often ignore covenants; covenants tend to become most relevant when times turn bad. When times are good, why be worried about something that only *might* happen? Why not just enjoy the good times for as long as they last? Besides, markets today have seen it all, so how bad could things really get anyway? While these sentiments may be offered in a sincere attempt to downplay market risks, the simple fact is that recent experiences in the credit markets in particular offer strong evidence that market risk is as great as it ever was, perhaps even greater. In Europe, for example, swap spreads have become much more volatile since the launching of a single currency. While a couple of explanations might be offered for this phenomenon, one could very well be the fact that with convergence of European currency risk such that intra-euro zone currency volatility has collapsed to zero, the preexisting euro zone currency volatility may have transformed itself into heightened interest rate sensitivity and credit-sensitive volatility. Borrowing from the second law of thermodynamics, which states that matter cannot be created or destroyed, only transformed, perhaps this can hold true (at least in part) for markets as well.

Until the market somehow finds a way to insulate itself from the types of volatility and market shock that have surfaced within the past couple of years, it appears that market protections have a role. Covenants do indeed have a role, and how well they can be strategically positioned within a portfolio depends to a large extent on the portfolio manager.

While euro zone members can be said to have achieved a convergence in exchange rate policy and considerable homogeneity with interest rate policy, other market factors are rather heterogeneous in nature as with bankruptcy laws. Yet even in the United States, these exists a long-established bankruptcy code detailing various steps that formally define the process of how a company proceeds in a bankruptcy scenario, but it is rare that the complete process is ever fully brought to bear; in so many instances a workout evolves and respective parties sit down to reach some kind of agreement.

Finally, in some instances a covenant may be implied. For example, an investor in an investment-grade sovereign nation typically does not demand a prospectus detailing the various promises the sovereign nation intends to keep when it issues debt. Rather, the assumption is (rightly or wrongly) that a sovereign nation will generally do everything it can to promote and maintain a deserved reputation in the marketplace for making good on its obligations. In many instances (though certainly not all), similar attitudes prevail toward the agencies of most federal governments, particularly if these agencies also come with Aaa/AAA ratings (implied or explicit).

Chapter 3 also touched on the importance of legal considerations when more complex products are created (as with synthetic collateralized loan obligations). Table 6.5 outlines some of the legal considerations that may

TABLE 6.5 Product and Legal Characteristics

Special-Purpose Vehicle	Equity ownership/ transfer rules	Debt ownership/ transfer rules	Minimum equity rules	Asset changes/ additions	Time-tranched debt	Subsequent debt issuance	Flexibility with asset types
(1) Special-purpose corporation	No	No	Yes	Yes	Yes	Yes	Yes
(2) Pay-through owner trust/master trust (Partnership)	No	No	Yes	Yes	Yes	Yes	Yes
(3) Grantor trust pass-through	No	No	N/A	No	N/A	No	Yes
(4) Real estate mortgage investment conduit (REMIC)	Yes	No	No	No	Yes	No	No
(5) Financial asset securitization investment trust (FASIT)	Yes	Yes	No	Yes	Yes	Yes	Yes

(1) A wholly owned corporation. Generally speaking, a contribution of assets in exchange for equity will be tax free to the transferor, though if cash or other property also is received in the exchange, then any gains might have to be recognized. Alternatively, any gains must be recognized immediately upon a sale of the assets as with CMOs. Gains or losses are recognized immediately unless the consolidated tax return deferred intercompany transaction timing rules apply.

(2) In any pay-through trust structure, the interests of the SPV consist of debt and equity, and this is a typical financing structure for time-tranched debt. The term "owner trust" usually is viewed as a pay-through trust structure typically taxed as a partnership. For tax purposes a master trust also is typically taxed as a partnership. Gains or losses usually are not recognized upon a transfer of assets to a partnership, though there are exceptions.

(3) The grantor trust pass-through structure usually is treated as an asset sale to the extent that the trust certificates are sold to third parties. The investment is an equity ownership in the assets, and no debt securities are issued.

(4) A REMIC is a collateralized mortgage obligation (CMO) issued after January 1, 1987, under legislation designed to eliminate certain tax and regulatory problems that limited issuer and investor participation in multiple series (tranche) CMOs. Gains or losses are recognized immediately upon a sale of the assets as with issued to third parties. For REMIC interests that are retained, gains or losses are amortized over the life of the security.

(5) In February 2000 the Internal Revenue Service released proposed regulations concerning Financial Asset Securitization Investment Trusts (FASITs), Congress authorized FASITs in 1996 to provide a nontaxable securitization vehicle for all types of debt instruments, including mortgage loans. The FASIT initially was seen as a potentially more flexible vehicle than the REMIC. A FASIT election may be made only by a "qualified arrangement," which includes a corporation, partnership, or trust or a segregated pool of assets. A FASIT may not be either a foreign entity or a U.S. entity or segregated pool if a foreign country or U.S. possession could subject its net income to tax. A FASIT must have one or more classes of debtlike "regular interests" and only one "ownership interest." The FASIT election must be made by the "eligible corporation" that owns the ownership interest in the permitted entity or segregated pool (the "owner"). For tax-reporting purposes, a FASIT is treated as a branch or division of the owner. Losses are not recognized, and special valuation rules apply for non-publicly traded assets that may give rise to a gain even when no economic gain exists.

255

be involved with the various special-purpose vehicles (SPVs) commonly created in support of launching complex products.

Again, the prospectus accompanying a structured product can be instructive about any relevant SPVs and what their particular role and responsibilities involve.

Finally, destabilizing events are not the sole purview of corporations; governments often take center stage as with the U.S. federal budget impasse in 1997. Outside of the United States, while certainly a debatable point, some Europeans may counter the accusation of being interventionist with the claim that the largest of state-supported bailouts of industries within the past 20 years or so actually occurred in the United States: Consider the Chrysler Corporation and the savings and loan industry.

Though originally intended to suggest how discrepancies may exist across certain perceptions and realities, the previously cited bailout examples also highlight how a credit call option may be said to be quietly embedded within the debt or equity of certain issuers' equity and/or debt, especially the debt and equity of large issuers.

The idea behind "too big to fail" has been around for a while, and can be described in a variety of different ways. One way follows: If you owe your bank $10,000 and cannot manage to pay it, you are in big trouble. But if you owe your bank $100 million and cannot pay it, your *bank* is in big trouble. If a given enterprise is perceived to be vulnerable enough to significant negative economic and/or political consequences, then there is a likelihood that extramarket forces (a government body or perhaps even a supranational body) may have to intervene. This was certainly the case in the United States with Chrysler in the 1980s and the savings and loan crisis in the 1990s.

What are of interest, certainly, are the various political and socioeconomic issues (and issues that can and do differ along cultural lines as well) that might prompt a government body to intervene in support of a particular credit event. When a particular industry type is thought to be in a special position to enjoy the bailout of an extramarket body, then it may be appropriate to view that industry type (or company) as having an invisible call embedded in its debt. That is, the government does not explicitly sell the industry or company a call option (which is in turn shared with equity and/or bond investors), but the likelihood of its stepping in to intervene could well be construed to imply the existence of a call-like support.

Because we are dealing with a less than explicit call option, we must contend with a list of vagaries. What is the strike price of the invisible call? Its appropriate volatility?

Rather than trying to focus on the minutiae of how such questions might be answered, perhaps it would be sufficient simply to highlight the variables that are deserving of consideration. Active investors interested in credit-sensitive products should consider which national industry types might be more likely than others to enjoy special financial treatment if worst-case scenarios were to surface. For that matter, since state and local governments also are in a position to offer financial assistance to industries, they should be considered too. And in certain situations, as with emerging market economies, sometimes extranational (perhaps even supranational) bodies might become involved. In recognition of different cultural perceptions of what is or is not a key industry (for our purposes, an industry deemed worthy of saving), these cultural considerations would have to factor into our thinking about embedded calls as we look across countries.

And just as we might evoke the notion of a credit call option embedded in certain bonds and equities of various companies, a call option might be said to exist in a country's currency. The central idea here is that certain countries in the world have economic and/or political ties to a "major" economic and/or political power, and thus enjoy particular amenities when/if any stress emerges. Such an economic/political relationship might be explicit, as between the west coast of Africa and France, where the exchange rate between the CFA (Communauté Financière Africaine) and the French franc is fixed and as such symbolizes the strong ties between western Africa and France, or less implicit though nonetheless real, as when the United States demonstrated its support when Mexico experienced economic and currency problems in 1994–1995.

These embedded calls have a price, and someone is paying for them. Arguably some part of the "price" may be paid by the weaker currency country (as when domestic priorities and policy ambitions may be subjugated to the priorities and policy ambitions of the stronger currency country), and some of the price may be paid by the stronger currency country (as when financial assistance is provided during both challenging times and other times).

This is all relevant because the worst-case scenario with any credit risk is the situation where a default occurs and there is zero recovery value potential. Note that the nature of the intervention provided to avoid or otherwise ease the effects of (potential) default does not necessarily have to be monetary. Support could come in many shapes, including a relaxing of regulatory constraints or tax breaks. Further, while the initial extramarket assistance might come relatively quickly, actually seeing the assistance take hold and with the desired effects might take much longer.

The previous paragraph cited regulatory and tax policy in the same sentence. Market regulation may be defined as any attempt to somehow influence or otherwise direct or guide someone's actions. By this definition, even a targeted tax policy could be viewed as a regulation of sorts, particularly if the tax policy provides some kind of break or incentive (or just the opposite) to a unique industry or type of business. Regulations do not necessarily have to be dictated by governmental decree. They might be imposed (or become effective merely by the power of suggestion) in a variety of different ways, as with special industry groups seeking to provide self-regulatory guidelines, or with rating agencies that may put forward their view on the desirable best practices of an industry or market sector. Regulations can be well defined or ad hoc, and may come with stiff fines and penalties or simple words of encouragement or warning. In short, a regulation can be anything that by intent seeks to promote or encourage a particular kind of desired behavior or outcome. Regulations may be intended to protect, to promote, or to deter certain behaviors. For our purposes here regulations can and do cause market participants to act in ways they may not otherwise; as such, regulations generally interfere with market efficiency, if "efficiency" is defined in the strictest sense of being the complete absence of any market frictions. Such an environment does not actually exist anywhere today, nor is it desirable.

It is presumed that in the absence of a particular regulation, the behavior of the targeted entity would otherwise be different. Whether this interference is seen as a good thing or a bad thing may well depend on which side of the regulation one is: the side being regulated or the side doing business with the regulated entity. Perhaps in some instances both sides see themselves as winners, while in other instances one side may be perceived to be a beneficiary while the other is somehow being held back. Table 6.6 presents examples of all possibilities.

In the United States (and in most other markets as well), two industry types that are heavily regulated are banking and insurance. This regulation extends to a variety of operations, including how they manage their capital and how they invest.

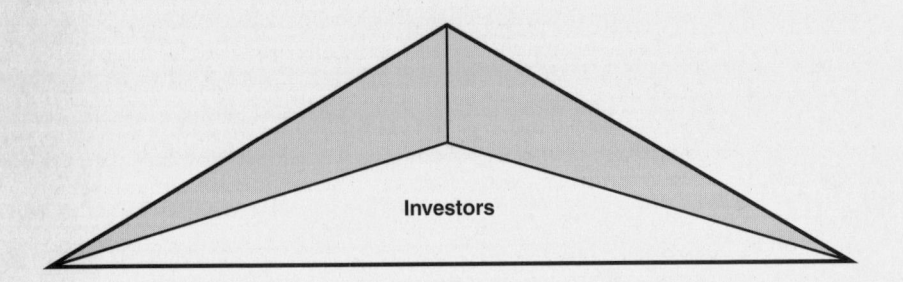

Investors

The previous section discussed how regulations can greatly impact issuers. This section addresses how investors may be subject to a variety of constraints, both self-imposed and imposed by others. For example, many fund managers voluntarily restrict their funds from being invested in certain types of derivatives, or they may face limits on how much they can leverage their

TABLE 6.6 Regulations by Point of View

	Regulated Entity	The Other Side
Positive view	May view regulation as a form of protection against such things as other firms trying to enter into the industry	May view regulation as protection against being sold an inferior good or service
Negative view	May see regulation as an impediment to entering other desirable business lines	May see regulation as preventing the ability to have access to a desired good or service

portfolio. Among industry types in the United States that are subject to more formal restrictions on the way they can invest, banking and insurance are most certainly at the top of the list. With banks, restrictions exist with investing in any type of equity product, as well as having to designate if the investments they have made are *held for portfolio* (a long-term investment) or *available for sale* (a short-term investment).

Another restriction on bank investments relates to credit considerations. In particular, banks often are required by the government where they operate to follow strict formulas for how much capital must be set aside relative to the types of securities they have purchased. Many times guidelines are taken directly from the Bank of International Settlements (BIS). For example, in 1988 the BIS released a document covering credit risk. The document outlines how different asset classes can be weighted in a capital-at-risk according to a security's riskiness. There are five risk weightings: 0 percent, 10 percent, 20 percent, 50 percent, and 100 percent. *OECD* (Organization for Economic Cooperation and Development) government debt or cash, for example, has a zero or low weight, loans on banks get 20 percent, while loans fully secured by mortgages on residential property are weighted at 50 percent. All claims on the private sector or on banks incorporated outside the OECD with a residual maturity of over one year are weighted at 100 percent.

To allow for a more dynamic approach to risk-based capital guidelines, the BIS has issued a new framework for credit risk. The new framework is designed to improve the way regulatory capital reflects underlying risk, and it consists of three pillars:

1. Minimum capital requirements
2. Supervisory review of capital adequacy
3. Market discipline

The area of minimum capital requirements develops and expands on the standardized 1988 rules. The risk-weighting system described above is replaced by a system that uses external credit ratings. Accordingly, the debt of an OECD country rated single-A will have a risk weighting of 20 percent while that of a triple-A will still enjoy a zero weighting. Corporate debt also will benefit from graduated weightings so that a double-A rated corporate bond will be risk-weighted at 20 percent while a single-A will be weighted at 100 percent. The committee also introduced a higher-than-100-percent risk weight for certain low-quality securities. A new scheme to address asset securitization was proposed whereby securitized assets would receive lower weightings relative to like-rated unsecuritized bonds. Further, the BIS indicated that more banks with more sophisticated risk management procedures in place could use their own internal ratings-based approach to form the basis for setting capital charges, subject to supervisory approval and adherence to quantitative and qualitative guidelines.

The supervisory review of capital adequacy attempts to ensure that a bank's risk position is consistent with its overall risk profile and strategy and, as such, will encourage early supervisory intervention. Supervisors want the ability to require banks that show a greater degree of risk to hold capital in excess of an 8 percent minimum capital charge.

Market discipline is hoped to encourage high disclosure standards and enhance the role of market participants in encouraging banks to carry adequate capital against their securities holdings. In sum, the BIS wants to specify explicit capital charges for credit and market risks and even seeks to enforce a charge for operational-type risks. Under the 1988 requirements, the BIS already made use of credit conversion factors and weightings according to the nature of counterparty risk.

The credit risk of derivatives is assessed by calculating the derivative's current replacement cost, plus an "add-on" to account for potential exposure. The "add-on" is based on the notional principal of each contract and varies depending on the volatility of the underlying asset and residual maturity of the contract. Foreign exchange contracts have higher weights than those of interest rates, and transactions with a residual maturity of more than one year bear higher weights than those under one year. The higher weights of the foreign exchange contracts are consistent with the relatively higher price volatility of currencies relative to interest rates. In further assessing the credit risk on derivatives, the BIS distinguishes between exchange-traded and over-the-counter products. Since the outstanding credit risk at exchanges is addressed with daily margin calls, exchange-traded contracts are exempt from credit risk capital.

In 1993 the Basle Committee proposed formulas for measuring market risk arising from foreign exchange positions and trading in debt and equity securities. The proposals were subsequently amended due to shortcomings in the way that the market risk of different instruments was to be treated, especially for derivatives. Key to the amendments was that the BIS Basle agreed to let banks use their own internal models to calculate capital charges for market risk. This is significant if only because it represents the first time that banking regulators moved from simple formulaic-type requirements to more sophisticated in-house models to determine regulatory capital. Banks that do not meet the criteria set down by the Basle Committee are not allowed to use their own internal models.

Another way that capital allocation decisions can be made, and especially at the product-type level, is with volatility measures. Again, simply put, the more price volatile one product type is relative to another, the less initial capital it might receive until it can show that its profitability makes it deserving of an even larger capital allocation. Various consulting firms derive their sole source of revenue from advising banking institutions on how they might best manage their operations in the context of regulatory requirements.

Value at Risk (VAR) refers to a process whereby fundamental statistical analysis is applied to historical market trends and volatilities so as to generate estimates of the likelihood that a given security's or portfolio's losses might exceed a certain amount. VAR is a popular risk-management vehicle for firms, where maximum loss amounts are set internally and are not permitted to be exceeded unless express permission is granted for doing so.

As stated, insurance companies are also subject to a variety of stringent rules of operation. Among the restrictions faced by insurance companies is a prohibition against investing in non-dollar-denominated securities, as well as having to evaluate potential purchases of mortgage-backed securities (MBSs).

Regarding insurance regulations pertaining to investment policy, this matter is generally handled on a state-by-state basis. To assist states with the drafting of appropriate law, the National Association of Insurance Commissioners (NAIC) has prepared so-called model laws. These proposals contain suggested limits or guidelines on various types of investments inclusive of mortgage products, securities denominated in currencies other than the dollar, securities lending, derivatives, and other matters.

Meantime, the Federal Financial Institutions Examination Council (FFIEC) has mandated three standard tests that CMOs must pass before a bank, savings and loan, or credit union can purchase a CMO security. The tests help to determine the level of interest rate risk and volatility of a CMO when subjected to interest rate changes. The three tests determine whether a CMO is high-risk, and thus ineligible to be purchased by these financial institutions.

Since some CMOs are structured to pay out a steadier level of cash flows over time, these would likely be more stable and predictable and tend to qualify for purchase under FFIEC tests. The FFIEC tests involve:

1. *An average life test.* The expected average life of the CMO must be less than or equal to 10 years.
2. *An average life sensitivity test.* The average life of the eligible CMO cannot extend by more than four years or shorten by more than six years with an immediate shift in the curve of plus or minus 300 basis points.
3. *Price sensitivity test.* The price of the eligible CMO cannot change by more than 17 percent for an immediate shift in the Treasury curve of plus or minus 300 basis points.

Certain employee pension funds are also subject to restrictions on the types of MBS and ABS that can be purchased. In 1974 the Employee Retirement Income Security Act (ERISA) was enacted giving the U.S. Department of Labor (DOL) the authority to define eligible ABS and MBS investments for employee benefit plans. The exemptions have been modified a few times since 1974, and generally permit employee benefit plan assets to be invested in pass-through certificates issued by grantor trusts, REMICs or FASITs holding fixed pools of certain types of secured debt obligations. These include single-family, commercial, or multifamily mortgage loans and loans secured by manufactured housing, motor vehicles, equipment and certain other limited types of property. Certificates backed by credit card receivables or any other types of unsecured obligation are not eligible for purchase. In 2000 some rather substantive changes were made to ease restrictions on purchases, and these are summarized in Table 6.7.

Figure 6.1 presents a brief summary of how financial products relate to investor classifications in the context of regulatory guidelines on investment restrictions.

Besides these explicit restrictions on how certain industry types may or may not invest, a variety of other formal and informal restrictions affect both investors and issuers on a day-to-day basis, without the benefit of an act of Congress. One informal restriction relates to the use of a particular cash flow type(s) such as derivatives. More formal restrictions can take the form of actual or anticipated reactions of the rating agencies, of peers and colleagues, or even of the financial press. Reputation can count for a great deal when it comes to the business of managing other people's money, and fund managers generally want to guard against adverse exposure whenever possible.

In at least one very real sense, the rating agencies themselves can be thought of as having a regulatory kind of influence on companies. Specifically, if one or more of the rating agencies were to frown on a particular use of capital, and if it were communicated that such usage could place the offending company in a position of being downgraded, this would most certainly weigh on a company's decision-making process. For example, when TruPs (or trust preferred securities) first came to market a few years ago as a hybrid of preferred stock and debt, rating agencies were quick

TABLE 6.7 Underwriter's Exemption Eligibility under ERISA

Aset Category	Eligible	Ineligible*
Residential home equity	LTV up to 125%; senior only; and rated AA– or better or LTV up to 100%; senior or subordinate; and rated BBB– or better	LTV over 125% or rated below BBB– or LTV over 100% but not over 125%; and (i) rated below AA– or (ii) subordinate
Commercial or multi-family (real estate secured), motor vehicles and manufactured housing	LTV up to 100%; senior or subordinate; and rated BBB– or better	LTV over 100% or rated below BBB–
Commercial or multi-family (not real estate secured) and and equipment	LTV up to 100%; senior only; and rated A– or better	LTV over 100% or rated below A– or subordinate
Home equity (revolving), credit cards, motor vehicles (leases/revolving), student loans and equipment (leases)	None	All

* Subordinate equity interests that satisfy Eligible LTV constraints are also eligible for purchase by insurance company general accounts under Department of Labor Class Exemption 95-60, regardless of their rating, as long as senior equity interests backed by the same asset pool are also eligible.

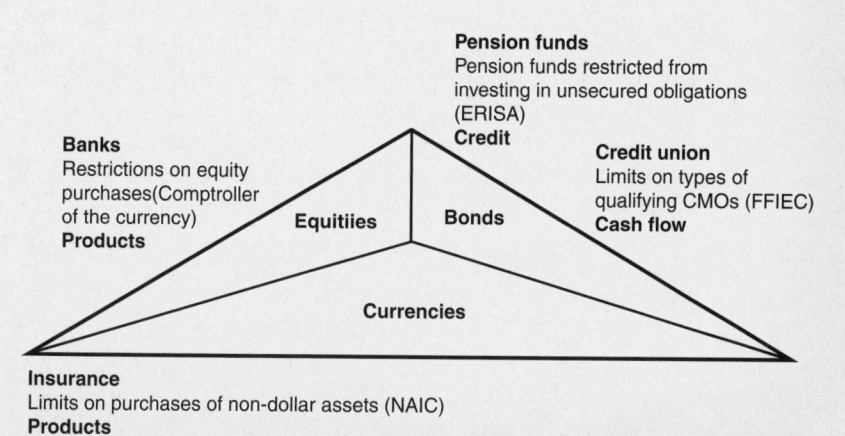

Pension funds
Pension funds restricted from investing in unsecured obligations (ERISA)

Banks
Restrictions on equity purchases(Comptroller of the currency)
Products

Credit union
Limits on types of qualifying CMOs (FFIEC)
Cash flow

Credit
Equitiies
Bonds
Currencies

Insurance
Limits on purchases of non-dollar assets (NAIC)
Products

FIGURE 6.1 Restrictions on cash flow, credit, and products by type of investing entity.

to respond with opinions about where they were best ranked relative to the issuer's capital structure. At the same time, they also issued explicit guidelines regarding how much of this product type they felt a given entity should issue.

Table 6.8, reprinted with permission from the Bank of International Settlements, summarizes various credit-related statutes as practiced within the United States.

In closing, investment rules and regulations—both those that are voluntarily imposed and those that are mandated by formal decree—will always be a key consideration for investors.

CHAPTER SUMMARY

The very existence of various market rules and regulations (inclusive of taxes) may serve to create pockets of price dislocation in the marketplace. From a pure classical economic viewpoint, this not very surprising. When economic agents act more in response to how someone else wants them to behave than to how they themselves might want to behave, distortions can well arise. When such distortions are a necessary side-effect of commonly accepted principles of sound behavior (as with protecting the risks that banks or insurance companies might take to the detriment of consumers who rely on their sound business practices), such rules and regulations typically are embraced as necessary and reasonable. What particular rules, regulations, and tax policies are helpful or not, and how best to create and enforce them, is a topic of considerable debate and review as long as there are markets.

Figure 6.2 offers a three-dimensional viewpoint to help reinforce the interrelationships presented in this chapter. Again, readers should think about how other product types might be placed here, not just as an academic exercise, but as a practical matter of how portfolios are constructed and managed.

With reference to the above mapping process, investors can view a variety of investment choices in the context of legal, regulatory, and tax environments, then make strategic choices according to their preferences and outlook regarding each category of potential risk and reward.

To bridge the first four chapters, Table 6.9 links products, cash flows, credit, and legal and regulatory matters.

While they are often thought of as a rather unexciting aspect of financial markets, tax, legal, and regulatory considerations are quite important, fluid, and deserving of very careful consideration.

TABLE 6.8 Partial List of Investor-Related Regulation in the United States

Year Adopted	Ratings-Dependent Regulation	Minimum Rating	Number of Ratings Required	Regulator/Regulation
1931	Required banks to mark-to-market lower-rated bonds	BBB	2	OCC and Federal Reserve examination rules
1936	Prohibited banks from purchasing "speculative securities"	BBB	Unspecified	OCC, EDIC, and Federal Reserve joint statement
1951	Imposed higher capital requirements on insurers' lower-rated bonds	Varies	N.A.	NAIC mandatory reserve requirements
1975	Imposed higher capital haircuts on broker/dealers below investment grade	BBB	2	SEC amendment to Rule 15c3-1: the uniform net capital rule for bonds
1982	Eased disclosure requirements for investment-grade bonds	BBB	1	SEC adoption of Integrated Disclosure System (Release #6383)
1984	Eased issuance of nonagency mortgage-backed securities (MBSs)	AA	1	Congressional promulgation of the Secondary Mortgage Market Enhancement Act of 1984
1987	Permitted margin lending against MBSs and (later) foreign bonds	AA	1	Federal Reserve Regulation T
1989	Allowed pension funds to invest in high-rated asset-backed securities	A	1	Department of Labor relaxation of ERISA restriction (PTE 89-88)
1989	Prohibited savings and loans from investing in below-investment-grade bonds	BBB	1	Congressional promulgation of the Financial Institutions Recovery and Reform Act of 1940
1991	Required money market mutual funds to limit holdings of low-rated paper	A1[1]	1[2]	SEC amendment to Rule 2a-7 under the Investment Company Act of 1940
1992	Exempted issuers of certain asset-backed securities from registration as a mutual fund	BBB	1	SEC adoption of Rule 3a-7 under the Investment Company Act of 1940

265

TABLE 6.8 Partial List of Investor-Related Regulation in the United States (continued)

Year Adopted	Ratings-Dependent Regulation	Minimum Rating	Number of Ratings Required	Regulator/Regulation
1994	Imposes varying capital charges on banks' and S&Ls' holdings of different tranches of asset-backed securities	AAA & BBB	1	Federal Reserve, OCC, FDIC, OTS Proposed Rule on Recourse and Direct Credit Substitutes
1998	Department of Transportation can extend credit assistance only to projects with an investment-grade rating	BBB	1	Transport Infrastructure Finance and Innovation Act 1998
1999	Restricts the ability of national banks to establish financial subsidiaries	A	1	Gramm-Leach-Bliley Act of 1999[3]

Source: Unless otherwise noted, the items in the table are reproduced from Richard Cantor and Frank Packer, "The Credit Rating Industry," *FRBNY Quarterly Review* (Fall 1994); 6. For other ratings-dependent regulation, refer to SEC Release No. 34-39457, File No. S7-33-97, pp. 1–8.

[1] Highest ratings on short-term debt, generally implying an A– long-term debt rating or better.

[2] If issue is rated by only one nationally recognized statistical rating organization (NRSRO), its rating is adequate: otherwise two ratings are required.

[3] Gramm-Leach-Bliley Act of 1999, Title I, p. 91.

Market Environment

Tax

A mapping process...

Cumulative preferred convertible stock

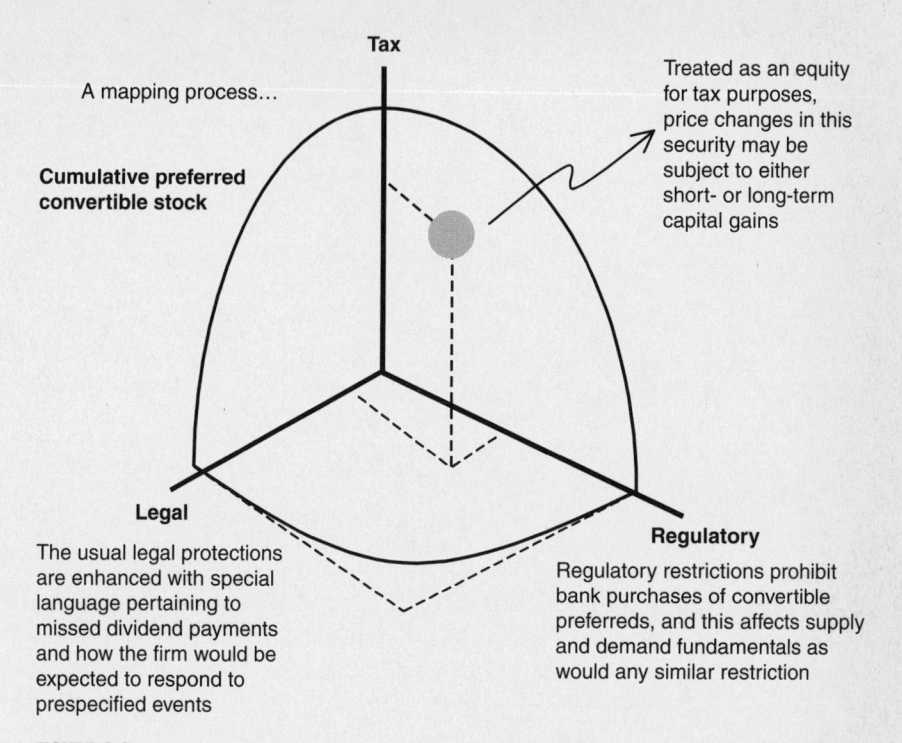

Treated as an equity for tax purposes, price changes in this security may be subject to either short- or long-term capital gains

Legal
The usual legal protections are enhanced with special language pertaining to missed dividend payments and how the firm would be expected to respond to prespecified events

Regulatory
Regulatory restrictions prohibit bank purchases of convertible preferreds, and this affects supply and demand fundamentals as would any similar restriction

FIGURE 6.2 Mapping process for cumulative preferred convertible stock in the context of tax and legal and regulatory considerations.

TABLE 6.9 Credit-Enhancing Strategies by Product, Cash Flow, and Legal/Regulatory/Tax

	Product	Cash Flow	Legal/Regulatory/Tax
Shorten maturity		√	
Change position in capital structure	√		
Collateralize		√	
Guarantees			√
Covenants			√
Wraps	√		

CONCLUSION

As a brief summary of the text, and as another conceptual way of thinking about market interrelationships, consider Figure 6.3.

Most continuums are presented as a horizontal line, with one main idea at one end and a contradicting idea at the opposite extreme. Yet in Figure 6.3 we present a continuum in the shape of a semicircle. The purpose for presenting bonds and equities in this circular context is to suggest that while bonds and equities are different product types, they are also closely related—at least more closely related than would be implied by placing them at opposite points of a horizontal continuum. Indeed, as has been referenced earlier in the text, the Achilles' heel of equities is the right conveyed to shareholders to vote on matters pertaining to the company, and the Achilles' heel of bonds is the presence of a maturity date.

In sum, while it remains popular in financial circles today to emphasize how different bonds are from equities, and how different these are from currencies, and so on, it is this author's view that financial products of all stripes have much more in common than not; there is much more to be gained pedagogically by emphasizing commonality as opposed to rifts. When an investor considers any financial product, there ought to be at least some cursory consideration of market risk, credit risk, and regulatory and tax issues,

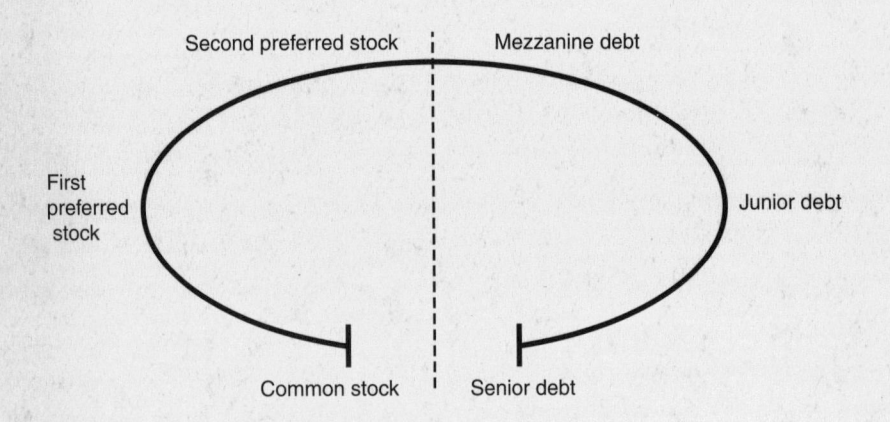

Common stock (CS) − Voting rights = Preferred stock (PS)

PS + Maturity date = Mezzanine debt (MD)

MD − Equity allocation + Maturity date (optional) = Junior debt (JD)

JD + Secured status + Maturity date = Senior debt

FIGURE 6.3 The debt/equity continuum as semicircular.

particularly since every financial product is affected by each of these elements. And for securities in the form of spot, a forward or future, or an option, these structures certainly share much in common across each and every type of financial instrument that they embody.

Perhaps the real conclusion here is that there is no conclusion, that readers are now in possession of a new toolbox filled with fresh perspectives of the marketplace, and as such are fully equipped to better understand existing products as well as engineer a financial innovation or two of their own.

Good luck to you!

Index

401k plans. *See* Retirement accounts
529 plans. *See* College savings accounts

A

A tranches, 141
Absolute return
  fund, 150
  investing, 150–153
ABSs. *See* Asset-backed securities
Accept delivery, 46
Add-on, usage, 260
Adjustable-rate mortgages (ARMs), 164–165
Agency bonds, 245
  taxable status. *See* U.S. federal agency bonds
  tax-adjusted total returns, 145t
Agency securities, tax-adjusted total returns, 244t
Aggressive growth, 150
Alpha, 161
American option, 145
Annualization term, 18
Appreciation, 8. *See also* Credit-related appreciation
Arbitrage. *See* Fixed income; Market neutral

ARMs. *See* Adjustable-rate mortgages
Asset-backed bonds, 91
Asset-backed instruments, 135fn
Asset-backed securities, 91, 103, 134–135
  servicer, 91
Asset-backed securities (ABSs), types, 262
Asset-liability management, 156
Asset-liability portfolio management, 156
Assets
  market value, 202
  stream, 156
  volatility, 202
Asymmetrical information, 203
At-the-money
  10–non-call-2, price volatility, 144
  call option, 215
  option, 63fn, 210, 213
  put, 208
  strike prices, 127
Available for sale, 259
Average life, 139
  prepayment rate, contrast, 139f
  sensitivity test, 262
  tests, 262

B

B tranches, 141
Backed-out. *See* Implied forward credit outlook
Bad debt, 24
Balanced funds, 155
Bank for International Settlements (BIS), 221, 259–260
Bankruptcies, 4
  scenario, 254
Bankruptcy-remote entity, 93
Banks, liabilities, 156
Basis points (bps), 8. *See also* Total return
  gain, 52
Basis risk, 114
Basis trade, 114–118, 210f
  creation, 114f
Basle Committee (1993), 260–261
Bear market environment, 102
Benchmark. *See* Market
  quantitative measure, 163
  risk, 238–240
  security, 28
Beta
  definition, 183
  industry types, 185f
  unity, value, 184
  usage, 182–204
Bid/offer spreads, 213
Binomial option model, tree, 59
BIS. *See* Bank for International Settlements

Black-Scholes application, 72f
Black-Scholes assumption. *See* Log-normality
Black-Scholes option pricing formula, 70
Blue chip stocks, 30
Bond-equivalent basis, 173
Bond-equivalent yield, 25, 174–175
Bonds. *See* Shorter-maturity bonds
  basis, 122f
  basket, 121fn
  cheapness/richness, 27fn
  coupon value, accruing, 37
  credit quality, 96f
  futures, 45–47
    CTD, 123
    price, 46–47
  indices, investment-grade portion, 169
  market, callable structures, 129
  portfolio construction, 234
  price
    risk, 172–182
    sensitivity, 189
  products, optionality variations, 134–150
  statistical methods, 205
  summary, 64
  total returns, 232
  uncertainty, layers, 25fn
  yield curve. *See* U.S. Treasury
Bonex bonds/securities, 86–87

Bonex clause, 86–87
Book value, 31
Bootstrapping effect, 43
Borrowings. *See* Longer-term borrowings; Short-term borrowings
Brady bonds, 159fn
 credit benefits, 149
Bullet bond, 70, 208
Business cycle, 5
Busted PAC, 142
Buy-and-hold-oriented investors, 244

C

C tranches, 141
Call option, 133, 203f, 256. *See also* At-the-money; Credit; Short call option; Synthetic call option
 calculation, 59t
 value, 53
Call payoff profile, 208f
Call value, 54–55
Callable bonds, 133, 149
 conceptual presentation, 130f
 creation, 129f
 issuing, 130
 payoff profile, 209
 price, definition, 199
Callable structures. *See* Bonds
Callables, 200. *See also* Discrete callables
 price, 133
Called away, 200

Canadian Treasury bills, 50–51
Capital, 91–97
 adequacy, supervisory review, 259
 allocation. *See* Risk
 amount, availabililty, 217
 base, 155
 exposure, 159
 flight, 85
 gains. *See* Long-term capital gains
 guidelines/restrictions, 217. *See also* Risk-based capital guidelines
 impact. *See* Collateralization
 preservation, 155
  fund, 154
 representation, 218
 requirements, 259
 return. *See* Return on risk-adjusted capital; Risk-adjusted return on risk-adjusted capital
 structure, 92, 202
 value, 205
Capital Asset Pricing Model (CAPM), 219
Capital-adjusted variables, 219–220
Carry (cost of carry), 35, 212. *See also* Negative carry; Positive carry
 component, 189
 duration, relationship, 190f
 options, 119

Carry (cost of carry) (*continued*)
  value, 116t, 118
    scenarios, 117f–119f
    zero value, 124
Carter Bonds, 84
Cash derivative, 92fn
Cash flow-paying product
  type, 117
Cash flows, 3, 15. *See also*
    Investor-specific
    cash flow
  appendix, 66–70
  combination, 209f
  diversification, 232
  interrelationships, 206–236
  intramouth, reinvestment, 165
  priority, 202
  profiles, 65f
  reinvestment, 226
  restrictions, 263f
  series, 156
  triangle, 147f
  types, 226–227
Cash flow-weighted average.
  See Yield
Cash settlement, 33
Cash-and-carry trade, 123
Cash/future combinations, 118
Cash-out value, 19
Cash-settled equity futures,
  47–51
CBO. *See* Collateralized bond
  obligation
CBOT. *See* Chicago Board of
  Trade

CDO. *See* Collateralized debt
  obligation
Ceilings, 217
Central bank authorities, 41
Century bonds, 3fn
Certificate of deposit (CD),
  6, 157
CFA. *See* Communauté
  Financière Africaine
Cheapest-to-deliver (CTD),
  115–118, 120fn. *See also*
  Bonds
  beneficial change, 121
Cheapness/richness. *See* Bonds
Chicago Board of Trade
  (CBOT), 77
  10–year Treasury bond
    future, 115
  bond futures contract, 115
  delivery process, 115
Chicago Mercantile
  Exchange, 35
Class A/B/C securities, 140
Clean prices, 37
  calculation. *See* Forward clean
    price calculation
Cleanup tranche, 141
CLO. *See* Collateralized loan
  obligation
Close out, usage, 212
CMOs. *See* Collateralized
  mortgage obligations
CMT. *See* Constant Maturity
  Treasury
Collateral. *See* General collateral

Collateralization, 89–91, 107.
    See also Overcollateralization
    capital, impact, 89–97
Collateralized bond obligation
    (CBO), 105
Collateralized debt obligation
    (CDO), 105–107. See also
    Nonsynthetic CDO;
    Synthetic CDO
Collateralized loan obligation
    (CLO), 105–106. See also
    Synthetic CLOs
Collateralized MBS, 135
Collateralized mortgage
    obligations (CMOs),
    164–165, 261
College savings accounts (529
    plans), 242
Communauté Financière
    Africaine (CFA), 257
Companies, geographical
    diversification, 87
Compounding frequency, 19
Constant Maturity Treasury
    (CMT) swap, 102–103
Constant Prepayment Rate
    (CPR), 138
Consumer Price Index (CPI), 12
Contract-eligible bond, 46
Conversion factor, 45
Convertible bond,
    transformation
    scenarios, 146f
Convertible preferred stock,
    145–146

Convertible-equity conversion
    price, 145–146
Convertibles, creation, 145f
Convexity, 172–182
    calculation, 180t
    risk, 197
    strategies, 169, 193f
Corporate securities, tax-adjusted
    total returns, 244t, 245t
Corporate settlement, 33
Correlation coefficient, 183–186
    decrease, 187
    generation, 182fn
Cost of carry. See Carry
Counterparty risk, 77, 80
Country-level default scenario, 88
Coupon cash flow, reinvestment,
    22, 223, 229fn
Coupon payments, 19, 173
    date, 131
Coupon reinvestment
    risk, 224
    uncertainty, 25
Coupon-bearing bonds, 25,
    96, 117
    form, 90
    price, 26fn
    spot purchase, 227
Coupon-bearing security, 18, 22
Coupon-bearing Treasury, 21,
    36, 176
    5-year, price cone, 230f
    12-month, 229
    bond, 42
        cash flows, 18fn

Coupon-bearing Treasury
(*continued*)
  reinvestment patterns,
    requirements,
    21fn, 22fn
  one-year, 230
Covenants, 250–253
  types, 251t
CPI. *See* Consumer Price Index
CPR. *See* Constant Prepayment
    Rate
Credit, 73
  call option, 257
  cone, 200, 201f
  considerations, 158
  conversion factors, 260
  default swap, 104
  dynamics. *See* Intramouth
    credit dynamics
  incremental risk, 223
  instrument. *See* Spot
  interrelationships, 216–217
  near-term outlook, 103
  quality, uncertainty, 22, 25
  rating, 74t, 79
    insurance, 75
  restrictions, 263f
  review, 75
  shocks, 79
  spread, 79
    increase, 100
    option, 100
  trades, 166
  watch, 75
  yield spreads, 60f

Credit absorbing vehicle, 101
Credit card receivables, 262
Credit derivatives, 75, 97–108
  issuer-specific types, 101
  profiles, 107t
  valuation, 99
Credit risks, 25, 75–89, 165, 190
  allocation methodology,
    216–217
  comparison, 225
  decrease, 226
  double-A, 78
  protection. *See* Downside
    credit risk protection
  quantification, 203
  security types, conceptual
    linking, 94f
Credit-enhanced bond, creation,
    147f, 148f
Credit-enhancing strategies, 267f
Credit-free securities, 79
Credit-linked note, 101, 105
  schematic, 101f
Credit-related appreciation, 149
Credit-related events, 99
Credit-related risks, layering, 93f
Credit-sensitive bond, 100
Credit-sensitive instrument. *See*
    Nonderivative credit-
    sensitive instrument
Credit-sensitive products,
    demand, 103
Credit-sensitive securities, 103
Creditworthiness, evaluation, 76
Crossover credits, 166

Index

CTD. *See* Cheapest-to-deliver
Cumulative preferred convertible stock, mapping process, 267f
Cumulative protection, 82
Currencies. *See* National currency; Nonnational currency; Planet currency acceptance. *See* Local currency; Sponsor currency
   controls, 87
   free flow, 85
   futures, opportunities, 51
   management, 158
   price cone, 233f
   rating. *See* Foreign currency rating; Local currency
   summary, 64
   swap, 249
Currency-enhanced securities, 129

D

Debt, 4. *See also* Bad debt; Distressed debt; Longer-dated debt; Shorter-dated debt
   continuum, 268f
   cushion, 95
   management, 85
Decapitalization, 250
Deep in-the-money, 144
Deep out-of-the-money, 144
Default
   definition, 75
   experiences, 74
   probability, 202–203
   rates, 99t
   scenario, 5. *See also* Country-level default scenario
   swap. *See* Credit
Deflation, 8
Delegated underwriting and servicing security (DUS), 142
Delivery. *See* Accept delivery; Make delivery
   definition, 118
   options, 46, 115–120, 120fn
   value, 121f
   process. *See* Chicago Board of Trade
   taking, 77
Delta. *See* Implied delta; Synthetic option
   hedge, 126
   movement, 210–211
   price sensitivities, 198f
   usage, 197, 210
Delta-adjusted amount. *See* Notional amount
Delta-neutral strategy, 126
Depreciation, 8
Derivatives, 7. *See also* Credit derivatives
Dirty prices, 37, 115, 174. *See also* U.S. Treasury note
   calculation. *See* Forward dirty price calculation

Discount
  currency, 49
  notes, 245
  process, 27
  rate, 26fn, 36
Discrete callables, 131–133
Distressed company, 5
Distressed debt, 24
Distressed securities, 151
Distressed/default situations, 248–249
Dividend-paying philosophy, 29
Dividends, 4
  formula, expected growth, 30
  payment, 47, 124
  yield, 48
DJIA. See Dow Jones Industrial Index
Dollar roll, 144
Dollar-euro exchange rate, 49
Domestic bond markets, Treasuries segments, 79
Double-A. See Credit risks
Double-B company, 201
Double-B corporate bond, 224f
Dow Jones Industrial Index (DJIA), 162
Dow Jones Utility Index, 162
Downside credit risk protection, 149
Downside protection, 146
Downside support, 148
Drift
  definition, 75, 98–99
  experiences, 74, 98
Due diligence, 5

Duration, 172–182. See also Macaulay's duration; Modified duration; Portfolio calculation. See U.S. Treasury bill; U.S. Treasury STRIPS relationship. See Carry
Duration-neutral positions, 245
DUS. See Delegated underwriting and servicing security

E

Economic cycles, 100
Economic hedge, 235
Economic weakness, 103
Efficiency. See Market
Embedded calls, 148, 257
Embedded optionality, 136
Embedded puts, 148
Embedded short options, 130
Emerging markets, 88, 151
Employee Retirement Income Security Act (ERISA), 262
  underwriters, exemption eligibility, 263t
Entities, triple-A ratings, 87
Equities, 227f
  bonds, similarities/differences, 7t, 98t
  buybacks, 250
  cash flows, 30f
  diversification, 227
  futures. See Cash-settled equity futures
  index futures, 47
  life cycle blend, 155
  market, preferred stock, 129

price cone, 232f
price risk, 182–204
returns, 232
statistical methods, 205
summary, 64
ERISA. *See* Employee Retirement Income Security Act
Euribor rate, 80
Euro
   creation, 204–205
   market, 49
   zone members, 254
Eurodollar-denominated securities, 205
Eurodollars, 80
   futures, 192, 205
   instruments, 192
   rate, 49
   spot, 192
European Central Bank, 85
European Community, 105
European option, 145
Eurorates, 49–50
   differential, 50
Euroyen yield, 80
Event-driven situations, 152
Events. *See* Credit-related events
Exchange, 35. *See also* Chicago Mercantile Exchange rate, 8. *See also* Dollar-euro exchange rate; Forward exchange rates
   transaction, 77
Exchange-traded contracts, 260
Exchange-traded option, 214
Exercise right, 129

Expected expenses, 220
   calculation, 221
Expected losses, 220
   calculation, 221
Expected return, 220
Extramarket forces, 256
Extramarket incentive, 57

F

Face amount, 20
Fallen angel, 201
Fannie Mae. *See* Federal National Mortgage Association
FASITs, 262
Fat-tail distributions, 68
Federal budgets, market control, 238–239
Federal Financial Institutions Examination Council (FFIEC), 261
Federal Home Loan Bank (FHLB), 243, 245–246
Federal Home Loan Mortgage Corporation (FHLMC), 129–130, 242
   pass-thrus, 136fn
Federal National Mortgage Association (FNMA), 129–130, 239, 242
   pass-thrus, 136fn
   product, 246fn
FFIEC. *See* Federal Financial Institutions Examination Council
FHLB. *See* Federal Home Loan Bank

FHLMC. *See* Federal Home Loan
  Mortgage Corporation
Financial engineering, 113
  appendix, 161–170
Financial fundamentals, 5
Financial guarantee
  schematic, 104f
Financial products, investing
  profile, 158–159
Financial Times Stock Exchange
  (FTSE), 162
Financing
  agreed-upon rate, 36
  rate, 36, 194
  risk, 189
  short-term rate, 39
Fixed income
  arbitrage, 151
  marketplace, 163
  products, outperformance, 205
  securities, 101, 205
    price change, effect, 181
Fixed-coupon par bond, 104
Fixed-rate product, 137
Flat price, 37fn
FNMA. *See* Federal National
  Mortgage Association
Foreign currency rating, 83–85
Forward agreement, 194
  payoff profile, 208
Forward clean price
  calculation, 38
Forward contracts,
  holders, 229fn
Forward dirty price
  calculation, 38

Forward duration value. *See*
  Securities
Forward exchange rates, 9
Forward formulas, 53t
Forward leaps, 40
Forward points, 50t
Forward price, 214
  strike price, contrast, 208
Forward rates, 44t
Forward settlement, 33
Forward spread (FS), 61f,
  133, 134f
  calculation. *See* Non-Treasury
    security
  interrelationships, 61f
Forward transaction, 124f. *See
  also* Offsetting forward
  transaction
Forward yields, spot yields
  (convergence), 191f
Forward-dated option, 199
Forward-forward arrangement,
  196
Forward/future profile,
  206–207
Forwards
  cash flow ownership,
    relationship, 40f
  futures, contrast, 34
  interrelationships, 56f
  markets, 79
  option, building-block
    approach, 56
  summary, 51–63
  undervaluation, 57
  yield value, 44

Freddie Mac. *See* Federal Home Loan Mortgage Corporation
Frequency, 19. *See also* Compounding frequency
FS. *See* Forward spread
FTSE. *See* Financial Times Stock Exchange
Fund management themes, 154t
Fund strategies, 169t
Funding sources, 247
Futures, 34–45. *See also* Bonds; Equity index futures
  cheap trading, 120
  contract. *See* Standard & Poor's 500
    physical settlement, 47
    unwinding, 35
  contrast. *See* Forwards
  opportunities. *See* Currencies
  summary, 51–63
  undervaluation, 57
  usage, 125f

G

G-7. *See* Group of Seven
G-10. *See* Group of Ten
Gamma, relation, 199f
Gap management, 157
GC. *See* General collateral
General collateral (GC), 196
Ginnie Mae. *See* Government National Mortgage Association
Global reserve currencies, 205
GNMA. *See* Government National Mortgage Association

Going long, 34
Gold standard, 7
Goods
  cost, subsidies, 11–12
  supply/demand, 11
  trade bans, 12
Government National Mortgage Association (GNMA), 136, 138
  pass-thrus, 136fn
Group of Seven (G-7), 67, 88
Group of Ten (G-10), 186
Growth funds, 154
Growth-type index, 154

H

Hedge. *See* Delta; Economic hedge
  funds, 150, 151, 221
Hedging. *See* Market neutral
Held for portfolio, 259
Hicks method, usage, 178
Historical volatility, 66–68
  formula, annualizing term, 67
  usage, 69
Holding companies, 252
Home mortgages, purchase, 130

I

Idiosyncratic risk, 219
IMF. *See* International Monetary Fund
Implied delta, 211
  definition, 212
Implied forward credit outlook, backed-out, 202

Implied repo rate, 123
Implied securities lending
  rate, 123
Implied value, 7
  value, calculation, 69
Implied volatility, 66–70, 232
Income. *See* Ordinary income
Income fund, 155
  types, 151
Income-oriented funds, 155
Incremental returns, 165
Incremental yield, 132
Indexed portfolio managers,
  167fn
Indexes
  adjustments, 163
  return, 153
India, long-term sovereign
  currency rating/short-term
  local currency rating, 88
Individual Retirement Accounts
  (IRAs), 242
Inflation, 8
Initial public offering (IPO),
  82–83, 152, 248
Institutional investor, 253
Interest paydown, pass-thru
  principal (relationship), 138f
Interest rate. *See* Short-term
    interest rates
  changes, 230
  decline, 135fn
  differential, 8
  futures, usage, 235
  increase, 209

parity, 8–9
  models, 232
  policy, homogeneity, 254
  swap, 101–102
    schematic, 103f
Interest rate-sensitive series,
  linkage/quantification,
  182–183
Internal strategic planning, 82
International fund, 157
International Monetary Fund
  (IMF) loans, 188
International Swaps and
  Derivatives Association
  (ISDA), 104
In-the-money. *See* Deep in-the-
    money
  call option, 63fn
  put option, 125
  value. *See* Options
Intramouth credit dynamics,
  166–167
Intrinsic value, 84, 125
Investment banks, 5, 249–250
Investment-grade bonds, 232
Investment-grade corporate
  securities, 103
  usage, 182
Investment-grade index, 166
Investor-related regulations,
  265t–266t
Investors, 4
  profile, 249
Investor-specific assets, 57
Investor-specific cash flow, 57

IPO. *See* Initial public offering
ISDA. *See* International Swaps and Derivatives Association
Issuers, 73
　profile, 19
　rating, 74

K

Kurtosis, 68

L

LEAPS. *See* Long-term Equity Anticipation Securities
Leaps. *See* Forward leaps
Leverage strategies, 165–166
Libor. *See* London Interbank Offered Rate
Liquidity premium, 44. *See also* Non-Treasury liquidity premium
Loan
　profiles, securitization, 90
　transaction, 122
Local currency, 6
　acceptance, 186
　rating, 83–84
Local market orientations, 252–253
Locking in, 227
Lockout, 141
　period, 131
　protection, 142
Log-normality, Black-Scholes assumption, 126

London Interbank Offered Rate (Libor), 49, 80
　cash investment, 104
　maturity, 97fn
　rates, 102, 104
Long option, 211
Long-dated security, 155
Longer-dated debt, 76
Longer-term borrowing, 76
Long-term bonds, 76
Long-term capital gains, 242
Long-term Equity Anticipation Securities (LEAPS), 190
Long-term investment, 259
Long-term loan, 157

M

Macaulay's duration, 174–175
Macaulay's methodology, usage, 178–179
Macro fund types, 151
Macro-oriented business-level exposure, protection, 235
Make delivery, 46
Mapping process, 144f. *See also* Cumulative preferred convertible stock
Margin account, 35
Market. *See* Secondary markets
　benchmarks, 203
　capitalization values, 48
　choppiness, near-term period, 52
　control. *See* Federal budgets
　discipline, 259

Market (*continued*)
  efficiency, 258
  environment, 241
  index, 153
  movement, 214
  participants, role
    enhancement, 260
  prices, attractiveness, 52
  regulation, 257
  risk, 205
    reduction, 190
  timing, 152
  transactions, 77fn
  value, actual worth (material
    difference), 57
  volatility, zero value, 71
Market neutral
  arbitrage, 151
  securities hedging, 152
Market-moving event, 67
Marking convention, 167
Maturities, 3
  date, 19, 131–132, 144, 175
    presence, 268
  rating. *See* Split maturity
    rating
  restrictions, 168
  yield, 26
MBSs. *See* Mortgage-backed
    securities
Mexico, default (1982), 102
Modeling conventions, 168
Modified duration, 175
  line, 177

price differences. *See*
    Present value
  values, increase, 176
Monetary authorities, 41
Money market
  instruments, 245
  yield, 26fn
Moody's Investors Service
  ratings, usage, 166
  statistical data, 98–99
  transition matrices, 100t
Mortgage-backed securities
  (MBSs), 103, 134, 139,
    164–165. *See also*
    Collateralized MBS;
    Overcollateralized MBS
  callable bond optionality,
    contrast, 136t
  cash flows, 136, 137f
  classes, 140
  life, 140
  market, 165
  pass-thru, 168
  pool, 140
  principal, 233
  purchases, 261
  types, 262
  usage, 182
  valuation, 137
Mortgages
  option-related dynamics, 134
  pool, 129
Moving average calculation, 68fn
Moving-mean calculation, 68fn

Multiple, 31
Multiplication, distributive
　　property, 26fn
Multistrategy fund types, 152
Municipal bonds, 247

N

NAIC. *See* National Association
　　of Insurance Commissioners
NASDAQ, 162
National Association of
　　Insurance Commissioners
　　(NAIC), 261
National currency, 188. *See also*
　　Nonnational currency
Negative carry, 117–120, 124
Net basis, 218
New York Stock Exchange, 162
Next day, definition, 16
Nikkei, 162
Nominal spread (NS), 61f,
　　133, 134f
　　interrelationships, 61f
Nominal yield
　　differences, 243
　　spread, calculation, 43
Nonbenchmark security, 28
Noncallable bond, 208
　　price, 199
Noncallable securities, 199
Non-cash-flow paying security,
　　206, 229
Nonderivative credit-sensitive
　　instrument, 100

Nondeveloped markets, 88
Nonfixed income securities, 38
Nonnational currency, 88
Non-par bond Treasury
　　security, 44
Non-pass-thru-type structures,
　　139
Nonsynthetic CDO, 106
Nonsystematic risk, 219
　　contrast. *See* Systematic risk
Non-Treasury bond, 24, 60
Non-Treasury instruments, 239
Non-Treasury liquidity
　　premium, 45
Non-Treasury par bond curve, 60
Non-Treasury products, 102
Non-Treasury security, 59, 102
　　forward spread calculation, 45
Not-for-profit entities, 241
Notional amount, 126
　　delta-adjusted amount, 127
Notional contract value, 192
Notional principal, 260
NS. *See* Nominal spread

O

OAS. *See* Option-adjusted spread
OECD. *See* Organization for
　　Economic Cooperation and
　　Development
Off-exchange transaction, 77
Offsetting forward transaction,
　　212
Off-the-run issue, 196

Off-the-run securities, 44fn
OLS. *See* Ordinary least squares
On special (special), 196, 240
On-the-run issue, 44fn, 196
On-the-run securities, 44fn
On-the-run Treasury, 44fn
Opportunistic fund types, 152
Opportunity cost, 194
Option-adjusted spread (OAS), 58–61, 133, 134f
  impact, 61f
  interrelationships, 61f
  pricing model, 200
  volatility, relationship, 200
Option-pricing model, modification, 69
Options
  building-block approach, 56
  deferred feature, 58
  interrelationships, 56f
  in-the-money value, 208
  model, tree. *See* Binomial option model
  strategies, 168
  undervaluation/over-valuation, 57
  usage, 125f
Option-type product, 214
Ordinary income, 242
Ordinary least squares (OLS) regression, 183fn
Organization for Economic Cooperation and Development (OECD), 259–260

Out-of-the-money, 125. *See also* Deep out-of-the-money
  call option, 63fn
  movement, 210
  put option, 63fn
Overcollateralization, 90
Overcollateralized MBS, 135
Overlay funds, 158
Over-the-counter (OTC)
  forward-dated transactions, 78
  market, 248, 253
  options, 168
  products, 168, 260
  transaction, 77
  Treasury options, 79

P

PACs. *See* Planned amortization classes
Par bond
  curve, 26, 43
  yield, 26
Par swap, 104
Pass-through security, 134, 226
Payments, timeliness, 22
Payoff profile, 127, 193, 206, 207f. *See also* Call payoff profile; Callable bonds; Forward agreement; Put payoff profile; Sigma; Variance; Volatility
  benefit, 208
Peer group, 5
Perpetual bond, 97
Perpetuals, coupons, 97fn

Planet currency, 188
Planned amortization classes
    (PACs), 140–142. *See also*
    Busted PAC
  application, 142f
Portfolio
  construction. *See* Bonds
  duration, 185
  emphasis, 152
  managers, 96, 162–164, 167fn.
      See also Indexed portfolio
      managers; Total returns
  forecast, 234
  product mix, 165
Positive carry, 118, 124
PPP. *See* Purchasing power parity
Predetermined life span, 3
Preferred stock, 144. *See also*
    Equities
  type, 145
Premium currency, 49
Prepayments, 129, 135
  rate. *See* Constant prepayment
      rate
  speed, 142
Present value, modified duration
    (price differences), 177
Present yield, 25
Price
  cone. *See* Coupon-bearing
      Treasury; Currencies;
      Equities
  risk, 223, 236. *See also*
      Equities
    currency classification, 187f

sensitivity. *See* Delta; Theta;
    Vega
  test, 262
  uncertainty, 18, 25
  values, contrast, 177t, 181t
  volatility, 226. *See* At-the-
      money
  yield, relationship, 200
Price to book value, 231
Price-depressing effect, 81
Price-earnings (P/E) ratio,
    150, 231
Price-lifting effect, 81
Price/yield relationship, 179–180
  comparison, 178f, 179f, 181f
Principal, 4
  balances, 234f
Principal payments, 135–137
Principal-coupon cash flows, 137
Priorities, 5–8
  ranking, 4
Probability
  profiles, 236f
  reduction, 235
  uncertainty, label, 222
  value, 139
Probability-weighted principal,
    140
Probability-weighted value, 140
Productivity, 8
Products, 3. *See also* Option-type
    product
  characteristics, 255t
  construction, 76
  interrelationships, 204–206

Products, 3 (*continued*)
  mix. *See* Portfolio
    rankings, continuum, 6f
    restrictions, 263f
Profit opportunities, 118
Profitability, 29
Promises, 3–8
Prospectus, usage, 250–253
Public Securities Association (PSA) model, 138
Purchasing power parity (PPP), 9–13
  models, 232
Put option, 147. *See also* In-the-money
  value, 53, 146
Put payoff profile, 208
Putable bonds, 148–149

Q

Quality option, 121fn

R

Raised debt, 86
RAROC. *See* Risk-adjusted return on capital
RARORAC. *See* Risk-adjusted return on risk-adjusted capital
Rating. *See* Issuers; Split maturity rating
  agencies, 74, 82, 97
  insurance. *See* Credit
Recoveries, 94t
  rates. *See* Weighted average discounted recovery rates

Reference curve, 45
Regression analysis, 219
Reinvested proceeds, 165
Reinvestment
  rates, 20–21, 41, 223fn, 229fn
  uncertainty, 18
Reinvestment risk, 195, 223, 236
  comparison, 225
  dispensing, 227
  uncertainty, 225
Relative return
  fund, 150
  investing, 153–159
    strategies, 161–164
Relative value, 27, 79
REMICs, 262
Repurchase (repo). *See* Reverse repo
  agreement, 123, 195
  financing. *See* Synthetic option
  market, 36, 79
  rate. *See* Implied repo rate
Residual tranche, 141
Retirement accounts (401k plans), 242
Return on risk-adjusted capital (RORAC), 219–220
Return profile, 194f
Reverse repo, 123, 124f
Rho risk, 127
Risk. *See* Benchmark; Credit risks; Price; Reinvestment risk
  adjustment, 218–219
  calculations, 221
  capital, allocation, 216f

conceptualization, 108f
limits, 217
macro context, 234–235
management, 161, 171, 222–225
  appendix, 238–240
  procedures, 260
measurement, 185
profile, 214
  conceptual mapping, 225f, 237f
tolerance, 221
variable, 197
Risk-adjusted return on capital (RAROC), 218–220
Risk-adjusted return on risk-adjusted capital (RARORAC), 219
Risk-adjusted variables, 219–220
Risk-based capital guidelines, 259
Risk-free asset, 211
Risk-free investment, 195
Risk-free product, 122
Risk-free rate, 194–197
Risk-oriented bondholders, 252
Risk/return profiles, 172, 205
Risk-reward trade-offs, 226, 235
Road shows, 83
Roll down, phenomenon, 239–240
Roll risk, 239
Roll-down risk, 239
RORAC. *See* Return on risk-adjusted capital

S

Sale price, 17
Same-day settlement, 33
Savings and loan crisis (1990s), 256
Scenario analysis, 233–234, 237
Secondary markets, 212
Securities
  face value, 211
  forward duration value, 191
  hedging. *See* Market neutral
  lending, 122–123
    market, 36
  prices, 231
  purchase, 248
  risk, 79
  risk/return profile, 159
Securities and Exchange Commission (SEC), 242
Securitization. *See* Loan profiles
Security-specific risk, 219
Selling short, 16
Senior structures, 201–202
Separately Traded Registered Interest and Principal Securities (STRIPS), 164–165
  30-year. *See* U.S. Treasury STRIPS
Servicer. *See* Asset-backed securities
Settlement
  agreement, 34
  dates, 15, 33, 175
Shareholders, 4
Short call option, 70
  price, 199

Short selling, 125
    fund types, 152
Short-dated liabilities, 157
Shorter-dated debt, 76
Shorter-maturity bonds, 78
Short-term bonds, 76
Short-term borrowings, 76
Short-term horizons, 192
Short-term interest rates, 41
Short-term investment, 259
Sigma, 161
    payoff profiles, 126f
Singapore, credit allocation, 218
Single-B company, 200–201
Single-C company, 201
Size restrictions, 168
Small caps, 162
Special. *See* On special
Special-purpose vehicles (SPVs), 93, 106, 256
Speed. *See* Prepayments
Split maturity rating, 76
Sponsor currency, acceptance, 186
Spot
    cash flow, 227–229
    credit instrument, 202
    interrelationships, 56f
    option, building-block approach, 56
    position, 215
    price, 15
    transactions, 77fn
    yields, 25
        convergence. *See* Forward yields
Spread. *See* Nominal spread; Swaps
    calculation. *See* Nominal yield difference, 44
    value, 29
SPVs. *See* Special-purpose vehicles
Standard & Poor's
    100 (S&P100), 162
    ratings, usage, 166
    statistical data, 98
    survey/report, 94–95
Standard & Poor's 500 (S&P500), 153
    change, 182
    equity index, 150
    futures contract, 48, 126
    price history, 185
    rally, 206
    returns, 161
    usage, 183–184
Standard deviation
    usage, 185
    zero value, 70–72
Standard error, 219
State-supported bailouts, 256
Strike price, 53, 71, 197, 202. *See also* At-the-money
    contrast. *See* Forward price objective, 211
STRIPS. *See* Separately Traded Registered Interest and Principal Securities
Subsidiaries, triple-A rating, 93
Swaps. *See* Constant Maturity Treasury; Currencies; Interest rate; Variance

dealers, 80–81
markets, 80–81
spread, 80
yields, 238–239
Synthetic balance sheet structure, schematic, 106f
Synthetic call option, 212
Synthetic CDO, 105
Synthetic CLOs, 254
Synthetic long forward, creation, 149f
Synthetic option
  creation, 209–211, 214
  delta, 211–213
  profile, 213f
  repo financing, 211
Systematic risk, 219. *See also* Nonsystematic risk; Unsystematic risk
  nonsystematic risk, contrast, 219t

T

T plus 3, 16
Tariffs, 12
Tax law, industry-specific categories, 246
Tax-adjusted total returns, calculations, 243
Tax-free funds, 155–156
Taylor series expansion, usage, 173
TED. *See* Treasury *versus* Eurodollar
Tennessee Valley Authority (TVA), 242, 243

Term structure, 22
Theta
  price sensitivities, 198f
  usage, 197
Third-party insurance, obtaining, 91
Timing option, 118
Total return-oriented portfolio manager, 156
Total returns
  analysis, 176
  basis points, 163
  calculation, 173t. *See also* Tax-adjusted total returns
  components, comparison, 233t
  funds portfolio managers, 153
  investing, 153
  relationship, 121f
Trade date, 33, 76–77, 115fn
  pay-in-full, 58
Trading
  records, 214
  rich/cheap, 28
Treasury *versus* Eurodollar (TED) spread, 205–206
Triple-B entity, 249
True worth, 16
Trust preferred securities (TruPs), 262
TVA. *See* Tennessee Valley Authority
Two-noncall-one, 131

U

Uncertainty
  conceptual mapping, 222f

Uncertainty (*continued*)
  degree, 226
  increase, 235
  label. *See* Probability
  layers. *See* Bonds
Uncollateralized loan, 90
Unsystematic risk, 219
Unwinding. *See* Futures
U.S. bond index, 182
U.S. Department of Labor (DOL), 262
U.S. dollar-denominated issues, 248
U.S. federal agency bonds, taxable status, 243t
U.S. Treasury bill
  3–month, 51
    cash flows, 17fn
  6–month, 42, 223f
    purchase, 236
  12–month-maturity, 229
  duration, calculation, 173
  finding, 195
  futures, 193
  investment, 41
  spot yield, 191
  total return, 224
  yield, 26
U.S. Treasury bonds, 84
  coupon cash flows, 23fn
  predisposition, 31
  rallying markets, 102
  two-year, 42, 191
  yield curve, 27
U.S. Treasury coupon-bearing securities, 225

U.S. Treasury note
  cash flow profile, 31fn
  dirty price, 175
U.S. Treasury obligations, 84
U.S. Treasury rates, 102
U.S. Treasury STRIPS, 175–176
  30–year, 172
  duration, calculation, 173–174
  yield, 178
U.S. Treasury zero-coupon bonds, 149

V

Value
  funds, 153
  investing, 157
  uncertainty, 202
Value at Risk (VaR), 261
Variance
  payoff profiles, 126f
  swap, 128
Vega
  price sensitivities, 198f
  usage, 197
Volatility, 53, 66. *See also* At-the-money; Historical volatility; Implied volatility
  calculations, 54fn
  increase, 200, 215
  outlook, 215
  payoff profiles, 126f
  price value calculation, 54
  reference, 128
  relationship. *See* Option-adjusted spread
  rolling series, 68fn

Index

spread. *See* Zero volatility spread
strategy
  creation, 125f
  execution, 192
  swap, 127–128
  value, 125, 229
  zero return, 193
  zero value, 55, 188

W

Weighted average discounted recovery rates, 95t
Weightings, linkage, 186
What-if scenarios, 244
Wilshire, 162
Worst-case scenarios, 257
Worth. *See* True worth

Y

YB. *See* Yield of benchmark
Yield. *See* Incremental yield; Spot
  cash flow-weighted average, 19fn
  curve, 26. *See also* U.S. Treasury bonds
  dynamic, 163
  inversion, 234
  differences. *See* Nominal yield
  enhancement, 156–157
  increase, 103
  references, 25
  relationship, 143f. *See also* Price
  spread, 24, 40, 79, 246fn. *See also* Credit
  calculation. *See* Nominal yield
  value. *See* Forwards
Yield of benchmark (YB), 28
Yield of nonbenchmark (YNB), 28
Yield-to-maturity, 25, 37
YNB. *See* Yield of nonbenchmark

Z

Z tranches, 141
Zero coupon security, price dynamics, 230
Zero volatility (ZV) spread, 59
Zero-coupon bonds. *See* U.S. Treasury zero-coupon bonds